Managing Business Ethics

Straight Talk About How to Do It Right

Second Edition

LINDA KLEBE TREVIÑO

Professor of Organizational Behavior

Smeal College of Business Administration
The Pennsylvania State University

KATHERINE A. NELSON

Senior Consultant
William M. Mercer, Inc.
Senior Fellow
The Wharton School
University of Pennsylvania

JOHN WILEY & SONS, INC.

New York • Chichester • Weinheim • Brisbane • Singapore • Toronto

ACQUISITIONS EDITOR	Ellen Ford
MARKETING MANAGER	Carlise Paulson
SENIOR PRODUCTION EDITOR	Christine Cervoni
SENIOR DESIGNER	Laura Boucher
COVER ILLUSTRATION	John S. Dykes/Stock Illustration Source, Inc.

This book was set in Garamond by Matrix Publishing Services and printed and bound by Courier Stoughton. The cover was printed by Lehigh Press.

This book is printed on acid-free paper. ♾

Library of Congress Cataloging-in-Publication Data
Treviño, Linda Klebe.
   Managing business ethics : straight talk about how to do it right
/ Linda Klebe Treviño, Katherine A. Nelson. — 2nd ed.
      p.   cm.
   Includes bibliographical references and index.
   ISBN 0-471-24652-2 (pbk. : alk. paper)
   1. Business ethics.   2. Business ethics—Case studies.
I. Nelson, Katherine A., 1948-   . II. Title.
HF5387.T734   1999
174'.4—dc21   98-37440
                                                                                CIP

Printed in the United States of America

10 9 8 7 6 5 4 3 2 1

Contents

SECTION (II) ETHICS AND THE INDIVIDUAL

Chapter 3   Common Ethical Problems   53

Chapter 4   Deciding What's Right: A Prescriptive Approach   79

Chapter 5   Deciding What's Right: A Psychological Approach   100

SECTION (III) ETHICS AND THE MANAGER

Chapter 6   Ethical Problems of Managers   127

Chapter 7   Managing for Ethical Conduct   148

SECTION (IV) ETHICS AND THE ORGANIZATION

Chapter 8   Ethical Problems of Organizations   179

Chapter 9   Ethics as Organizational Culture   204

Chapter 10   Creating an Ethical Organizational Culture: Model Ethics Programs   246

SECTION (V) ETHICS AND THE WORLD

Chapter 11   Managing for Ethical Conduct in a Global Business Environment   289

Appendix   Integrative Case: Manville Corporation   320

Index   331

Preface

WHY DOES THE WORLD NEED ANOTHER BUSINESS ETHICS TEXT?

The popular business press is replete with feature stories describing how companies are clamoring for educational institutions to make business education more relevant. "Give us graduates who have been trained in how to manage, lead, communicate, and exercise sound judgment," the business people being interviewed all seem to say. As a result, universities across the country are scrambling to design new courses that incorporate leadership, communications skills, the basics of human resources management, and ethics. We've heard similar sentiments from students, employees, and corporate executives. That's why we wrote this book; we want to make the study of ethics relevant to real-life work situations.

This book is different from other business ethics texts in several key ways:

First, it was written by an unusual team. Linda Treviño is Professor of Organizational Behavior at The Pennsylvania State University. She is widely published, has many years of experience in teaching students and executives in university settings, and also has experience as a corporate consultant on ethics and management issues. Kate Nelson is an ethics consultant who designs ethics programs for corporations, government agencies, and professional associations. She has over twenty years of journalism and management experience, has presented ethics programs at many colleges and universities, and is a senior fellow at Wharton. We think this diverse mix of theory and practice makes the book unique.

Second, the approach of this book is the most pragmatic we've seen, and that approach is a direct response to complaints and suggestions we've heard from the students, employees, and corporate executives we mentioned earlier. "Make it real," they have said. "Tell us what we need to know to effectively manage people. Take the mystery out of this subject that seems so murky. Get to the point." This book starts with the assumption that ethics in organizations is about human behavior in those organizations. We believe that behavior results from a number of factors, many of which can be influenced by managers and the organizations themselves. As a result, this book is organized into sections about individuals, managers, and organizations, the ethical dilemmas they face, and how they might solve them. It also features philosophical and psychological factors of decision making, corporate culture, how managers can influence employees' behavior, what corporations are doing to encourage ethical behavior, and international business ethics.

Third, we have used a different mix of examples than is found in conventional business ethics texts. Most texts focus on high-level, corporate dilemmas: "Should senior executives be paid at a particular level? Should this industry do business in China? Should American environmental laws apply to American companies operating overseas?"

Although these are interesting issues, the vast majority of students and employees will never have to face them. However, they will have to hire, manage, assess performance, discipline, fire, and provide incentives for staff, as well as produce quality products and services, and deal effectively and fairly with customers, vendors, and other stakeholders. As a result, although we do feature a number of the classic corporate ethics cases, the vast majority of cases in this book reflect the kinds of problems that most people will encounter during the course of their careers. All of the "hypothetical" cases in this text are based on actual incidents that have happened somewhere—it's the real stuff that goes on every day in offices across the country.

Fourth, this book was developed with the help of students at a number of universities and with guidance from numerous managers and senior executives from various corporations and organizations. We have incorporated the latest research on ethics and organizational behavior into this text, and much of the material that appears within these pages has been tested in both university and corporate settings.

Fifth, we believe this book is easy to use because it's organized to be flexible. It can be used alone to teach an ethics course, or it can be used as a supplement to a more conventional, philosophical text. The sections in this book basically stand alone and can be taught in a different sequence than is presented here, and it also has many cases and vignettes you can use for class discussion. The instructor's guide provides resources to help teach this course, such as outlines, overheads, discussion questions, and additional cases for class discussion, and it supplies references to many other resources that can be used to teach the course.

A NOTE TO STUDENTS

This book was written for you. We have listened to your complaints and your wish lists and have tried to pare this complicated subject down to a digestible size. The cases that appear in this book all happened to people just like you, who were not as prepared to deal with the dilemmas as you will be after taking this course. Before you get into this, we have one suggestion: know that regardless of how large an organization you find yourself in, you're not some little cog in a giant wheel. You have the power to change not only your own behavior and knowledge of ethics, but also the behavior and knowledge of the people you work with. Use that power: the job you save may be your own.

ACKNOWLEDGMENTS

It takes a lot of work by a lot of people to make a project like this come together. We would like to begin with some joint thank-you's. Then, because this process has been so meaningful for each of us, we would like to separately share our more personal thanks.

We both offer our heartfelt appreciation to current and former executives—in particular, Kent Druyvesteyn, Joe Paterno, Shirley Peterson, Vin Sarni, Carl Skooglund, and Larry Axline—who agreed to share their valuable time and advice, some of them on multiple occasions. Their wisdom can be found throughout this book. They helped bring the subject of managing business ethics to life.

We also wish to thank Gary Weaver (University of Delaware and formerly Penn State doctoral student) for being our philosophy adviser, Dennis Gioia (Penn State faculty member and dear friend) for sharing his Pinto Fire Case and especially his reflections, and Richard Daley and Scott Hibbard (University of Montana) for contributing the Manville case.

John Wiley & Sons, Inc. is a fine publisher with a superb team. These people encouraged, nudged, nudged, and nudged again. We have many Wiley people to thank for making this project a success, but especially Tim Kent, the editor of our first edition and Ellen Ford, the editor of this edition.

The book's reviewers also contributed significantly to making this a better book. Our thanks go to James Weber (Duquesne University), Diane Swanson (Kansas State University), David Jacobs (American University), and Bruce Charnov (Hofstra University).

We also want to thank our students and particularly Penn State undergraduate and MBA students who provide us with excellent feedback and advice semester after semester.

SPECIAL ACKNOWLEDGMENTS—FROM LINDA K. TREVIÑO

Many special people have helped along the path that brought me to the writing of this book. I'd like to begin by thanking my mentors in the doctoral program at Texas A&M University's management department. Many thanks to Stuart Youngblood (now at Texas Christian University), Don Hellriegel, Richard Woodman, Dick Daft (now at Vanderbilt University), and Mary Zey (Sociology Department), who encouraged my early theorizing and research in business ethics. They told me to go with my gut and to do what was important—and they supported my every step.

I would like to thank the colleagues who have worked with me on empirical research over the years and who have been partners in learning about the management of business ethics: particularly Gail Ball, Ken Butterfield, Don Mc-

Cabe, Bart Victor, and Gary Weaver. This learning has contributed to the book in important ways.

Shortly after becoming a faculty member at Penn State, I had the good fortune to meet my friend and co-author, Kate Nelson. I was intrigued by a brief *Wall Street Journal* article about Kate's work at Citibank (you'll read more about that later). We met and became fast friends, who (believe it or not) loved talking about business ethics. We decided to write an article together, and the rest, as Kate says, is history. Kate brought the real world into this book. She was also willing to tell me when I was getting too academic (not her words exactly). It became more and more clear to me that we were supposed to write this book together, and I'm very glad we did. Thanks, Kate!

The article became a book proposal that we first shared with publishers at the Academy of Management meeting in 1992. Shortly thereafter, Bill Oldsey (formerly publisher at John Wiley & Sons, Inc.) showed up in my office at Penn State. His enthusiasm for the book was immediate and infectious. I want to thank Bill for the special part he played in this incredible journey.

Finally, I want to thank the light of my life, Dan, for the inspiration, love, and support he provides every day of my life and for being one of the most ethical human beings I know. Also I want to thank family members, colleagues, and many dear friends not only for cheering me on (as usual), but also for their many contributions to this book. They have served as readers and interviewees. They have provided clipping services and offered ideas for cases. They were there when I was overwhelmed. I can't thank them enough.

SPECIAL ACKNOWLEDGMENTS—FROM KATHERINE A. NELSON

I began to care about ethics and integrity as a very young child and as part of a family where "doing it right" was the only way to go. As a result, my biggest debt is to my parents, Harry R. and Benadette Prendergast Nelson, and my brother, James V. Nelson. My parents worked tirelessly, carefully, and lovingly to set me on the right path. Jim's generosity and enthusiastic support of his older sister have encouraged me not only to teach ethics, but also to write this book. I'm grateful to Jim's wife, Susan, for her many encouraging words of support when I was ready to tear my hair out and for giving our family our two most precious additions, Conor and James Nelson. My extended family has also done much to hone my sense of right and kindness—my grandparents, my aunts, uncles, cousins—and I am grateful to them.

Thanks also to my inner circle of friends, who provided valuable encouragement, advice, and moral support: Ann Frazier-Hedberg, Carol Dygert, Jan Tunney, John and Kathy Worgul, and the Rev. Bill Martin and his wife Gail.

Many thanks to Wharton, where I'm a senior fellow, and particularly to Dr. Thomas A. Donaldson and Dr. Thomas W. Dunfee, who are not only world-class ethicists, but who are also superior human beings and cherished friends. And I'm grateful to all of the nuns who watched over me from grammar school through college—the Sisters of Charity in Emmitsburg, Maryland, and Riverdale, New York, especially Sister Cecilia Connelly.

Thanks also go to the many managers who, each in his or her own way, taught me that business ethics needn't be an oxymoron: Cal Asher, formerly of the Utica (NY) *Observer-Dispatch;* Charlie Fohlin, formerly of Honeywell Information Systems in Wellesley, Massachusetts; Tom Brown, formerly of Merrill Lynch in White Plains, New York; and Christopher York, Don Armiger, Peter Thorp, Judith Fullmer, Henry Morales, Jerry Lieberman, Michael Brooks, Michael Silverman, Peter Carey, and Jane Shannon—all currently or formerly with Citibank in New York City.

A special thank you goes to my husband, Stephen J. Morgan—an honorable man if there ever was one—who has proven to me that princes really do exist.

Of course, a final thank you goes to my co-author, Linda Treviño, for her dear, dear friendship and for working with me to produce this book in what, in comparison to accounts from other writing teams, was an almost painless experience.

INTRODUCTION TO BUSINESS ETHICS

Introducing Straight Talk About Managing Business Ethics: Where We're Going and Why

INTRODUCTION

This book began with a fortuitous phone call back in 1987 that resulted in a friendship. Linda Treviño, professor of organizational behavior at Penn State University, noticed a small article on the front page of the *Wall Street Journal*. The piece described a game to teach business ethics that had been developed at Citicorp, the nation's largest commercial bank. As someone who teaches ethics to business students, and who cares deeply about preparing students to think about ethics and manage their conduct in corporations, she decided to find out more about Citicorp's game. She called the game's developer, Kate Nelson, a vice president and head of human resources communications at Citicorp. The rest, as they say, is history.

We began a dialogue and over time discovered that we had a lot in common. We had both learned that many students—whether on a campus or in a corporation—felt intimidated by the subject of ethics. We had both listened to their frustrations: "Why does this have to be so mysterious? This is hopeless; there's nothing we can do about the behavior of people who report to us. Give us some guidance. Tell us what we should be doing. Don't frame business ethics in terms of Aristotle. Tell us what will be expected of us at General Electric, Ford, and Bank of America. Advise us on what to do when something goes wrong, and how to prevent that from happening." In many ways, this book is a response to those concerns.

Before writing the book, however, we had to make several decisions. First, would such a big undertaking be a worthwhile effort? Could we take the mystery out of business ethics? Could we address the cynicism that we had both encountered? Did we have something unique to say? Would it make any difference? We became convinced that we could write a book that would teach something unique and that we could do it in a fun and practical way.

TAKING AWAY THE MYSTERY

We want to take the mystery out of business ethics. In other situations (romance, for example?) mystery may stimulate interest. But mystery only serves to make ethics inaccessible to most students and managers. For most people, the word "ethics" means something esoteric and far-removed from reality. But organizational ethics isn't mysterious. It's about *us*—people making decisions in organizations every day. All of us belong to organizations. We're members of schools, fraternities, sororities, clubs, sports teams, religious organizations, and work organizations. As members of these organizations, we frequently find ourselves facing ethical dilemmas—*situations concerning right and wrong where values are in conflict.*

As a student, you may have observed a friend cheating and wondered what to do. Which is the more important value—sticking by a friend, or complying with the honor code that requires you to turn in a cheater? In a work setting, perhaps you've been tempted to do something you believe is wrong (i.e., lie to a customer about a delivery date) because your boss encourages you to focus on short-term financial results. Which is more important—honesty to the customer or adhering to your boss's expectations? Loyalty is an important value for most of us. But, what happens when one of your employees (a good friend) hasn't been meeting agreed-on performance expectations for some time? Which is more important—loyalty to the organization or loyalty to your friend? All of these examples represent values in conflict. All are ethical dilemmas.

Until about ten years ago, we knew so little about the topic of organizational ethics that a book like this probably couldn't have been written. With rare exceptions, knowledge was limited to a few surveys saying that, yes, ethics is a problem. But, in recent years, researchers have begun to rigorously study organizational ethics. Although there's much left to learn, we're beginning to understand the factors that influence ethical conduct in organizations, and what works and what doesn't in ethics management. That's the kind of information we'll share with you so that you'll understand yourself and others better, and you'll be a better manager who is able to influence others' behavior in an ethical direction.

MOVING BEYOND CYNICISM

Cynicism has become an epidemic throughout society and is manifested in a "contemptuous mistrust" of business leaders.[1] Irving Kristol, writer, educator, and editor, said, "One of the reasons the large corporations find it so difficult to persuade the public of anything is that the public always suspects them of engaging in clever public relations instead of simply telling the truth."[2] Such cynical attitudes toward business have been exacerbated in recent years by repeated organizational restructurings, accompanied by high executive compensation and massive layoffs.[3]

Unfortunately, this cynicism extends to managers themselves. Since the classic studies of business ethics conducted in the 1960s and 1970s,[4] managers have repeatedly reported their own cynicism—the pressure they feel to compromise their personal ethical standards on the job, and they're even more cynical about their peers' ethics than their own.[5] They blame business's preoccupation with gain, the lack of reinforcement of ethical behavior, competition, the existence of generally accepted unethical practices in certain industries, a sense that only results are important to superiors, and the ineffective enforcement of ethics codes. Among all managers, those at lower levels have reported feeling the most pressure to compromise their ethics.[6]

Many of our readers are business school students, the future managers of business enterprises. We're concerned that cynicism may be a problem in this group. Surveys suggest that many business students believe that they'll be expected to check their ethics at the corporate door or that they will be pressured to compromise their own ethical standards in order to succeed.[7]

The media may be responsible for undergraduate students' cynical view of American business. Think about the depiction of business and its leaders in movies and on television. The Media Research Center conducted a survey of 863 network TV sitcoms, dramas, and movies from 1995 to early 1997. Nearly 30 percent of the criminal characters in these programs were business owners or corporate executives. Entrepreneurs were represented as drug dealers ("Beverly Hills, 90201"), kidnappers ("Nash Bridges") or sellers of defective gear to the military.[8] *Fortune* magazine calls this "the rise of corporate villainy in prime time."[9] Academic research on the representation of business in movies suggests that cynicism toward American business increased after study participants viewed the film *Roger & Me* which depicted ruthless plant closings and layoffs at General Motors.[10] Imagine the cumulative effect of viewing countless movies and television programs that portray business as corrupt and business leaders as ruthless and unethical.

We are happy to say that our MBA students seem less cynical. This is probably because most of them have spent several years in the business world. They know, from experience, that business organizations vary from the highly ethical to the highly unethical and that business people vary as well. They also know that they would prefer to work for an ethical organization and to deal with individuals they can trust to follow through on their commitments. For our cynical readers, we want to help by doing two things: (1) by empowering managers with the tools they need to address ethical problems and manage for ethical behavior and (2) by providing positive examples of people and organizations who are "doing things right." We agree with Coach Joe Paterno, Penn State's legendary football coach whose program is known for integrity. He said this in response to our questions about cynicism. "I don't care what cynical people say. I don't really pay attention. These are small people who . . . don't have the confidence or courage to do it the right way. And when they see someone doing it the right way, deep down they feel guilty. They'd rather say that it can't be done . . . , that everybody cheats. I hear that all the time. 'Fine,' I say. 'You think what you want.' I know what I do. People around me know. You've got to just run your organization. You can't worry about what these cynical people say."

Tools to Manage Unethical Behavior

With so much focus on negative events, people can become cynical because they feel helpless to influence these events. They feel overwhelmed by the pressures they perceive to be pushing them and others inexorably toward self-interested behavior at the expense of their higher aspirations. The "mystery" of organizational ethics contributes to this feeling of helplessness. How can we do anything about something we don't understand? We hope to dispel this feeling of helplessness, and simultaneously reduce the cynicism by offering conceptual and practical tools for managing ethics.

Focus on the Positive and the Ethical

We'd also like to focus on the positive and the ethical in people and in organizations. We're not Pollyannas: we see plenty of real-world examples to inspire us to keep ourselves and our organizations moving in a positive and ethical direction.

Ethical conduct is alive and well at work. In an *Industry Week* survey, three out of four respondents claimed that their company's code of ethics, or ethics in general, actually means something to them in their day-to-day work, and that figure is up from an earlier survey.[11] Employees are clearly looking for positive guidance from their organizations so that they can feel good about the work they do every day.

Many organizations are acknowledging that they're not islands, isolated from the larger communities that surround them. In fact, they know that they function best within healthy communities. The leaders of these organizations have been referred to as "enlightened capitalists."[12] They reject the notion, dominant in the 1980s, that business's sole responsibility is to maximize profits. Although they're true believers in the free market system, these "enlightened capitalists" acknowledge that the free market system can also produce negative side effects such as pollution and "poverty-amid-plenty."[13] They believe that it's better for business to voluntarily help solve these problems than to be forced to do so by the government. One corporate lawyer estimated that a new law results in 200 to 300 pages of regulations—all of which have to be followed by the corporations affected by the law. Furthermore, enlightened business leaders argue that business has a responsibility to address certain social problems because of its unique abilities, and because a healthy social environment is a prerequisite for a healthy business environment. Therefore, they maintain that a business that serves its multiple stakeholders best (i.e., customers, employees, the community—essentially, any party who has a stake in what the organization does and how it performs) also serves its shareholders best in the long run.[14]

ISN'T BUSINESS ETHICS JUST A FAD?

Management researchers began to study business ethics during the 1960s by conducting surveys of managers' attitudes toward business ethics.[15] Some thought that business ethics was just a fad then (related to media attention to the burgeoning consumer rights movement, for example)—that interest in the topic would quickly fade. But research has found that management fads generally last only about 10 years,[16] and interest in business ethics has climbed for more than 30 years. This interest is fueled in part by regular media coverage of ethical lapses in the business community. Examples include the federal savings and loan disaster, Wall Street insider trading scandals, the Exxon Valdez oil spill, Beech-Nut's sale of a chemical concoction as pure apple juice, Archer Daniels Midland's price fixing, Denny's and Texaco's racial discrimination, Mitsubishi's sexual harassment, and the tobacco industry's reluctance to acknowledge the health hazards of smoking.

But ethical lapses aren't limited to business; ethical problems affect every institution of our society. For example, in the 1970s, the Watergate scandal focused attention on ethical problems in government. This focus continued with questions about the faulty decision making that led to the *Challenger* disaster, check-writing scandals in Congress, Irangate, Whitewater, sexual harassment in the military, and questionable election fundraising tactics.

Religious, educational, philanthropic, and sports organizations haven't been immune. Catholic priests have sexually abused children, students have cheated on exams and plagiarized papers, philanthropic organizations have spent contributors' funds irresponsibly, and student athletes have run afoul of National Collegiate Athletic Association (NCAA) rules. Although we don't want to leave it to the media to define ethical business practice, the media's continuing interest in business ethics suggests that ethics isn't just a fad.

Articles and books have also proliferated in the academic and professional press, suggesting that these communities are becoming increasingly interested in ethics as well. And organizations of every kind are addressing the "ethics problem" in a number of ways. Many of them are establishing high-level ethics committees, drafting codes of ethical conduct, and conducting ethics training programs. Such ethics initiatives have increased quite steadily since the 1970s.[17]

The wider American community also seems very interested in ethics and values these days. Perhaps the best examples of their interest are William Bennett's (former Education secretary under Ronald Reagan) best-selling *Book of Virtues*[18] and the popularity of radio talk show hosts such as "Dr. Laura Schlesinger" who dispenses advice in response to callers' moral dilemmas. So, in addition to focusing on the negative—the ethical lapses—there seems to be a need in our society also to focus on the positive—models of positive ethical conduct in private and public life.

As we've seen, interest in ethics reflects the reality of life in all sectors of our society, and it has continued to grow over the past 30 plus years. Ethical lapses are a part of human behavior that's here to stay. That's one reason why we wrote this book. If the ethics "problem" isn't just a fad, then managers have an ongoing concern that they must anticipate, understand, and manage. We also believe that the interest in ethics as a positive force hasn't been adequately tapped in the business world. Although they do not get as much media attention, there are many positive examples of business people doing good and doing well. We want to share those too.

CAN BUSINESS ETHICS BE TAUGHT?

Before launching a book-writing effort, we also needed to be convinced that we could actually teach our readers something. Despite growing interest in ethics and ethics training, dissenters from both the business and academic communities[19] have raised serious questions about whether ethics can or should be taught. Felix Rohatyn, a noted New York investment banker, said that ethics can't be taught past the age of 10. Lester Thurow, former dean of the Massachusetts Institute of Technology's Sloan School of Management, echoed this view when he stated that business schools can do little if students haven't already learned ethics from their families, clergy, previous schools, or employers.[20]

In the wake of the insider trading scandals of the 1980s, Mr. Thurow and a chief operating officer of a large Wall Street investment firm claimed on a television news program that educational institutions or business organizations could have done little about the unethical individuals who participated in insider trading. These people just hadn't been raised with the proper values.

If they're correct, ethics education is a waste of time and money. Bad apples are just tainted people who can't be trained or rehabilitated. Therefore, resources should be devoted to identifying and discarding bad apples, not educating them.

Aren't Bad Apples the Cause of Ethical Problems in Organizations?

In part, the belief that ethics can't be taught is driven by the assumption that ethical problems are caused by such "bad apples" and that unethical behavior in organizations can be traced to a few "bad apples" that spoil it for the rest of us. According to this belief, people come to organizations as either good or bad and organizations can do little to change them. All they can do is attempt to hire people of good character and get rid of the bad ones who slip through the selection system.

This "bad apple" idea[21] is appealing because unethical behavior can then be blamed on bad individuals. Although it's unpleasant to fire people, it's relatively easier to discard a "bad apple" than to search for some organizational problem that caused the apple to rot.

Garry Trudeau's (1987) Doonesbury cartoon treatment of Dennis Levine, who was convicted of insider trading, reflected this bad apple view. In the cartoon, Levine is totally unresponsive to an ethics counselor's attempts to appeal to his sense of morality.

> Scot, Ethics Counselor: ". . . and since everyone else was doing it, you figured using insider information was okay?"
>
> Levine: "Yeah, like the golden rule says."

Scot: "Uh, the golden rule? Which golden rule is that?

Levine: "Do unto others before they do it unto you first."

Scot: "Okay, ethically, you seem to be a little rusty . . . Why don't we review a few basic moral questions, okay? What's the opposite of wrong?"

Levine: "Poor."

Trudeau portrays Levine as a "bad apple" who is totally unresponsive to the counselor's attempt to appeal to some basic understanding of right and wrong. Levine, the "bad apple," just doesn't "get it."

Despite the appeal of the "bad apple" idea, character is a poorly defined concept, and when people talk about it, they rarely define what they mean. They're probably referring to a complex combination of traits that are thought to guide individual behavior in ethical dilemma situations. If character guides ethical conduct, training shouldn't make much difference because character is thought to be relatively stable, meaning that it's difficult to change, persists over time, and guides behavior across different contexts. Character develops slowly as a result of upbringing and the accumulation of values that are transmitted by schools, families, friends, and religious organizations. Therefore, people come to educational institutions or work organizations with an already defined good or poor character. Good apples will be good and bad apples will be bad.

In fact, people do have predispositions to behave ethically or unethically (we'll talk about these in Chapter 5). And sociopaths can certainly slip into organizations with the sole intent of helping themselves to the organization's resources, cheating customers, and feathering their own nests at the expense of others. They have little interest in "doing the right thing." When this type of individual shows up in your organization, the best thing to do is to discard the bad apple, making an example of the incident to those who remain.

But discarding "bad apples" won't necessarily solve an organization's problem with unethical behavior. The organization must also scrutinize itself to determine if there's something rotten in the organization that's spoiling the apples. You'll learn in this book that most people aren't guided by a strict and consistent internal moral compass. Rather, they look outside themselves for cues about how to think and behave, particularly when the circumstances are ambiguous or unclear as they are in many ethical dilemma situations. At work, the organizational culture transmits many cues about how one should think and behave. Executive leadership, norms, role models, reward systems, and many other components of the organizational culture combine to let people know what they're expected to do. Although much more subtle, this is as much an educational process as explicit ethics training.

So, another view suggests that "bad apples" may turn bad because they're spoiled by "bad barrels"— something in the organization that not only condones, but may even require unethical behavior. These are not bad folks to begin with. But their behavior can easily turn bad if they believe that their boss or their organization expects them to behave unethically. In this view, an organization that's serious about supporting ethical behavior and preventing misconduct must delve deeply into its own cultural norms and practices to search for systemic causes of unethical behavior. Management must take responsibility for the messages it sends or doesn't send about what's expected. If ethics problems are rooted in the organization's culture, discarding a few "bad apples," without changing that culture isn't going to solve the problem. An effective and lasting solution will rely on management's systematic attention to all aspects of the organization's culture and what it is explicitly or implicitly "teaching" organizational members.

Shouldn't Employees Already Know the Difference between Right and Wrong?

A belief associated with the good/bad apple idea is that any individual of good character should already know right from wrong and should be able to be ethical without special training. You probably think of yourself as an individual of good character. So, think about the following real dilemma.

You're the VP of a medium-sized organization that uses chemicals in its production processes. In good faith, you've hired a highly competent person to ensure that your company complies with all environmental laws and safety regulations. This individual informs you that a chemical the company now uses in some quantity is not yet on the approved EPA list, although it's undergoing review and is scheduled to be placed on the approved list in about three months because it's been found to be safe. You can't produce your product without this chemical, yet you're not supposed to use the chemical until it's approved. Waiting for approval would require shutting down the plant for three months, putting hundreds of people out of work, and threatening the company's very survival. What should you do?

The solution isn't clear cut, and good character isn't enough to guide decision making in this case. As with all ethical dilemmas, values are in conflict here—obeying the letter of the law versus keeping the plant open and saving jobs. The decision is complicated by the fact that the chemical has been found to be safe and is going to be approved in a matter of months. As in many of today's business decisions, this complex issue requires the development of occupation-specific skills and abilities. For example, some knowledge in the area of chemistry, worker safety, and environmental laws and regulations would be essential. Basic good intentions aren't enough.

James Rest, a scholar in the areas of professional ethics and ethics education, argued convincingly that "to assume that any 20-year-old of good general character can function ethically in professional situations is no more warranted than assuming that any logical 20-year-old can function as a lawyer without special education."[20] Good general character (whatever that means) doesn't prepare an individual to deal with the very special ethical problems that are likely to arise in one's career. Individuals must be trained to recognize and solve the unique ethical problems of their particular occupation. That's why many professional schools (business, law, medicine and others) have added ethics courses to their curricula.

So, although individual characteristics are a factor in determining ethical behavior, good character alone simply doesn't prepare people for the special ethical problems they're likely to face in their jobs or professions. Special training can prepare them to anticipate these problems, recognize ethical dilemmas when they see them, and provide them with frameworks for thinking about ethical issues in the context of their unique organizations.

Aren't Adults' Ethics Fully Formed and Unchangeable?

Another false assumption guiding the view that business ethics can't be taught is the belief that one's ethics are fully formed and unchangeable by the time one is old enough to enter college or a job. However, moral psychology research has found that this is definitely not the case.[23] Moral judgment develops throughout childhood and young adulthood in a complex process of social interaction with peers, parents, and other significant persons, and this development continues at least through young adulthood. In fact, young adults in their twenties and thirties in moral development educational programs have been found to advance in moral reasoning even more than younger individuals.[24] Given that most people enter professional education programs and corporations during young adulthood, the opportunity to influence their moral reasoning clearly exists.

Business school students may need ethics training more than most. Research has found that students in business ranked lower in moral reasoning than students in philosophy, political science, law, medicine, and dentistry.[25] And undergraduate business students and those aiming for a business career have been found to be more likely to engage in academic cheating (test cheating, plagiarism, etc.) than students in other majors or those headed toward other careers.[26] At a minimum, professional ethics education can direct attention to the ambiguities and ethical gray areas that are easily overlooked without it. Consider this comment from a 27-year-old Harvard student after a required (since 1988) nine-session ethics module in Decision Making and Ethical Values at the beginning of the Harvard MBA program.

> Before, [when] I looked at a problem in the businessworld I never consciously examined the ethical issues in play. It was always subconscious and I hope that I somewhat got it. But that [ethics] was never even a consideration. But now, when I look at a problem, I have to look at the impact. I'm going to put in this new ten-million-dollar project. What's going to be the impact on the people that live in the area and the environment. . . . It's opened my mind up on those things. It's also made me more aware of situations where I might be walking down the wrong path and getting in deeper and deeper, to where I can't pull back.[27]

It should be clear from the above arguments that ethics *can be taught*. Ethical behavior relies on more than good character. Although good upbringing may provide a kind of moral compass that can help the individual determine the right direction and then follow through on a decision to do the right thing, it's certainly not the only factor determining ethical conduct. In today's highly complex organizations, individuals need additional guidance. They can be helped to recognize the ethical dilemmas that are likely to arise in their jobs; the rules, laws, and norms that apply in that context; reasoning strategies that can be used to arrive at the best decision; and an understanding of the complexities of organizational life that can conflict with one's desire to do the right thing. For example, businesses that do defense-related work are expected to comply with a multitude of laws and regulations that go way beyond what the average person can be expected to know.

The question of whether ethics should be taught remains. Many still believe that ethics is a personal issue that should be left to individuals. Similar to attempts to proselytize about religion, they see attempts to teach ethics as inappropriate efforts to impose certain values and to control behavior. But we believe that it is an employer's responsibility to teach employees what they need to know in order to recognize and deal with the ethical issues they are likely to face in their jobs. Failure to do so is like failing to teach a machinist how to operate a machine properly. It's just poor management.

Defining Ethics

Some of the controversy about whether ethics can or should be taught may stem from disagreement about what we mean by ethics. Ethics can be defined as "a set of moral principles or values," a definition that portrays ethics as highly personal and relative. I have my moral principles, you have yours, and neither of us should try to impose our ethics on each other.

But we believe that a better definition of ethics is the principles, norms, and standards of conduct governing an individual or group. We expect work organizations to govern work-related conduct. They prescribe all kinds of behavior including what time to arrive and leave the workplace, whether smoking is allowed on the premises, how customers are to be treated, and how quickly work should be done. Prescriptions about ethical conduct aren't much different. Work organizations prescribe how employees should fill out expense reports, and they define what they consider to be a conflict of interest or bribe. If we use this definition, ethics becomes an extension of good management. Leaders identify appropriate and inappropriate conduct, and they convey their expectations to employees through ethics codes, training programs, and other communication mechanisms.

According to Carl Skooglund, vice president and ethics director at Texas Instruments, "ethics is the ground rules of how we are going to relate to other people — the expectations and understandings that define how we are going to deal with others. And by others we mean customers, suppliers, governments, communities, but most of all, one another. When you think about ethics in that context, ethics can be taught because we sure can teach what our expectations and understandings ought to be."

In most cases, individual employees will agree with their company's expectations and prescriptions. For example, who would disagree that it's wrong to steal company property, lie to customers, dump cancerous chemicals in the local stream, or comply with regulations on defense contracts? At times, however, an employee may find the organization's standards inconsistent with his or her own moral values or principles. For example, a highly religious employee of a health maintenance organization may object to offering abortion as an alternative when providing genetic counseling to pregnant women. Or, a highly devoted environmentalist may believe that his or her organization should go beyond the minimum standards of environmental law when making decisions about how much to spend on new technology or on environmental cleanup efforts. These individuals may be able to influence their employers' policies. Otherwise, the person's only recourse may be to leave the organization for one that is a better values match.

Good Control or Bad Control?

Whether or not we prefer to admit it, our ethical conduct is influenced (and, to a large degree, controlled) by our environment. In work settings, leaders, managers, and the entire cultural context are an important source of this influence and guidance. If, as managers, we allow employees to drift along without our guidance, we're unintentionally allowing them to be "controlled" by others. If this happens, we're contributing to the creation of "loose cannons" who can put the entire organization at risk. Guidance regarding ethical conduct is an important aspect of controlling employee behavior. It can provide essential information about organizational rules and policies, and guidance about behavior that is considered to be appropriate or inappropriate in a variety of situations.

But should organizations be "controlling" their employees in this way? B.F. Skinner,[28] the renowned late psychologist, argued that it's all right, even preferable, to intentionally control behavior. He believed that all behavior was controlled, intentionally or unintentionally. Therefore, what was needed was more intentional control, not less. Similarly, ethical and unethical behavior in organizations is already being controlled explicitly or implicitly by the existing organizational culture (see Chapter 9). Therefore, organizations that neglect to teach their members "ethical" behavior, may be tacitly encouraging "unethical behavior" through benign neglect. It's the organization's responsibility to provide guidance through explicit guidance and through the support of the organization's formal and informal cultural systems (see Chapter 9). The supervisor who attempts to influence the ethical behavior of subordinates shouldn't be viewed as a meddler, but as a part of the natural management process.

To summarize, we believe that educational institutions and work organizations should teach people about ethics and guide them in an ethical direction. Adults are open to, and generally welcome, this type of guidance. Ethical problems are not caused entirely by "bad apples." They're also the product of "bad barrels"—organizational systems that either encourage unethical behavior or, at least, allow it to occur. Making ethical decisions in today's complex organizations isn't a simple task. Good intentions and a good upbringing aren't enough. The special knowledge and skill required to make good ethical decisions in a particular job may be different from what's needed to resolve personal ethical dilemmas, and this knowledge and skill must be taught and cultivated.

THIS BOOK IS ABOUT MANAGING ETHICS

Now that we've (hopefully) convinced you that ethics is a worthwhile topic that can and should be taught, we need to discuss our somewhat unique approach to teaching business ethics. This book takes a managerial approach to business ethics. Between us, we have many years of experience in management, in consulting, and in management teaching and research. Based on this experience, we begin with the assumption that business ethics is essentially about human behavior, and that if we understand human behavior in an organizational context, we can better understand and manage our own and others' ethical conduct. Kent Druyvesteyn, vice president for ethics at General Dynamics from 1985 to 1993, made a clear distinction between philosophy and management in his many talks with students and executives over the years. As he put it, "I am not a philosopher and I am not here to talk about philosophy. Ethics is about conduct."

We agree with Mr. Druyvesteyn. After years of study and experience, we're convinced that most people need a management approach to help them deal with organizational ethics. As with any other management problem, managers need to understand why people behave the way they do so that they can influence this behavior. Most managers want the people with whom they work to be productive, to produce high quality products, to treat customers well, and to do all of this in a highly ethical manner. They also want and need help accomplishing these goals.

Therefore, we rely on a managerial approach to understanding business ethics. We introduce concepts that can be used to guide managers who want to understand their own ethical behavior and the behavior of others in the organization. And we provide practical guidance to those who wish to lead their department or organization in an ethical direction.

Consider this diagram:

First, we're defining ethical behavior in business as behavior that is consistent with the principles, norms, and standards of business practice that have been agreed upon by society. Although some disagreement exists about what these principles, norms, and standards should be, we believe that there is more agreement than disagreement. Many of the standards have been codified into law. Others can be found in company and industry codes of conduct and international trade agreements.

The ethical decision-making process involves three basic steps: moral awareness (recognizing the existence of an ethical dilemma), moral judgment (deciding what's right), and ethical behavior (taking action to do the right thing). We propose that all of these steps are influenced by two types of factors: characteristics of individuals and characteristics of organizations. Most ethics texts focus on individuals. They teach about philosophical theories that can help individuals analyze the ethics of a given situation—to make good moral judgments (the middle stage in the process). The idea is that ethical behavior will improve if people acquire these conceptual tools that can help them make sound ethical decisions. Business people know that deciding what's right represents an essential part of organizational ethics, and we agree. Therefore, we introduce some of the most useful philosophical theories designed to guide moral judgment in Chapter 4. But we also believe that acquiring these decision-making tools provides only a small part of the knowledge needed to improve business ethics. Sometimes people aren't even aware that they are facing an ethical dilemma. Even if they do, cognitive limitations and biases often limit their ability to make the best moral judgment (see Chapter 5). Furthermore, even when people know the right thing to do, they find it difficult to do the right thing because of group or organizational pressures. Therefore, our approach focuses on individuals and organizations—on ways to manage your own conduct and the conduct of other people in the organization, especially those who report to you. (Chapter 7 covers group and organizational influences, and Chapter 9 emphasizes the role of organizational culture.)

You'll notice from the diagram that we believe both characteristics of individuals and characteristics of organizations affect ethical behavior in organizations. But organizational factors are emphasized in the book because they are the factors managers can influence the most.

BRINGING ETHICS DOWN TO SIZE

Most ethics texts focus almost exclusively on "big" dilemmas that reflect a corporate position: "Should the company market this product or do business in China? Are executive compensation plans fair and equitable?" We include corporate-level examples, too, because they're important. But this book is also loaded with examples that reflect the ethical dilemmas facing individual employees and managers at all levels (see especially Chapters 3 and 6). "Should you blow the whistle on your employer? Should you accept a gift from a supplier? Should you hire your spouse's company to provide an important service to your firm?"

ETHICS AND THE LAW

You'll find many references to the law in the pages that follow. By including these references, we certainly don't mean to imply that the only guiding principle for deciding what's right should be whatever is legal. Perhaps the easiest way to think about the relationship between business ethics and the law is in terms of a Venn diagram. If we think of the law as reflecting society's minimum norms and standards of business conduct, we can see that there is a great deal of overlap between what's legal and what's ethical. Generally speaking, most people believe that law-abiding behavior is also ethical behavior. But there are many standards of conduct agreed upon by society that are not codified in law. For example, conflicts of interest may not be illegal, but they are generally considered to be unethical in our society and are commonly covered in codes of ethics. So, the domain of ethics includes the legal domain but extends beyond it to include the ethical standards and issues that the law does not address. Finally, there are times when you might encounter a law that you believe is unethical. For example, not so long ago racial discrimination was legal in the United States. Therefore, the legal and ethical domains certainly overlap to a large degree, but not completely. It is conceivable to think of something as being legal and unethical, or unethical but not covered by any law.

RELATIONSHIP BETWEEN
ETHICS AND LAW

HOW THE BOOK IS STRUCTURED

The present chapter of the book introduces our approach. Chapter 2 begins with (and attempts to answer) the question many students ask, "Why Be Ethical?" We describe concrete examples showing that people at all levels (from employees to managers to society) care about ethics, and that your success in business can depend on how well you can manage ethics.

The second section of the book focuses on ethics from an individual perspective. Chapter 3 categorizes the common ethical problems individuals face in work organizations. Chapter 4 presents the reader with an overview of some basic philosophical theories that have formed the underpinning for the traditional study of business ethics. It also suggests a list of practical decision-making steps individuals can follow to evaluate an ethical dilemma and decide on a course of action. Chapter 5 presents a more psychological approach to individual ethical decision making. It provides a kind of "reality check" for Chapter 4, suggesting that human cognitive limitations and biases can interfere with the ideal decision-making process (see diagram above). Chapter 5 also suggests that people do have predispositions to behave in certain ways when faced with ethical dilemma situations.

In Section III, we develop our management perspective on business ethics. Chapter 6 presents common ethical problems managers face when dealing with their subordinates, their superiors, and their peers and provides advice on what factors to consider when you're confronted with one of them. Chapter 7, "Managing for Ethical Conduct," introduces management concepts that can help explain the group and organizational pressures that influence people to behave ethically or unethically. We also provide practical advice for managers about how to use these management concepts to encourage ethical conduct and discourage unethical conduct in their employees.

Section IV is entitled "Ethics and the Organization." It begins with a chapter entitled, "Ethical Problems of Organizations." Although some people question whether corporations are moral entities, there are clearly ethical issues that can be classified as organizational level rather than managerial level. This chapter classifies those, using a stakeholder perspective, and provides examples of them. Chapter 9 focuses on business ethics as an organizational culture phenomenon. It provides a comprehensive overview of how an organization can build a culture that reflects a concern for ethics, and how it can change its culture to be more supportive of ethical conduct. Chapter 10 follows with practical advice on how organizations can design an ethics infrastructure, and effective communications and training programs. It also includes examples of successful programs various companies have implemented to encourage ethical conduct among their employees. Many of these examples resulted from interviews we conducted with top managers in these companies.

Section V wraps up the book with a chapter on international business ethics. Chapter 11 extends our discussion of business ethics to the global business environment. Although global examples appear throughout the book, this is an important enough issue to warrant its own chapter.

CONCLUSION

We hope that reading this book gives you a better understanding of how you can promote ethical behavior in yourself and others. An understanding of ethics is critical to all of us because good ethics represents the very essence of a civilized society. Ethics is the bedrock on which all of our relationships are built; it's about how we relate to our employers, our employees, our co-workers, our customers, our communities, our suppliers, and one another. Ethics is not about the connection we have to other beings—we are all connected—rather, it's about the quality of that connection. That's the real bottom line.

DISCUSSION QUESTIONS

1. Before reading this chapter, did you think of ethics as "just a fad?" Why or why not? What do you think now? Why?

2. Have you been cynical about business and its leaders? Why or why not? (See cynicism exercise that follows.) How does cynicism affect you, as a business student or as a manager?

3. We defined ethical behavior as "behavior that is consistent with the principles, norms and standards of business practice that have been agreed upon by society." What happens if society hasn't agreed? And what happens if you're doing business in a society different from your own? How would you define ethical behavior then?

4. Apply the "bad apple" idea to your own experience by citing an example of unethical conduct you observed. Was it the fault of a bad apple, was there "something rotten" in the barrel that contributed to the problem, or was it a combination of the two?

5. Can you think of something that is legal but unethical, or something that is ethical but illegal?

6. Cite an example of a situation you're familiar with where the "right" answer just wasn't obvious. What would a decision maker need to know in order to arrive at an acceptable solution?

7. Are you convinced that business ethics can and should be taught? Why or why not?

EXERCISE

Your Cynicism Quotient

Answer the following questions as honestly as you can. Circle the number between 1 and 5 that best represents your own beliefs about business.

		Strongly Disagree			Strongly Agree	
1.	Financial gain is all that counts in business.	1	2	3	4	5
2.	Ethical standards must be compromised in business practice.	1	2	3	4	5
3.	The more financially successful the business person, the more unethical the behavior.	1	2	3	4	5
4.	Moral values are irrelevant in business.	1	2	3	4	5
5.	The business world has its own rules.	1	2	3	4	5

		Strongly Disagree				Strongly Agree
6.	Business persons care only about making profit.	1	2	3	4	5
7.	Business is like a game—one plays to win.	1	2	3	4	5
8.	In business, people will do anything to further their own interest.	1	2	3	4	5
9.	Competition forces business managers to resort to shady practices.	1	2	3	4	5
10.	The profit motive pressures managers to compromise their ethical concerns.	1	2	3	4	5

Add the total number of points. The maximum is 50 points. Total _____

The higher your score, the more cynical you are about ethical business practice. Think about the reasons for your responses. Be prepared to discuss them in class.

NOTES

1. O'Toole, J. 1991. Do good, do well: The business enterprise trust awards. *California Management Review:* Spring, 9–24.

2. Olasky, M. N. 1985, 1986. Ministers or panderers: Issues raised by the public relations society code of standards. *Journal of Mass Media Ethics* 1, no. 1.

3. Employee cynicism: An examination using a contract violation framework. *Human Relations* 49: 1395–1418.

4. Baumhart, R. C. 1961. How ethical are businessmen? *Harvard Business Review* 39 (4): 6–8.

   Brenner, S. N., and Molander, E. A. 1977. Is the ethics of business changing? *Harvard Business Review* 55: 57–71.

5. Carroll, B. 1975. Linking business ethics to behavior in organizations. *S. A. M. Advanced Management Journal* 43: 3, 4–11.

   Jones, T. M., and Gautschi, F. H. 1988. Will the ethics of business change? A survey of future executives. *Journal of Business Ethics* 7: 231–248.

   Lincoln, D. J., Pressley, M. M., and Little, T. 1982. Ethical beliefs and personal values of top level executives. *Journal of Business Research* 10: 475–487.

   Posner, B. Z., and Schmidt, W. H. 1987. Ethics in American companies; A managerial perspective. *Journal of Business Ethics* 6: 383–391.

   Posner, B. Z., and Schmidt, W. H. 1992. Values and the American manager. *California Management Review,* Spring: 80–94

6. Baumhart, R. C. 1961. How ethical are businessmen? *Harvard Business Review* 39 (4): 6–8.

Baumhart, R. C. 1968. An honest profit: What businessmen say about ethics in business. New York: Holt, Rinehart and Winston.

Brenner, S. N., and Molander, E. A. 1977. Is the ethics of business changing? *Harvard Business Review* 55: 57–71.

7. Wood, J. A., Longenecker, J. G., McKinney, J. A., and Moore, C. W. 1988. Ethical attitudes of students and business professionals: A study of moral reasoning. *Journal of Business Ethics* 7: 249–257.

DeSalvia, D. N., and Gemmill, G. R. 1971. An exploratory study of the personal value systems of college students and managers. *Academy of Management Journal* 14: 227–238.

Lane, M. S., Schaupp, D., and Parsons, B. 1988. Pygmalion effect. *Journal of Business Ethics* 7: 223–229.

Fulmer, R. M. 1968. Business ethics: A view from the campus. *Personnel Administrator* 45 (2): 31–39.

Jones, T. M., and Gautschi, F. H. 1988. Will the ethics of business change? A survey of future executives. *Journal of Business Ethics* 7, 231–248.

8. Elber, L. 1997. Bad guys wear business suits; businessmen and women get a bad rap on television. *Centre Daily Times,* June 27, p. 22C.

9. Villains of prime time; Business is TVs newest bad guy. 1997. *Fortune,* July 7: 32.

10. Bateman, T. S., Sakano, T., and Fujita, M. 1992. Roger, me, and my attitude: Film propaganda and cynicism toward corporate leadership. *Journal of Applied Psychology* 77: 768–771.

11. Benson, T. E. 1991. Industry ethics edge upward. *Industry Week,* September 16: 18, 20.

12. O'Toole, J. 1991. Do good, do well: The business enterprise trust awards. *California Management Review,* Spring: 9–24.

13. Ibid.

14. Ibid.

15. Baumhart, R. C. 1961. How ethical are businessmen? *Harvard Business Review* 39 (4): 6–8.

16. Abrahamson, E. 1997. Proceedings of the Academy of Management.

17. Weaver, G., Treviño, L.K., and Cochran, P., in press. Corporate ethics practices in the mid-1990s: An empirical study of the Fortune 1000. *Journal of Business Ethics.*

18. Fineman, J. 1994. Virtuecrats. *Newsweek,* June 13: 31–36.

19. Levin, M. 1990, Ethics courses: Useless. *New York Times,* November 25.

20. Hanson, K. O. 1988, Why we teach ethics in business school. *Stanford Business School Magazine,* February: 14–16.

21. Treviño, L. K., and Youngblood, A. 1990. Bad apples in bad barrels: A causal analysis of ethical decision-making behavior. *Journal of Applied Psychology* 75 (4): 378–385.

22. Rest, J. R. 1988. Can ethics be taught in professional schools? The psychological research. *Easier Said Than Done,* Winter.

23. Ibid.

24. Rest, J. R., and Thoma, S. J. 1986. Educational programs and interventions. In *Moral development: Advances in research and theory.* J. Rest, ed. New York: Praeger, 59–88.

25. Best, J. R. 1987. Moral judgement: An interesting variable for higher education research. Paper for the Annual Convention for the Association for the Study of Higher Education, Baltimore, MD: November 21.

26. McCabe, D., and Treviño, L. K. 1993. Academic dishonesty: Honor codes and other situational influences. *Journal of Higher Education* 64: 522–538.

27. Piper, T.R., Gentile, M.C., and Parks, S. D. 1993. Can ethics be taught? Boston: Harvard Business School.

28. Skinner, B. F. 1971. *Beyond freedom and dignity*. New York: Knopf.

CHAPTER 2

Why Be Ethical?
(Why Bother? Who Cares?)

INTRODUCTION

It's impossible to know what John might have accomplished if he had lived. Since he was a brilliant young tax lawyer, he might have helped you structure your finances or defended you in court. He surely would have been the friendly, decent kind of neighbor you leave your key with when you leave town. Unfortunately, we'll never know.

We haven't created John or made him up. He was a son, a brother, a husband, and he became a father one month after he died in 1978. He was 32 years old. He died because some people who worked for a leading corporation never thought about how their product could affect him—or if they did think about it, they didn't care enough.

John unloaded sheets of asbestos during the summer between college and law school. Ten years later, asbestos particles killed him. The manufacturer knew before John was born that asbestos could cause fatal lung diseases and cancers in workers who handled it. But for decades they warned no one. And John, along with ship builders, brake repairers, and others, paid a terrible price—their lives.

Why be ethical? Why bother? Who cares? As individuals we must care about ethics because people like John will no longer contribute to our society; because our toddlers have sipped apple juice that contained no apples; our sisters have had birth control devices that maimed them; our coastlines have been scarred by oil spills.

As workers, we care about ethics because most of us prefer to work for ethical organizations. We want to feel good about ourselves and the work we do. As managers, we must be concerned about the ethics of the people who report to us. More than just our jobs depend on this concern—recent legislation has made managers liable for the criminal activities of their subordinates.

Organizations must care about ethics because their members depend on them to help define the boundaries of acceptable and unacceptable behavior.

Also, ethical lapses can cost an organization dearly, in shattered customer confidence, increased government regulation, and huge fines.

Finally, no matter what our role, we must bother about ethics because we're people first. We live in a world community—we're all inextricably connected to each other and to the environment and our future depends on our caring enough.

THE MOTIVATION TO BE ETHICAL

Classical economists assume that practically all human behavior, including altruism, is motivated solely by self-interest—that humans are purely rational economic actors who make choices solely on the basis of cold cost/benefit analyses. But there is much evidence to suggest that people also act for altruistic or moral purposes that seem to have little to do with cost/benefit analyses.[1] For example, people will:

mail back lost wallets to strangers, cash and all

help strangers in distress

donate blood marrow for strangers, or a kidney to a family member

In his book, *The Moral Dimension,* Etzioni[2] cited many more examples and research evidence to document his claim that human action has two distinct sources: the pursuit of pleasure or self-interest, and moral commitments. Accordingly, most human decisions are based on ethical and emotional considerations as well as rational economic self-interest. They're motivated by both economic and moral concerns.

Therefore, we begin this chapter with an important assumption—that, as members of society, all of us have moral and ethical concerns as well as self-interested economic concerns. You will see in this chapter that people and organizations care about ethics for reasons that stem from both of these sources. For example, organizations may be interested in being ethical in order to avoid criminal liability or a bad reputation, or they may be interested in being ethical just because they believe it's the right thing to do.

THE MEDIA FOCUS ON ETHICS AND CORPORATE REPUTATION

If you believe that the media focus attention on issues people care about, then lots of people must care about ethics. In recent years, the media spotlight has focused on the problem of serious ethical lapses in every type of organization—business, government, educational, religious, sports, and others. We've all heard about insider traders, businesses that overcharge the government, government employees who steal or misuse funds, academics who falsify their research results, students who cheat, ministers who steal from their congregations, athletes who take bribes, and companies that exploit poor workers in developing countries.

Hollywood, society's most powerful image maker, has generally portrayed business people as sleazy, greedy, and heartless. Who can forget J.R. Ewing, who "slithered across the TV screen as the vile head of Ewing Oil" on the TV series "Dallas," or Michael Douglas as Gordon Gecko, the unscrupulous corporate raider who corrupted a young stockbroker in the film *Wall Street?*[3] Charles Brown, former chairman of AT&T, asked, "When was the last time you watched a TV sitcom in which a business person was the hero?"[4]

But can the media really influence an organization's image? The answer is yes. Since 1982, *Fortune* magazine has conducted an annual "most admired corporations" survey, based on ratings provided by senior executives, outside directors, and financial analysts. Using these survey data along with additional data, an academic study investigated the relationship between media coverage and change in corporate image or reputation.[5] Overall, more positive media coverage meant a more positive corporate reputation. And for companies that began with poor reputations, positive media exposure was associated with significant image improvements.

But does reputation really matter? According to *Business Week*, "business has a huge stake in the way the rest of society perceives its ethical standards." On the negative side, scandals give business "a black eye"[5] and cost money. For example, in response to media reports that raised questions about Dow Corning's breast implants, the stock of Corning, Inc., one of the two corporate parents, declined by about 15 percent, despite the fact that the implants represented only around 1 percent of Dow Corning's business, and insurance coverage seemed adequate to cover potential lawsuits.[7] Similarly, Exxon faced years of negative media scrutiny after the Exxon Valdez oil spill.

Business isn't the only kind of organization that can be negatively affected by media exposure and a bad reputation. Since the 1940s, the United Way has been the "blue chip of charities." In 1992, the United Way's reputation as a trusted community philanthropic organization was severely damaged when the extravagances of its leader were aired in the press. President William Aramony resigned amid charges of nepotism and misuse of agency funds to support his lavish lifestyle. For the United Way, reputation translates into dollars contributed to its funding coffers. After the scandal, the organization (both at national and community levels) struggled to regain its lost public trust. Reports suggest that the United Way network raised $66 million less in 1992 than in 1991. In attempts to regain the public trust, United Way appointed a new president, implemented new cost controls and accountability measures, and established an ethics program. For United Way, "doing business differently" is now seen as a matter of the organization's survival.[8] However, recent reports suggest that the organization is still reeling from the scandal along with changes in the way Americans give to charity. The result—4.5 million former donors (20 percent) have simply stopped giving to the United Way, and many of the remaining 17.7 million now give less.[9]

On a more positive note, a favorable corporate reputation "may enable firms to charge premium prices, attract better applicants, enhance their access to capital markets, and attract investors."[10] In its March 2, 1998 issue, *Fortune* magazine reported that if an investor had bought $1,000 worth of stock in its top ten most admired companies and reinvested the dividends, that investment would have compounded into $146,419 today—three times more than a similar investment in the Standard & Poor's 500 would have produced. But top financial performance alone does not get a company into the ranks of the "most admired." The most admired companies have great leaders, outstanding employee relations, and they have stayed out of legal and ethical trouble. Southwest Airlines is on the 1998 list of America's most admired companies. Herb Kelleher, the CEO, says, "we pay just as good wages and benefits as other airlines, but our costs are lower because our productivity is higher, which is achieved through the dedicated energy of our people. It's sheer willpower—no mechanical tricks." In explaining how Southwest can empty and refill a plane in 20 minutes when it takes other airlines an hour, Kelleher says, "We've got exactly the same equipment. The difference is, when a plane pulls into a gate, our people run to meet it." The leaders of the most admired companies are in love with their businesses. Kelleher says, "I love it, I love it—I sure as heck do."[11]

The media generally ignores the millions of routine but ethical transactions that must occur every day if society is to function effectively. However, the media spotlight does shine on those particularly positive or negative events that are considered to be newsworthy. Organizations that find themselves in the media spotlight will find their reputations either enhanced or sullied by this media attention.

MANAGERS CARE ABOUT ETHICS

Managers care about ethics in part because they face the thorny problem of how to prevent and manage unethical behavior in their ranks. Ask any manager for examples and be prepared to spend the day. As just one example of self-interested unethical behavior, the U.S. Chamber of Commerce estimates that workplace theft costs U.S. businesses up to $40 billion each year and employees are thought to be responsible for much of it.[12] In addition to self-interested behavior, employees may engage in unethical behavior because they think (rightly or wrongly) that it's expected. Or, they simply may not know that they are doing something that's considered to be unethical.[13]

Whatever its source, subordinates' unethical behavior is a management problem that won't go away. It may become even more of a challenge as restructuring reduces management layers, leaving fewer managers to supervise more workers. With more workers to supervise, the manager can't directly observe behavior. Restructuring is also increasing the number of part-time or contingency workers. These workers are likely to feel less loyalty to the organization and may be more prone to engage in unethical behaviors such as theft.

Furthermore, more workers may cross the ethical/unethical behavior line in response to fierce business competition and strict focus on the bottom line. Employees may believe that they can help the company succeed (at least in the short term) by fudging sales figures, abusing competitors, or shortchanging customers. Those who are potential layoff candidates are also more likely to flirt with impropriety.[14] Many perceive the message to be "reaching objectives is what matters and how you get there isn't that important."[15] Therefore, today's managers may have to work even harder to communicate that ethical conduct is expected, even in the midst of aggressive competition.

Finally, many managers understand the positive long-term benefit a reputation for ethics can bring to business dealings. Carl Skooglund, vice president and ethics director at Texas Instruments, had this to say, "We try to explain to people why ethics has a positive benefit. It is far more than just keeping you out of trouble, or mitigating your sentences with a judge. There are very positive, even competitive reasons to be ethical. If you walk into a relationship and somebody says, 'I know you, I know your track record, I can trust you,' that's important. Two years ago, in a survey that we sent out to employees, I received an anonymous comment from somebody who said, 'A reputation for ethics which is unreproachable is a silent partner in all business negotiations.' I agree and it works in all personal and business relationships. An unethical company is very difficult to do business with. You can't trust them. You're never sure if a commitment's a commitment. At TI, our customers have told us that they can be sure of one thing: once TI commits, we're going to break our tail to make it happen. That's an easy company to do business with."

EXECUTIVE LEADERS CARE ABOUT ETHICS

Many business executives care about ethics and about business's image in society. John Akers, former chairman of the board of IBM, wrote that "No society anywhere will compete very long or successfully with people stabbing each other in the back; with people trying to steal from each other; with everything requiring notarized confirmation because you can't trust the other fellow; with every little squabble ending in litigation; and with government writing reams of regulatory legislation, tying business hand and foot to keep it honest. . . . There is no escaping this fact; the greater the measure of mutual trust and confidence in the ethics of a society, the greater its economic strength."[16]

Robert D. Haas, chairman and CEO of Levi Strauss & Co., discussed the importance of company values this way:

> Levi has always treated people fairly and cared about their welfare. The usual term is "paternalism." But it is more than paternalism, really—a genuine concern for people and a recognition that people make this business successful.
>
> In the past, however, that tradition was viewed as something separate from how we ran the business. We always talked about the "hard stuff" and the "soft stuff." The soft stuff was the company's commitment to our work force. And the hard stuff was what really mattered; getting pants out the door.
>
> What we've learned is that the soft stuff and the hard stuff are becoming increasingly intertwined. A company's values—what it stands for, what it's people

believe in—are crucial to its competitive success. Indeed, values drive the business. . . . Values are where the hard stuff and the soft stuff come together.[17]

Joe Paterno, Penn State University's legendary football coach, said the following in an interview about his program's reputation for integrity.

It makes good sense to be ethical—to be honest. If there's a rule, I insist that we adhere to the rule. If my people say, "Hey the other guy is breaking the rule, I say in the short run, it may hurt us, but in the long run we'll be way ahead of them." It may mean we have to work a little harder. Instead of calling on 10 players to recruit five, we may have to call on 15 or 20. . . . It's certainly doable because we're doing it. I don't care if it's in football or in business. You've got to have enough guts and enough confidence in your ability to do it right. . . . There's a difference between success and excellence in the sense that it's easy to make money. It's easy to win. You can manipulate, cut corners. But, I think you have to have a standard that you believe in and stay with it. We're in it for the long run. This isn't a get-rich-quick kind of operation. If we were in business, we wouldn't play games with the company to get the stock up in the next three years. We'd be in it for the long haul. And, we'd be a better company. Once you establish that, the stockholders or the fans love you.

We believe that, although intertwined with the "hard stuff," organizational ethics is a distinct managerial concern that must be addressed by management at all levels of the organization. Top management's role is particularly important. The leaders of America's business organizations don't "leap from bed in the morning in order to maximize the risk-adjusted present value of streams of future cash flows." Their role is "not simply financial and administrative, but social, political, and moral."[18] This book will provide insight into this moral leadership role and its importance in creating and maintaining the organization's ethical culture (see Chapter 9).

EMPLOYEES CARE ABOUT ETHICS—EMPLOYEE ATTRACTION AND COMMITMENT

Organizations are concerned about their ability to hire and retain the best workers. The evidence suggests that employees are more attracted to and more committed to ethical organizations. "People who know that they are working for something larger with a more noble purpose can be expected to be loyal and dependable, and, at a minimum, more inspired."[19]

Recent studies confirm that it may be important to consider how potential and current employees are affected by the organization's ethics. In a survey conducted by *Working Woman* magazine, "a strong majority of those polled said that they would not work for a company with a history of environmental accidents, insider trading or worker accidents, or a law firm that defends known racketeers."[20] In another survey conducted by a national opinion research firm, ethical corporate behavior, honest company communications, and respectful treatment ranked among employees' five top-ranked goals, before good pay, which was eleventh on the list, and job security, which ranked fourteenth. Ethical corporate behavior was ranked so high because "workers translate the ethics of the company into how they're personally treated." People "want to be proud of where they work.." They "don't want to work for bandits, and when companies get negative publicity for their activities, workers suffer."[21]

Academic studies[22] have found that workers are more attracted to socially responsible firms.[23] They are also more committed to organizations that have a "benevolent climate"—one that focuses on the welfare of employees and the community, while organizational commitment is lower in "egoistic" climates (based on self-interest and people being out for themselves). Employees are also more committed to organizations whose top managers represent high ethical standards and whose reward systems support ethical conduct and discipline unethical conduct.[24] Yet another survey found that managers who believed their senior management to be credible (i.e., honest and competent) reported positive attachments to their organization.[25]

For a concrete example, let's look again at Levi Strauss & Co. Turnover among managers at headquarters in San Francisco is just 1.5 percent a year. Here's what Ruth Meyler, associate general counsel, was quoted as saying in *Fortune* magazine, "The company where I worked before partook of the classic dog-eat-dog ethos. When you got dressed in the morning, metaphorically speaking, you had to put on your breastplate and helmet and have your musket loaded. At Levi Strauss, you are the same person at the office and at home. I find that extraordinarily important.[26]

INDIVIDUALS CARE ABOUT ETHICS—REPUTATION COUNTS

Employees are not just organizational drones. They are individual human beings who are concerned about their relationships and their personal reputations. In today's work environment, success depends on one's ability to work effectively with others. Trust greases the wheels of working relationships with peers across departments and on project teams. We disagree with the old adage that "nice guys (or gals) finish last." If it looks like bad guys (or gals) come out ahead, this is generally a short-run result. A reputation for being difficult to work with, dishonest, or mean usually catches up with you as co-workers withhold important information and promotions go to others. Given the importance of relationships to effectiveness in business today, one's reputation for integrity is an essential ingredient for success and personal satisfaction.

In our interview with Carl Skooglund, vice president and ethics director at Texas Instruments, he talked about a story he tells college recruits who visit Texas Instruments. "I quote Helen Hayes. (She was quoted on the radio, and I almost wrecked the car copying it down.) She made a statement that applies to anybody who is a parent, a teacher, a manager, a supervisor, a spouse, anybody who is in a position of trust. She said, 'When they call you a star, you are obligated to conduct yourself above reproach. People give you their hearts and their trust, and you have no right to let them down.' I tell the recruits, look, there are going to be decisions you have to make. There are going to be times when things will be given to you. There are going to be times when things will be taken away—perhaps even your job. But throughout your professional life, there is one thing that nobody can ever take away from you unless you make the decision to let them take it away from you, and that is your integrity."

DOES SOCIETY CARE? BUSINESS AND SOCIAL RESPONSIBILITY

Most of this book is about ethics inside organizations. But we also need to consider business's role in society and whether business has social as well as financial responsibilities. A rich literature on corporate social performance suggests reasons why corporations must be socially, as well as financially, responsible.[27] First, from an economic perspective, business must use its power responsibly or risk losing it. Businesses are responsible to multiple stakeholders. Recall that a stakeholder was defined in Chapter One as any party (e.g., customers, employees, suppliers, the government, stockholders, the community) who has a stake in what the organization does and how it performs.[28] These stakeholders often have the power to interfere with a firm's autonomy and economic freedom. For example, employees can strike, customers can boycott products, and the government can pass laws and regulate a firm's activities. In this economic perspective on social responsibility, corporations must be socially responsible in order to avoid economic harm and in order to maintain the legitimacy granted by society.[29]

A second duty-based perspective argues that businesses have an ethical responsibility to stakeholders that goes beyond avoiding economic harm. Responsible executives have a duty to care about justice and stakeholder rights because it is the right thing to do. This perspective supports corporate policies and practices that go beyond legal or regulatory requirements, such as the development of quality products that contribute to societal welfare, human resource practices that treat employees fairly, manufacturing processes that protect the environment, and contributions to help the firm's community. These

Figure 1   Corporate Social Responsibility Pyramid

(Reprinted by permission, from the Foundation for the School of Business at Indiana University, *Business Horizons,* July/August, 1991.)

policies and practices may "pay" especially in the long term. For example, the best employees may be attracted to firms that treat people well. But, those who argue for the duty-based perspective would say that the positive duty exists whether or not an economic payoff results.[30]

Obviously, the biggest corporate social responsibility challenges come when ethical responsibility and economic responsibility conflict. For example, if the long-term economic interests of the firm require that employees be laid off, a duty-based perspective would require that the layoffs be carried out in a fair and just manner.

Corporate social responsibility (CSR) has been conceptualized as a pyramid constituting four kinds of responsibility that must be considered simultaneously: economic, legal, ethical, and philanthropic.[31] (See Figure 2.1.)

Economic Responsibilities

Economic responsibilities refer to business's primary function as a producer of goods and services that consumers need and want, while making an acceptable profit. This responsibility is considered to be primary, because without financial viability the other responsibilities become moot issues.

Milton Friedman is the most outspoken proponent of the argument that management's sole responsibility is to maximize profits for shareholders. Yet, even he states that management should "make as much money as possible while conforming to the basic rules of society, both those embodied in the law and those embodied in ethical custom."[32] Interestingly, this statement tacitly embraces two of the three additional components of the corporate social responsibility pyramid: legal and ethical responsibility.

Legal Responsibilities

In addition to its economic responsibilities, business is expected to carry out its work in accordance with the law and government regulations. The law guiding business practice can be viewed as a fundamental precept of the free enterprise system and as coexisting with economic responsibilities.

Ethical Responsibilities

Obviously, not every societal expectation has been codified into law. Therefore, ethical responsibilities encompass the more general responsibility to do what's right and avoid harm. For example, PPG Industries, Inc. has a Worldwide Code of Ethics. On their website (ppg.com), they say "PPG's ethics go beyond the legal code. Compliance with the law is the absolute minimum expected of a PPG associate, no matter where he or she works. All PPG associates are expected to behave in a manner which is not only lawful but also morally acceptable to all of the constituencies with whom we have dealings."

Vin Sarni, former CEO of PPG, said:"It is not enough to simply say that our conduct is lawful. The law is the floor. Compliance with it will be the absolute minimum with respect to the PPG associate, no matter where he or she works. Our ethics go beyond the legal code. . . .That's not just waving the flag. We live that. And, I personally believe that we have a competitive advantage from being that way."

In 1993, when GM claimed that its sidesaddle fuel tank design (placed outside the truck frame in order to carry more fuel) met all federal regulations, a Georgia jury apparently wasn't convinced that the company had met its ethical obligation to avoid harm. In the case of a 17-year-old who was killed when his pickup truck's gas tank exploded, the jury found the company negligent and awarded the boy's parents over $100 million in punitive damages.

Given its problematic history (more than 150,000 lawsuits alleging health problems from exposure to asbestos), the Manville Corporation (formerly Johns-Manville) now goes above and beyond its legal responsibilities with regard to product safety. In addition to complying with U.S. law by placing warning labels on all of its fiberglass products, Manville puts warning labels on fiberglass products being shipped to Japan. The company did this despite the fact that such warnings are not required by local law, and despite the fact that the company was advised against it by the Japanese government because the warnings might result in cancer fears. Tom Stephens, chairman, president, and chief executive officer (CEO), said, "But a human being in Japan is no different from a human being in the U.S. We told them we had a policy. We had to have a label." Although the company lost 40 percent of its sales to Japan in one year, it was later able to rebuild its Japanese business.[33]

Thus, the ethical responsibility category frequently interacts with the legal category, pushing the expansion of legal responsibilities, and placing expectations on business persons to function at a level above the law. Social responsibility involves how business organizations manage both their legal and ethical obligations.

Philanthropic Responsibilities

Finally, philanthropic responsibilities involve the corporation's active involvement in activities that promote human welfare or goodwill. This generally includes donations of time and money, such as donations to the United Way, or mentoring programs for disadvantaged youth. Because philanthropy is considered by many people to be a voluntary or discretionary aspect of corporate social responsibility, failure to be philanthropic is generally not considered to be unethical. On the other hand, in American culture, those with wealth (including wealthy businesses) are expected to share their good fortune. Andrew Carnegie, the nineteenth-century steel baron who gave millions to charity, claimed that "he who dies rich dies thus disgraced." In a 1990s version of the same belief, broadcasting tycoon Ted Turner pledged $1 billion to the United Nations in 1997 to help refugees, and he challenged other wealthy business people to follow his lead.

Government Regulation of Business

Government regulation is one way that society shows that it cares about responsible conduct in business. Consider recent changes in health care in the United States. Market forces have helped to reduce inflation in health care costs as managed care companies compete for patients. But citizens have called upon states and the federal government to intervene with regulations that limit the financial incentives these companies can give to doctors and that bar them from excluding people with preexisting medical conditions. In a recent book by Robert Kuttner entitled *Everything for Sale; the Virtues and Limits of Markets,* the author argued that regulated competition is the wave of the future. According to Kuttner, regulation is necessary because, as a society, we have commitments to certain public purposes such as universal access to electricity (even in unprofitable rural areas) and health insurance (even for otherwise uninsurable cancer or AIDS patients). Furthermore, in some markets, consumers don't have choices, as when there is only one local cable-TV company or when economies of scale make competition inefficient. (For example, it wouldn't be efficient to string multiple power lines to every home.). Sometimes, in order to create competition, monopolies (such as the former AT&T) need to be restrained through regulation. Finally, government is responsible for preventing serious risks to our system (for example, by regulating the financial services industry) and for holding companies accountable for the "externalities" they create. Externalities are costs to society, such as air and water pollution, that are produced by companies but that are not reflected in the company's cost structure.[34] As consumers, we rely on our representatives in government to hold companies accountable for their actions. We want to be sure that our air, food, and water are safe, that airlines don't skimp on maintenance or pilot training, and that physicians who work for managed care companies put patient care ahead of profits.

Is Socially Responsible Business Good Business?

We don't have a perfect answer to this question. There's anecdotal evidence on both sides. For example, we can probably all name individuals who have "gotten ahead" the unethical way. Despite our desire to believe otherwise, unethical managers can be successful, and unethical organizations can be profitable, at least in the short term.

On the other hand, one can also point to highly ethical organizations that have been extremely profitable. In an attempt to demonstrate a positive link between good ethics and firm financial performance, James Burke, former CEO of Johnson & Johnson, compiled a list of major companies with a reputation for ethics and social responsibility. The group, including such recognized names as J&J, Coca-Cola, Gerber, IBM, Deere, 3M, Xerox, J.C. Penney, and Pitney Bowes, grew at a rate of 11.3 percent annually from 1950 to 1990, while the growth rate for Dow Jones industrials as a whole was only 6.2 percent for the same period.[35]

Many business leaders argue that ethics pays in the long term. For example, Norman Augustine, chairman of Lockheed Martin (formerly CEO of Martin Marietta), a large defense contractor, recounted a situation when the company's ethics were on the line. When competing on a government contract, the company received a brown paper bag containing their competitor's bid. They immediately turned it over to the U.S. government and told the competitor about it. The company lost the contract, employees lost jobs, and shareholders lost money—huge short-term losses. But Augustine is convinced that the loss was only short term. "We helped establish a reputation that, in the long run, will draw us business. . . it always pays off in the long term."

Over the years, studies that have attempted to document the relationship between social responsibility and financial performance have shown both positive and negative relationships.[36] When positive correlations were found, it wasn't clear whether social responsibility led to increased financial performance or whether higher financial performance provided firms with more slack resources that they could then devote to social performance. Recent research suggests that both are likely to be true.[37] A recent study used an index of eight attributes of corporate social responsibility as rated by the firm Kinder, Lydenberg, Domini, an independent service that assesses corporate social performance of companies in the Standard & Poor's 500, based on firms' responses to key stakeholder interests. Firms with strong financial performance were rated higher on corporate social performance, suggesting that companies that do well financially allocate more resources to social concerns—they "do good by doing well." Those that are not in good financial health may not have the funds to engage in philanthropy or other discretionary social performance activities. The study also found that financial performance depends on good social performance, suggesting that firms also "do well by doing good." The authors termed this the "good management theory," arguing that good social performance is related to other good managerial practices. It is likely that these relationships are linked in what the authors termed a "virtuous circle" in which good corporate social performance feeds financial performance and good financial performance makes it possible to continue good corporate social performance. Clearly, being socially responsible doesn't harm the firm's bottom line as some economists have suggested in the past. In fact, the study's findings suggest that a firm's relationships with key stakeholders (e.g., employees, community, natural environment) are important to its financial performance.[38]

A recent study has also found that socially irresponsible and illegal corporate behavior are associated with substantial negative stock market returns. The author synthesized the results of 27 studies that covered over 2,000 incidents of socially irresponsible or illegal behavior. Across these studies, stock prices decreased significantly in response to socially irresponsible or illegal acts,[39] thereby decreasing shareholder wealth. These results suggest that there are definitely costs to being socially irresponsible.

The research we just reviewed supports the idea that social responsibility can be financially rewarding and that irresponsibility can be costly. But we would like to propose that business people may have another reason to believe in "good ethics" and social responsibility—because they're people first, who value their good reputations and the opinion of their friends, family, and community. They're guided by a moral compass that points them in an ethical direction, as well as a financial compass that points them toward consideration of the costs and benefits of a decision. As one business person put it, "I can only really speak for myself, and to me, my word is the most important thing in my life and my credibility as an individual is paramount. All the other success we have had is secondary."[40]

Michael Josephson clearly separated good ethics from good business when he said:

> Goodness does not guarantee winning. And unless we can teach that to people, they are always going to look for the angle . . . ethics [is a] separate, independent evaluation of conduct. . . . Ethics is like your skin—it goes with you everywhere. Ethics is a moral perspective that asks you to judge your conduct in terms of what's right and wrong, what's decent, what's good, what's honest, what's honorable. The reason to be ethical is simply that it's the right thing to do.[41]

You've probably heard of Malden Mills, the Massachusetts manufacturer of Polarfleece and Polartec fabrics. On December 11, 1995, while the CEO was celebrating his 70th birthday, the company experienced a catastrophic industrial fire that wiped out three of four factories in Lawrence, Massachusetts. The fourth building was saved due to the heroic efforts of 27 union employees who fought the fire all night. No one was killed in the fire, thanks to the efforts of employees who checked attendance sheets, made a human chain, and dragged their fellow employees to safety. After the fire, CEO Aaron Feuerstein carried the welfare of his employees, customers, and the Lawrence community on his shoulders. "There is no way I would throw 3,000 workers into the street—no way I would take Lawrence, Massachusetts and condemn them to economic oblivion."[42] He quickly announced that he would keep his 3,000 jobless employees on the payroll for a month, which he extended to two months, and then three months, while the factory was being rebuilt. Feuerstein paid out a total of more than $15 million in wages and benefits to jobless employees after the fire. Employees jumped to the challenge. Just a few weeks after the fire, productivity was even higher than it had been before the fire because of employees' creativity and willingness to work "25 hours a day."[43] By summer, almost all of the employees had returned to work, and the 400 unemployed got extended health benefits, help finding work, and a promise of a job when the new plant opened. Feuerstein received accolades from the workforce and the media, and an invitation from President Bill Clinton to attend the State of the Union Address.

Many in the business community thought Feuerstein should have pocketed the insurance money and moved the company somewhere with lower labor costs, perhaps overseas. But *Fortune* magazine praised Feuerstein as an astute businessman in his handling of the disaster. He treated his employees as an asset rather than an expense, cultivated their loyalty, and bet on the company's future. Feuerstein says that Malden Mills has been successful when other U.S. textile companies have failed because of employees' product innovation and production quality. Malden Mills' research and development and production employees literally saved the company in the early 1980s when the bottom dropped out of the market for artificial furs, the company's mainstay at the time. Employees used their expertise to create and manufacture high-quality Polarfleece and Polartec, synthetic fabrics that are engineered to fit specific customers' needs. Malden Mills holds patents for the fabrics and for the machines used to manufacture them. The latest application is a new line of expensive upholstery fabrics, snapped up at a recent European trade show. Productivity is high, and customers such as Eddie Bauer, Lands' End, L.L. Bean, North Face, and Patagonia are extremely loyal. The decision to rebuild the factory was also a rational one because insurance covers the replacement cost of a factory only if it is rebuilt. If he hadn't replaced the factory, Feuerstein might have had to settle for the depreciated value of the burned building and its contents. And moving the factory overseas would have risked losing the quality advantage. Finally, Feuerstein took advantage of a mountain of free media attention from *People* and *Parade* magazines, TV news magazines such as "Dateline," and more.[44] Feuerstein and Malden Mills were the focus of media attention again in September 1997 when the rebuilt plant was opened. Almost all employees were back at work, and their love for the CEO was obvious.

According to *Fortune,* "any idiot with a strong enough stomach can make quick money, sometimes a lot of it, by slashing costs and milking customers, employees, or a company's reputation. But clearly that's not the way to make a lot of money for a long time. The way to do that is to create so much value that your customers wouldn't dream of looking for another supplier. Indeed, the idea is to build a value creation system of superior products, service, teamwork, productivity, and cooperation with the buyer."[45] This view jives with Feuerstein's philosophy. In a 1997 talk to management professors at their annual Academy of Management meeting, Feuerstein said that his business objective is to win by creating a better-performing, higher-quality product that is different from what competitors are making. But, to do that, you have to have the right people, trust, and understanding. You have to extend to your people the loyalty you want them to extend to you. Clearly, Feuerstein is an accomplished businessman. But he is also driven by deeply held moral beliefs. In that same talk to business professors, he quoted the Bible (in Hebrew!) on the responsibility of a rich man not to praise himself for his riches, and to do kindness, justice, and charity in the community. Given his moral beliefs, he believed that he had no choice but to rebuild his factories.

So, to Feuerstein, the question "Is socially responsible business good business?" is tautological. Good business doesn't refer to just the financial bottom line. It refers to business that does well financially by producing superior and unique products that meet customers' needs AND by being responsible to employees and the community.

Socially Responsible Investors

A new breed of shareholder cares about both the financial and social bottom line of business. "Socially responsible" investors insist that their investments meet ethical as well as financial criteria. They "put their cash where their conscience is." Although the social criteria vary, many shun certain types of industries, such as nuclear energy, weapons, and tobacco, while they support companies that use energy wisely, protect the environment, and market safe products and services. They may also consider the firm's human resource practices such as female and minority advancement, day care, or profit-sharing. Books such as *The Better World Investment Guide*[46] provide ethical investors with specific company evaluations based on ethical criteria. A number of brokers, financial planners, and mutual funds are also now serving these investors' needs. A trade association, the Social Investment Forum, reported that socially responsible investing grew from $40 billion in 1984 to over $600 billion in 1995. They listed 55 funds that use some ethical screen and manage $12 billion for investors (see www.socialinvest.org for the study). What does all of this mean for business ethics? It means that, at least for this group of investors, shareholders' interests are no longer distinct from employee, customer, and community interests. They're all interconnected.[47]

Social Responsibility Rewarded—The Business Enterprise Trust

The Business Enterprise Trust (BET) is an organization established to acknowledge the hundreds of individuals and business organizations exhibiting "courage, integrity and social vision" in their work. BET awards, given annually since 1990, have focused on companies that produce socially responsible products, support philanthropic projects, engage in enlightened personnel practices, and more. Following are representative awardees who are highlighted on the BET website (www.betrust.org).

> The aging owners of the Orchard Corporation passed up lucrative acquisition offers until they found a buyer who pledged not to sell off assets to finance the acquisition, and who was willing to let the company continue its people-oriented "open communications policy."[48]
>
> The McKay Nursery Company in Waterloo, Wisconsin, created an employee stock ownership plan for all of its employees, including its seasonal employees who are migrant laborers. Most of these employees return year after year and are taking advantage of this opportunity to save for retirement.
>
> Donna Klein and Marriott International in Washington, D.C., developed the Associate Resource Line (ARL), a 24-hour counseling telephone line aimed at the company's 100,000 plus low-income workers. This multilingual hotline helps these employees with social service-related issues such as child care, substance abuse, domestic violence, and immigration and naturalization. As a result, the company has significantly reduced turnover, absenteeism and tardiness among these employees, and customer service has improved.

Others have been nominated for providing community services that go way beyond traditional philanthropy. A prime example is GE Plastics' (a division of General Electric) "Share to Gain" program, implemented for the first time at the company's division meetings in 1989. GE had recently acquired Borg-Warner Chemicals, and company representatives decided that some kind of team-building activity was needed to help Borg-Warner attendees get to know GE employees and their culture. Forsaking the usual annual meeting events (golf, fishing, and sailing) GE Plastics planned something entirely new—an opportunity for people to get to know each other by "sharing a hard day's work for a good cause." Five community sites in San Diego, California, were chosen based on their desperate need for repair. After meticulous planning, hundreds of people worked together to totally renovate each facility in a single eight-hour day. The events were a tremendous success by all accounts. The facilities were renovated, the participants built new friendships and working relationships, and felt good about what they had accomplished together.

Trust and the Benefits of Self-Governance

A more elusive benefit of ethics in organizations is trust. Many in the business community believe that, although difficult to document, trust has both economic and moral value. The introductory statement to the Disney code of ethics states that, "[The] public trust, above all else, is the basis for the remarkable success of the Disney organization." John Shad, former chair of the Securities and Exchange Commission, claimed that brokers annually trade $40 trillion in securities on the telephone, in a highly efficient system with almost no fraud or cheating.[49]

Individuals and organizations build trust accounts that work something like a bank account.[50] You make deposits and build your trust reserve by being honest and by keeping commitments. You can draw on this account and even make mistakes as long as the reserve is maintained. Having a trust reserve allows the individual or organization the flexibility and freedom to act without scrutiny, saving a great deal of time and energy in all types of relationships. Imagine a marriage that is based on trust. The partners go about their daily business without feeling any need to check up on each other or to hire private detectives to confirm the other's whereabouts.[50] The same is true of trust-based business relationships where a handshake seals a deal, and a business partner's word is considered to be a contract. Corporations also build trust with their customers. Johnson & Johnson made a huge contribution to its trust account when it recalled all Tylenol from store shelves after the poisoning crisis in 1982 (a situation discussed in more detail in Chapter 8). Despite no recall requirement and huge recall costs, the company put its customers first.

However, trust accounts are easily overdrawn. And when they are, all flexibility disappears. Every word and action is carefully checked and double checked for signs of dishonesty. In organizations, lawyers are hired, contracts are drawn up and signed, and CYA (cover your "you know what") memos fly. Ethics scandals have breached the public's trust in a number of institutions, including business. When trust is breached, the public typically calls for more government intervention and punishment of rule violators. Government intervention means less self-governance and more government control; interference that organizations view as costly.

In 1988, Gary Edwards, then executive director of the Ethics Resource Center, testified before the Armed Services Committee of the U.S. House of Representatives on the topic of self-governance in the defense industry. He made the following link between trust and self-governance.

> Ideally, self-governance sets and achieves ethical standards higher than the requirements of the law and, in so doing, draws on and nourishes a moral force in its employees altogether different from the spirit of grudging compliance with—or adversarial evasion of—externally imposed legal requirements. When self-governance is effective, public trust is merited and secured, When self-governance fails, a measure of economic freedom is lost as government moves to protect the public interest and re-establish its trust."[52]

Avoiding the Costs of Criminal Liability

In addition to all of the other reasons for being ethical, the law presents a crystal clear cost-based reason.[53] Until recently, criminal law focused on the individual defendant rather than the corporation, and fines on corporations were relatively modest. However, since the mid-1980s the trend has been toward increasing fines for both individuals and organizations convicted of felony crimes. The U.S. Congress created the U.S. Sentencing Commission in 1984 in response to criticism of judicial discretion in sentencing, and perceived disparities between sentences for "white-collar" and other types of crimes. In 1987, the Commission imposed Federal Sentencing Guidelines for individual offenders. These guidelines limited judicial sentencing discretion and mandated some incarceration for virtually every felony offender.

In November 1991, the Commission issued its new sentencing guidelines for organizations convicted of federal crimes. The organization can be convicted even if only one employee is caught breaking the law. The guidelines cover most federal crimes including fraud, antitrust, securities, tax, bribery, and money-laundering offenses, and they impose a schedule of mandatory fines. "Virtually without exception, the Guidelines require a convicted organization to make restitution and to pay a substantial fine (which is not tax deductible)."[54] The guidelines even include a provision calling for a "corporate death penalty." The provision was used by federal prosecutors in the case of American Precision Components Inc., a Farmingdale, N.Y., company that sold ordinary nuts and bolts to government contractors as highly tested space components.[55] The company agreed to divest all of its assets.

Corporate criminal misconduct is costly. Firms' stock prices drop in the short term in response to announcements of allegations of corporate crime and in response to announced penalties.[56] A recent study also found that financial performance suffers significantly over the five years following a conviction.[57]

Perhaps most important for our discussion, fines and other sanctions can vary widely depending on whether management reports itself and cooperates with investigative authorities and depending on whether the company has a program in place to prevent and detect illegal behavior. Therefore, the same crime can be subject to a wide range of penalties. The minimum fine under the Guidelines is $250, and the maximum is $290 million or even more if the crime meets certain criteria. (For more specific information about how fines are determined, see the tables at the end of the chapter.) The Guidelines also provide that a defendant organization that doesn't have an effective legal compliance program should be put on corporate probation. Some of the recommended conditions of probation include requiring that the organization: publicize (at its own expense and as directed by the court) the fact of its conviction, and the nature of the punishment; periodically report to the court regarding financial condition and operating results; submit to periodic, unannounced reviews of books and records, and interrogation of employees by court-appointed experts (paid by the organization); and inform the court of any material adverse change in business conditions or prospects.

According the U.S. Sentencing Commission's 1996 Annual Report, more and more firms are being sentenced under the guidelines. In 1996, 157 organizations were sentenced. Fraud was the most frequent offense, followed by environmental waste discharge, money laundering, and antitrust cases. Firms sentenced ranged in size from five employees to a publicly traded company with 8,500 employees and annual revenues in excess of $1 billion. Fines were levied on 119 organizations. Three corporations were fined $25 million (the largest fine levied in 1996) for environmental offenses. None of the fined firms had an effective compliance program in place, and none had reported themselves. Sixty percent of companies sentenced in 1996 were placed on probation.

Clearly, organizations have an incentive to develop effective legal compliance programs. Although these programs vary somewhat, the framework provided by the Sentencing Guidelines has guided their development. The requirements include making legal compliance the responsibility of high-level

TABLE 2.1 Seven Requirements for Due Diligence and an Effective Compliance Program

1) Establishing compliance standards reasonably capable of preventing criminal conduct

2) Assigning specific high-level individuals with responsibility to oversee those compliance standards

3) Exercising due care to ensure that discretionary authority is not delegated to individuals with a propensity to engage in illegality

4) Taking necessary steps to communicate compliance standards and procedures to all employees, with a special emphasis on training and the dissemination of manuals

5) Taking reasonable steps to achieve compliance with written standards through monitoring, auditing, and other systems designed to detect criminal conduct, including a reporting system free of retribution to employees who report criminal conduct

6) Consistently enforcing the organization's written standards through appropriate disciplinary mechanism, including, as appropriate, discipline of individuals responsible for failure to detect an offense

7) After an offense is detected, taking all reasonable steps to respond and to prevent future similar conduct

officers, communicating rules through written materials and training, establishing monitoring and reporting systems, and disciplining offenders and those responsible for not detecting offenses (among other requirements). (See Table 2.1 for the full list of requirements.)

It should be clear by now that the misconduct of a single employee can put an entire organization at risk and that the development of an effective compliance program can help an organization prevent trouble with the law. However, problems can arise if an organization's "ethics" program focuses exclusively on legal compliance. Employees often view compliance programs as symbols of management's mistrust or of management's attempt to cover itself at employees' expense. Employees are more likely to accept a compliance program if it is seen as part of an organization's more positive focus on ethics and values. We will talk more about specific organizations' ethics and compliance programs in Chapter 10.

ETHICS AND THE NEW ORGANIZATIONAL PARADIGM

The old joke that business ethics is an oxymoron may be outmoded. The concepts of business and ethics may be more compatible today than some might think. The emerging business paradigm encompasses individual and group empowerment, responsibility, removal of distinctions between workers and managers, harmony, cooperation, teamwork, trust, honesty, and integrity.[58]

Paradigm Shift

The word "paradigm" comes from the Greek word for "pattern." In this context, the word "paradigm" refers to the pattern we use for looking at and understanding the world—our shared, fundamental assumptions about the nature of work and business and their place in society.

The old business paradigm is mechanistic and analytical, and is represented by traditional ideas about hierarchy, control, scientific management, assembly lines, and the primacy of quantitative analysis. In the best-selling book, *In Search of Excellence,* Tom Peters attacked the old model and touched a nerve. The old model wasn't flexible enough to adapt quickly to the speed of information and changes in the environment. American business was conducted like a football game, where players follow calls from the sidelines.

According to Noel Tichy of the University of Michigan business school, a better model may be a rugby game that "requires tremendous communication, continuous adjustment to an uncertain environment, and problem solving without using hierarchy."[59] The old paradigm no longer works in an age of global knowledge enterprises, instant communication, and ecological limits. When the old paradigm no longer works, paradigm shift occurs.

Paradigm shift isn't about simple reform—a change within the existing paradigm that retains its old assumptions. Rather, it's about a complete transformation of these underlying assumptions and their replacement by new ones.[60] According to *Fortune* magazine, the new paradigm "takes ideas from quantum physics, cybernetics, chaos theory, cognitive science, and Eastern and Western spiritual traditions to form a world view in which everything is interconnected."[61]

The New Business Paradigm—People and Work

The twin focus of the new paradigm is on people and interconnectedness. Work organizations are viewed as communities, and employees are members of these communities. People spend many of their waking hours in the work setting and devote much of their energy to work-related activities. This means that work is an important source of meaning in people's lives.[62] In these new corporate communities, intuition and spiritual values are valued alongside analytical skills. Network structures that place customers and employees at their centers are replacing the rigid hierarchies of the past. Business is no longer just about products and bottom line profits. The words products and profits join with words like meaning and values. In a study of Fortune 1000 executives conducted by Cornell's Johnson Graduate School of Management, executives were asked which characteristics would be most important for corporate leadership a decade from now. "Compassionate" was number two, right behind "team builder." Executives also strongly agreed that corporations have a responsibility to address social concerns. It's interesting to note that MBA students ranked compassionate near the bottom of their list of important leader characteristics. "Results oriented" was at the top. MBAs were also more likely than executives to say that maximizing profits was a company's overriding responsibility, and they were less likely to agree that corporate leaders should consider all stakeholders in policy making.[63]

Some of America's most successful CEOs have not only bought these new paradigm ideas, they're selling them. Max DePree, CEO of Herman Miller, in his bestselling book, *Leadership Is an Art,* wrote of a "covenant" (not a contract) between company and employee. According to DePree, this covenant helps employees feel part of a community and provides the basis for superior management.[64]

Robert Haas, CEO of Levi Strauss has expressed it this way: "We are not doing this [values-based strategy] because it makes us feel good—although it does. We are not doing this because it is politically correct. We are doing this because we believe in the interconnectedness between liberating the talents of our people and business success."[65]

Jan Carlzon, former president and CEO of Scandinavian Airlines System, talked about the power of respect, trust, and love (yes, love) in management. He believes that if employees are treated with love, respect, and trust they will contribute to the firm's success in their 50,000 "moments of truth" with customers each day. If love, respect, and trust are used to motivate people, they will dare to take risks, even to make mistakes. If fear is the motivator, they won't. The implications for organization ethics are profound. In the new paradigm, individuals are assumed to be whole systems. Therefore, they're not only allowed to take their values to work, they must do so.

The New Business Paradigm—Interconnectedness

Similarly, organizations are viewed as integral parts of an interconnected world community and ecosystem. In an ecosystem, one doesn't exploit workers, customers, or the environment, because the negative effects of exploitation are tacitly understood. They harm everyone.

The sense that corporations are part of the broader community and ecosystem has manifested itself in the expansion of social responsibility beyond an individual organization's boundaries. For example, Sears has said that it won't import forced-labor products from China. Dow Chemical asks its international suppliers to conform to U.S. standards on pollution and safety that are frequently tougher than local laws. Levi Strauss & Co. has ditched some suppliers that didn't measure up to its tough conduct standards, and has exacted reforms from many others. Home Depot distributed a questionnaire to its worldwide suppliers, asking whether any factory in the supply chain employs children or prison convicts.[66]

The new paradigm has clearly shifted perceptions of social responsibility beyond the corporation's front door—to its suppliers and their suppliers both here and abroad. Each corporation is viewed as part of an expanded network of organizations that can affect all of the people and environments that are directly or indirectly touched by its activities.

CONCLUSION

This chapter was designed to pique your interest in business ethics. Hopefully, we have convinced you that lots of people care about it, and that it's worth bothering about. The remainder of the book aims to help you understand ethics from a managerial perspective, explaining how this aspect of the organizational world actually works and what you can do to manage it. It will also provide practical decision-making guidance for facing your own ethical decisions and for helping others do the same.

DISCUSSION QUESTIONS

1. Do you think business ethics/social responsibility is important? Why or why not?

2. Identify reasons why an organization would be interested in being ethical and then classify those reasons in terms of whether they represent moral motivation or economic motivation.

3. Choose a company and identify its key stakeholders.

4. Think about the four types of corporate social responsibility. Do you agree that they should be represented by the pyramid? Why or why not? What are the implications of stopping at a particular pyramid level? For example, would it be all right if a company took its sole responsibility to be financial responsibility to its shareholders? Financial responsibility and legal responsibility? Can you think of a better way to graphically represent a company's social responsibility?

5. Think about the television programs and films you've seen recently in which business was portrayed in some way. How were business and business people portrayed? Is there anything business could or should do to improve its media image? Some businesses try to stay out of the limelight. Why might that be? What do you think of that strategy?

6. Do you believe that employees are more attracted and committed to ethical organizations? Are you? Why or why not? Make a list of the companies you would prefer to work for and the reasons why. Are there also companies that you would refuse to work for? Why? Are there ethically "neutral" companies that don't belong on either list?

7. Do you think organizations should be concerned about the new sentencing guidelines? Should they be doing anything differently because of them?

8. Discuss the new organizational paradigm. Have you seen examples of it? Counterexamples?

CASE 2.1

River Blindness[67]

Merck & Co. Headquartered in New Jersey, Merck & Co. is one of the largest pharmaceutical companies in the world. In 1978, Merck was about to lose patent protection on its two best-selling prescription drugs. These medications had been a significant part of Merck's $2 billion in annual sales. Because of this, Merck decided to pour millions into research to develop new medications. During just three years in the 1970s, the company invested over $1 billion in research and was rewarded with the discovery of four powerful medications. Profits, however, were never all that Merck cared about. The son of the founder of Merck, George W. Merck, said, "We try never to forget that medicine is for people. It is not for the profits. The profits follow, and if we have remembered that, they have never failed to appear. The better we have remembered that, the larger they have been." This philosophy was at the core of Merck & Co.'s value system.

River Blindness

The disease onchocerciasis, known as "river blindness," is caused by parasitic worms that live in the small black flies that breed in and about fast-moving rivers in developing countries in the Middle East, Africa, and Latin America. When a person is bitten by a fly (and some people are bitten thousands of times a day), the larvae of the worm can enter the person's body. The worms can grow to almost two feet long and can cause grotesque growths on an infected person. The real trouble comes, however, when the worms begin to reproduce and release millions of microscopic baby worms into a person's system. The itching is so intense that some infected persons have committed suicide. As time passes, the larvae continue to cause severe problems, including blindness. In 1978, the World Health Organization estimated that more than 300,000 people were blind because of the disease, and another 18 million were infected. In 1978, the disease had no safe cure. There were two drugs that could kill the parasite, but both had serious, even fatal, side effects. The only measure being taken to combat river blindness was the spraying of infected rivers with insecticides in the hope of killing the flies. However, even this wasn't effective since the flies had built up an immunity to the chemicals.

Merck's Ethical Quandary

Since it takes $200 million in research and 12 years to bring the average drug to market, the decision to pursue research is a complex one. Since resources are finite, dollars and time have to go to projects which hold the most promise, both in terms of making money so a company can continue to exist and in alleviating human suffering. This is an especially delicate issue when it comes to rare diseases, when a drug company's investment could probably never be recouped because the number of people who would buy the drug is so small. The problem with developing a drug to combat river blindness was the flip side of the "orphan" drug dilemma. There were certainly enough people suffering from the disease to justify the research, but since it was a disease afflicting people in some of the poorest parts of the word, those suffering from the disease were too poor to purchase the medication.

In 1978, Merck was testing a drug for animals called "ivermectin" to see if it could effectively kill parasites and worms. During this clinical testing, Merck discovered that the drug killed a parasite in horses that was very similar to the worm that caused river blindness in humans. This, therefore, was Merck's dilemma: company scientists were encouraging the firm to invest in further research to determine if the drug could be adapted for safe use with humans.

Case-Based Questions

1. Think about the definition of stakeholders from Chapter One—any parties with a stake in the organization's actions or performance. Who are the stakeholders in this situation?

2. What are the potential costs and benefits of such an investment?

3. If a safe and effective drug could be developed, the prospect of Merck recouping its investment was almost zero. Could Merck justify such an investment to shareholders and the financial community?

4. If Merck decided not to conduct further research, how would it justify such a decision to its scientists? How might the decision to develop the drug, or not to develop the drug, affect employee loyalty?

5. How would the media treat a decision to develop the drug? Not to develop the drug? How might either decision affect Merck's reputation?

6. Think about the decision in terms of the corporate social responsibility pyramid. Did Merck have an ethical obligation to proceed with development of the drug? Would it matter if the drug had only a small chance to cure river blindness? Or does this decision become a question of philanthropy?

7. How does Merck's value system fit into this decision?

   If you were the senior executive of Merck, what would you do?

Another Short Case for Discussion

You have a long-standing consulting relationship with a large consumer products company. This company represents 50 percent of your consulting revenues and is clearly your most important client. The CEO has called to ask you to commit a significant amount of time over the next couple of months to assist with a large merger project. The company is merging with a large conglomerate whose primary business is the sale and distribution of tobacco products. The CEO is relying on you to assist in facilitating a smooth integration of the two companies. You promised yourself that, since your father died of lung cancer, you would never work for a tobacco company. Is there a way that you can accept the consulting assignment and still keep your promise to yourself? How will you handle this if you decide that you cannot work for the tobacco company?

⬯ **APPENDIX** ⬯

How Fines Are Determined under the U.S. Sentencing Guidelines

Exact penalties are based on a base fine and the "culpability score" assigned by the court. The base fine is the greatest of the following: the pretax gain from the crime, the amount of intentional loss inflicted on the victim(s), an amount based on the Sentencing Commission's ranking of the seriousness of the crime (ranging from $5,000 to $72.5 million). This amount is then multiplied by a number that depends on the culpability score. The culpability score ranges from 0 to 10, and the multipliers range from .05 to 4 (see Table 2.1).

Every defendant starts at a culpability score of 5 and can move up or down depending on aggravating or mitigating factors (see Table 2.2 for these factors). The presence of aggravating factors can cause the culpability score to increase. These aggravating factors include (1) organizational size, combined with the degree of participation, tolerance, or disregard for the criminal conduct by high-level personnel or substantial authority personnel in the firm, (2) prior history of similar criminal conduct, and (3) role in obstructing or impeding an investigation.

The presence of mitigating factors, however, can cause the culpability score to drop. In order to decrease the culpability score, the organization must have in place an "effective program to prevent and detect violations of the law." If the court determines that the organization has such a program, 3 points can be removed from the base culpability score of 5. Besides having an effective compliance program in place, the culpability score can be substantially reduced if the organization reports the criminal conduct promptly after becoming aware of the offense and before imminent government investigation. According to the

TABLE 2.2   Method for Determining Minimum and Maximum Fines

Culpability score	Minimum multiplier	Maximum multiplier
10 or more	2.00	4.00
9	1.80	3.60
8	1.60	3.20
7	1.40	2.80
6	1.20	2.40
5	1.00	2.00
4	0.80	1.60
3	0.60	1.20
2	0.40	0.80
1	0.20	0.40
0 or less	0.05	0.20

Guidelines, an organization that reports its own misconduct, cooperates with authorities, and accepts responsibility can have as many as 5 points subtracted from the base culpability level of 5 (see mitigating factor no. 2).

The mitigating factors that reduce the culpability score have important implications for the way companies manage ethical conduct. For example, many believe that overseeing an "effective" program for preventing and detecting legal violations is a full-time job for at least one person. It would likely involve the development of a conduct code, training programs, scrutiny of reward sys-

TABLE 2.3   Aggravating and Mitigating Factors That Can Increase or Decrease Culpability Scores

Aggravating Factors—result in an increase to the base level of 5

1. The size of the organization coupled with the degree of participation, tolerance, or disregard for the criminal conduct by "high level personnel" or "substantial authority personnel." In a firm with greater than 5000 employees, this factor can result in an increase of as much as 5 points.

2. Prior history: Organizations that have been either civilly or criminally adjudicated to have committed similar conduct within the past five years can have as many as 2 points added.

3. Obstructing, impeding, (or attempting to obstruct or impede) during the investigation, prosecution, or something can result in 3 points added.

Mitigating Factors—result in downward departures from the base level of 5

1. Having an effective program to prevent and detect violations of the law can result in a downward departure of 3 points.

2. Self-reporting, cooperating, and accepting responsibility for the criminal conduct can result in a downward departure of 5 points.

tems, the development of communication systems, detection systems, and so on. Practical information about how organizations are actually implementing ethics programs will be discussed in more detail in Chapter 10.

NOTES

1. Etzioni, A. 1988. *The moral dimension: Toward a new economics.* New York: Free Press.

2. Ibid.

3. Grover, R. 1988. Bad guys wear pinstripes. *Business Week,* October 21: 61–63.

4. Fusco, M.A.C. 1988. Ethics game plan: Taking the offensive. *Business Week Careers,* Spring/Summer:51.

5. Wartick, S. L. 1992. The relationship between intense media exposure and change in corporate reputation. Spring: 33–49.

6. Yes, business and ethics do go together. 1988. *Business Week,* February 15: 118.

7. Labich, K. 1992. The new crisis in business ethics. *Fortune,* April 20: 167–176.

8. Segal, T., and Del Valle, C. 1993. They didn't even give at the office. *Business Week,* January 25: 68–69.

9. Johnston, D.C. 1997. United Way, faced with fewer donors, is giving away less. *New York Times,* November 9, p. 1, Column 6.

10. Fombrun, C., and Shanley, M. 1990. What's in a name? Reputation building and corporate strategy. *Academy of Management Journal, 333:* 233–256.

11. Stewart, Thomas A. 1998. America's most admired companies. *Fortune,* March 2: 71–82.

12. Zemke, R. 1986 Employee theft. How to cut your losses. *Training,* May: 74–78.

13. Collins, J. 1990. Why bad things happen to good companies and what can be done. *Business Horizons,* November December: 18–22.

14. Hager, B. 1991. What's behind business' sudden fervor for ethics. *Business Week,* September 23: 65.

15. Labich, K. 1992. The new crisis in business ethics. *Fortune,* April 20: 167–176.

16. Akers, J. F. 1989. Ethics and competitiveness—putting first things first. *Sloan Management Review,* Winter: 69–71.

17. Howard, R. 1987. Values make the company: An interview with Robert Haas. In @CT:Leaders on leadership. W. Bennis, ed. Boston: Harvard Business School, 33–54.

18. Badaracco, J. L., Jr. 1992. Business ethics: Four spheres of executive responsibility. *California Management Review,* Spring: 64–79.

19. Channon, J. 1992. Creating esprit de corps. In *New traditions in business.* J. Renesch, ed, San Francisco: Berrett—Koehler Publishers. 53–68.

20. Sandroff, R. 1990. How ethical is American business? *Working Woman Magazine,* September: 113–116.

21. Kleiman, C. 1989. Heading the list of worker wishes isn't more money! *The Morning Call,* October 2: B10.

22. Cullen, J. B., and Victor, B. 1993. The effects of ethical climates on organizational commitment: A multilevel analysis. Unpublished manuscript.

23. Turban, D. B., and Greening, D. W. Corporate social performance and organizational attractiveness to prospective employees. *Academy of Management Journal,* 40: 658–672.

24. Treviño, L. K., Butterfield, K. D., and McCabe, D. in press. The ethical context in organizations: Influences on employee attitudes and behaviors. *Business Ethics Quarterly.*

25. Posner, B. Z., and Schimdt, W. H. 1992. Values and the American manager. *California Management Review,* Spring: 80–94.

26. Sherman, S. 1997. Levi's: As ye sew, so shall ye reap. *Fortune,* May 12: 104–114.

27. Swanson, D. 1995. Addressing a theoretical problem by reorienting the corporate social performance model. *Academy of Management Review* 20: 43–64.

28. Freeman, E. 1984. *Strategic management: A stakeholder approach.* Boston: Pitman/Ballinger.

29. Davis, K. 1973. The case for and against business assumption of social responsibilities. *Academy of Management Journal* 16: 312–322.

    Wood, D. J. 1991. Corporate social performance revisited. *Academy of Management Review* 16: 691–718.

30. Swanson, 1995, op. cit.

31. Carroll, A. B. 1991. The pyramid of corporate social responsibility: Toward the moral management of organizational stakeholders. *Business Horizons* 34 (4): 39–48.

32. Friedman, M. 1970. The social responsibility of business is to increase its profits. *New York Times,* September 13: 122–126.

33. Singer, A. W. 1993. Can a company be too ethical? *Across the Board,* April: 17-22.

34. Kuttner, R. 1997. Everything for sale. *Fortune,* March 17: 92–94.

35. Labich, K. 1992. The new crisis in business ethics. *Fortune,* April 20: 167–176.

36. Aupperle, K. E. Carroll, A. B., and Hatfield, J. D. 1985. An empirical examination of the relationship between corporate social responsibility and profitability. *Academy of Management Journal* 28: 449–459.

    McGuire, J. B., Sundgren, A., and Scheeweis, T. 1988. Corporate social responsibility and firm financial performance. *Academy of Management Journal* 31: 854–872.

    Ullman, A. H. 1985. Data in search of a theory. a critical examination of the relationships among social performance, social disclosure, and economic performance of U.S. firms. *Academy of Management Review* 10: 3, 540–447.

37. Waddock, S. A., and Graves, S. B. 1994. The corporate social performance-financial performance link. Paper presented at the Academy of Management meeting, August, Dallas.

38. Waddock, S. A., and Graves, S. B. 1997. The corporate social performance-financial performance link. *Strategic Management Journal* 18: 303–319.

39. Frooman, J. 1997. Socially irresponsible and illegal behavior and shareholder wealth. *Business & Society* 36 (3): 221–249.

40. Bhide, A., and Stevenson, H. H. 1990. Why be honest if honesty doesn't pay. *Harvard Business Review,* September October: 121–129.

41. Josephson, Michaael S. 1989. Ethics in a legalistic society. *Exchange,* Fall: 3–7.

42. Feurestein, A. 1997. Presentation at the Academy of Management annual meeting, Boston.

43. Ryan, M. 1996. They call their boss a hero. *Parade,* September 8: 4–5, p. 5.

44. Teal, T. 1996. Not a fool, not a saint. *Fortune,* November 11: 201–204.

45. Ibid.

46. Alperson, M., Marlin, A. T., Schorsch, J., and Will, R. 1991. *The better world investment guide.* New York: Prentice-Hall.

47. Melton, J. 1996. Responsible investing; $639 billion and counting. *Co-Op America Quarterly,* Spring, 13.

48. O'Toole, J. 1991. Do good, do well: The business enterprise trust awards. *California Management Review,* Spring, 9–24.

49. Kuhn, J. W. 1992. Ethics in business: What managers practice that economists ignore. *Business Ethics Quarterly* 2 (3): 304–315.

50. Covey, S. R. 1989. *The 7 habits of highly effective people.* New York: Simon & Schuster.

51. Ibid.

52. Center Director Testifies Before Congress Report.

53. Adapted from a speech given by attorney Steven Alan Reiss, 1992.

54. Reiss, S. A. 1992. Speech given at the Conference Board meeting on Business Ethics, 1992.

55. *United States v. American Precision Components Inc.,* 93–450.

56. Strachan, J. L., Smith, D. G., and Beedles, W. L. 1983. The price reaction to (alleged) corporate crime. *Financial Review* 18 (2): 121–132.

    Wier, P. 1983. The costs of antimerger lawsuits. *Journal of Financial Economics* 11: 207–224.

57. Baucus, M. S., and Baucus, D. 1997. Paying the piper: An empirical examination of longer-term financial consequences of illegal corporate behavior. *Academy of Management Journal* 40: 129–151.

58. Rose, F. 1990. A new age for business? *Fortune,* October 8: 156–164.

59. Ibid.

60. Garfield, C. 1992. Second to none: Business in the ecological age. *Noetic Sciences Review,* Winter: 15–19.

61. Rose, F. 1990. A new age for business? *Fortune,* October 8: 156–164.

62. Badaracco, J. L., Jr. 1992. Business ethics: Four spheres of executive responsibility. *California Management Review,* Spring: 64–79.

63. Dyckman, T. R. 1996. Bottom line: Compassion. *Centre Daily Times,* December 1: 5A.

64. Miller, H. 1991. Should your company save your soul? *Fortune,* January 14: 33.

65. Haas, R. 1994. Managing by values. *Fortune,* August 1: 46–52.

66. McCormick, J., and Levinson, M. 1993. The supply police. *Newsweek,* February 15: 48–49.

67. Bollier, D. 1991. *Merck & company.* Stanford, CA: The Business Enterprise Trust.

ETHICS AND THE INDIVIDUAL

CHAPTER 3

Common Ethical Problems

INTRODUCTION

The bad news about business ethics is: your career can be irrevocably damaged if you mishandle an ethical issue. But there's also good news: many ethical issues in business are quite predictable. You can be fairly certain that during the course of your career, you'll run into myriad ethical problems such as a customer who asks for a special deal or terms, or questions about the appropriate use of corporate resources, or discrimination of one sort or another. Since ethical issues are somewhat predictable, you have a better chance of dealing appropriately with ethical problems if you think about what's likely to happen before it occurs.

Before we get into a discussion of ethical issues, however, it's important to look at the relationship that exists between you and your employer. Although most people don't sign a contract the day they join a company or organization, there is a contractual relationship of sorts between workers and employers. Both parties have expectations, and rights, and offer consideration to the other. Your employer pays you in salary and benefits to perform a job, and your organization expects you to behave in a certain way; you have a responsibility to be "part of the family" and exhibit loyalty and other corporate "virtues" and to refrain from other, less desirable behaviors. On the other hand, you expect not only a salary for the work you perform, but also a certain modicum of fairness. Most people expect employers to treat them decently and to provide an appropriate work environment. Whenever we discuss the employer/employee contract in this chapter, it's this complicated set of expectations that we're referring to.

So what are some typical ethical problems? We've compiled some of the more obvious dilemmas and have divided them into broad categories, including human resources issues, conflicts of interest, customer confidence issues, and the use of corporate resources. We will address a number of specific topics under each broad category. To make it easy to follow, each topic contains the following information:

What is it?—a definition of the issue.

Why is it an ethical problem?

Professional costs—possible penalties for ethical or legal transgressions.

Special notes—some topics may include important information related to the topic.

HUMAN RESOURCES ISSUES

It's difficult to overstate how important it is for a company to effectively manage its people. Human resources—the employees who make up an organization—are any corporation's most important and expensive investment, and are the underpinning of an organization's success or failure. Barbara Toffler[1] found that 66 percent of the ethical issues encountered by the managers she interviewed involved managing human resources or internal organizational processes. In addition, the widest legal exposure for many companies may involve violations or perceived violations of the employer employee contract.

In the United States, there's currently a shortage, not just of workers, but of workers with the skills necessary to fill highly skilled jobs. As a result, corporations are actively designing programs to attract, motivate, and retain qualified employees.

Probably the most effective way to retain qualified employees is to create a working environment where people feel appreciated. People who like to come to work may be significantly more productive than workers who feel their efforts are unappreciated, their management doesn't care about them, or their ideas don't count. Productivity, which is at the very heart of competitiveness, can exist only when employees are respected by management and when employees are encouraged to respect one another.

We use the term *human resources issues* to describe the problems that occur when people work together. They can include discrimination, sexual or other types of harassment, performance evaluation, hiring, firing, or simply "how people get along." (Performance evaluation—including appraisals, discipline, hiring, firing, and layoffs—will be discussed in Chapter 6.)

The word to remember when considering human resources issues is fairness, and most corporate policy is constructed to build fairness into the system. When we talk about fairness, we mean equity, reciprocity, and impartiality—the way most people think about what is "fair."[2] Something is said to be equitable when something is divided between two people according to the worth and gains of the two individuals: "If they received equal shares, did they work equally hard?" Most people think it's unfair when two people have performed the same duty and they receive a different share of the reward. Another measure of fairness is reciprocity, or the fairness of exchanges: "You did this for me and I'll do that for you." Most people perceive it as being unfair if one person fails to hold up his or her part of a bargain. The third measure of fairness is impartiality: "Is the person who's going to listen to my story biased in some way, or has he or she prejudged the situation?" Most people think of fairness as being inconsistent with prejudice and bias.

Most protective legislation and corporate human resources policy try to incorporate those elements. The goal is to hire, treat, promote, appraise, and lay off or fire employees based solely on their qualifications and not on factors like sex, race, or age. The goal is to level the playing field and create a fair environment where performance is the only factor that counts (equity), where employer employee expectations are understood and met (reciprocity), and where prejudice and bias are not factors (impartiality).

Discrimination

You and Lisa met five years ago when you were hired into the management training program of a large utility. Although you're now in different parts of the organization, you have managed to stay close over the years. Lisa recently had a baby and plans to take advantage of the full six months of maternity leave the company offers. She told you that she's definitely coming back to work after her leave and that her department has promised to hold her job for her. Meanwhile, you've seen a posting for her job on the company's website. You run into one of Lisa's colleagues in the hall and ask about the posting. He says, "Oh yeah, they're going to fill that job. But don't tell Lisa. She's got five more months to be a happy Mom. Besides, they'll find something for her to do if she decides to come back."

Since discrimination by race, religion, national origin, sex, and age is prohibited by federal law in the United States, many companies have defined policies prohibiting any kind of discrimination. Unfortunately, there can be quite a gulf between where corporate policy leaves off and reality begins. When people from various backgrounds get together to provide a service or manufacture a product, there surely will be people who have conscious or unconscious biases toward various groups, and others who are simply ignorant of the effect their behavior has on others.

What Is it?

Discrimination occurs whenever something other than qualifications affects how an employee is treated. Unequal treatment—usually unfavorable can take many forms. Older workers who suddenly find themselves reporting to younger ones can be resentful since they feel younger workers lack experience. Younger employees can be tempted to ignore advice from older workers, who they feel are "out of touch." The attitudes toward age will most likely become increasingly important over the next decade as the general population grows older.

Racial, ethnic, religious, or sexual stereotypes can creep into the behavior of even the most sophisticated individuals. The importance of being able to manage different types of people can't be overstated. In the United States, ethnic and racial minorities are growing faster than the population as a whole. By the year 2000, almost 85 percent of the new entrants into the workforce will be women, minorities, or immigrants.[3]

In the case involving Lisa, the new mother, her maternity leave could result in discrimination. Although pregnant employees are protected by law (see "Why Is It an Ethical Problem?" which follows), in this case her time away from her job is clearly being viewed as a liability. Of course, employers have the right to replace workers who are on extended leaves because of illness, disability, or other reasons such as finishing an education. The problem in Lisa's case is that her department seems to be doing an end run around her by keeping her in the dark while her job is filled. If Lisa knew what the department's plans were, she might shorten her leave, or arrange a part-time working situation for a few months. But unless her colleague tells her what he has found out, the job she left won't be the one she comes back to. It's simply not fair to keep Lisa in the dark.

Discrimination can be a subtle or not-so-subtle factor not only in working relationships, but also in hiring, promotions, and layoff decisions. People who don't fit a "corporate profile" may be passed over for advancement because they're female, or a member of a minority group, or for other reasons that may or may not be covered in protectionist legislation. Surely there are many barriers in the workplace—not just the glass ceiling that refers to barriers to female advancement. There probably are also barriers for people who are over 50 years old, or who have medical problems, or who are short, disabled, overweight, bearded, balding, or homosexual—any quality that varies from the "norm." And some employers create job requirements, which could automatically eliminate certain employees, not because of their qualifications, but because of personal circumstances.

Why Is It an Ethical Problem?

Discrimination is an ethical issue—beyond any legal protections—because it's at the core of fairness in the workplace. Fairness is a critical commodity because it's viewed in the United States as an "inalienable" right.[4] Our government has attempted to ensure fairness and justice; the word "trust" is on every piece of currency, and the Pledge of Allegiance declares "with liberty and justice for all." In addition, our entire legal system has justice and the protection of individual rights as its cornerstone. Consequently, people expect fairness from organizations in general, but specifically from their employers.

Costs

Victims of discrimination can file under Title VII of the Civil Rights Act of 1964 with the Equal Employment Opportunity Commission (EEOC), or bring suit under tort or contract law. This legislation specifically prohibits discrimination based on race, religion, sex, color, and national origin. Groups specifically protected by Title VII include women, African Americans, Hispanics, Native Americans, and Asian-Pacific Islanders. (Also, some states and local communities have added more protections—like sexual orientation and marital status—to that list.) The Pregnancy Discrimination Act of 1978 prohibits discrimination against pregnant women. The 1967 Age Discrimination in Employment Act extends protection to people 40 years of age and older. The 1973 Rehabilitation Act was the first federal legislation to protect disabled Americans against discrimination by federal, state, local governments, agencies, and contractors. The Americans with Disabilities Act (ADA) of 1990 extended protection to the private sector by requiring all companies with more than 15 employees to make reasonable accommodations in order to employ workers with disabilities. Although the law doesn't list conditions or diseases that are protected—since people react so differently to disease, and some may be disabled and some may not be—some conditions are specifically included or excluded. HIV infection, for example, is considered a disability, and people who have it are protected by the ADA law.

Discrimination lawsuits can be costly for employers not simply in terms of legal fees and damages and media coverage. The morale of victims certainly suffers as they endure discrimination lawsuits, but the morale of other employees can also suffer. Imagine how the thousands of employees of Texaco must have felt when their company was under siege for a discrimination lawsuit. (You'll read more about this case in Chapter 6.) It's embarrassing for employees when the company they work for is publicly accused of wrongdoing.

If you're an individual accused of discriminating against another employee, the least you'll endure is an investigation. If you're found guilty, you'll probably be penalized or even fired. If you're found innocent, you or your accuser will most likely be counseled about your behavior and its effects, and one or both of you may be transferred to another area. If you manage someone who has been accused of discrimination, expect a lot of questions concerning why you were unaware of it or tolerated it. If you were aware of it and didn't do anything about it, be prepared for disciplinary action, particularly if a lawsuit results.

Special Note

The many programs that train employees to "value diversity" can seem to be at odds with the efforts to assimilate various groups and especially with the laws and policies that prohibit discrimination. Learning to appreciate differences flies in the face of what many of us are taught from the time we're children—we should "fit in." Not only are many of us taught to downplay our own uniqueness in an effort to blend in, but also we're taught to ignore differences in other people. We usually are taught "not to notice" different colors, religions, accents, ways of dressing, and physical disabilities or abilities. Even sexual differences, which can be hard to ignore, have been played down in the not-too-distant past.

Valuing diversity means treating people equally while incorporating their diverse ideas. Discrimination means treating people unequally because they are, or appear to be, different. Valuing diversity is a positive action, while discrimination is a negative action. Valuing diversity tries to incorporate more fairness into the system, while discrimination incorporates unfairness into the system. The key to valuing diversity is understanding that different doesn't mean deficient and it doesn't mean less. Different means different.

Harassment—Sexual and Otherwise

The U.S. Senate confirmation hearings of Clarence Thomas's nomination to the Supreme Court focused American business and workers on the issue of sexual harassment. One result of that incident was an overnight increase in the number of corporations offering sexual harassment training to sensitize employees to the issue. Another result was a growing apprehension on the part of employees—especially men—toward workers of the opposite sex. Sometimes the line between friendly and offensive is blurry.

> One of your co-workers is Joanne, a computer whiz with an offbeat style and a great sense of humor. Two of Joanne's favorite "targets" are you and Bill, another co-worker who tends to be quite standoffish in his business relationships. Joanne is the department clown and is forever goading you and Bill—you, because you're a great audience and clearly think she's hilarious; Bill, because she likes to try to get him to be more approachable. Joanne frequently alludes to sexual subjects and has called both you and Bill "little alley cats" and "studs." While Joanne's behavior doesn't offend you at all, you're surprised when Bill approaches you in the men's room and bitterly complains about Joanne's constant teasing.

What Is it?

Federal law has defined two types of sexual harassment: Quid Pro Quo and Hostile Work Environment.

Quid Pro Quo means that sexual favors are a requirement—or appear to be a requirement—for advancement in the workplace. Hostile Work Environment means that a worker has been made to feel uncomfortable because of unwelcome actions or comments relating to sexuality. This type of sexual harassment is especially murky because sexual harassment of this type is like beauty: it's in the eye of the beholder. What constitutes sexual harassment for one person, may not for another. Putting your arm around a person's shoulder may feel like harassment to one individual, whereas someone else may be comfortable with such a gesture. This type of sexual harassment includes not only physical gestures, but also can include remarks of a sexual nature—even compliments—and displays of sexually provocative material, like nude or revealing photographs displayed in an office.

In both types of sexual harassment, the decision about whether the behavior constitutes sexual harassment is determined from the point of view of a "reasonable" person and the harasser's intentions aren't considered, which is why sexual harassment issues can be confusing. Since sexual harassment is determined by the reaction of the victim, you have to consider—not what you mean by your comments or actions—but how they might be interpreted by the other person

Most people will readily agree that kissing someone or patting someone on their rear end could be construed by some as being sexual harassment. But are you sexually harassing someone if you compliment her appearance, or touch his arm, or make jokes of a sexual nature?

In Joanne's case, she hasn't done a very good job of considering exactly who her audience is and how each of her two co-workers might react to her jokes. While you might think it's funny to be called a little stud, Joanne probably should think more carefully about how someone like Bill might react to being called a name with sexual connotations. Is Joanne out of line? Is Bill overreacting? According to the law, it doesn't matter if you and Joanne think Bill is overreacting. The yardstick used to determine whether sexual harassment occurred will be how uncomfortable a reasonable person would be with Joanne's comments, and not what Joanne intended with her remarks.

Why Is It an Ethical Problem?

Harassment (sexual or otherwise) is a form of discrimination and is therefore an ethical issue because it unfairly focuses job satisfaction, advancement, or retention on a factor other than the ability to do the job. Most instances of sexual harassment have nothing to do with romance and everything to do with power and fairness.

Costs

Victims of sexual harassment can file under Title VII of the Civil Rights Act of 1964 with the Equal Employment Opportunity Commission (EEOC), or bring suit under tort or contract law. An employer can be held liable for an employee's sexual harassment activities if the employer has knowledge of the conduct and has done nothing to correct it. As a result, most companies take a sexual harassment charge very seriously.

Most companies will launch an immediate investigation if someone is accused of sexually harassing another employee. If this is a first-time event and the incident that prompted it is not determined to be lewd or an assault—think of the scenario featuring Joanne that was discussed earlier—the employee may be warned, disciplined, or transferred to another area. (However, in some major companies a first-time offense is enough to get someone fired.) If the behavior is judged to be lewd or forceful, or if there's evidence that the employee has demonstrated a pattern of behavior, the employee will most likely be fired, and often very quickly. (One corporation was able to conduct an investigation, find evidence of a pattern, and terminate the harasser in less than 48 hours.) If the accused is found innocent, or if it's determined that a misunderstanding exists between the two parties, the accused and the accuser will probably be counseled by human resources professionals and, if necessary, one of them may be transferred to another area. The manager of a sexual harasser can expect a lot of questions concerning why he or she was unaware of it. If the manager was aware of it and didn't do anything about it, he or she should be prepared for disciplinary action, particularly if a lawsuit results.

Sexual harassment lawsuits are very expensive for corporations. Awards to victims have been substantial as is the toll such charges can take on co-workers' morale and on the ability to hire qualified candidates. For example, in June 1998, Mitsubishi Motors' North American division agreed to pay $34 million in the biggest sexual harassment settlement ever obtained by the U.S. government. The settlement was based on charges brought by 350 female factory workers at an Illinois factory. The women alleged that co-workers and supervisors kissed and fondled them, called them "whores" and "bitches," posted sexual graffiti and pornography, demanded sex, and retaliated if they refused. They also complained that managers did nothing to stop the harassment. In addition to paying the fine, Mitsubishi fired 20 workers and disciplined others, agreed to provide mandatory sexual harassment training, revise its sexual harassment policy, and investigate future sexual harassment allegations within three weeks. Compliance will be monitored by a three-person independent panel.

CONFLICTS OF INTEREST

People and corporations are naturally involved in a tangle of relationships—both personal and professional. Your personal reputation, and the reputation of your company, are inextricably tied to how well you handle relationships with other employees, customers, consultants, vendors, family, and friends. Your ability to act impartially, and look as if you are acting impartially, are key to your fulfilling your end of the employer employee contract.

> Your daughter is applying to a prestigious Ivy League university. Since admission to the school is difficult, your daughter has planned the process carefully. She has consistently achieved high marks, taken preparatory courses for entrance exams, and has participated in various extracurricular activities. When you tell one of your best customers about her activities, he offers to write her a letter of recommendation. He's an alumnus of the school and is one of its most active fundraisers. Although he's a customer, you also regularly play golf together, and your families have socialized together on occasion.

What Is It?

A conflict of interest occurs when your judgment or objectivity is compromised. The appearance of a conflict of interest—when a third party could think your judgment has been compromised—is generally considered to be just as damaging as an actual conflict.

In the case of a customer offering to do a favor for you—or your daughter or other member of your family—some of the questions you'll need to ask yourself include: Would your customer's offer influence your business relationship? Could someone think your business judgment had been compromised by accepting your customer's offer? Is your relationship more than just a business one, so that accepting an offer could be interpreted as a simple act of friendship?

Some corporations have a policy that permits the acceptance of favors from customers or vendors if there's also a "friendship" present; and friendship is usually defined by these companies as a long-standing relationship that's well known in the community. For example, in small towns where everyone knows everyone else, many customers will be friends and it's unrealistic to expect anything else. Other organizations (including government agencies) would discourage accepting a favor like this one under any circumstances. Things to consider when making your decision in this case include: how long you've been friends with your customer, how well known the relationship is in your community, his knowledge of your daughter's qualifications, and whether your customer expects anything in return for his recommendation or if the letter is simply a gesture of friendship with no strings attached. How would his recommendation be perceived by others?

Almost every business situation can involve conflicts of interest. A conflict can occur when a vendor lavishly entertains you or when you entertain a customer—if the object is influence. Both situations could prompt an observer to think that a special deal or advantageous terms are part of the relationship. Conflicts of interest can occur when people who report to you observe that you have an especially close friendship with one of their co-workers. Conflicts can occur when you're asked to judge the creditworthiness of your neighbor or if you perform consulting work for your employer's competitor. They can involve accepting hand-tooled cowboy boots from an advertising agency, being sponsored for membership in an exclusive private club by a consulting company, or allowing a supplier to give you a discount on equipment for your home when you place an order for your office.

Common conflicts of interest include:

Overt Bribes or Kickbacks

Anything that could be considered a bribe or kickback is a clear conflict of interest. It doesn't matter whether the bribe or kickback is in the form of money or something else of substantial value that is offered in exchange for access to specific products, services, or influence.

Subtle "Bribes"

These can be interpreted to include gifts and entertainment. Most corporate policy places a ceiling of $25–$100 on the gifts employees can accept from, or give to, customers or vendors. Reciprocity is one yardstick used for determining whether entertainment is acceptable. If you can't reciprocate with the same kind of entertainment being offered to you, it's probably inappropriate to accept it. For example, if a vendor offers you tickets to the Super Bowl, or a weekend of golf, or dinner for four at a $200-per-person restaurant, it's probably inappropriate for you to accept under any circumstances. The emphasis on reciprocity is to maintain a fair, even playing field for all vendors, so that you (as a purchaser) will be unbiased when making a decision about a vendor. As mentioned earlier, both reciprocity and impartiality are elements of fairness.

Accepting discounts on personal items from a vendor will also be interpreted as a conflict. The formula to use when determining whether to accept a discount is simple: if it's a formal arrangement between your company and a supplier and is offered to all employees, it's probably acceptable; if the discount is being extended only to you, it's not acceptable.

Influence

Your relationship with someone by itself can constitute a conflict of interest. For example, if you're in charge of purchasing corporate advertising and your cousin or neighbor or college friend owns an advertising agency, it will be considered a conflict if you make the decision to hire that firm. That doesn't preclude the firm from bidding, but it does preclude you from making the decision. If a decision involves anyone with whom you have a personal relationship, you should ask someone else to make it. Another way to avoid the appearance of a conflict in a situation like this one, which is charged with issues of partiality, is to arrange for a "blind" competition, where the identity of various bidders is known only by someone not involved in the decision-making process. However, since any decision made by you in such a case will be suspect—even in blind evaluations—you should include other employees in the decision-making process.

Privileged Information

As an employee, you're naturally privy to information that would be valuable to your employer's competitors. That's why it's generally considered a conflict of interest if you hold a full-time job for ABC Insurance Company and decide to do some consulting work for XYZ Insurance Company. There are certainly exceptions to this rule of thumb: if you're a computer programmer at Green's Restaurant, it probably isn't a conflict to wait on tables at Red's Restaurant. Two factors could make such a situation acceptable: if the work you perform at your second job doesn't compromise the work you do at your first one, and if both employers are aware of your activities.

In addition, it can appear as if you're involved in a conflict if you and a close relative or friend work for competitors or if one of you works for an organization—such as a media company—which might have a particular interest in your company's activities. One good way to handle this is to let your manager know if a close relative or friend works for an organization which might be problematic. Full disclosure removes substantial risk from the situation.

Why Is It an Ethical Problem?

The basis of every personal and corporate relationship is trust, and it exists only when individuals and corporations feel as if they're being treated fairly, openly, and on the same terms as everyone else. Conflicts of interest erode trust by making it look as if special favors will be extended for special friends and that attitude can enhance one relationship, but at the expense of all others.

Costs

Depending on the offense, myriad federal and state laws cover conflicts of interest. Certain professions, such as banking, accounting, law, religion, and medicine, have special obligations—often spelled out in professional codes of ethics—commonly referred to as "fiduciary" responsibilities. These professions are widely know as "trust" professions, meaning that these practitioners have been entrusted with sensitive, confidential information about their clients. Fiduciary responsibilities concern the obligations resulting from relationships that have their basis in faith, trust, and confidence.

If you're suspected of a conflict of interest, the least you can expect is an investigation by your company. If it determines that your behavior demonstrates a conflict or the appearance of a conflict, you may be warned, disciplined, or even fired depending on the nature of your behavior. If you've accepted a bribe or kickback, you could face termination and even arrest. Being involved in a conflict of interest means that your judgment has been compromised and it can severely damage your professional reputation.

CUSTOMER CONFIDENCE ISSUES

We've all heard the saying, "The customer is always right," and companies like L.L. Bean and Wal-Mart have benefited by weaving that slogan into the fabric of their corporate cultures. But excellent customer service is more than being able to return a defective refrigerator or having cheerful customer service representatives (although that helps). Excellent customer service also means providing a quality product or service at a fair price, honestly representing the product or service, and protecting the customer's privacy.

What Is It?

Customer confidence issues include a range of topics including confidentiality, product safety and effectiveness, truth in advertising, and special fiduciary responsibilities.

> You work for a consulting company in Atlanta. Your team has recently completed an analysis of Big Co., including sales projections for the next five years. You're working late one night when you receive a call from an executive vice president at Big Co. in Los Angeles, who asks you to immediately fax her a summary of your team's report. When you locate the report, you discover that your team leader has stamped "For internal use only" on the report cover. Your team leader is on a hiking vacation and you know it would be impossible to locate him. Big Co. has a long-standing relationship with your company and has paid substantial fees for your company's services.

Confidentiality

Privacy is a basic customer right. Privacy and the obligation to keep customer information in confidence often go beyond protecting sales projections or financial information. It can also mean keeping in strict confidence information concerning acquisitions, mergers, relocations, layoffs, or an executive's health or marital problems. In some industries, confidentiality is so important an issue that companies prohibit their employees from publicly acknowledging a customer relationship. In the financial services industry, for example, it's common practice to refuse to divulge that XYZ Company is even a customer.

In the case involving Big Co., an executive is demanding access to a confidential report. First, are you absolutely certain that the caller is indeed a Big Co. executive? If you have verified her identity, do you know whether she has clearance from Big Co. to examine your team's report? If she does have clearance, is your team's report in a format that your company wants to share with Big Co., or does it need revision? Whenever you see "For internal use only," that's what it means, and it can be enormously risky to release the report to anyone—including the customer—without permission from someone within your company who has responsibility for that client. In a case like this one, you should track down someone who's in a position of authority in your company—your manager's manager perhaps—before you override the warning on the report and release any information.

On occasion, third parties may ask for customer information. For example, a reporter or a client may ask you about customer trends. It's never acceptable to discuss specific companies or individuals with a third party, or provide any information that might enable a third party to identify a specific customer. If you want to provide information, you can offer aggregate data from a number of companies, as long as the data provided doesn't allow any one customer to be identified.

You're the head of marketing for a small pharmaceutical company that has just discovered a very promising drug for the treatment of Alzheimer's disease. You have spent months designing a marketing campaign that contains printed materials and medication sample kits for distribution to almost every family physician and gerontologist in the country. As the materials are being loaded into cartons for delivery to your company's representatives, your assistant tells you that she has noticed a typographical error in the literature that could mislead physicians and their patients. In the section that discusses side effects, diarrhea and gastrointestinal problems are listed as having a probability of 2 percent. It should have read 20 percent. This error appears on virtually every piece of the literature and kits, and ads containing the mistake are already on press in several consumer magazines.

Product Safety

Another basic customer right is product safety, and there's probably no issue that will more seriously affect a corporate or an individual's reputation. When we think of product safety, we usually think of it as being an organizational issue. But many of the ethical disasters that have product safety as the core issue started out as small problems that mushroomed. Especially in service businesses, where the "products" are delivered by individuals to individuals, product safety is a critical issue. As a result, product safety is every employee's issue, as well as being an organizational issue. (We'll read more about this as an organizational problem in Chapter 8.)

In the case concerning the typographical error about a new drug's side effects, the head of marketing faces a nasty dilemma. If she reproduces all of the printed material, it surely will be at a very great cost to this small company, and it will result in a significant delay in getting the drug to physicians. However, since many elderly people are prone to gastrointestinal upsets and many can become very ill and even die as a result, this typo is a significant one and the material cannot go out as is. Certainly the ideal solution would be to redo all of the marketing materials. However, if time and financial considerations prohibit that, there are other solutions. One solution might be to quickly produce a "correction" to be inserted into every kit. Also, a letter could be distributed to every physician with an explanation of the correction, as well as a discussion of how important quality and full disclosure are to your company. This solution will still be costly, but not nearly as costly as doing nothing and letting the kits go out with an error. What do you suppose would be the cost of even one wrongful death lawsuit? How about a class action? How about the accompanying publicity?

In another case, a large financial firm was excoriated in 1994 when its brokers sold shares in questionable partnerships to individual investors, who later lost substantial sums on their investments in the partnerships. As a result, the firm not only suffered repeated lashings in the press, but it paid enormous fines as well, and its reputation has suffered greatly. Although this may not be the kind of situation we ordinarily think of when we consider product safety, people have suffered because a firm's salespeople overstated the soundness of a "product." In this case the product was advice, and the public, the press, and the courts deemed once again that the "safety" of a product or service is an important consumer right.

Truth in Advertising

There are many salespeople who simply exaggerate their product's (or service's) benefits to consumers. Do fast sports cars automatically turn every young man into a James Dean? Will investing in a certain bond ensure you a safe retirement? Hype is generally a part of most sales pitches, and most consumers expect a certain amount of hype. There are other cases, however, when fudging the truth about a product is more than just hype—it's unfair. (Like product safety, truth in advertising is an issue for both organizations and individuals.)

Imagine that your financial firm is offering a new issue—a corporate bond with an expected yield of 7–7.5 percent. In the past, offerings like this one have generally been good investments for clients, and you have sold the issue to dozens of large and small clients. You're leaving on a two-week vacation and only have a few hours left in the office, when your firm announces that the yield for the bond has been reduced; the high end will now be no more than 7 percent. The last day of the issue will be next week, while you're away on vacation. What should you do?

The fact is that your customers have been misled (albeit unintentionally) about the yield on that particular bond, and now you are under an obligation to tell the truth about the instrument before the issue closes. Why? Because another basic consumer right is to be told the truth about the products and services purchased. Failure to tell the truth about a product can be devastating for an organization, and it also can cause big problems for the company employees who are involved in perpetuating the false information.

Special Fiduciary Responsibilities

As discussed earlier in this chapter, certain professions, such as banking, accounting, law, religion, and medicine, have special obligations to customers. The law and the judicial system have recognized these special obligations, and they are spelled out in the codes of ethics for those professions.

> For 12 years, you've been the financial advisor for an elderly man in his late 70s who is an active investor of his own portfolio and for a trust that will benefit his two children. In the last few months, you've noticed a subtle, yet marked, change in his behavior. He has become increasingly forgetful, has become uncharacteristically argumentative, and seems to have difficulty understanding some very basic aspects of his transactions. He has asked you to invest a sizable portion of his portfolio and the trust in what you consider to be a very risky bond offering. You are frank about your misgivings. He blasts you and says that if you don't buy the bonds, he'll take his business elsewhere.

If you work for a large electronics chain, it's not your responsibility to assess the mental stability of a customer who's purchasing a new television. You're selling; he's buying. However, individuals in fiduciary professions have a responsibility to protect their customer's assets—and that entails "knowing" their customers; frequently, that can mean assessing behavior and saving customers from themselves. In most cases, if a customer wants to make a risky investment against your advice, there's little you can do but wish him or her well. Who knows? You might be wrong, and the customer might make a fortune. However, if a financial professional sees clear signs of incompetence in a long-time customer who's suddenly interested in making a risky bet, he or she is under some obligation to seek help. The case involving the mental stability of a long-time customer is one of the most common dilemmas encountered by financial advisors. The advisor could try again to dissuade the client from making the investment, or involve the firm's senior management in negotiations with the client. The advisor could contact a member of the client's family—one of the children perhaps—and explain his or her reservations. The advisor could also possibly contact the client's lawyer or accountant, who are also bound by confidentiality constraints because of the fiduciary nature of their professions. However, most financial executives will agree that something must be done to try to help this long-time customer.

Why Is It an Ethical Problem?

We use the term *customer confidence issues* as an umbrella to address the wide range of topics that can affect your relationship with your customer. These are ethical issues because they revolve around fairness, honesty, and respect for others and customer relationships can't survive without those basics of trust.

Costs

There are severe corporate and individual penalties regarding truth in advertising and product safety, and more may be on the way. In addition to fines and imprisonment, the publicity in cases where product safety is a factor is generally staggering, as is the public's reaction. Even if a company is exonerated in the long run, the publicity generated by these situations can be seriously damaging, and it can take years for a company to recover, especially if there's evidence of wrongdoing and consumers feel that the organization has violated a public trust.

The fastest way to lose customers or clients is to violate their basic rights to honesty, a quality product or service, or confidentiality. And, obviously, losing customers will short-circuit any career. In addition, if you belong to a profession with special fiduciary responsibilities, violating customer trust or confidentiality can result in disciplinary action or censure.

USE OF CORPORATE RESOURCES

As discussed in the introduction, you and your employer have a special relationship, and each owes the other a modicum of loyalty based on that relationship. In addition, since you're a corporate representative, you're considered an "agent" of your company. This means that your actions can be considered as actions of the corporation. This section of the chapter presents the flip side of an earlier section on Human Resources Issues—your employer's responsibilities to you are described in that section, and your responsibilities to your employer are described here.

What Is It?

The use of corporate resources involves your fulfilling your end of the employer employee "contract." It means being truthful with your employer and management, and being responsible in the use of corporate resources, including its finances and reputation.

> A young woman who works for you is moving with her husband to another city, where she'll be looking for a new job. She's an excellent worker and when she asks you for a reference, you're glad to do it for her. She specifically asks for a written recommendation on your corporate letterhead.

Use of Corporate Reputation

Whenever you identify yourself as an employee of your company, people can infer that you are speaking on behalf of it, which is why you have to be careful how you link yourself to your company. For example, if you use corporate letterhead to write a recommendation for someone or simply to complain to the telephone company, it can be construed as a "corporate" position. Consequently, corporate letterhead should be used only for corporate business. If, as in the case of the recommendation, you need to identify yourself as an employee, use your personal stationery and attach your business card. The objective is to differentiate between your personal opinions and any official stance of your organization.

Recommendations, in particular, present a challenge for employers and individuals. Many companies attempt to check with former employers when hiring someone. This can present a problem since most companies prohibit their personnel from officially supplying this type of information because of lawsuits that have resulted from employer-supplied recommendations. (Many employers will supply only the following information concerning former employees: name, date of employment, and job title. And most employers will require your written consent before they supply any salary information to a third party.)

Similarly, if you're asked to make a speech, write an article, serve on the board of a nonprofit organization, or participate in any activity that would identify you (and your personal opinions) with your company, be sure to get permission from your manager, the legal department, or human resources. You may unwittingly be supporting a position or organization with which your company may not wish to be associated. For example, while it might seem like a great idea for you to serve on the board of your local ASPCA, if you work for a pharmaceutical company that tests drugs on animals, you may be placing your employer in an embarrassing position. Of course, you can serve on the board as a private citizen, but not as an employee of XYZ Drug Company unless you've received corporate authorization.

> You're an employment counselor at a large outplacement firm. Your company is currently negotiating with Black Company to provide outplacement services to 500 employees who are about to lose their jobs as the result of a layoff. Your neighbor and good friend is a reporter for the local newspaper, who mentions to you over coffee one Saturday that she's writing a story about Black Company. According to her sources, 1,500 employees are about to lose their jobs. You know her numbers are incorrect. Should you tell her?

Dealing with the press—even when the reporter is a friend or relative—is a tricky business and shouldn't be attempted by a novice. In a case like the one above, where you may think your friendly reporter might have incorrect numbers, silence is truly the best policy. Her numbers may in fact be correct, and your numbers may represent only the employees who are eligible for outplacement services, not the total number who are losing their jobs.

Another issue that can be confusing to business people is what "off the record" means. For the most part, off the record means that a reporter won't quote you directly or attribute any remarks to you. You can't, however, tell a reporter that your remarks are off the record after the fact. The way to tell a reporter that remarks are off the record is to inform him or her before you offer your information. But the very best way to make sure something is off the record is to keep your mouth shut in the first place. Reporters with the best of intentions can very innocently get their sources into trouble by providing information that only the source would know, thereby identifying the source.

If you are contacted by the press, immediately contact your company's public relations department. Unless you're trained to answer press inquiries and receive authorization to do it, you should never comment to the press. It's easy to innocently supply confidential information or cast a negative light on your company when you're untrained to deal with probing or ambiguous questions posed by a skilled journalist.

You've been working very long hours on a special project for the chairman of your company. Your company policy states that employees who work more than 12 hours in one day may be driven home by a company car at company expense. Policy also states that employees who work longer than two hours past the regular end of their day can receive a meal delivered to the office at company expense. You and your colleagues who are also working on the project are arriving at the office at 8:00 A.M. and order dinner at 7:00 P.M.; then you enjoy dinner and conversation for an hour and are driven home by company cars. Is this OK?

Corporate Financial Resources

In a game entitled "Where Do You Draw the Line—An Ethics Game," produced by Similc II, players explore the differences between taking $10 worth of pencils from their company and distributing them to poor children, making $10 worth of personal long-distance calls at work, and taking $10 from their company's petty cash drawer. Is there a difference among these scenarios, or are they pretty much the same thing? Most people eventually conclude that all of them, regardless of the employee's intentions, involve stealing $10 worth of corporate resources. The bottom line is that corporate equipment and services should be used only for company business. Whether it involves making personal phone calls, completing expense reports, appropriating office supplies, sending personal mail through the company mail room, or using copy equipment to print a flyer for your scout troop, personal or inappropriate use of corporate resources is unethical and violates most corporate policy.

In a case like the one above where you and colleagues are working long hours to complete a special project for the company's chairman, you are following corporate policy to the letter, so your actions are probably acceptable to most organizations. However, if you and your co-workers are stretching out the last hour of dinner so that you can take a company car home, you're getting into ethical hot water. Are you also stretching out their work in order to have a free meal? If you would have no problem explaining your actions to the chairman, or if you wouldn't mind if he or she sat in on one of those dinner hours, then the meals and the cars are perfectly acceptable. The important thing is to treat your company's resources with as much care as you would your own.

Your manager is being transferred to another division of the company in early January. He calls a meeting in early November and asks that every department head delay processing all invoices until after January 1. He wants to keep expenses low and revenues high so that his last quarter in your area shows maximum revenue.

Providing Honest Information

Another key issue concerns truth. Although everyone will agree that telling the truth is important, someday you may have a manager who says something like, "These numbers look too negative—let's readjust them so it looks better to senior management." Many managers feel it necessary to put a positive spin on financials before submitting them up through the ranks. As a result, some companies have suffered serious financial penalties because their numbers have been positively spun on so many succeeding levels, they bear no resemblance to reality by the time they reach the top. "Fudging" numbers can have serious consequences since senior management may make crucial decisions based on flawed data. (Corporations are fined by regulators if inaccurate financial information is submitted to regulators or incorporated into formal financial statements.) If you're asked to skew any kind of corporate information, you may want to consult with someone outside of your chain of command such as the legal, human resources, or audit department.

In the case about a manager wishing to delay paying expenses until after he leaves the area, such creative bookkeeping not only harms the person who is taking his place in January, it also harms the vendors who are relying on prompt payment of their invoices. It's grossly unfair to ask vendors to wait almost 60 extra days before getting paid. One solution might be to approach the other department heads and gain their cooperation in refusing to follow your manager's request. Another course of action would be to relate the incident to the audit department, who would surely be interested in your manager's shenanigans.

Why Is It an Ethical Problem?

Your use of corporate resources is an ethical issue because it represents fulfilling your end of the employer–employee contract—and its roots are in fairness and honesty.

Costs

Obviously, if you've stolen corporate assets or filed an inflated expense report, you'll almost certainly be fired, and you may be arrested. If you have divulged confidential information to another corporation (as in supplying a recommendation for a former employee), your company may be placed at risk for a lawsuit.

If you fail to uphold your end of the employer–employee loyalty contract, your career at your company can be short-circuited. Most corporate cultures place tremendous importance on honesty, loyalty, and teamwork. Generally, successful corporations are communities, where a sense of family has been encouraged. Just as family members try to protect one another and keep family information private, the company community tries to encourage the same behavior. Individuals who violate the "family" trust by squandering resources, being dishonest, or misusing the "family" reputation, are frequently isolated or even banished.

WHEN ALL ELSE FAILS—BLOWING THE WHISTLE

A section on ethics and the individual wouldn't be complete without a discussion of what happens when you suspect wrongdoing within your organization. If your organization's activities are keeping you awake at night, you may have to report it—blow the whistle—and you need to proceed with great caution.

How not to blow the whistle might be best illustrated in a case that involves a high-level investment banker who discovered that some of his colleagues were engaged in unethical dealings with several customers. The investment banker brought the situation to the attention of his manager, who told him to forget it. Determined to raise the issue, the banker wrote an irate memo outlining the situation and naming names to his company's CEO. The banker copied the memo to several other top managers. Even though there were only three levels of management between the banker and the CEO, and even though the banker was right about his colleagues and they were eventually fired, the banker was also fired.

In another large, multinational company, a young trainee in an Asian country felt he was being treated unfairly by his local management. In a pique of anger, he wrote a long message outlining his grievances on his company's electronic mail system. Although he addressed his message to the company CEO, president, and head of human resources (all three senior managers were based in New York), he copied everyone else on the system—approximately 30,000 managers worldwide. The trainee was fired, not because of the message, but because of how he communicated it. The head of human resources commented, "He was being groomed for management, and we couldn't have someone with such poor judgment in that role. If he had complained only to senior management, he would have been heard, he would have been protected, and we would have corrected the situation. After copying the world with his complaint, we felt he was a loose cannon and we had no choice but to get him out."

Unless you want to be branded as someone with poor judgment, you have to be very careful about how you raise ethical concerns. Usually, the CEO is one of your last resorts, and he or she should be approached only after you've exhausted every other internal resource and are ready to go outside the company to resolve the issue. An exception to this would be in a company like PPG Industries, where the former CEO, Vince Sarni, asked and encouraged employees to contact him directly with issues. A hotline for that purpose sat on his desk, and he personally answered that phone.

So how do you blow the whistle? First, let's talk about when. A long-time customer approaches you for financing for a new business venture. The customer offers as collateral a piece of property he has purchased in a rural location for the purpose of building a housing development. You send an appraiser to the property and he accidentally discovers that this property holds toxic waste. You're sure this customer is unaware of the waste; in fact, the waste is migrating and in a few years will invade the water table under a nearby farmer's fields. You explain the situation to your manager, who naturally instructs you to refuse to accept the property as collateral, but he also forbids you to mention the toxic waste to the customer. "Let them find out about it themselves," he says. Do you alert the customer to the toxic waste? Do you alert government regulators?

When Do You Blow the Whistle?

Let's assume first that your concern involves a serious issue. Reporting toxic materials, for example, is a serious issue, because of the potential for harm. One of your colleagues padding an expense report a bit probably isn't as serious. Once you've informed your manager about a fudged expense report, your responsibility is probably fulfilled. However, one colleague fudging an expense report is a far cry from a group of employees systematically altering all of their expense reports with their manager's knowledge. If you suspect something of that magnitude, of course you should report it to someone outside of your chain of command such as your internal auditor.

Many might disagree with this approach, but few people in business have the time to be "on patrol." Once a manager is alerted, it's his or her responsibility to deal with issues like expense reports, except in extraordinary circumstances. This could be termed "picking your battles," and responding appropriately to your gut feelings. Chapter 4 will provide detailed decision-making tools that can help you decide what to do in a particular ethical dilemma. But, for now, let's consider a number of simple triggers that can help you to determine if an issue is serious.

Some of the triggers to help you determine if an issue is serious enough to be raised beyond your immediate manager include an issue that involves truth, employee or customer (or other stakeholder) rights, trust, harm, your personal reputation, or the reputation of your organization, and whether the law is being broken or compromised. In the toxic dump case, for example, harm could certainly result, customer (and other stakeholder) rights are involved, your organization's reputation is at risk, a public trust may be violated, and law may very well be compromised or broken if you keep quiet about toxic wastes under a proposed housing development. A situation like that has all the earmarks of a serious ethical dilemma.

Suppose your manager asks you to supply inaccurate numbers in a financial report to another level of management. That situation involves not only a breach of truth, but also potential harm and could damage your reputation. It's a serious issue that you'll probably want to report.

How to Blow the Whistle

Let's assume that you're dealing with a serious issue, you've assembled the facts, they're accurate to the best of your knowledge, you've asked your peers or your manager for advice, and there's a law or company policy about to be violated or one of the other triggers discussed earlier indicates a serious problem. Now what?

1. Approach your immediate manager first. If your manager tells you to ignore a situation or belittles your concern, approach him or her again. The second time you approach your manager, you may want to write a memo and spell out your concerns in black and white so it's more difficult for your manager to ignore or dismiss them. Frequently, writing a memo will be enough to convince your manager that this is serious and you'll get a more favorable response. You should also do some soul searching to make sure your decision to pursue this issue is an objective one, and not based in any feeling of revenge you might have for your manager, co-workers, or company. Also, you should find out exactly how your company wants issues raised and if there is a special process for doing it. If there is, follow the process to the letter.[5]

2. Now is the time to discuss the issue with your family. Since any whistleblowing activity can affect not only you, but also your family, it's imperative that your family know what's going on. It's also the time to document your activities. Obtain copies of correspondence that relate to the issue and any memos you've written in an attempt to alert management. It's also a good idea to keep a diary to track activities related to the issue and describe any conversations you've had concerning the issue.[6] If you receive no satisfaction from your manager, it's time to go to the next level of management. The most diplomatic way of going around your manager is to say to your manager something like, "I feel so strongly about this that I'd like a meeting with you and your manager to discuss it." The positive aspect of asking your manager to go with you to the next level is that he or she won't feel betrayed and you'll appear to be a team player. The negative aspect is that your manager may forbid you to approach his or her manager. If that happens, or if you're still not satisfied after meeting with the next level of management, you'll need to consider going outside of your chain of command.

3. If your company has an ethics officer, department, or ombudsman, now is the time to contact that person. It's also a good idea to do some research to find out if your state has any special legislation regarding whistleblowing. Your state may have legislative protection for whistleblowers, but it may require you to follow certain procedures in order for you to be protected.[7]

4. If your company has no formal ethics department, you'll need to think about areas outside of your chain of command that would be the most receptive to your concerns. If your issue is human resources related—if it involves relationships or activities within your company like discrimination or sexual harassment— approach your human resources officer or department. If the issue is business related—if it involves external relationships such as those with customers, vendors, regulators, and the like— you can still approach human resources, but a better choice would probably be the legal department or your company's internal auditors. Obviously, if the issue involves the law or an actual or potential illegality, you should contact the legal department. And if the issue concerns a financial matter, it's probably better to approach your organization's auditors. Most auditors have a system of internal checks they can trigger which will confirm or refute your suspicions and even protect you. Also, some auditors in some industries have an underground network of sorts; there are relationships that exist among auditors from various organizations. They can investigate situations very quietly and keep the situation from blowing out of proportion if that's indicated and appropriate.

Since the role of human resources, legal, and audit departments is to protect the corporation, they should be receptive to any concerns that could put the company at risk. If, however, the activity you're concerned about has been approved or condoned by the highest levels of management, these internal departments may go along with "business as usual." And since their role is to protect the company, you are likely to find that their first allegiance is to the company, and not to you.

It's usually safe to approach these departments, but it's not completely without risk. You can reduce the risk if you can persuade one or more of your colleagues to join you in the process. Having an ally can encourage lawyers and auditors to take you more seriously. It may also be wise to consult your personal lawyer at this point in the process. According to Hoffman and Moore[8], he or she can "help you determine if the wrongdoing violates the law, aid you in documenting information about it, inform you of any laws you might be breaking in documenting it, assist you in deciding to whom to report it, make sure reports are filed on time, and help you protect yourself against retaliation."

5. Once you've approached your management, the ethics office (if your company has one), and human resources, legal, and audit, you should have received some satisfaction. The vast majority of whistleblowing cases are resolved at one of those levels.

However, if you're still concerned, the risks to you personally escalate significantly from this point on. Your last resort within your company would be your organization's senior management, including the CEO, president, or board of directors. Obviously, you should contact whoever has a reputation for being most approachable. Understand that your immediate management will most likely be irate if you approach senior management. However, if you're right about your concerns, you may end up a big hero if the issue you're raising is a localized problem and senior management is unaware of what's going on.

Before contacting your senior management, be sure to have your facts straight and documented. (This is where a diary and copies of correspondence will be useful.) If you're wrong, few people are going to understand or forgive you. You may be harassed, reprimanded, or penalized, or there may be some pretext found to fire you.

6. If you've raised the concern all the way to the top of your company, still have a job, and are still unsatisfied, your only choice now is to go outside. If your company is part of a regulated industry, like defense contractors and commercial banks, you can contact the regulators who are charged with overseeing your industry. Or you can contact the press.

However, if you've already contacted numerous individuals in your company, it won't take a genius for people to figure out who is talking outside of the company. Even if you contact the press or the regulators anonymously, your co-workers probably will be able to figure out who's talking.

Recent legislation has made it easier and more lucrative for employees to blow the whistle when companies are government contractors or when the federal government has somehow been defrauded. Under the False Claims Act, whistleblowers who report corporate wrongdoing to prosecutors can be awarded 15 to 30 percent of whatever damages the federal government recovers, which are to be three times the damages the government has sustained. Since the government has recovered $1.13 billion in the last ten years, this has become a powerful incentive for some employees to tell all to prosecutors.[9] For guidance in this area, there are several whistleblower web sites that can answer myriad questions; just use the keyword "whistleblower" on your internet search engine.

7. There are situations that might be so disturbing to you that you may have no alternative but to quit your job. The toxic dump situation described earlier might just be one of those situations. And frankly, the stress involved in blowing the whistle is so intense that you might consider quitting your job after step 3 or 4. Whistleblowing is so stressful that in one study,[10] one-third of the whistleblowers surveyed would advise other people not to blow the whistle at all.[11] Many people, however, would find it extremely difficult, and perhaps im-

possible, to live with certain situations on their conscience. The knowledge of a toxic dump about to poison private wells would probably be almost impossible to live with for most people. When knowledge becomes unbearable, blowing the whistle and ultimately quitting your job may be the only solution.

CONCLUSION

This chapter has highlighted some of the most common ethical problems you might encounter during your career, and provided some advice on raising issues if you feel the need. Although ethical problems can be very difficult to evaluate, it can be easier to decide what to do when you've spent some time thinking about them ahead of time—before they happen. In the next two chapters, we'll examine tools you can use to help you evaluate dilemmas, and decide what to do.

MORE CASES FOR DISCUSSION

Human Resources Issue

Your division has formed a committee of employees to examine suggestions and create a strategy for how to reward good employee ideas. The committee has five members, but you are the only one who is from a minority group. You're pleased to be part of this effort since appointments to committees such as this one are viewed generally as a positive reflection on job performance. At the first meeting, tasks are assigned and all the other committee members think you should survey minority members for their input. During the weeks that follow, you discover that several committee meetings have been held without your knowledge. When you ask why you weren't notified, two committee members tell you that survey information wasn't needed at the meetings and you'd be notified when a general meeting was scheduled. When you visit one committee member in his office, you spot a report on the suggestion program that you've never seen before. When you ask about it, he says it's just a draft he and two others have produced. How would you handle this?

Conflict of Interest Issue

You've just cemented a deal between a $100 million pension fund and Green Company, a large regional money manager. You and your staff put in long hours and a lot of effort to close the deal and are feeling very good about it. You and three of your direct reports are having lunch in a fancy restaurant to celebrate a promotion, when the waiter brings you a phone. A senior account executive from Green is on the phone and wants to buy you lunch in gratitude for all your efforts. "I'll leave my credit card number with the restaurant owner, he says. "You and your team have a great time on me." Describe three courses of action you might take and the pros and cons of each.

Customer Confidence Issue

You're working the breakfast shift at a fast-food restaurant when a delivery of milk, eggs, and other dairy products arrives. There's a story in the local newspaper about contaminated milk that has been distributed by the dairy which has supplied a delivery of milk to your restaurant. When you read the article more closely, you discover that there's a problem with only a small portion of the dairy's milk, and the newspaper lists the serial numbers of the containers that are problems. When you point out the article to your manager, he tells you to forget it. "If you think we've got time to go through every carton of milk to check serial numbers, you're crazy," he says. "The article says right here that the chances are minuscule that anyone has a contaminated carton." He also explains that not only doesn't he have the workers to check the milk, but also destroying the milk would require him to buy emergency milk supplies at the retail price. So, he tells you to get back to work and forget about the milk. He says, "I don't have the time

or the money to worry about such minor details."

Use of Corporate Resources Issue

You work for Red Co. You and a colleague, Pat Brown, are asked by your manager to attend a week-long conference in Los Angeles. At least 25 other employees from Red Co. are attending, as well as many customers and competitors from other institutions. At the conference, you attend every session and see many of the Red Co. people, but you never run into Pat. Although you've left several phone messages for her, her schedule doesn't appear to allow room for a meeting. However, when you get back to the office, the department secretary, who's coordinating expense reports, mentions to you that your dinner in L.A. must have been quite the affair. When you ask, "What dinner?", she describes a dinner with 20 customers and Red Co. employees that Pat paid for at a posh L.A. restaurant. When you explain that you didn't attend, she shows you the expense report with your name prominently listed as one of the attendees. Describe at least two ways in which you could handle this situation.

DISCUSSION QUESTIONS

1. Have antidiscrimination laws helped or hurt the fair treatment of workers?
2. Is diversity management an ethical issue? *3rd party* ✓
3. Is sexual harassment as important an issue for men as it is for women?
4. What conditions would make accepting a gift from a vendor or a client acceptable?
5. Describe the conditions under which you could hire a college friend.

6. Why do certain professions—bankers, accountants, lawyers, physicians, clergymen, and women have fiduciary responsibilities?

7. What would you do if a former subordinate asked you to write him/her a letter of reference on corporate letterhead?

✓ 8. Do employers have a responsibility to alert other employers to an employee's wrongdoing by supplying an unfavorable reference? Why or why not? Discuss the conflict between community responsibility and self-protection.

9. What conditions would have to be present for you to blow the whistle about unethical conduct you observed at work? How would you go about it?

NOTES

1. Toffler, B. 1986. *Tough choices: Managers talk ethics.* New York: John Wiley & Sons, 12.

2. Wilson, J. Q. 1993. *The moral sense.* New York: The Free Press, 55–78.

3. Rice, F. 1994. How to make diversity pay. *Fortune,* August 8, 79.

4. Sheppard, B., Lewicki, R., and Minton, J. W. 1992. *Organizational justice: The search for fairness in the workplace.* New York: Lexington Books.

5. Webber, R. 1989. Whistleblowing. *Executive Excellence,* July: 9–10.

6. Ibid.

7. Dunkin, A. 1991. Blowing the whistle without paying the piper. *Business Week,* June 3, 138–139.

8. Hoffman, W. M., and Moore, J. M. 1984. *Business ethics: Reading and cases in corporate morality.* New York: McGraw-Hill, 257

9. Rothracker, Rick. 1997. Whistle-Blower Law Reap Big Payoffs for U.S. Treasury, *Legi-Slate,* August 29, 1997: 1.

10. Soeken, K. L., and Soeken, D. R. 1987. A survey of whistleblowers: Their stressors and coping strategies. *Proceedings of the Hearing on H.R. 25* (pp. 156–166). Washington, D.C.: U.S. Government Printing Office.

11. Miceli, M., and Near, J. 1992. *Blowing the whistle.* New York: Lexington Books, 303.

CHAPTER 4

Deciding What's Right:
A Prescriptive Approach

INTRODUCTION

There are two ways to think about individual ethical decision making—a prescriptive approach and a descriptive approach. The prescriptive approach, derived from philosophy, offers decision-making tools (ways of thinking about ethical choices) that prescribe what decision you should make as a "conscientious moral agent"[1] who thinks carefully about moral choices. They're designed to help you make the best possible ethical decision. In this chapter we'll introduce some of these and explain how you can integrate them and use them in a practical way.

We know, however, that people don't always make the best decision. Prescriptions aren't always followed. So, it's helpful to understand how people's minds really work—how people really make decisions. The psychological approach, discussed in the next chapter, relies on psychological research and describes how people actually make ethical decisions. It focuses in particular on the cognitive biases and limitations that often keep us from making the best possible decisions. Hopefully, if we understand both approaches, we can improve our ethical decision making.

Many ethical choices are clear-cut enough for us to be able to decide what to do rather quickly because they pit "right" against "wrong." Is deciding whether to embezzle corporate funds a tough ethical dilemma? Not really, because embezzling is stealing and it's wrong, period. There's not much of a dilemma there. But things can get pretty murky in situations where two or more important values, rights, or obligations conflict and we have to choose between equally unpleasant alternatives. Consider the following dilemma.

The Layoff

You're the plant manager in one of ABC Company's five plants. You've worked for the company for 15 years, working your way up from the factory floor after the company sent you to college. Your boss just told you in complete confidence that the company will have to lay off 200 workers. Luckily, your job won't be affected. But a rumor is now circulating in the plant, and one of your workers (an old friend who now works for you) asks the question, "Well, Pat, what's the word? Is the plant closing? Am I going to lose my job? The closing on our new house is scheduled for next week. I need to know!" What will you say?

This is a true ethical dilemma because two values are in conflict. Two "right" values that can create significant conflict are truth and loyalty. As illustrated in the case, telling the truth to your friend means that you may have to break your promise to be loyal to the company that has treated you so well. In this chapter, we'll introduce conceptual tools that are designed to help you think through ethical dilemmas from multiple perspectives. None of the approaches is perfect. In fact, they may lead to different conclusions. The point of using them is to get you to think carefully and avoid falling into a solution by accident.

PRESCRIPTIVE APPROACHES TO ETHICAL DECISION MAKING IN BUSINESS

Philosophers have been wrestling with ethical decision making for centuries. We certainly don't intend to provide a philosophy course here, but we can distill some important principles that can guide you in your ethical decision making. In this section, we'll outline some of the major contemporary approaches that we think can provide you with the most practical assistance.[2] We'll then incorporate them into a series of steps that you can use to evaluate ethical dilemmas, and we'll apply these steps to the short layoff case.

Focus on Consequences (Consequentialist Theories)

One set of philosophical theories is categorized as consequentialist (sometimes referred to as teleological, from the Greek *telos* or goal). When you're attempting to decide what's right or wrong, consequentialist theories focus attention on the results or consequences of the decision or action.

Utilitarianism is probably the best known consequentialist theory. According to the principle of utility, an ethical decision should maximize benefits to society and minimize harms. What matters is the net balance of good consequences over bad.

A utilitarian would approach an ethical dilemma by identifying the alternative actions and their consequences. For example, what would be the consequences (societal harms and benefits) of my telling my friend what I know about the layoff? What would be the consequences (societal harms and benefits) of not sharing what I know? This would be followed by a kind of mental calculation of all the costs and benefits of these consequences. For example, one cost of telling my friend would be that he or she might tell others and send the plant into chaos. A potential benefit might be that I would retain the trust of a valued friend. The "best" decision would be the one that yielded the greatest net benefits for society, and the "worst" decision would be the one that yielded the greatest net harms for society. So, if more people would be ultimately hurt than helped if Pat informs her friend of the impending layoff, a utilitarian would conclude that Pat shouldn't tell.

The utilitarian approach can be extremely helpful in thinking through an ethical dilemma. Don't we generally look at the consequences of our own and others' actions in trying to decide what's right? And don't we consider who will benefit and who will be harmed? When the state decides to build a new highway through your property, aren't they using a utilitarian rationale when they argue that the benefits to the community (increased development, reduced traffic, fewer accidents, etc.) outweigh the harm to the few property holders who will be inconvenienced by an eyesore in their back yard?

But a challenge involved in using a strictly consequentialist approach is that it is often difficult to obtain the information required to evaluate all of the consequences for all individuals who may be directly or indirectly affected by an action or decision. When, in business, do you have ALL of the facts? And even if you have all of the information, it can be extremely cumbersome to have to calculate all of the harm and benefits every time you encounter a new ethical dilemma. Try it. Can you list all of the potential harm and benefits for all of those who may be directly or indirectly involved in the layoff situation described above? It's relatively easy to list the potential harm and benefits to yourself. But can you envision all of the potential harm and benefits to all of the other people who may be involved? Remember, according to utilitarianism, an ethical decision should maximize benefits and minimize harm to society. So it isn't acceptable to just think of harm and benefits to yourself and those close to you.

Another difficulty with this type of approach is that the rights of a minority group can easily be sacrificed for the benefit of the majority. For example, slaveholders in the old South argued that the greatest good would be served by maintaining the system of slavery.

Nevertheless, the utilitarian approach remains particularly important to ethical decision making in business for a variety of reasons. First, utilitarian thinking—through its descendant, utility theory—underlies much of the business and economics literature. Second, on the face of it, most of us would admit that considering the consequences of one's decisions or actions is extremely important to good ethical decision making. In fact, studies of ethical decision making in business have found that business managers generally rely on a utilitarian approach.[3] So, the remaining question is whether other kinds of considerations are also important.

Focus on Duties, Obligations, and Principles (Deontological Theories)

The word "deontological" comes from the Greek *deon* or duty. Rather than focusing on consequences, deontological approaches would ask, "what is Pat's duty now that she knows about the layoff?" Deontologists base their decisions about what's right on broad, abstract universal principles such as honesty, promise keeping, fairness, rights (to safety, privacy, etc.), justice, and respect for persons and property. According to some deontological approaches, some moral principles are binding, regardless of the consequences. Therefore, some actions would be considered wrong even if the consequences of the actions were good. In other words, a deontologist focuses on doing what is "right" (based on moral principles such as honesty), whereas a utilitarian focuses on doing what will maximize societal welfare. An auditor taking a deontological approach would insist on telling the truth about a company's financial difficulties even if doing so might cause more harm than good and risk putting the company out of business, whereas a utilitarian auditor would weigh the societal harms and benefits before deciding what to do.

Some deontological theories focus on rights rather than duties or principles. The concept of rights goes back to classical Greek notions of "natural rights" that emerge from "natural law." Rights can be thought of as "negative rights" such as the limits on government interference with citizens' right to privacy or the pursuit of happiness. Or rights can be thought of in more positive terms, such as the individual's rights to health and safety. The rights of one party can conflict with the rights of another party, as when the rights of a company to seek profits for its shareholders conflict with the rights of a community to clean air or water. Furthermore, the rights of one party are generally related to the duties of another. So, if we agreed that communities have the right to clean water, businesses would have the duty to protect that right.

So, how does a deontologist determine what rule, principle, or right to follow? Some rely on Western biblical tradition or moral intuition for guidance. For example, the Golden Rule, familiar to many of us, provides an important deontological guide: "Do unto others as you would have them do unto you." In our layoff situation, the Golden Rule would suggest that Pat should tell her friend what she knows because she would want her friend to do the same for her if the situation were reversed.

The German philosopher, Emmanuel Kant, provides a particular mode of deontological thinking about ethical choices through his "categorical imperative": "Act as if the maxim of thy action were to become by thy will a universal law of nature." This mode of thinking asks whether the rationale for your action is suitable to become a universal law or principle for everyone to follow. For example, if you break a promise, the categorical imperative asks, "is promise breaking a principle everyone should follow?" No, if everyone did this, promises would become meaningless. In fact, they would cease to exist.

A practical deontological question to ask yourself might be, "what kind of world would this be if everyone behaved this way or made this kind of decision in this type of situation?" What kind of world would this be if everyone broke promises at will?

In a further application of the categorical imperative, think about the following example. A number of physicians are recruited to participate in a large-scale multicenter study to investigate the survival rates of breast cancer victims who are being treated with a new drug. Strict rules are developed regarding inclusion of patients in the study. Only those who have had surgery within the last three months can be included. Dr. Smith has a patient who hears about the study and wants very much to participate. Because Dr. Smith thinks that the drug could really help this patient, he agrees to include her even though her surgery took place six months ago. He changes the dates on her charts to conform with the study requirements and reasons that this one little change shouldn't affect the study results.

According to the categorical imperative, we must ask whether the rationale for Dr. Smith's action (helping his patient by breaking the study rules) is suitable to become a principle for all to follow. The answer is no. What if a number of other doctors did the same thing as Dr. Smith? What if those involved in medical research followed their own preferences or motives rather than the rules guiding the study? Society would be unable to rely on the results of medical research. What kind of a world would it be if researchers were routinely dishonest? It would be one where we simply couldn't rely on the integrity of scientific research, and most of us would deem that kind of world unacceptable.

A major challenge of deontological approaches is deciding which duty, obligation, right, or principle takes precedence because, as we said earlier, ethical dilemmas often pit these against each other. What does the deontologist do if one binding moral rule clashes with another? Can it be determined which is the more important right or principle? Because the U.S. Constitution is based on a rights approach, many U.S. public policy debates revolve around questions such as these. For example, the abortion debate rests on the question of whether the rights of the mother or the fetus should take precedence.

Another difficulty of deontological approaches involves the difficulty of arguing for a rule or principle that, if followed in a particular situation, will have devastating consequences. That's where consequentialist and deontological approaches conflict. For example, what if Pat determines that telling her friend what she knows (in accordance with the principles of honesty and respect for her friend as a person) could have devastating consequences for the company as a whole? In response to this concern, some philosophers argue that deontological principles (i.e., truth telling, promise keeping) don't have to be regarded as absolute. For example, one could violate a rule or principle for a good reason (according to Kant, a reason that you would be willing to accept for anyone in the same position).[4]

policy

Focus on Integrity (Virtue Ethics)

The virtue ethics approach focuses more on the integrity of the moral actor than on the moral act itself. Although virtue ethics as a philosophical tradition began with Aristotle, a number of contemporary ethicists (including business ethicists) have brought it back to the forefront of ethical thinking.[5]

A virtue ethics perspective considers primarily the actor's character, motivations, and intentions. This doesn't mean that principles, rules, or consequences aren't considered at all, but they're considered in the context of assessing the actor's character and integrity. For example, one's character may be assessed in terms of principles such as honesty, in terms of rule following (did this actor follow his profession's ethics code?) or in terms of consequences (as in the physician's agreement to, above all, do no harm).

In virtue ethics, character is very much defined by one's community. Therefore, it's important to think about the community or communities within which business people operate. Think about yourself. What community or communities would you look to for help in deciding whether you were a business person of integrity? Your professional association? Your church? Your family? Your peers within your company? Would the communities you identify be different if you were evaluating your nonwork self?

Virtue ethics may be particularly useful in determining the ethics of an individual who works within a professional community that has well-developed norms and standards of conduct. For example, the accounting profession has developed a code of conduct for professional accountants. Being a virtuous accountant would mean abiding by that code of professional responsibility. The same goes for financial consultants who are certified and who agree to abide by specific professional rules and standards.

A virtue ethics approach allows the decision maker to rely on relevant community standards without going through the complex process of trying to decide what's right in every situation using deontological or consequentialist approaches. The assumption is that the community has already done this type of thinking. However, what if the community hasn't done this type of thinking? Or what if the community is just wrong? Furthermore, the usefulness of virtue ethics in business may be limited because in many areas of business there is limited agreement about what the standards are. There is no universal code of conduct for all business managers to follow.

These are just a few of the philosophical approaches that may be applied in ethical dilemma situations. We've introduced the ones we feel have the most practical benefit to business managers, and, admittedly, we've introduced them in a rather general way, without many of the nuances developed by philosophers over the years. We've suggested that all of the approaches have limitations. No one of them, by itself, provides perfect guidance in every situation. Obviously, if all of the approaches lead to the same solution, the decision is a relatively easy one. The tough ones arise when the approaches conflict.

We don't have a perfect solution. We certainly won't resolve the academic controversies over the "best" philosophical approach here. But we believe that all of the approaches we've presented suggest important factors to keep in mind in making business ethics decisions. Therefore, we offer the following eight steps that rely on all of the types of analysis just discussed.[6] Before presenting them, we'd like to offer a caveat. The eight steps suggest a linear decision-making process that is necessarily inaccurate. Ethical decision making is often not linear. But it will be helpful to cover all of these points, even if not in this particular sequence.

EIGHT STEPS TO SOUND ETHICAL DECISION MAKING IN BUSINESS

1. Gather the Facts

The philosophical approaches don't tell us to gather the facts. But they seem to assume that we'll complete this important step. You might be surprised at how many people jump to solutions without having the facts. Ask yourself, "How did the situation occur? Are there historical facts that I should know? Are there facts concerning the current situation that I should know?"[7]

Fact gathering is often easier said than done. Many ethical choices are particularly difficult because of the uncertainty involved in them. Facts may simply be unavailable. For example, in our layoff case, Pat may not have good information about the legal requirements on informing workers about layoffs. Also, she may not have enough information to determine how long it would take these 200 workers to find new jobs. But recognizing these limitations, you should attempt to assemble the facts that are available to you before proceeding.

2. Define the Ethical Issues

Many of us have knee-jerk responses to ethical dilemmas. We jump to a solution without really thinking through the ethical issues and the reasons for our response (we'll talk more about why in Chapter 5). For example, in the layoff case, one person might say, "Oh, that's easy, promise-keeping is the ethical issue. Pat has to keep her promise to her boss and protect her job." Another person might say that honesty is the key ethical issue. "Pat just has to tell the truth to her friend."

So, our second recommendation is, don't jump to solutions without first identifying the ethical issues or points of values conflict in the dilemma. There are generally multiple ethical issues that go back to the deontological, or principle-based, theories we just discussed. For example, in the case above, one ethical issue has to do with the rights, of the workers and the company. How would you define workers' rights to know about the plant closing in advance. How much advance notice is appropriate? What does the law say? Another ethical issue has to do with the company's right to keep the information private. Furthermore, what is the company's obligation to its workers in this regard? At a more personal level, there are the ethical issues related to principles such as honesty, loyalty, and promise keeping. Is it more important to be honest with a friend or to keep a promise to one's boss? Does one owe more loyalty to a friend or to one's boss? Can you think about the situation from a justice or fairness perspective? What would be fair to the company and to those who would be laid off?

Points of ethical conflict may go back to the conflict between consequentialist and deontological approaches. For example, if I tell the truth (consistent with the principle of promise keeping), bad things will happen (negative consequences). A consequentialist would think about the ethical issues in terms of harms or benefits. Who is likely to be harmed? Who is likely to benefit from a particular decision or action? A virtue ethics approach would suggest thinking about the ethical issues in terms of community standards. Does your relevant community identify a particular action as wrong? Why or why not?

Our inclination is to stop with the first ethical issue that comes to mind. For example, in our layoff case, we might be inclined to stop with the issue of loyalty to a friend. Challenge yourself to think of as many issues as you possibly can. Here's where talking about the problem with others can help. Present the dilemma to co-workers, to your spouse, or to friends you respect. Ask them whether they see other issues that you may have missed.

3. Identify the Affected Parties

Both consequentialist and deontological thinking involve the ability to identify the parties affected by the decision. The consequentialist will want to identify all those who are going to experience harm and benefits. The deontologist might want to know whose rights are involved and who has a duty to act in the situation.

Being able to see the situation through others' eyes is a key moral reasoning skill. Lawrence Kohlberg called this skill role taking. Frequently, you have to think beyond the facts provided in a case in order to identify all affected parties. It often helps to begin with the individuals in the case who are immediately affected (e.g., Pat, the worker, Pat's boss) and then to progressively broaden your thinking to incorporate larger groups. For example, in this case, you might include the other workers, the local community, the rest of the company, and society in general. As you think of more and more affected parties, additional issues will probably come to mind. For example, think about the local community. If this is a small town with few other employers, fairness to the entire community becomes an issue. Shouldn't they have as much time as possible to plan for the impact of this plant closing? Try to put yourself in their shoes. How would they argue their case? How would they feel?

In Chapter 1, we introduced the concept of stakeholders, all of those who have a stake in what an organization does and how it performs. Stakeholders can include owners, managers, customers, employees, suppliers, the community, the government, the natural environment and, of course, stockholders. In the context of ethical decision making in business, we should identify the stakeholders affected by the decision and ask how they are affected. Try to make your thinking as broad as possible here. Some of the stakeholders affected by the decision may not even be born yet. The best concrete example of unborn stakeholders might be "DES daughters." In the 1940s, DES, a synthetic estrogen, was prescribed for pregnant women who seemed to be in danger of miscarrying. By 1971, it became clear that DES produced a birth defect in the daughters of these women. Because of the birth defect, DES daughters were more likely to develop vaginal cancer, especially between the ages of 15 and 22. They also had a higher than normal rate of cervical cancer.[8]

Once stakeholders are identified, role-playing can help you to see the issue from different stakeholder perspectives. In your classroom or your department, get individuals to seriously play the relevant roles. You may be surprised at how perspectives change based on this simple exercise. What decision would you reach if you were someone else in the situation? This step incorporates the Golden Rule: Treat others as you would like others to treat you. Imagine yourself as each of the players in a decision situation. What decision would they reach and why?

Another consideration may be to ask whether you can "test" a potential decision with affected parties before your prospective course of action is made final. The objective is to gauge how various audiences will react, and to be able to adjust or fine-tune a decision along the way.[9] One question you could ask yourself is, how would this or that stakeholder react if this decision were made public? For example, imagine that ABC Co. (in our layoff case) had another thriving plant in another location. However, in the decision-making process, it was assumed that employees wouldn't want to relocate because of their ties to the local community. Wouldn't it be best to ask them their preferences than to assume what they would want to do?

4. Identify the Consequences

After identifying the affected parties, think about the potential consequences for each of these parties. This step is obviously derived from the consequentialist approaches. It isn't necessary to identify every possible consequence. But you should try to identify consequences that have a relatively high probability of occurring and those that would have particularly negative consequences if they did occur (even if the probability of occurrence is low). Who would be harmed by a particular decision or action? For example, in our case, telling the truth to the worker might cause Pat to lose her job, which would have negative consequences for her entire family (especially if she's a single mother). However, it would give her worker (and presumably others who would be told) the benefit of more time to look for a new job, perhaps saving many families from negative financial consequences. Can you determine which solution would accomplish the most net good? A popular version of utilitarianism asks the question, "which decision or action will produce the greatest good for the greatest number of people?" Would telling a lie to your friend benefit the most people? Or would it be better for all affected parties if you were to tell the truth?

Long-term Versus Short-Term Consequences In business decisions, it's particularly important to think in terms of short-term AND long-term consequences. Are you confident that your position will be as valid over a long period of time, even if circumstances or people change? In this case, is the long-term health of the company and the people who will remain employed more important than the short-term consequences to the 200 workers who will be laid off?

Symbolic Consequences In business, it's also extremely important to think about the potential symbolic consequences of an action. Every decision and action sends a message; it stands for something. What message will a particular decision or action send? What will it mean if it is misunderstood? For example, if Pat doesn't tell her worker the truth, and he finds out later that she knew, what will the symbolic message be to this worker and the others who work for Pat—that she's more interested in saving her own hide than in taking care of them?

Consequences of Secrecy If a decision is made in private in order to avoid some negative reaction, think about the potential consequences if the decision were to become public. For example, the public has been outraged by the fact that tobacco companies may have hidden their knowledge of the negative health effects of cigarette smoking.[10]

5.   Identify the Obligations
   Identify the obligations involved and the reasons for each. For example, consider Pat's obligation toward the affected parties. When identifying Pat's various obligations, be sure to state the reasons why she has this duty or obligation. Think in terms of values, principles, character, or outcomes. For example, if you're considering Pat's obligation to keep her promise to her boss, your reasoning might go like this: "Pat shouldn't break her promise to her boss. If she does, the trust between them will be broken. Promise keeping and trust are important values in superior/ subordinate relationships."
   This step, and the obligations you identify, may vary depending on the people involved and the roles they play. For example, our faith in our financial system depends in part on auditors' obligation to tell the truth about a company's financial difficulties. Similarly, our faith in science as an institution depends on the integrity of the scientific data and how scientists report it. So, the auditor and the scientist have a particularly strong obligation to tell the truth.

6.   Consider Your Character and Integrity
   In thinking about what you should do in an ethical dilemma, it can also be useful to consider what your relevant community would

consider to be the kind of decision that an individual of integrity would make in the situation. You have to begin by identifying the relevant community. Then, you have to determine how community members would evaluate the decision or action you're considering.

A method that can help you with this process is known as the disclosure rule. It asks whether you would feel comfortable if your activities were disclosed in the light of day in a public forum like *The New York Times* or some other medium. Obviously, *The New York Times* assumes a general community standard. It's important for you to determine which medium is the appropriate one in your situation. But, in general, if you don't want to read about it in *The New York Times,* you probably shouldn't be doing it. If you would be embarrassed to have someone read about your activities in the newspaper—or if you'd be uncomfortable telling your parents, children, spouse, or clergy about your decision—you probably should rethink it.

Boris Yavitz, the former dean of Columbia University's Graduate School of Business, offered another version of the test for New Yorkers: "Unless you would do it in Macy's department store window at high noon, don't do it." And Thomas Jefferson expressed it like this: "Never suffer a thought to be harbored in your mind which you would not avow openly. When tempted to do anything in secret, ask yourself if you would do it in public. If you would not, be sure it is wrong."

This kind of approach can be especially valuable when a decision needs to be made quickly. Suppose someone in your organization asks you to misrepresent the effectiveness of one of your company's products to a customer. You can immediately imagine how a story reporting the details of your conversation with the customer would appear in tomorrow's paper. Would you be comfortable having others read the details of that conversation? The ideal is to conduct business in such a way that your activities and conversations could be disclosed without your feeling embarrassed.

Another method might be to ask a question asked by the Seneca people (one of the original five nations of the great Iroquois Confederacy located in the northeastern United States and southeastern Canada) in their guidelines for self-discipline: "how will I be remembered when I'm gone?"[11] Americans don't often think about this question, but it's a good one. Will you be remembered as an individual of integrity or not?

7. Think Creatively about Potential Actions

Before making any decision, be sure that you haven't unnecessarily forced yourself into a corner. Are you assuming that you have only two choices, either "a" or "b"? According to Jack Edwards, vice president of Cummins Engine Company, who spoke at the 1994 Conference Board meeting on ethics, it's important to look for creative alternatives. Perhaps if you've been focusing on "a" or "b," there's another answer "c." For example, he told the story of an American business person who received an extravagant gift from a foreign supplier. This situation could easily be conceptualized as an "a" or "b" situation. Should I accept the gift (which is against company policy), or should I refuse it (which will likely be interpreted as a slap in the face by this important supplier). The "c" solution was to accept the gift as a gift to the company that would be displayed in the headquarters entrance.

In another overseas location, the company was having difficulty with local children cutting through a wire fence and stealing valuable electronic components. The "a" or "b" solution was to arrest or not arrest these young children when they were caught. After involving the community, the managers involved were able to arrive at a "c" solution. They discovered that the children were stealing because there weren't enough classrooms at the local school, leaving the children with little to do but get into trouble. Cummins made classrooms available on their site. The mayor provided accreditation, books, and teachers. This "c" solution cost the company very little and accomplished a great deal. Three hundred and fifty students were accommodated, the stealing problem disappeared, and Cummins became a valued corporate citizen.

8. Check Your Gut

    The emphasis in these steps has been on a highly rational fact-gathering and evaluation process once you know that you're faced with an ethical dilemma. But don't forget your gut. Empathy is an important emotion that can signal awareness that someone might be harmed. And intuition is gaining credibility as a source for good business decision making. We can't always say exactly why we're uncomfortable in a situation. But years of socialization have likely made us sensitive to situations where something isn't quite right. So, if your gut is bothering you, give the situation more thought. In fact, this may be your only clue that you're facing an ethical dilemma to begin with. So, pay attention to your gut. But don't let it make your decision for you. Once you know you're facing an ethical dilemma, use the rational decision-making tools developed here to guide your decision making.

PRACTICAL PREVENTIVE MEDICINE

Doing Your Homework

There's no doubt that you'll encounter ethical dilemmas—every employee probably encounters hundreds of them during a career—the only thing in doubt is when. Your mission is to be as prepared as much as possible before you run into a problem. The more informed you are, the more effective you'll be in protecting yourself and your employer. The best way to do that is to learn the rules of your organization and your profession, and to develop relationships that can help you if and when the need arises.

You can learn the rules in various ways. First, read your company's code of ethics (if it has one) and policy manual. Since most policy manuals are huge, you obviously can't memorize one. But if you skim the contents, some of the rules will sink in—you may not remember the exact policy, but you'll probably remember at least that one exists and where to find it.

Second, ask questions. Managers, executives, and peers will admire your initiative when you ask what they think is "important around here." Since many organizational standards are unwritten and they differ from company to company, the only way you'll find out about them is by asking. While you're asking questions, query your co-workers (including management) about what kinds of ethical situations are most common in your organization and how your organization generally handles those issues. Ask your manager how to raise ethical issues within your organization. Since he or she will certainly tell you to raise an issue with him or her first, be sure to find out how you raise an issue in his or her absence. This not only gives you a roadmap for raising issues, but it also sends a signal to your manager that ethics are important to you.

Finally, develop relationships with people who are outside of your chain of command. Get to know people in human resources or personnel, legal, audit, and other departments who might be able to provide information, help you raise an issue or determine if something even is an issue, or vouch for your credibility in a crisis. You might also want to join a professional group or association. Many professions have developed ethical standards—apart from those that may exist in your company—and it can be very helpful to know other people in your profession to confidentially consult with if a crisis arises in your company. Some may say that this is being political, but we think it's just plain smart to network with people outside of your immediate job and company. It's the difference between being a victim of circumstance and having the power, the knowledge, and the network to help manage circumstances.

Frankly, after you've done your homework and learned about your company's standards and values, you may find that your values and your employer's values are in conflict. If the conflict is substantial, you may have no choice but to look for work in another organization.

When You're Asked to Make a Snap Decision

Many business people place value on the ability to make decisions quickly, and as a result many of us can feel pressure to make up our minds in a hurry. This can be a particular issue when people are inexperienced for whatever reason—this may be their first job or a new one, or they may have changed companies or industries—and they may feel a need to prove their competence by making decisions quickly. Obviously, that can be dangerous. The ethical decision-making tools described earlier in the chapter assume that you'll have some time to devote to the decision. Therefore, consider the following guidelines when a quick decision seems called for:

1. Don't underestimate the importance of a hunch to alert you that you're facing an ethical dilemma. As we said earlier, your gut is your internal warning system. As one senior executive at a multinational computer company said, "The gut never lies." When your gut tells you something's wrong, consider it a warning siren.

2. Ask for time to think it over. Most snap decisions don't have to be that way. Say something like, "Let me think about it and I'll get right back to you." Bargaining for time is a smart way to give yourself a break—then you can really think about the decision and consult with others. It's better to take the time to make a good decision than it is to make a bad decision quickly and have lots of time to regret it. Would you rather be known as cautious or reckless?

3. Find out quickly if your organization has a policy that applies to your decision.

4. Ask your manager or your peers for advice. You should consider your manager the first line of defense when you encounter an ethical dilemma. Regardless of your level within the organization, you should never hesitate to ask for another opinion. This is where the network comes in handy. If you have friends in human resources or the legal department, you can float the issue with them on a casual basis to see if there even is an issue.

5. Use *The New York Times* test (the disclosure rule). As we said earlier, this is a quick-check kind of test. If you'd be embarrassed to have your decision disclosed in the media or to your family, don't do it.

> You're upgrading your department's data processing capabilities and have just placed an order for four personal computers and two laser printers with a computer company representative. When you mention that you wish you had a printer at home like the ones you just ordered, the representative tells you that because of your large order, she can give you a 50 percent discount on a printer for your home. However, all items must be ordered now. You feel that this is not quite right, but you're not sure why.

In this case, the employee could have real doubt about whether or not to accept a 50 percent discount on a printer for his home. Even though he feels funny about the offer, he might be thinking that he does a lot of work at home, so accepting a discount on a personal printer could be justified. And since the computer representative made the offer after the order was placed, there's no conflict of interest—his decision to purchase obviously wasn't influenced by the offer of a discount.

But he should listen to his gut, which is feeling that this isn't quite right. He can first stall the computer representative by telling her he'll get back to her later in the day or tomorrow. He can find out what his company policy says about making purchases. (Many companies would equate the discount with a gift and forbid accepting it unless it's available to all employees.)

Suppose he finds nothing in the policy manual to prohibit the discount, and other workers have said "go for it." Then he can use *The New York Times* test. How would the public react to his decision? Some people would probably think that his order was influenced by the offer of a discount. He knows that's not true, but it might be difficult to convince other people of that. This is called an appearance of a conflict of interest, and as discussed in Chapter 3, an appearance can be as damaging as an actual conflict. If someone could think your judgment has been affected by a relationship or, in this case a discount, it could be viewed as the appearance of a conflict and should be avoided. Appearances are extremely important in business and may not be accounted for by the philosophical tools provided earlier in the chapter. Whether you appear to be fair may be as important as whether you're really fair.

The bottom line is: If you think that your decision could be misinterpreted or if someone could think the objectivity of your decision has been compromised, rethink the decision. The representative's offer can be refused politely by saying something like, "My company doesn't allow personal discounts," or "I just don't feel right about it."

If you ever feel that accepting a favor from a vendor will place you under an obligation to the vendor in the future, be very careful. For example, a public relations manager, Mary, described an incident with a printing company (we'll call it Type Co.) sales representative who was trying to get her business. Type Co. already did business with a number of departments within her company, but Mary was satisfied with her current printer and saw no reason to switch. Just before the holidays, Type Co. sent a miniature television to Mary and to all of Type Co.'s other clients in her company. She immediately felt that the gift was inappropriate, but to check out her judgment, she called one of Type Co.'s other clients in her company. Mary's colleague assured her that there was nothing wrong with accepting the gift and that it was simply a token of good will. (If Mary had been friendly with one of her company's lawyers or human resources managers, she would probably have received very different advice.) However, Mary was still uneasy and sent the television back.

When asked why she returned the gift, Mary said, "I felt like I was being bribed to do business with Type Co." Mary listened to her internal warning system, despite what her colleague said. A reader of *The New York Times* would probably agree that Mary was being bribed to do business with Type Co.

CONCLUSION

This chapter has presented a prescriptive approach to individual ethical decision making. When you're confronted with an ethical choice, you should find it helpful to inform your choice by considering the ideas and steps offered in this chapter. The end-of-chapter questions and case should give you some practice in applying these ideas and steps to real ethical dilemmas.

However, the prescriptive approach needs to be complemented by the descriptive approach offered in Chapter 5. In the next chapter, you'll learn about psychological research that can help us understand how people actually make ethical decisions—the individual characteristics and cognitive processes that impact the decisions people make.

DISCUSSION QUESTIONS

1. If you had to choose just one of the philosophical approaches discussed in this chapter to guide your decision making, which would you choose? Why?

2. Think about an ethical dilemma situation that you've faced. Apply the eight steps recommended in this chapter. Does it change your thinking about the situation? Would it change your action?

3. Some corporations and other organizations have designed ethical decision-making tests that incorporate some of the principles and systems described in this chapter. For example, Carl Skooglund, vice president and ethics director at Texas Instruments, outlines the Ethics Quick Test recommended for use by Texas Instrument employees:[12]
   a. Is the action legal?
   b. Does it comply with your best understanding of our values and principles?
   c. If you do it, will you feel bad?
   d. How will it look in the newspaper?
   e. If you know it's wrong, don't do it, period!
   f. If you're not sure, ask.
   g. Keep asking until you get an answer.

   Think about this list in terms of the decision-making guides discussed in the chapter. Which ones are being used here? Which are not? What recommendations, if any, would you make to alter this list? If you had to make up a list for your company, what would be on it? Why?

   Do the same with the Rotary International Four-Way Test:
   a. Is it the truth?
   b. Is it fair to all concerned?
   c. Will it build good will and better relationships?
   d. Will it be beneficial to all concerned?

   Think about the rest of the Seneca people's guidelines for self-discipline.[12] Could they serve as guides for ethical decision making in business? Why or why not?
   a. Am I happy in what I'm doing?
   b. Is what I'm doing adding to the confusion?
   c. What am I doing to bring about peace and contentment?
   d. How will I be remembered when I am gone?

4. What limitations, if any, can you think of to the prescriptions provided in this chapter? Can you think of reasons why they might not work?

CASE 4.1

Pinto Fires

by Dennis A. Gioia

On August 10, 1978, three teen-age girls died horribly in an automobile accident. Driving a 1973 Ford Pinto to their church volleyball practice in Goshen, Indiana, they were struck from behind by a Chevrolet van. The Pinto's fuel tank ruptured and the car exploded in flames. Two passengers, Lynn Marie Ulrich, 16, and her cousin, Donna Ulrich, 18, were trapped inside the inferno and burned to death. After three attempts Lynn Marie's sister, 18-year-old Judy Ann, was dragged out alive from the driver's seat, but died in agony hours later in the hospital.

They were merely the latest in a long list of people to burn to death in accidents involving the Pinto, which Ford had begun selling in 1970. By the time of the accident, the car had been the subject of a great deal of public outcry and debate about its safety, especially its susceptibility to fire in low-speed rear-end collisions. This particular accident, however, resulted in more media attention than any other auto accident in U.S. history. Why? Because it led to an unprecedented court case in which the prosecution brought charges of reckless homicide against the Ford Motor Co.—the first time that a corporation had been charged with criminal conduct, and the charge was not negligence, but murder. At stake was much more than the maximum penalty of $30,000 in fines. Of immediate concern, a guilty verdict could have affected 40 pending civil cases nation-

wide and resulted in hundreds of millions of dollars in punitive damage awards. Of perhaps greater concern, however, were larger issues involving corporate social responsibility, ethical decision making by individuals within corporations, and ultimately, the proper conduct of business in the modern era.

How did Ford get into this situation? The chronology begins in early 1968 when the decision was made to battle the foreign competition in the small car market, specifically the Germans, but also the growing threat from the Japanese. This decision came after a hard-fought, two-year internal struggle between then-president Semon "Bunky" Knudsen and Lee Iacocca, who had risen quickly within the company because of his success with the Mustang. Iacocca strongly supported fighting the competition at their own game, while Knudsen argued instead for letting them have the small car market so Ford could concentrate on the more profitable medium and large models. The final decision ultimately was in the hands of then-CEO Henry Ford II, who not only agreed with Iacocca, but also promoted him to president after Knudsen's subsequent forced resignation.

Iacocca wanted the Pinto in the showrooms by the 1971 model introductions, which would require the shortest production planning period in automotive history to that time. The typical time span from conception to production of a new car was more than 3 1/2 years; Iacocca, however, wanted to launch the Pinto in just over 2 years. Under normal conditions, chassis design, styling, product planning, advance engineering, component testing, and so on, all either were completed or nearly completed prior to tooling of the production factories. Yet, because tooling had a fixed time frame of about 18 months, some of these other processes were done more or less concurrently. As a consequence, when it was discovered through crash testing that the Pinto's fuel tank often ruptured during rear-end impact, it was too late (in other words, too costly) to do much about it in terms of redesign.

A closer look at the crash-test reports reveals that Ford was aware of faulty fuel tank design. Eleven Pintos were subjected to rear-end collisions with a barrier at average speeds of 31 miles per hour to determine if any fuel would be lost after impact. All eight of the Pintos equipped with the standard fuel tank failed. The three remaining cars, however, survived the test because special measures had been taken to prevent tank rupture or fuel leakage. These measures included a plastic baffle placed between the axle housing and the gas tank, a steel plate between the tank and the rear bumper, and a rubber lining for the gas tank.

It should be noted that these tests were done under guidelines established by Federal Motor Vehicle Safety Standard 301, which was proposed in 1968 by the National Highway Traffic Safety Administration (NHTSA), but not officially adopted until the 1977 model year. Therefore, at the time of the tests, the Pinto met the required standards. Standard 301 had been strenuously opposed by the auto industry, and specifically Ford Motor Co. In fact, the lobbying efforts were so strong that negotiations continued until 1976, despite studies showing that hundreds of thousands of cars burned every year, taking 3,000 lives annually; the adoption of the standard was projected to reduce the death rate by 40 percent. Upon approval of Standard 301 in 1977, all Pintos were provided with a rupture-proof fuel tank design.

Despite the crash-test results, Ford decided to go with its gas tank design. Because the typical Pinto buyer was assumed to be extremely price conscious, Iacocca set an important goal known as "the limits of 2,000"—the Pinto could not cost more than $2,000 and could not weigh more than 2,000 pounds. Thus, to be competitive with foreign manufacturers, Ford felt it could not spend any money on improving the gas tank. Besides, during the late 1960s and early 1970s, American consumers demonstrated little concern for safety, so it was not considered good business sense to promote it. Iacocca echoed these sentiments when he said time and time again "Safety doesn't sell," a lesson he had learned after a failed attempt to add costly safety features to 1950s Fords.

Ford had experimented with placing the gas tank in different locations, but all alternative locations reduced usable trunk space. A design similar to that of the Ford Capri was successful in many crash tests at speeds over 50 miles per hour, but Ford felt that lost trunk space would hurt sales too much. One Ford engineer, when asked about the dangerous gas tank said, "Safety isn't the issue, trunk space is. You have no idea how stiff the competition is over trunk space. Do you realize that if we put a Capri-type tank in the Pinto, you could only get one set of golf clubs in the trunk?"

The last of Ford's reasons for not making adjustments to the fuel tank design, however, was unquestionably the most controversial. After strong lobbying efforts, Ford and the auto industry in general convinced NHTSA regulators that cost/benefit analysis would be an appropriate basis for determining the feasibility of safety design standards. Such an analysis, however, required the assignment of a value for a human life. A prior study had concluded that every time someone died in an auto accident there was an estimated "cost to society" of $200,725 (detailed in the exhibit entitled, "What's Your Life Worth?")[13]

Having this value in hand, Ford calculated the cost of adding an $11 gas tank improvement versus the benefits of the projected 180 lives that would be saved (via an internal memo entitled "Fatalities Associated with Crash-Induced Fuel Leakage and Fires"). This is presented in the exhibit labeled "The Cost of Dying in a Pinto."[14] As is demonstrated, the costs outweigh the benefits by almost three times. Thus, the cost/benefit analysis indicated that no improvements to the gas tanks were warranted.

Having decided to go ahead with normal production plans, the Pinto's problems soon surfaced. By early 1973, Ford's recall coordinator received field reports suggesting that Pintos were susceptible to "exploding" in rear-end collisions at very low speeds (under 25 miles per hour). Reports continued to indicate a similar trend in subsequent years, but no recall was initiated despite the mounting evidence. At every internal review, those responsible decided not to recall the Pinto.

Prior to the Indiana accident, the most publicized case concerning the Pinto's gas tank was that of Richard Grimshaw. In 1972, Richard, then 13, was riding with a neighbor on a road near San Bernardino, California, when they were hit from the rear. The Pinto's gas tank ruptured, causing the car to burst into flames. The neighbor was burned to death in a crash that was survivable—if there had been no fire. Richard suffered third-degree burns over 90 percent of his body and subsequently underwent more than 60 operations, with only limited success. A civil suit was settled in February 1978, when a jury awarded a judgment of over $125 million against Ford, most of which consisted of punitive damages (later reduced to $6 million by a judge who nonetheless accused Ford of "callous indifference to human life"). This judgment was based on convincing evidence that Ford chose not to spend the $11 per car to correct the faults in the Pinto gas tanks that its own crash testing had revealed.

The Pinto sold well until the media called special attention to the Pinto fuel tank story. As a consequence, in June 1978, in the face of pressure from the media, the government, pending court cases, and the potential loss of future sales, Ford ordered a complete recall of all 1.5 million Pintos built between 1970 and 1976. During the 1980 Indiana trial that resulted from the fatal accident of 1978, differing views continued to be expressed about the Pinto fires case. Ford representatives argued that companies must make cost/benefit decisions all the time.

They claimed that it is an essential part of business, and even though everyone knows that some people will die in auto accidents, buyers want costs held down; therefore, people implicitly accept risks when buying cars.

In a scathing article accusing Ford of criminally mismanaging the Pinto problem, investigative reporter Mark Dowie framed the case in a different and rather more sensational way, with this often-quoted speculation: "One wonders how long the Ford Motor Company would continue to market lethal cars were Henry Ford II and Lee Iacocca serving twenty-year terms in Leavenworth for consumer homicide."[15]

The Cost of Dying in a Pinto

Printed below are figures from a Ford Motor Co. internal memorandum on the benefits and costs of an $11 safety improvement (applicable to all vehicles with similar gas tank designs) which would have made the Pinto less likely to burn.

Benefits

Savings:180 burn deaths, 180 serious burn injuries, 2,100 burned vehicles.

Unit Cost:$200,000 per death, $67,000 per injury, $700 per vehicle.

Total Benefit: 180 X ($200,000) +

180 X ($67,000) + 2,100 X ($700) = $49.5 million.

Costs

Sales:11 million cars, 1.5 million light trucks.

Unit Cost:$11 per car, $11 per truck.

Total Cost: 11,000,000 X ($11) + 1,500,000 X ($11) = $137 million.

Case-Based Questions

Put yourself in the role of the recall coordinator for Ford Motor Co. It's 1973 and field reports have been coming in about rear-end collisions, fires, and fatalities. The decision you must make is whether or not you should act to recall the automobile.

1. Identify the relevant facts.

2. Identify the pertinent ethical issues/points of ethical conflict.

3. Identify the relevant affected parties.

4. Identify the possible consequences of alternative courses of action.

5. Identify relevant obligations.

6. Identify your relevant community standards that should guide you as a person of integrity.

7. Check your gut.

8. What will you decide?

Another Short Case for Discussion

As a counselor in an outplacement firm, you've been working with Irwin for six months to find him a new position.

During that time, he has completed extensive assessment work to determine if he's in an appropriate profession or if he might benefit from a career change. The results of the assessment indicate that Irwin has low self-esteem, probably could benefit from psychotherapy, and is most likely ill-suited for his current profession. Irwin has been actively interviewing for a position that's very similar to two others he has held and lost. He desperately wants and needs this job. The company where he's interviewing happens to be one of your most important clients. You receive a call from the head of Human Resources at the company, who tells you that Irwin suggested she call you for information about his abilities, interests, and personality style as measured by the assessment process. She also asks you for a reference for Irwin. Since he has, in effect asked that you share information with this woman, is it okay for you to give her an honest assessment of Irwin? What are your obligations to Irwin, to your client in this case? Is there a way for you to be honest, yet not hurt Irwin's chances to obtain this job? Or is that important? What will you do?

NOTES

1. Rachels, J. 1983. *The elements of moral philosophy*. New York: McGraw-Hill.

2. Peach, L. 1994. An introduction to ethical theory. In *Research Ethics: Cases and Materials*, R. L. Penslar, ed. Bloomington: Indiana University Press.

3. Fritsche, D. J., and Becke, H. 1984. Linking management behavior to ethical philosophy—An empirical investigation. *Academy of Management Journal* 27: 166–175.

4. Rachels, *The elements of moral philosophy*.

5. Solomon, R. C. 1988. *Ethics and excellence*. New York: Oxford University Press.

6. Bebeau, M. 1994. Developing a well-reasoned moral response to a moral problem in scientific research ethics. Paper distributed at the Teaching Research Ethics conference, Poynter Research Center for the Study of Ethics and American Institutions, Bloomington: Indiana University, May 1994.

7. Nash, L. 1989. Ethics without the sermon. In *Ethics in Practice*, K. R. Andres, ed. Boston: Harvard Business School Press.

8. Larson, D. E. 1990. *Mayo clinic family health book*. New York: William Morrow.

9. Nash, L. 1989. Ethics without the sermon. In *Ethics in Practice*, Andres, ed.

10. Messick, D. M., and Bazerman, B. 1994. Ethics for the 21st century: A decision making perspective. Unpublished manuscript.

11. Steiger, B. 1984. *Indian medicine power*. Atglen, PA: Whitford Press, 92.

12. Skooglund, C. 1992. Ethics in the face of competitive pressures. *Business Ethics Resource*, Fall: 4.

13. Dowie, M. 1977. How Ford put two million fire traps on wheels. *Business and Society Review* 23: 51–55.

14. Ibid.

15. Ibid.

CHAPTER 5

Deciding What's Right:
A Psychological Approach

INTRODUCTION

Chapter Four introduced prescriptive ethical theories. These theories, developed by philosophers, have been designed to help individuals decide what they should do in response to ethical dilemmas. But people don't always even recognize the ethical dimensions of the issue or situation they face. When they do, they don't always make the best decisions. And even when they identify the best decision, they may not have the will to follow through. Research in psychology points to some reasons why. This chapter focuses on the psychology of individual ethical decision making. As opposed to discussing what individuals should do, it introduces the psychological factors—the individual differences and cognitive processes that influence how people think and what they actually do in response to ethical dilemmas. It also discusses some of the cognitive barriers that can keep well-intentioned people from good ethical decision making and suggests some ways to overcome these barriers.

MORAL AWARENESS AND MORAL JUDGMENT

If a decision maker is to engage in moral judgment processes (like those discussed in Chapter Four), she or he must first recognize the ethical nature of the situation at hand.

MORAL AWARENESS → MORAL JUDGMENT

We refer to this initial step in the ethical decision-making process as moral awareness. With moral awareness, a situation or issue is interpreted as a moral or ethical issue. It is an important step that shouldn't be taken for granted because awareness of the ethical nature of the situation is far from automatic. Consider the following example.

You've just started a new job in the financial services industry. One afternoon, your manager tells you that he has to leave early to attend his son's softball game, and he asks you to be on the lookout for an important check that his boss wants signed before the end of the day. He tells you to do him a favor—simply sign his name and forward the check to his boss. To a naive employee, this may seem like a straightforward and easily accommodated request. But if the company trained you well, you would immediately be aware of the ethical nature of the situation. Your manager has asked you to engage in forgery, a serious ethical lapse, especially in the financial services industry. Recognizing the moral nature of the situation would likely lead to some very different thinking about what to do.

A recent study found that people are more likely to recognize the moral nature of an issue or decision if they believe that their co-workers will consider it to be ethically problematic, if moral language is used to present the situation to the decision maker, and if the decision is seen as having the potential to produce serious harm to others.[1]

Let's take these factors one at a time. First, if you believe that your co-workers are likely to see a decision as ethically problematic, it probably means that the issue has been discussed, perhaps in a company-sponsored ethics training program or informally among co-workers. Such discussions prime you to think about situations in a particular way. When a similar situation arises, it triggers memories of the previous ethics-related discussion and you are more likely to categorize and think about the situation in those terms.[2] Using the forgery example, perhaps a company training program actually presented a similar problem to your work group and you all agreed that signing the check would be inappropriate. Having participated in such a discussion, you would recognize that your peers believe that signing the check would be ethically problematic and you would be more likely to see your boss's request as an "ethical" problem.

Second, situations can be represented or "framed" in different ways—using moral language or more neutral language. Using moral language (words like integrity, honesty, fairness, propriety—or lying, cheating, stealing) will more likely trigger moral thinking because these terms are attached to existing cognitive categories that have moral content. For example, if the manager in the example above had asked you to forge the check for him, the word "forge" would more likely trigger legal or ethics-related concerns than if he simply asked you to sign the check (more neutral language). In response to the term *forgery,* you would more likely wonder if signing the check was wrong, if anyone was being hurt, and what the consequences would be if you did or didn't do it.

Finally, an issue or situation that has the potential to produce serious harm to others is likely to be seen as an ethical issue. In the forgery example, if forging the check would result in serious harm to customers, you would more likely see it as a serious issue than if no one would be harmed. Thomas Jones[3] proposed that individuals are more likely to recognize the ethical nature of issues that are morally intense. Moral intensity of an issue is higher when the consequences for others are potentially large, these consequences are relatively immediate and likely to occur, and the potential victims are psychologically or physically close to the decision maker. For example, a decision to leak toxic chemicals into the local water supply is highly likely to harm many people in one's own community. Such a decision is morally intense, and therefore the decision maker is likely to see it as an ethical issue. In contrast, a decision that might require laying off a few individuals in a foreign subsidiary would be less likely to trigger moral awareness. Only a few people would be affected, the consequences will occur in the future, and these individuals are both psychologically and physically distant from the decision maker.

This research suggests that managers can encourage employees' moral awareness by providing training and by talking with employees about the types of ethical issues they're likely to face and why these issues are ethically problematic, by encouraging employees to have these discussions themselves, by using moral language in these interactions, and by encouraging employees to think about the consequences of their actions and to take responsibility for the consequences of the decisions they make. By doing these things, managers can help their employees to be more morally aware —more able to recognize ethical issues when they arise.

INDIVIDUAL DIFFERENCES, MORAL JUDGMENT, AND ETHICAL BEHAVIOR

Once people are aware of the ethical dimensions of a situation or decision, they engage in moral judgment processes that can contribute to ethical conduct. Much of this book focuses on the situational pushes and pulls that influence thought and action. For example, people follow leaders or their peers. They tend to do what's rewarded. Yet, despite these powerful pushes and pulls, people do bring something of themselves to situations. Heroes emerge when you least expect it. People blow the whistle despite severe negative consequences. Others embezzle funds or lie to customers despite all of management's efforts to support good conduct. How can we explain these ethical and unethical behaviors? Very simply, ethical conduct is influenced by both situational pushes and pulls AND characteristics of the individual that we'll call individual differences.

When people are hired, they come with personalities—individual predispositions to think and behave in certain ways. Research has uncovered a number of individual traits that influence the way people think and behave in response to ethical dilemmas.

Cognitive Moral Development

The best explanation for moral judgment and action based on individual characteristics comes from the moral reasoning research of Lawrence Kohlberg.[4] When people behave morally, they must, among other things, decide what course of action is morally right (as we just discussed), and they must choose the morally right path over others.[5] In other words, if they decide that blowing the whistle is the morally right path, they must follow through and do it.

Kohlberg's moral reasoning theory is a cognitive developmental theory that focuses primarily on how people decide what course of action is morally right. His research began by following 58 American boys ranging in age from 10 to 16 years old. He interviewed them every three years over a 12-year period, asking for their open-ended responses to hypothetical moral dilemmas. Their responses were analyzed and resulted in new understanding of how moral reasoning gradually changes from middle childhood to adulthood.

The resulting cognitive moral development theory proposes that moral reasoning develops sequentially through three broad levels, each composed of two stages. As individuals move forward through the sequence of stages, they can comprehend all reasoning at stages below their own but cannot comprehend reasoning more than one stage above their own. Development through the stages results from the cognitive disequilibrium that occurs when an individual perceives a contradiction between his or her own reasoning level and the next higher one. This can occur through training but generally occurs through interaction with peers and life situations that challenge the individual's current way of thinking. According to Kohlberg, the actual moral decision isn't as important as the reasoning process used to arrive at it. However, he argued that the higher the reasoning stage, the more ethical the decision because the higher stages are more consistent with prescriptive ethical principles of justice and rights (like those discussed in the deontological approach, Chapter Four).

Kohlberg's theory has been successfully applied to studies of adults in business settings.[6] For example, Weber interviewed business managers about their responses to the following hypothetical dilemma:[7]

Evelyn worked for an automotive steel casting company. She was part of a small group asked to investigate the cause of an operating problem that had developed in the wheel castings of a new luxury automobile and to make recommendations for its improvement. The problem did not directly create an unsafe condition, but it did lead to irritating sounds. The vice-president of engineering told the group that he was certain that the problem was due to tensile stress in the castings. Evelyn and a lab technician conducted tests and found conclusive evidence that the problem was not tensile stress. As Evelyn began work on other possible explanations of the problem, she was told that the problem had been solved. A report prepared by Evelyn's boss strongly supported the tensile stress hypothesis. All of the data points from Evelyn's experiments have been changed to fit the curves, and some of the points which were far from where the theory would predict have been omitted. The report "proved" that tensile stress was responsible for the problem.

A number of questions were presented to the interviewees. For example, they were asked whether Evelyn should contradict her boss's report and why. We will use this hypothetical dilemma to understand the theory and how responses to the above question (along with others) help to identify an individual's placement in Kohlberg's moral reasoning stage framework. Table 5.1 outlines the levels and stages involved.

TABLE 5.1 Levels of Cognitive Moral Development According to Kohlberg

Stage	What is considered to be right
LEVEL I—PRECONVENTIONAL	
Stage 1—*Obedience and Punishment Orientation*	
Sticking to rules to avoid physical punishment. Obedience for its own sake.	
Stage 2—*Instrumental Purpose and Exchange*	
Following rules only when it is in one's immediate interest. Right is an equal exchange, a fair deal.	
LEVEL II—CONVENTIONAL	
Stage 3—*Interpersonal Accord, Conformity, Mutual Expectations*	
Stereotypical "good" behavior. Living up to what is expected by peers and people close to you.	
Stage 4—*Social Accord and System Maitenance*	
Fulfilling duties and obligations of the social system. Upholding laws except in extreme cases where they conflict with fixed social duties. Contributing to the society or group.	
LEVEL III—POSTCONVENTIONAL OR PRINCIPLED	
Stage 5—*Social Contract and Individual Rights*	
Being aware that people hold a variety of values; that rules are relative to the group. Upholding rules because they are the social contract. Upholding nonrelative values and rights regardless of the majority opinion.	
Stage 6—*Universal Ethical Principles*	
Following self-chosen ethical principles of justice and rights. When laws violate principles, act in accord with principles.	

Adapted from Kohlberg, L. (1976) Moral stages and moralization: The cognitive-developmental approach. In T. Lickona (Ed.), *Moral development and behavior: Theory, research, and social issues.* New York: Holt, Rhinehart and Winston, pp. 34–35.

Level I At level I (labeled the preconventional level and including stages 1 and 2), a person views rules as imposed and external to the self. The decision about what's right is explained in terms of rewards and punishments and the exchange of favors. Stage 1 individuals are guided by obedience for its own sake. Avoiding punishment is the key consideration. It's easy to imagine a small child thinking, I should share my toy with my brother because if I don't Mom will yell at me. A stage 1 response to the Evelyn situation might argue that it would be wrong to contradict her boss because she must obey her superiors and she would certainly be punished if she disobeyed.

At stage 2, concern for personal reward, satisfaction, and a sense of duty to oneself are important. In addition, a kind of market reciprocity is considered. What is right may be judged in terms of a "you scratch my back, I'll scratch yours" reciprocity. A stage 2 child might think that if I share my toy with my brother, he might share his with me later. A stage 2 response in the Evelyn situation might argue that Evelyn should support her boss because he is responsible for her performance appraisals, and if she lets this one go, he might overlook some of her problems from the past. Also, if her boss has been kind or helpful to her in the past, she may express some obligation to repay the favor.

Level II   At level II (labeled the conventional level and including stages 3 and 4), the individual has internalized the shared moral norms of society or some segment like a family or work group. What's morally right is explained in terms of living up to roles and the expectations of relevant others, fulfilling duties and obligations, and following rules and laws. Kohlberg's research placed most American adults at this level and Weber's research found that most managers' responses to the Evelyn dilemma were at level II, stages 3 and 4.

At stage 3, what's morally right is thought to be that which pleases or helps others or is approved by those close to you. Interpersonal trust and social approval are important. For example, a stage 3 response to the Evelyn dilemma might say that Evelyn shouldn't contradict her boss because she would be perceived as disloyal by her boss and might lose the social approval and trust of her boss and peers. On the other hand, what if Evelyn shares her dilemma with close family members whose opinions are important to her, and they feel strongly that she must contradict her boss? In this case, she would likely reason that she should contradict her boss because the people she trusts believe it's the right thing to do.

At stage 4, the perspective broadens to consider society. The individual is concerned about fulfilling agreed-upon duties and following rules or laws that are designed to promote the common good. Therefore, a stage 4 response might say that Evelyn should contradict her boss because of her duty to society. What if the noises do represent a safety problem? She has a responsibility as a good member of society to report it. She would feel particularly strongly about this if she were aware of product safety laws that required her to report the problem.

Level III   Finally, we come to level III (postconventional, sometimes called principled reasoning—stages 5 and 6). The principled individual has gone beyond identification with others' expectations, rules, and laws to make decisions more autonomously and consistent with principles of justice and rights. It's important to remember that very few adults in our society actually reach stage 5 and that stage 6 is thought to be a theoretical stage only.

At stage 5, the emphasis is still on rules and laws because these represent the social contract, but stage 5 thinking considers the possibility of changing the law for socially useful purposes. And a stage 5 individual would take into account moral laws above society's laws, such as considering what decision would create the greatest societal good. A stage 5 Evelyn might reason that she should contradict her boss because doing so would be consistent with the ethical principle of the greatest societal good, particularly if she considered safety of the automobiles to be a potential problem. Her responsibility goes beyond that of a good law-abiding member of society. A stage 5 Evelyn is also responsible to principles of justice and rights. So, even if there is no law requiring her to report what she knows, a stage 5 Evelyn would consider the rights to safety of the potential automobile consumers as an important reason for her to tell.

People often mistakenly think that ANY principle qualifies as "principled" thinking in Kohlberg's theory. But Kohlberg is quite precise about the kinds of principles that qualify as "principled" thinking, and he details how a researcher would score an interview to determine an individual's stage. Without going into too much detail here, level three principles are principles of justice and rights generally consistent with the kind of principles introduced in Chapter Four under deontological theories.

To understand Kohlberg's theory, you must remember that it is a cognitive theory. What counts is the reasoning processes involved in a decision, not the decision itself. So, a stage 1 individual and a stage 5 individual may make the same decision, but their reasons for making it are very different.

Are Women and Men Different?

In 1982, Carol Gilligan published *In a Different Voice,* a widely publicized book about women's cognitive moral development. Gilligan, who had been Kohlberg's student, claimed that Kohlberg's theory was flawed because he had studied only boys and then had simply applied the same theory to girls. Her own research with girls led Gilligan to question the exclusive focus on justice in Kohlberg's higher stages. She found that people raise both justice and care concerns when describing moral conflicts. She also found that males focused almost exclusively on justice considerations and that a care focus was almost exclusively a female phenomenon. Females were more likely to use a "morality of care" that emphasized relationships—raising issues related to caring for others, responsibility to others, and the continuity of interdependent relationships.[8]

Gilligan's claims have received a great deal of attention, particularly in the child and adolescent development fields. But their applicability to adults working in business organizations is limited. Gilligan's own research[9] comparing the moral reasoning of male and female medical students found no significant difference between the genders, suggesting that both men and women are strongly influenced by the powerful cultural norms of medical practice. Similarly, an interview study of business managers[10] based on Gilligan's theory, found no gender differences. All but one of the managers (male and female) who described a moral conflict at work based their moral reasoning on rights. Finally, cognitive moral development studies based on Kohlberg's theory and conducted by many other researchers over the years have found only trivial gender differences. When differences have been found, females generally have scored higher than men.[11]

We can now begin to address the second requirement for ethical behavior—doing what's right. Recall that to behave morally, people must first decide what course of action is morally right (probably depending to a large degree on their stage of moral development), and then they must choose the morally right path over others.[12]

Looking Up and Looking Around.[13]

We've already learned that most adults are at the conventional level of cognitive moral development (level II), meaning that they're highly susceptible to external influences. Their decision about what's morally right, and therefore their likely action, is inextricably linked with what others think, say, and do. We call this looking up and looking around for ethical guidance.

These individuals aren't autonomous decision makers who strictly follow an internal moral compass. They look up and around to see what their superiors and their peers are doing and saying, and they use these cues as a guide to action. Therefore, most people are highly likely to do what's expected of them as a result of the reward system, role expectations, authority figure demands, and group norms. That's why the remainder of this book focuses so heavily on these external influences and why it's so important that managers structure the work environment to support ethical conduct. The large majority of employees will be looking for guidance and they'll do what's right if guided and supported along those lines.

Autonomous Principled Thinking and Action

Higher stage thinking is more independent of these external influences. The postconventional principled thinker (level III, representing a minority of people) has developed his or her own justice and rights-based principles that guide ethical decision making. Research has demonstrated that these people are also more likely to behave consistently with their own principle-based decisions—they'll carry through and do what they think is right. More principled individuals also have been found to be less likely to cheat, more likely to resist pressure from authority figures, more likely to help someone in need, and more likely to blow the whistle on misconduct.[14] But it's important for managers to remember that level III individuals are rare. Autonomous decision making based on principles of justice and rights is the exception rather than the rule.

The bottom line for managers is this. Cognitive moral development theory and research tell us that most of the people you manage are going to be strongly influenced by what you do, say, and reward. They are looking up and looking around for guidance from you and their peers, and they're likely to follow what they see around them. Therefore, it's your responsibility to structure the work environment in a way that supports ethical conduct. If you avoid this responsibility, these people will look elsewhere for guidance, and the guidance they receive may not support ethical conduct at all.

Those few individuals who have reached principled levels of moral reasoning should be singled out to lead key decision-making groups. They can be identified with the use of instruments that have been developed by cognitive moral development researchers. Research on ethical decision making in groups suggests that when less principled individuals lead a group, the group's ethical decision-making performance decreases. On the other hand, groups with leaders higher in moral reasoning either improve or stay the same.[15]

Moral reasoning can also be increased through training. Over the years, Kohlberg, his students, and colleagues have designed training approaches based on cognitive moral development theory. In this type of training, facilitators give participants hypothetical ethical dilemmas for discussion. The facilitator promotes movement through moral reasoning stages by challenging participants' thinking and by exposing individuals to reasoning higher than their own. This creates cognitive conflict, leading the participant to question and eventually revise his or her own reasoning. Research has supported the effectiveness of this type of training with adults in dental, medical, and business schools.[16] So, managers may want to consider incorporating these ideas into their firms' ethics training.

LOCUS OF CONTROL

Another individual characteristic that has been found to influence ethical conduct is locus of control.[17] Locus of control refers to an individual's perception of how much control he or she exerts over the events in life. Locus of control can be thought of as a single continuum from a high internal locus of control to a high external locus of control. An individual with a high internal locus of control believes that outcomes are primarily the result of his or her own efforts, whereas an individual with a high external locus of control believes that life events are determined primarily by fate, luck, or powerful others. Locus of control is not something a person is born with. It develops over time through interaction with other people and the social environment. Therefore, although it is thought to be relatively stable, one's locus of control can shift. For example, if someone with a very high internal locus of control became a prisoner of war with little chance of escape, he or she would likely develop a more external focus over time.

External Locus of Control ←——————————————→ Internal Locus of Control

Relationship to Ethical Conduct

How is locus of control related to ethics? First, individuals with a high internal locus of control see the relationship between their behavior and its outcomes more clearly than do those with an external locus of control. They see themselves as in control of things that happen. Therefore, they're more likely to take responsibility for the consequences of their actions. It would be more difficult for such an individual to say, "well, it's not my responsibility. I just work here" or "I'm just following orders." Studies have found that internals are more likely to help another person, even if there's a penalty for doing so.[18]

Internals see themselves as in charge of their own fates. Therefore, they should also be less willing to be pressured by others to do things they believe to be wrong. One interesting study asked subjects to complete a story in which the main character was pressured to violate a social norm.[19] The more internal the subject's locus of control, the more likely the story completion had the hero resisting the pressure. In an obedience to authority experiment (explained in more detail in Chapter Seven), externals were more likely to give apparently (but not really) harmful electric shocks to someone if told to do so by the experimenter.[20]

For managers, it may be helpful to know where your workers fit on the locus of control continuum. It can help you understand how they think and how they react to a variety of situations, including ethical situations. For example, workers who constantly blame bad luck and other external factors for performance failures or ethical lapses may be doing so because of an external locus of control—that's the way they view the world. You can work with such individuals to help them see the relationship between their actions and the outcomes by consistently holding them responsible and accountable for what they do. As a result, their locus of control may shift over time and they will take more responsibility for the consequences of their actions.

COGNITIVE BARRIERS TO GOOD ETHICAL JUDGMENT

Individual differences aside, all human beings share certain ways of thinking about the world. The steps offered in Chapter Four assume a rational ethical decision-making process, prescribing how an ethical decision should be made. However, studies of human decision making have found that actual decision making falls short of this rational ideal. Although people intend to be rational in their decision making, for a variety of reasons they're not. In recent years, psychologists have discovered a number of weaknesses and biases in how people make decisions.[21] Some of these have direct implications for ethical decision making in organizations[22] and for the advice given in Chapter Four. Think of this part of the chapter as a kind of "reality check.." If you're going to manage your own and others' ethical behavior, you need to understand how people really think in addition to how they should think.

As a backdrop for your thinking, recognize that the cognitive weaknesses and biases we will be discussing operate primarily because people try to reduce uncertainty and simplify their world. Although uncertainty is a fact of organizational life, business people want very much to deny the uncertainty they face. Therefore, they tend to act as if the world is rational and they're in control. Being "in charge" and able to predict events is a highly valued characteristic, especially in business. But this focus on being in charge is an illusion that can get managers into trouble. What if you really don't know all of the facts—what the risks are—who the potential affected parties are—what all the consequences of your decisions are? You'll see in this chapter that the best way to avoid decision-making weaknesses and biases is to become aware of them and to incorporate steps into your decision making that are explicitly aimed at reducing their impact.

Script Processing—The Pinto Fire Case

Dennis A. Gioia is a management scholar and an expert on social cognition in organizations, who has provided us with a rare opportunity to look inside the head of someone who was involved in a widely publicized business ethics situation. He has analyzed his own thoughts and behavior as recall coordinator at Ford Motor Company shortly after the Ford Pinto was introduced in both an article in the *Journal of Business Ethics*[23] and personal reflections that you'll find at the end of this chapter.

In the summer of 1972, Gioia graduated with an MBA. His value system included opposition to the Vietnam War and deep concerns about the ethical conduct of business. "I cultivated my social awareness; I held my principles high; I espoused my intention to help a troubled world; and I wore my hair long. By any measure I was a prototypical `Child of the '60's."[24] A car enthusiast, Gioia was hired by the Ford Motor Company to be a "Problem Analyst." One year later he became Ford's Field Recall Coordinator, in charge of coordinating all current recall campaigns and identifying developing problems.

In analyzing his participation in the decision NOT to recall the Pinto, Gioia suggests that his behavior was highly influenced by script processing. Scripts are cognitive frameworks that guide human thought and action. Although they are generally not written down, scripts contain information about the appropriate sequence of events in routine situations. For example, most of us have a fairly complex script for how to behave in a fancy restaurant, from approaching the maître d', to tasting the wine, to choosing a fork to use, to the appropriate tip to leave. Information processing is made much more efficient because a cognitive script allows the individual to call on an established behavior pattern and act automatically without contemplating every decision or action in great detail. Active thinking is not required because the situation fits the mental prototype, which triggers the script and the prescribed behaviors. According to Gioia, this is something like "cruising on automatic pilot." Many of us discover that we have been cruising on automatic pilot when we drive to a familiar destination, but we can't recall how we got there. We were following an established behavior pattern. The route was so familiar that we didn't have to think about it anymore. Somehow we were magically there. Similar things happen at work. Behaviors become routinized and we do them pretty much without thinking.

Given the huge information load expected of someone who was simultaneously managing hundreds of files on potential safety problems, scripts provided a great information processing advantage. Rather than treating every potential problem situation as unique, Gioia could save time and mental energy by making quick and efficient decisions about problems as they arose. As early reports about the Pinto began to trickle in, they didn't raise any red flags because they fit the scripted criteria for a "normal" accident. Therefore, he filed the claims automatically and gave seemingly more important problems his active attention.

In addition to its contribution to information processing efficiency, however, script processing clearly has disadvantages. Gioia admittedly "looked right past" potential problems because he had seen similar information patterns hundreds of times before. The scripted definition of a crisis case was not met by the information he received, so the Pinto wasn't singled out for attention. Consistent with research on script processing, he selectively perceived information that was consistent with the script and ignored information that didn't fit the pattern.

Muffled emotions can also become part of a script. Many jobs require the control of emotions, particularly negative emotions. The recall coordinator's job fit this category. In order for him to function in his job every day, Gioia's emotions had to be squelched to some degree. Even when one event penetrated his script, it didn't lead to recall of the Pinto. He had received a photograph of a burned Pinto and subsequently saw the burned hulk of an actual automobile. These powerful visual images moved him to bring the case before members of the Field Recall office. However, at the meeting, it became clear that the characteristics of the Pinto problem didn't meet the group's shared scripted criteria for a recall. For example, only a few field reports had come in about the Pinto, compared to the many more field reports that would generally support a recall decision. All members, including Gioia, voted not to recall.

Script processing can be particularly problematic for ethical decision making. First, ethical decision making requires active consideration of the moral dimensions of the situation and a "custom" decision, tailored to the complexities of that particular case. Yet, Gioia argues that in many situations organizational members are not even aware that they are dealing with an ethical dilemma. In terms of our previous discussion, they are morally unaware. They handle situations by following scripts that are likely to exclude ethical considerations. In other words, ethical dilemmas do not lend themselves to "automatic pilot" decisions. Yet, the realities of our hectic work lives make this sort of default decision making very common.

Cost/Benefit Analysis

Frequently, in addition to the cognitive processing limitations of individual decision makers, institutionalized decision-making processes can powerfully influence the decisions that are made by individuals or groups. In the Pinto fire case, a controversial decision-making process was used to justify the decision not to change the gas tank design. The National Traffic Safety Association had approved the use of cost/benefit analysis to establish automotive safety design standards. This involved the assignment of a dollar value for a human life, deemed to be approximately $200,000 in 1970. As an internal memo revealed, Ford had tabulated the costs of altering the tank design (for all similarly designed vehicles) to be $137 million, or $11 per vehicle. The benefits were calculated to be $49,530,000. These included the savings to society that would be accrued by preventing 180 deaths at $200,000 each, plus 180 projected burn injuries at $67,000 per injury and 2,100 burned cars at $700 per car. Using the cost/benefit analysis made the decision look straightforward. The costs of redesign outweighed the benefits and would therefore not be undertaken. Moral considerations didn't figure into the equation.

Attempts to reduce complex decision making to quantitative terms aren't uncommon, especially in a highly competitive business environment. In this way, complex decisions can be simplified, an apparent advantage. Assigning a value to human life is also still done by government agencies. For example, the Environmental Protection Agency values the life of a thirtysomething worker at about $5 million when it assesses its regulations.[25] But, the potential disadvantages of reducing the value of human life to quantitative terms should be clear. Such simplification removes moral criteria from the decision-making process.

The Pinto Fire example also points to the importance of multiple selves and role behavior that will be discussed more in Chapter Seven. Gioia was an idealistic young student, but he admittedly dropped his idealism at the corporation door, picking it up on his way out each day. In performing his job of recall coordinator, the role expectations and guiding scripts were more influential. As he says:

> The recall coordinator's job was serious business. The scripts associated with it influenced me more than I influenced [them]. Before I went to Ford I would have argued strongly that Ford had an ethical obligation to recall. After I left Ford, I now argue and teach that Ford had an ethical obligation to recall. But, while I was there, I perceived no obligation to recall and I remember no strong ethical overtones to the case whatsoever. It was a very straightforward decision, driven by dominant scripts for the time, place, and context.

Clearly, these processes that individuals and organizations use to simplify complex decisions can have significant implications for the ethical decisions managers make. Although script processing and quantitative decision-making criteria clearly help us to do our jobs more efficiently, they can also strip ethical considerations from the decision-making process.

One way to address this problem is to make ethical considerations part of the script. Gioia suggests that this may be possible, although he warns that "it will take substantial concentration on the ethical dimension of the corporate culture (see Chapter Nine), as well as overt attempts to emphasize ethics in education, training, and decision making before typical organizational scripts are likely to be modified to include the crucial ethical component."[26] You can help your subordinates by working with them to make the scripts explicit and to analyze them for their ethical components.

You can also require decision-making groups to analyze the ethical aspects of their decisions and to include this analysis in their report(s). Just as environmental impact statements are now a routine part of many business decisions, an ethical analysis could require that managers focus on the influence of a particular decision on stakeholders' rights and consequences for the community or communities affected by the decision. You can also require groups to justify their decision-making process (e.g., decision-making criteria and weighting) in moral as well as quantitative terms.

Thinking about Fact Gathering

In Chapter Four, we advised you to "get the facts" as an important first step in good ethical decision making. But be aware that your thinking about the facts is likely to be biased. Research evidence suggests that you may look for the wrong ones or stop looking too soon because you think you already have all the facts you need.

We know that most people, including business students and business executives, are overconfident about their knowledge of the facts. For example, in research studies, people were asked factual questions. Then they were asked to judge the probable truth of their answers. In response to the question, "Is Rome or New York farther north," most people chose New York, and they believed that the probability was about 90 percent that they were right. Actually, they were wrong. Rome is slightly north of New York. Being overconfident can make you fail to search for additional facts or for support for the facts you have.[27]

Even if you gather additional facts or support, another cognitive bias termed the confirmation trap[29] may influence your choice of which facts to gather and where to look. All of us have the tendency to look for information that will confirm our preferred answer or choice and to neglect to search for evidence that might prove us wrong. If you're a pharmaceutical executive who wants to believe that a new product is safe, you're more likely to ask your managers something like, "Does it meet all FDA regulations?" In this case, the executive expects and will probably get a confirming response, and a quick decision to go ahead with the drug can be made. However, the meeting might take a very different turn if the executive asks, "What health and safety problems are still possible with this drug?"[29]

In an attempt to overcome these limitations and biases, it's important that you consciously try to think of ways you could be wrong. Incorporate questions in your individual and group decision-making processes such as, "How could I/we be wrong?" "What facts are still missing?" and "What facts exist that might prove me/us to be wrong?" You may still miss some important facts, but you'll miss less of them than if you didn't ask these questions at all.

Thinking about Consequences

In Chapter Four, we also introduced consequentialist theories, and we advised you to think about all the potential consequences of your decision for a wide variety of stakeholders. Who can argue with such sage advice? But psychologists have found a number of problems with how people think about consequences.

Reduced Number of Consequences

Psychologists have found that one way people simplify their decisions and make them more manageable is to reduce the number of consequences they consider. They're especially likely to ignore consequences that are thought to affect only a few people. But consequences that affect only a few people can be serious. For example, a highly beneficial drug may have beneficial consequences for many and adverse consequences for only a few people. But what if those few people could die from side effects of the drug?[30] Obviously, you wouldn't want to ignore such serious consequences no matter how few people are affected. In attempting to consciously deal with this situation, it helps to consult a broad range of people who have a stake in the decision you're making. Invite input from all interested parties, especially those who disagree with you and those with the most to lose. Ask them what consequences they're concerned about and why. Then, incorporate these consequences in your decision making.

Consequences as Risk

One way to think about consequences is to think in terms of decision making about risk. Research suggests that people tend to underestimate potential risks because of an illusion of optimism. They overestimate the likelihood of good future events and underestimate the bad. People also generally believe that they're less susceptible to risks than others. This belief is supported by the illusion of control, the general belief that we really are in charge of what happens. And if we think we can control events, we also think bad things are less likely to happen. This illusion of control has been demonstrated to exist in MBA students from top U.S. business schools, suggesting that managers are certainly vulnerable.[31] Managers whose judgment is influenced by these cognitive biases are likely to underestimate the risk facing the firm as a result of a particular decision. But if managers ignore risks, they're also ignoring important consequences. So, it's important to recognize this tendency to ignore risk, and design risk analysis into your decision-making processes.

Even if we attend to risks, we still have difficulty thinking about them in a completely rational way. One tendency that can contribute to downplaying risk was already discussed—the tendency to attend to information that will help to confirm the decision we would prefer to make (confirmation bias). In the famous space shuttle *Challenger* disaster, everyone knew that there was risk. The question was how much, and was it too much? Many economic and political factors were pushing NASA to launch this shuttle with the teacher on board. Researchers now believe that the confirmation bias may have influenced decision makers to focus on the information that confirmed their preference, which was to launch and to discount available information about risks that would have supported a delay.[32]

Consequences over Time—Escalation of Commitment

The prescription to think about consequences also fails to take into account the fact that decisions are not isolated choices but often become part of a series of choices within the context of a larger decision or project. Consider the following scenario:

> You finally graduated from college and landed a great job, and you invested most of your savings in the car of your dreams—a used BMW. But in a short time, the car began having mechanical problems. Every time you brought it to the mechanic, he claimed that it was fixed for good, but the problems continued and your bank account was being drained. Should you quit trying to fix the car?

Because you've already made the decision to buy the car and you've already invested a lot of money in it, your tendency will be to continue to be committed to this previously selected course of action. This tendency has been called "escalation of commitment to a losing course of action" or "throwing good money after bad."[33] A perfectly rational decision maker would consider the time and expenses already invested as "sunk costs." They aren't recoverable and shouldn't be considered in a decision about what to do. Only future costs and benefits should be considered. But this is difficult. Norms in our society and in our organizations support trying, persistence, and sticking with a course of action. Also, if others are involved, we're likely to feel the need to justify our original decision—whether it was to buy a car, a piece of equipment, or land.

One way to overcome escalation of commitment is, as with many biases, to recognize that it exists and try to adjust for it. Ask yourself explicit questions about whether you're committed to a decision just because failure would make your original decision look bad. Ask yourself, "If I took over the project today, with no personal investment, would I support the project?" Another approach is to bring in outsiders and ask for their opinions or turn the project over to them completely. That gets your own ego completely out of the decision-making process.

Thinking about Integrity

In Chapter Four, you were also advised to think about your own integrity—to ask yourself what a person of integrity would do in the particular situation facing you. But cognitive biases can get in the way here too. If your thoughts about yourself are controlled by illusion rather than reality, how can you make a good decision about your integrity? The basic idea here is that individuals prefer to think positively about themselves. They're likely to unconsciously filter and distort information in order to maintain the positive self image they prefer.

Psychologists know that people have an illusion of superiority. Surveys have found that people tend to think of themselves as more ethical, fair, and honest than most other people.[34] It's obviously an illusion when the large majority of individuals claim to be more honest than the average person, or more ethical than their peers. It's a little like Garrison Keillor's mythical Lake Wobegon where ALL the children are above average. There isn't a whole lot you can do here except to try to be honest with yourself.

Thinking about Your Gut

Finally, in Chapter 4, we advised you to listen to your gut. But in this chapter, we've spent a great deal of time telling you that your gut may well be wrong—led by cognitive limitations and biased thinking.

We think that your gut can still be useful in alerting you that something might be wrong—that you're facing an ethical dilemma—in the first place. But once that decision is made, you should temper your gut with the knowledge gained in this chapter and the rest of the book. Hopefully, the combination of your gut and an informed brain will help you to make better decisions.

Emotions in Ethical Decision Making

Finally, we should acknowledge the importance of emotions in ethical decision making. People often decide to take action because they feel empathy or anger, not because they have rationally decided on the best course of action. For example, consider how GM's managers handled a four-year legal battle with VW over their allegation that a 56-year-old GM executive, Jose Lopez, took 20 boxes of GM proprietary documents when he left GM to join Volkswagen in 1993. In 1992, Lopez had been GM's worldwide purchasing czar who was known for his ability to cut costs ruthlessly. The missing documents included information about GMs suppliers and their prices for auto parts, as well as information about upcoming Opel car models. *Fortune* magazine referred to the four-year legal battle that ensued as a tale of "betrayal" and "revenge." Lou Hughes was head of GM Europe whose Opel subsidiary competed fiercely with Volkswagen. Hughes was furious that Lopez would take proprietary documents to a competitor. He insisted that there would be no settlement with VW as long as Lopez remained there. When asked what he hoped to gain from the litigation, Hughes replied, "Look, this is not a question of business. This is a question of ethics."[35] Years of investigation yielded no hard evidence to suggest that anyone at VW had actually used secret GM information. *Fortune* suggested that at the time "one might have expected GM to act pragmatically, find some face-saving exit, and return its attention to the car business."[36] That might have been the "rational" cool-headed thing to do. Instead, they escalated the fight, bringing a racketeering suit that was expected to drag on for years and cost tens of millions of dollars. When pragmatic board members questioned the action, the board chairman insisted that the company had to pursue the suit because it "had been terribly wronged." "Some things aren't measured in time and money. They're just who we are."[37] Finally, in January 1997, the two companies settled the case. Lopez, who had already resigned from Volkswagen, was barred from doing any work for VW through the year 2000. Volkswagen paid GM $100 million and agreed to buy $1 billion worth of GM parts over seven years. *Fortune* magazine asked, "But what, in the end did the long, bitter, and costly struggle accomplish? In the cold light of day, the answer seems simple and shocking: not much."[38] A huge company devoted years of attention and spent millions of dollars because its managers were morally outraged that their former friend had betrayed them.

Clearly, anger and other emotions can influence thoughts and actions. Whether that is good or bad depends on whether the emotion leads to "right" or "wrong" action. If empathy leads you to think about the consequences of your actions, that's a good thing. If moral outrage leads you to seek justice, that's good as well. But moral outrage can also lead to a desire for revenge, and that may be the time to bring cooler heads to the decision. Those who are not as emotionally involved should be able to offer a more rational and more balanced assessment of the situation at hand. In the GM–Volkswagen case, those pragmatic board members may have been right to support a quick settlement of the case.

CONCLUSION

This chapter has introduced you to individual differences that can influence ethical decision making. The chapter has also outlined the cognitive limitations and biases that can interfere with good ethical decision making. Hopefully, knowing about these and how they can be overcome will help you to be a better individual decision maker. Much of the remainder of the book will move beyond this focus on the individual decision maker to a focus on the group and organizational influences that can have a profound influence on your decisions and actions.

Personal Reflections on the Pinto Fires Case

by Dennis A. Gioia

The last chapter ended with a provocative case highlighting some of the sordid events in the history of the Pinto fires problem. As the authors have indicated in this chapter, I was involved with this infamous case in the early 1970s. They have asked me to reflect on lessons learned from my experience.

I take this case very personally, even though my name seldom comes up in its many recountings. I was one of those "faceless bureaucrats" who is often portrayed as making decisions without accountability and then walking away from them—even decisions with life-and-death implications. That characterization is, of course, far too stark and superficial. I certainly don't consider myself faceless, and I have always chafed at the label of bureaucrat as applied to me, even though I have found myself unfairly applying it to others. Furthermore, I have been unable to walk away from my decisions in this case. They have a tendency to haunt—especially when they have such public airings as those involved in the Pinto fires debacle have had.

But why revisit 20-year-old decisions, and why take them so personally? Here's why: because I was in a position to do something about a serious problem . . . and didn't. That simple observation gives me pause for personal reflection and also makes me think about the many difficulties people face in trying to be ethical decision makers in organizations. It also helps me to keep in mind the features of modern business and organizational life that would influence someone like me (me!, of all people, who purposefully set out to be an ethical decision maker) to overlook basic moral issues in arriving at decisions that, when viewed retrospectively, look absurdly easy to make. But they are not easy to make, and that is perhaps the most important lesson of all.

The Personal Aspect

I would like to reflect on my own experience mainly to emphasize the personal dimensions involved in ethical decision making. Although I recognize that there are strong organizational influences at work as well, I would like to keep the critical lens focused for a moment on me (and you) as individuals. I believe that there are insights and lessons from my experience that can help you think about your own likely involvement in issues with ethical overtones.

First, however, a little personal background. In the late 1960s and early 1970s, I was an engineering/MBA student; I also was an "activist", engaged in protests of social injustice and the social irresponsibility of business, among other things. I held some pretty strong values that I thought would stand up to virtually any challenge and enable me to "do the right thing" when I took a career job. I suspect that most of you feel that you also have developed a strongly held value system that will enable you to resist organizational inducements to do something unethical. Perhaps. Unfortunately, the challenges do not often come in overt forms that shout the need for resistance or ethical righteousness. They are much more subtle than that, and thus doubly difficult to deal with because they do not make it easy to see that a situation you are confronting might actually involve an ethical dilemma.

After school, I got the job of my dreams with Ford and, predictably enough, ended up on the fast track to promotion. That fast track enabled me to progress quickly into positions of some notable responsibility. Within two years I became Ford's vehicle recall coordinator, with first-level responsibility for tracking field safety problems. It was the most intense, information-overloaded job you can imagine, frequently dealing with some of the most serious problems in the company. Disasters were a phone call away, and action was the hallmark of the office where I worked. We all knew we were engaged in serious business, and we all took the job seriously. There were no irresponsible bureaucratic ogres there, contrary to popular portrayal.

In this context, I first encountered the neophyte Pinto fires problem—in the form of infrequent reports of cars erupting into horrendous fireballs in very low-speed crashes and the shuddering personal experience of inspecting a car that had burned, killing its trapped occupants. Over the space of a year, I had two distinct opportunities to initiate recall activities concerning the fuel tank problems, but on both occasions I voted not to recall, despite my activist history and advocacy of business social responsibility.[39]

The key question is how, in the space of two short years, could I have engaged in a decision process that appeared to violate my own strong values—a decision process whose subsequent manifestations continue to be cited by many observers as a supposedly definitive study of corporate unethical behavior? I tend to discount the obvious accusations: that my values weren't really strongly held; that I had turned my back on my values in the interest of loyalty to Ford; that I was somehow intimidated into making decisions in the best interests of the company; that despite my principled statements I had not actually achieved a high stage of moral development, and so on. Instead, I believe a more plausible explanation for my own actions looks to the foibles of normal human information processing.

I would argue that the complexity and intensity of the recall coordinator's job required that I develop cognitive strategies for simplifying the overwhelming amount of information I had to deal with. The best way to do that is to structure the information into cognitive "schemas," or more specifically "script schemas," that guide understanding and action when facing common or repetitive situations. Scripts offer marvelous cognitive shortcuts because they allow you to act virtually unconsciously and automatically, and thus permit handling complicated situations without being paralyzed by needing to think consciously about every little thing. Such scripts enabled me to discern the characteristic hallmarks of problem cases likely to result in recall and to execute a complicated series of steps required to initiate a recall.

All of us structure information all of the time; we could hardly get through the work day without doing so. But there is a penalty to be paid for this wonderful cognitive efficiency: we do not give sufficient attention to important information that requires special treatment because the general information pattern has surface appearances that indicate that automatic processing will suffice. That, I think, is what happened to me. The beginning stages of the Pinto case looked for all the world like a normal sort of problem. Lurking beneath the cognitive veneer, however, was a nasty set of circumstances waiting to conspire into a dangerous situation. Despite the awful nature of the accidents, the Pinto problem did not fit an existing script; the accidents were relatively rare by recall standards, and the accidents were not initially traceable to a specific component failure. Even when a failure mode suggesting a design flaw was

identified, the cars did not perform significantly worse in crash tests than competitor vehicles. One might easily argue that I should have been jolted out of my script by the unusual nature of the accidents (very low speed, otherwise unharmed passengers trapped in a horrific fire), but those facts did not penetrate a script cued for other features. (It also is difficult to convey to the layperson that bad accidents are not a particularly unusual feature of the recall coordinator's information field. Accident severity is not necessarily a recall cue; frequently repeated patterns and identifiable causes are).

The Corporate Milieu

In addition to the personalized scripting of information processing, there is another important influence on the decisions that led to the Pinto fires mess: the fact that decisions are made by individuals working within a corporate context. It has escaped almost no one's notice that the decisions made by corporate employees tend to be in the best interest of the corporation, even by people who mean to do better. Why? Because socialization processes and the overriding influence of organizational culture provide a strong, if generally subtle, context for defining appropriate ways of seeing and understanding. Because organizational culture can be viewed as a collection of scripts, scripted information processing relates even to organizational-level considerations. Scripts are context bound; they are not free-floating general cognitive structures that apply universally. They are tailored to specific contexts. And there are few more potent contexts than organizational settings.

There is no question that my perspective changed after joining Ford. In retrospect, I would be very surprised if it hadn't. In my former incarnation as a social activist, I had internalized values for doing what was right as I understood rightness in grand terms; but I had not internalized a script for applying my values in a pragmatic business context. Ford and the recall coordinator role provided a powerful context for developing scripts—scripts that were inevitably and undeniably oriented toward ways of making sense that were influenced by the corporate and industry culture.

I wanted to do a good job, and I wanted to do what was right. Those are not mutually exclusive desires, but the corporate context affects their synthesis. I came to accept the idea that it was not feasible to fix everything that someone might construe as a problem. I therefore shifted to a value of wanting to do the greatest good for the greatest number (an ethical value tempered by the practical constraints of an economic enterprise). Doing the greatest good for the greatest number meant working with intensity and responsibility on those problems that would spare the most people from injury. It also meant developing scripts that responded to typical problems, not odd patterns like those presented by the Pinto.

Another way of noting how the organizational context so strongly affects individuals is to recognize that one's personal identity becomes heavily influenced by corporate identity. As a student, my identity centered on being a "good person" (with a certain dose of moral righteousness associated with it). As recall coordinator, my identity shifted to a more corporate definition.

This is an extraordinarily important point, especially for students who have not yet held a permanent job role, and I would like to emphasize it. Before assuming your career role, identity derives mainly from social relationships. Upon putting on the mantle of a profession or a responsible position, identity begins to align with your role. And information processing perspective follows from that identity.

I remember accepting the portrayal of the auto industry and Ford as "under attack" from many quarters (oil crises, burgeoning government regulation, inflation, litigious customers, etc). As we know, groups under assault develop into more cohesive communities that emphasize commonalities and shared identities. I was by then an insider in the industry and the company, sharing some of their beleaguered perceptions that there were significant forces arrayed against us and that the well-being of the company might be threatened.

What happened to the original perception that Ford was a socially irresponsible giant that needed a comeuppance? Well, it looks different from the inside. Over time, a reasonable value for action against corporate dominance became tempered by another reasonable value that corporations serve social needs and are not automatically the villains of society. I saw a need for balance among multiple values, and as a result my identity shifted in degrees toward a more corporate identity.

The Torch Passes to You

So, given my experiences, what would I recommend to you, as a budding organizational decision maker? I have some strong opinions. First, develop your ethical base now! Too many people do not give serious attention to assessing and articulating their own values. People simply do not know what they stand for because they haven't thought about it seriously. Even the ethical scenarios presented in classes or executive programs are treated as interesting little games without apparent implications for deciding how you intend to think or act. These exercises should be used to develop a principled, personal code that you will try to live by. Consciously decide your values. If you don't decide your values now, you are easy prey for others who will gladly decide them for you or influence you implicitly to accept theirs.

Second, recognize that everyone, including you, is an unwitting victim of his or her own cognitive structuring. Many people are surprised and fascinated to learn that they use schemas and scripts to understand and act in the organizational world. The idea that we automatically process so much information so much of the time intrigues us. Indeed, we would all turn into blithering idiots if we did not structure information and expectations, but that very structuring hides information that might be important—information that could require you to confront your values. We get lulled into thinking that automatic information processing is great stuff that obviates the necessity for trying to resolve so many frustrating decisional dilemmas.

Actually, I think too much ethical training focuses on supplying standards for contemplating dilemmas. The far greater problem, as I see it, is recognizing that a dilemma exists in the first place. The insidious problem of people not being aware that they are dealing with a situation that might have ethical overtones is another consequence of schema usage. I would venture that scripted routines seldom include ethical dimensions. Is a person behaving unethically if the situation is not even construed as having ethical implications? People are not necessarily stupid, ill-intentioned, or Machiavellian, but they are often unaware. They do indeed spend much of their time cruising on automatic, but the true hallmark of human information processing is the ability to switch from automatic to controlled information processing. What we really need to do is to encourage people to recognize cues that build a "Now Think!" step into their scripts—waving red flags at yourself, so to speak—even though you are engaged in essentially automatic cognition and action.

Third, because scripts are context-bound and organizations are potent contexts, be aware of how strongly, yet how subtly, your job role and your organizational culture affect the ways you interpret and make sense of information (and thus affect the ways you develop the scripts that will guide you in unguarded moments). Organizational culture has a much greater effect on individual cognition than you would ever suspect (see Chapter Nine).

Last, be prepared to face critical responsibility at a relatively young age, as I did. You need to know what your values are and you need to know how you think so that you can know how to make a good decision. Before you can do that, you need to articulate and affirm your values now, before you enter the fray. I wasn't really ready. Are you?

DISCUSSION QUESTIONS

(Note that these questions apply to Gioia's reflections as well as the rest of the chapter.)

1. Steven F. Goldstone, chairman and CEO of RJR Nabisco (one of four big U.S. cigarette manufacturers), said, "I have no moral view of this business . . . I viewed it as a legal business. You shouldn't be drawing a moral judgment about a business our country says is perfectly legal and is taxed like crazy by it"(Goldberg, p. 41). Think about Goldstone's statement in terms of moral awareness. What might happen if he began thinking about his business in moral, and not just legal, terms?

2. Evaluate yourself in terms of cognitive moral development and locus of control. What does this tell you about your own ethical decision making? Do the same for someone you know well.

3. Identify a situation in which you have used script processing in a work or other life situation.

4. What does it mean to say that everyone is a victim of his or her cognitive structures? Think about cognitive moral development, locus of control, and Gioia's actions in the Pinto Fires case.

5. Do you believe that scripts can override one's value system?

6. Answer the question posed in the reflections: Is a person behaving unethically if the situation was not even construed in ethical terms—if there was no moral awareness?

7. What does it mean to say that organizational culture is a collection of scripts?

8. Who should make the decision about taking risks with others' lives in designing products?

9. Should someone be permitted to place a value on a human life? Should a company? Should the government?

10. How do you feel about the use of cost/benefit analysis where human life is part of the cost calculation? Might the infusion of moral language have changed the decision makers' thinking? For example, what if decision makers had talked about their responsibility for killing 180 human beings?

11. Given that all automobiles are unsafe to some degree, where do you draw the line on product safety? How safe is safe enough—and who decides?

Another Short Case for Discussion

Mary, the director of nursing at a regional blood bank, is concerned about the declining number of blood donors. It's May, and Mary knows that the approaching summer will mean increased demands for blood and decreased supplies, especially of rare blood types. She is excited, therefore, when a large corporation asks to host a series of blood drives at all of its locations, beginning at corporate headquarters. Soon after Mary and her staff arrive at the corporate site, Mary hears a disturbance. Apparently, a pretty young nurse named Peggy was drawing blood from a male donor with a very rare blood type when the donor fondled her breast. Peggy jumped back and began to cry. Joe, a male colleague, sprang to Peggy's defense and told the male donor to leave the premises. To Mary's horror, she also learned that the male donor was a senior manager with the corporation. What is the ethical dilemma in this case, and what values are in conflict? How should Mary deal with Peggy, Joe, the male donor, and other representatives of the corporation?

NOTES

1. Butterfield, K., Treviño, L .K., and Weaver, G. 1997. Moral awareness in business organizations: a model and field test. Unpublished working paper.
2. Fiske, S. T., and Taylor, S. E. 1991. *Social cognition*. 2nd ed. New York: McGraw-Hill.
3. Jones, T. M. 1991. Ethical decision making by individuals in organizations: An issue-contingent model. *Academy of Management Review*16: 366–395.
4. Kohlberg, L. 1969. Stage and sequence: The cognitive-developmental approach to socialization. In *Handbook of socialization theory and research,* D. A. Goslin, ed. Rand McNally, 347–380.
5. Rest, M. 1986. *Moral development; Advances in research and theory*. New York: Praeger.
6. Treviño, L. K., and Youngblood, S. A. 1990. Bad apples in bad barrels: A causal analysis of ethical decision-making behavior. *Journal of Applied Psychology* 75 (4): 3768–385.
   Weber, J. 1988. The relationship between managerial value orientations and stages of moral development: Theory development and empirical investigation with behavioral implications. Unpublished dissertation, The University of Pittsburgh.
7. Ibid.
8. Gilligan, C. 1982. *In a different voice*. Cambridge, MA: Harvard University Press.
9. Gilligan, C., and Attanuci, J. 1988. Two moral orientations. In *Mapping the moral domain,* C. Gilligan, J. V. Ward, and J. M. Taylor, eds. Cambridge, MA: Harvard University Press, 73–86.
10. Derry, R. 1987. Moral reasoning in work-related conflicts. *Research in Corporate Social Performance and Policy* 9: 25–50.
11. Rest, M. 1986. *Moral development; Advances in research and theory*. New York: Praeger.
12. Ibid.
13. This phrase was used with different meaning by R. Jackall in *Moral Mazes* by Oxford University Press.
14. Treviño, L. K.1992. Moral reasoning and business ethics. *Journal of Business Ethics* 11: 445–459.

15. Dukerich, J., Nichols, M. L. Elm, D. R., and Vollrath, D. A. 1990. Moral reasoning in groups: Leaders make a difference. *Human Relations* 43: 473–493.

16. Treviño, L. K. 1992. Moral reasoning and business ethics. *Journal of Business Ethics* 11: 445–459.

17. Rotter, J. B. 1966. Generalized expectancies for internal versus external control of reinforcement. *Psychological Monographs: General and Applied* 80:1–28.

18. Midlarski, E. 1971. Aiding under stress: the effects of competence, dependency, visibility, and fatalism. *Journal of Personality* 39: 132–149.

    Midlarski, E., and Midlarski, M. 1973. Some determinants of aiding under experimentally induced stress. *Journal of Personality* 41: 305–327.

    Ubbink, E. M., and Sadava, S. W. 1974. Rotter's generalized expectancies as predictors of helping behavior. *Psychological Reports* 35: 865–866.

19. Johnson, R. C., Ackerman, J. M., Frank, H., and Fionda, A. J. 1968. Resistance to temptation and guilt following yielding and psychotherapy. *Journal of Consulting and Clinical Psychology* 32: 169–175.

20. Propst, L. R. 1979. Efforts of personality and loss of anonymity on aggression: A reevaluation of deindividuation. *Journal of Personality* 47: 531–545.

21. Bazerman, M. H. 1994. *Judgment in managerial decision making.* New York: John Wiley & Sons.

22. Messick, D. M., and Bazerman, M. 1994. Ethics for the 21st century; a decision-making perspective. Unpublished manuscript. The International Consortium for Executive Development Research.

23. Gioia, D. 1992. Pinto fires and personal ethics: A script analysis of missed opportunities. *Journal of Business Ethics* 11(5,6): 379–389.

24. Ibid.

25. Raeburn, Paul. 1997. Saving lives doesn't have to cost a bundle. *Business Week,*. July 14: 29.

26. Gioia, Pinto fires and personal ethics.

27. Messick and Bazerman, Ethics for the 21st century.

28. Bazerman, *Judgment in managerial decision making.*

29. Messick and Bazerman, Ethics for the 21st century.

30. Ibid.

31. Ibid..

32. Ibid.

33. Staw, B. M., and Ross, I. 1987. Understanding escalation situations. In *Research in Organizational Behavior,* Vol. 9, B. M. Staw and L. L. Cummings, eds. Greenwich, CT: JAI Press.

34. Messick and Bazerman, Ethics for the 21st Century.

35. Elkind, P. 1997. Blood feud. *Fortune,* April 14: 90–102.

36. Goldberg, J. 1998. Big tobacco's endgame. *New York Times Magazine,* June 21: 36–42, 58–60, 41.

37. Ibid., p. 97.

38. Ibid., p. 102

39. See Gioia, Pinto fires and personal ethics, for a more thorough description and analysis of my experience.

ETHICS AND THE MANAGER

CHAPTER 6

Ethical Problems of Managers

INTRODUCTION

Ethical issues for individual employees and managers are very different, since managers are responsible for the entire range of human resources activities such as hiring, firing, disciplining, and performance evaluation. Also, since managers are responsible for employee supervision, the courts can hold them accountable for the activities and behavior of the people who report to them. Finally, because managers are role models for the workers in their department, it's critical that managers be able to discuss the ethical implications of decision making and provide advice to employees who find themselves in an ethical quandary. These facts of corporate life have frustrated many managers. "How can I possibly manage the ethics or morality of the people I manage? Is it even possible to manage ethics? Where are the special pitfalls for me as a manager?" In this chapter, we're going to examine what responsibilities managers have and how you as a manager can influence your direct reports to make ethical decisions.

MANAGING THE "BASICS"

Perhaps there's never been more competition to hire and retain qualified workers than in today's marketplace. The result: managers need to be proficient at hiring the best people, evaluating their performance, disciplining them, and even terminating a worker who is an unsatisfactory performer.

Hiring and Work Assignments

After two years of complex negotiations and hand-holding, your bank has finally signed Big Holding Co. as a client. Big Holding has three main divisions: a chemicals business in Louisiana, a heavy equipment division outside of Cleveland, and an agricultural business in Iowa. Since the business is so enormous, you assign three junior employees to the company—one employee per division. Jim Patterson, a talented chemical engineer will head the effort for the chemicals business.

When you and your three employees meet with the senior management team from Big Holding to plot long-term strategy, the chief financial officer pulls you aside to chat. "You shouldn't send Jim to Louisiana," he says. "There have been numerous violent incidents there involving people of his race, and I would be afraid for his safety. Why don't you assign him to one of the other divisions, and send someone else down South?"

You're planning to hire a new marketing manager and one of the leading candidates is very short. He's so short that he could be classified as a dwarf and would have difficulty doing things like reaching light switches. If you hired him, his office would have to be modified, although that really isn't much of a problem. The real problem is your concern about how your customers would react. The specific job he's applying for requires extensive customer contact, and his appearance is frankly disconcerting. On the other hand, his credentials are excellent and he's certainly qualified for the job.

A manager hires, or brings new people into the organization, and determines employee work assignments once employees are on the job. The new people may be permanent employees, or they may be part-time employees, temporary workers, or consultants.

Federal law prohibits discrimination based on race, religion, sex, color, ethnic background, and age, and it protects those who are pregnant or handicapped. In the first example above, which involves an African-American male, the correct answer is not as clear-cut as it may appear. The worker is certainly qualified for the job—and he should be given the opportunity to be assigned to the part of the business he seems most qualified to manage. Although federal legislation supposedly protects him from discrimination, the element of danger in this case caused at least one company to reassign an employee in a very similar case; and the young man, one of the organization's brightest stars, left in a matter of weeks.

Another solution might have been to give the employee the choice of whether to go or accept another assignment. Many senior managers who have reviewed this case have suggested that one way to handle this situation may be to say, "Here are the facts as I know them—it's your decision and I'll support whatever you decide." Other managers have suggested doing some research to determine whether your customer is honestly relating a troublesome situation or is actually discriminating against one of your employees. Or perhaps there is another agenda of which you are unaware. Whatever your customer's reasons, some prudent research might give you a better understanding of his motivations.

In the second example, which involves a very short candidate, many people might think that the solution is even more ambiguous. He is "certainly qualified" for the job, and his size may very well include him in protectionist handicapped legislation. But the larger issue is: what qualities should determine whether or not an individual should be hired?

All protectionist legislation—at all levels—points to the answer, as does the concept of fairness. Hiring, promotions, and terminations should be based on ability, period. However, it's one thing to ignore someone because of your own prejudice and quite another to hesitate to put someone in a situation where they might suffer discrimination from an external audience that's out of your control such as your customers. It's difficult to say whether you're doing someone a favor by setting him or her up for possible failure in an environment that's hostile.

Prejudice is difficult to overcome. Everyone has biases: some people don't like very tall people, or very short people, or fat ones, or skinny ones, or old ones, or young ones. Others have biases against brown eyes, or blue eyes, or eyes with wrinkles, or big noses, or aquiline noses, or balding heads, or hair that appears to be too long. Some people like individuals from certain schools or from particular parts of the country. What if someone interviews for a job and he is just plain unattractive, or she's deaf, or he had cancer three years ago, or she speaks English with an accent? Do those qualities have anything to do with an ability to do the job, or with talent?

Some employers have a "corporate profile" in mind when they hire, especially when they're trying to fill positions with "extensive public contact." Some large Fortune 100 companies are well known for their penchant for hiring certain types of employees. They look for healthy, young people with regular features, moderate height, a medium build, and no discernible accents. Do employers with a conscious, or subconscious "corporate profile" think that the public or their customers are somehow homogeneous? If history had used a "corporate profile" as a yardstick, Abraham Lincoln, Benjamin Franklin, Marian Anderson, Albert Einstein, Sammy Davis, Jr., and Franklin Roosevelt may have been relegated to positions with "no public contact."

Talent and ability come in a variety of packages. When managers use anything other than those two factors to evaluate qualifications for hiring, promotions, or work assignments, they shortchange not only the individual, but also their employer. And they may help to perpetuate stereotypes in the workplace.

Performance Evaluation

You were recently promoted to manager of a department with five professionals and two clerical staff. One of the professionals, Joe, is a nice guy, but he simply hasn't been able to match the performance of the others in the department. When he tells you he's been interviewing for another job in a different part of your company, you pull his personnel file and see that the person who previously managed the department had rated Joe's performance as "good to excellent." You frankly disagree. Joe has asked you for a recommendation. Based on the written appraisals, you could give him a good one—but your personal observation is at odds with the written evaluations. Joe's prospective manager—your peer in another department—asks for your opinion. What do you say?

When we talk about performance evaluation, we're really talking about two things. First, there's a written assessment of an employee's performance. Most large companies have a formal performance appraisal system, with forms to standardize the process, and a mandate to complete a written evaluation on every employee usually once each year. These written appraisals usually have some influence on any salary adjustments, and they usually become part of the employee's permanent personnel file. Second, there's the informal process of performance evaluation that ideally is an ongoing process throughout the year. When a manager gives continuous feedback—when objectives are stated and then performance against those objectives is measured—employees generally aren't surprised by the annual written performance appraisal.

Why is continuous evaluation important? A training manager in New York City tells a story about the importance of accurately and continuously appraising performance. "Imagine you're bowling," he says. "A bed sheet is stretched across the lane and you can't see what you're doing. Your manager is the only person who can tell you how you're doing. What would happen if your manager told you how you were doing only occasionally or once a year? How would your performance be affected if he or she told you about your performance only when you got gutter balls? What would happen if he or she only commented just when you did well?" It's only when your manager gives you consistent feedback—reflecting the complete range of your behavior—that you can improve your performance.

The problem with performance evaluation is that most managers hate to do it. It's certainly easier to recognize an employee's achievements than his or her shortcomings, but many managers are so busy that they forget to recognize either. Pointing out an employee's deficient performance is extremely difficult for most managers. It's such a thorny issue that in a survey of 4000 Fortune 500 executives, five out of seven executives said that they would rather lie to employees about performance than confront them about performance problems.[1]

In the example above, the manager thinks Joe has been inaccurately (and perhaps even dishonestly) evaluated in the past. Since most employers require a rating of "good" or "satisfactory" before an employee can transfer to another job, the manager will probably feel pressure to supply such a recommendation so Joe can qualify for the transfer. This is a common problem. Many organizations have employees like Joe, who are less than stellar performers, but who are never confronted with their poor performance. In Joe's company, no manager has been brave enough to bite the bullet and either try to get Joe to improve his performance or initiate the termination process. It's easier to pass Joe along to someone else—to turn him into a Ping-Pong ball, bouncing from department to department, never really improving his performance because no one will confront him with the truth. And because his written appraisals have been less than honest, prospective managers get buffaloed into thinking Joe's performance is adequate. It's a vicious cycle and a real disservice to the employee, his or her co-workers, and the organization.

One good way to ensure continuous performance evaluation is to establish a formal system with the employees who report to you, whether or not your company requires it, and certainly more often than once each year. Meet with each employee every six months or every year, and jointly agree to job objectives and how to measure success for each objective. Then meet monthly with each employee and discuss how the employee is meeting his or her objectives. When objectives and measurement standards are established in advance and progress is tracked, it's much easier for employees to perform. They know what the target looks like, how to get there, and how they'll know when they've met it. An ongoing process eliminates the need to blast a nonperformer once a year and can greatly reduce misunderstanding, resentment, and charges of discrimination or bias.

Probably the best way to handle the situation with Joe is to be honest with him. "I can't write you the kind of letter you want for the following reasons. [Spell out the performance problems.] We can either wait until you get your performance on track, or I can write you a letter that reflects my honest evaluation of your work at this time. It's up to you."

Discipline

Steven is a salesman who reports to you, the regional director of sales for an office supply company. He has a great track record and has consistently surpassed his sales targets, but he has a terrible flaw. He's not on time for anything. He's late both for meetings with you and lunches with clients, and the problem extends to his paperwork. His expense reports, sales reports—everything is handed in a day or sometimes even a week late. As his manager, you've counseled him about his tardiness, and he has improved. Now instead of being 15 minutes late for a meeting, he's only 5 minutes late. And instead of submitting his expenses a week late, they're only two days late. His lateness seems minor in view of his achievements, but it's driving you and his co-workers crazy.

Most managers view disciplining employees as something to be postponed for as long as possible. Many people in a work environment try to ignore a worker's shortcomings in the hope that the situation will improve. Discipline, however, is important for a number of reasons: not only to ensure worker productivity, but also to set the standard that certain behaviors are expected from all employees, and to meet the requirements of the U.S. Sentencing Guidelines. As we discussed in Chapter Two, the Sentencing Guidelines specify that all employees in an organization must receive consistent discipline for similar infractions. For example, in the case of employee theft, a secretary and a senior vice president must be treated in the same way. The Guidelines are violated if one receives a slap on the wrist and the other is suspended or fired.

In the case of Steven, the late salesman, you as a manager could be tempted to view disciplining his lateness as nit-picking. He's a star after all, right? However, to expect promptness from all of your other employees and not from Steven is unrealistic and unfair.

Research has given us clues about the most effective ways to discipline employees. First, the discipline must be constructive and done in a professional manner. For example, although you might be tempted to scream at Steven and call him a jerk, that's not going to change his behavior. It's much more effective to meet with him, explain the consequences of his lateness, and focus the discussion on his behavior, not on him personally.

Second, the discipline should be done privately. Employees should never be criticized in front of other employees. It's just as embarrassing as being criticized in public by your parent or your spouse, and it encourages nothing but hard feelings. Those discussions should always be held behind closed doors.

Third, employees should have input into the process and be encouraged to explain their side of the story. The entire idea of "team" management revolves around individuals being encouraged to share their view of a situation. The real problem may not be with the particular employee you want to discipline. Steven, for example, may be late with reports because people are late in submitting data to him. To solve problems at the simplest point, it's wise to ask for an employee's explanation.

Finally, discipline should be appropriately harsh and consistent with what other employees have received for similar offenses. This aspect of discipline is perhaps the most important in terms of ensuring good performance in the future.[2]

For example, a highly respected financial professional (let's call her Beth) was fired from her position at a large manufacturing company for providing an inaccurate calculation in a report to senior management. The head of human resources for the bank gave Beth a Herculean task: to use a new formula to calculate the company's pension obligations on all current employees. The assignment was given at 6:00 P.M. on a Tuesday, and the report needed to be written, typed, and copied for a senior management meeting the next morning at 9:00 A.M. Beth and her secretary stayed at the office all night long, doing calculations, writing the report, and finally preparing it for the meeting the next morning. When one of the senior managers discovered an error in one of the complex calculations, Beth was summarily fired by the head of human resources. It sent a huge message, not only to Beth, but to the entire human resources department. Other mistakes had been made—even by the head of human resources—and those errors had been punished with a reprimand, certainly not a firing. And, of course, the impossible deadline constituted an extenuating circumstance in everyone's opinion except the head of human resources. The effects of unreasonable discipline are far reaching, and that's why discipline needs to be appropriate to the offense and consistent with what others have received.

In the case of Steven, the late salesman, unless you're willing to be consistent and accept tardiness in all other employees, Steven's behavior needs to be addressed.

Terminations

You're a manager in a large commercial bank. You discover that Patricia, a loan officer who reports to you, has forged an approval signature on a customer loan, which requires signatures from two loan officers. When you confront Pat with the forgery, she apologizes profusely and says that her husband has been very ill. The day she forged the signature, he was going into surgery and she just didn't have time to find another loan officer to sign the authorization for the loan. Pat has been with your bank for 15 years and has a spotless record.

Terminations come in many varieties and none of them are pleasant. There are terminations for cause—meaning that an individual has committed an offense that can result in instant firing. "Cause" can represent different things to different companies, but generally theft, assault, cheating on expense reports, forgery, fraud, and gross insubordination (including lying about a business matter) are considered to be "cause" in most organizations. Many companies define "cause" in their employee handbooks.

In the case above, Patricia will most likely be fired for cause. In banking, there are few things as sacred as a signature, and a professional with 15 years of banking experience would certainly be expected to know this. Forgery of any kind cannot be tolerated in a financial institution. It's a sad case, and any manager would feel compassion for Patricia. However, some offenses are unpardonable in a financial institution, and this is probably one of them.

There are also terminations for poor performance. This type of firing is most often based on written documentation such as performance appraisals and attendance records. Many employers have a formal system of warnings that will occur before someone is actually terminated for poor performance. A verbal warning is usually the first step in the process, followed by a written warning, and then termination. The process can differ from company to company.

Then there's downsizing, which is just a fancy word that means layoffs. Layoffs can result from many kinds of reorganizations such as mergers, acquisitions, and relocations, or they can be the result of economic reasons or changes in business strategy. A layoff can result from a decision to trim staff in one department or from a decision to reduce head count across the company. Whatever the reason, layoffs are painful, not only for the person losing his or her job, but also for the co-workers who'll be left behind. Co-workers tend to display several reactions: they exhibit low morale; they become less productive; they distrust management; and they become extremely cautious.[3]

In addition, layoff survivors are generally very concerned about the fairness of the layoff. They need to feel that the downsizing was necessary for legitimate business reasons; that it was conducted in a way that was consistent with the corporate culture; that layoff victims received ample notice; and that the victims were treated with dignity and respect. If management provided "a clear and adequate explanation of the reasons for the layoffs," survivors will be more likely to view the layoffs as being fair.[4] These are just a few reasons why layoffs have to be handled well.

Whatever the reason for a termination, you can take certain steps as a manager to make it easier for the employee being terminated and for yourself.[5] Again, the main goals are to be fair and to allow the employee to maintain personal dignity.

1. Do your homework before you meet with the employee. Prepare a brief explanation of why this termination is necessary and have ready an explanation of the severance package being offered to this employee, including financial and benefits arrangements. It's also helpful

to check the calendar and consult with your company's public relations department to ensure you're not firing someone on his birthday or on the day she receives recognition from an industry group or professional association.

2. If at all possible, you should arrange to have an outplacement counselor or human resources professional on hand to meet with the employee after you have spoken to him or her. Most outplacement counselors advise managers to give the bad news to terminated employees early in the day and early in the week, if possible. This gives the employee time to meet with a counselor if necessary. (Obviously, this advice doesn't apply to employees who are fired for cause.)

3. It's generally a good idea to terminate someone on neutral ground, in a conference room for example, rather than in your office. In that way, you can leave if the situation becomes confrontational. If possible, try to assess what the employee's reaction might be. If you're about to fire a violent person for cause (like assaulting a co-worker), you might want to have security nearby when you deliver the news.

4. Speak privately with each individual, and do it face to face, not by e-mail, telephone, or in a meeting or other kind of public forum. When you deliver the news, be objective, don't be in any way abusive, be compassionate, do it quickly (if possible), and never, never get personal.

5. Finally, keep all information about the termination private. Never discuss the reasons for a firing with anyone who doesn't have a need to know. The exception to this advice is when numerous layoffs occur. Survivors—co-workers who are left behind—will require some explanation of why layoffs were needed. In this case, you might want to speak about general, never specific or personal, reasons for the layoff. (For more information on downsizing, see Chapter 8.)

Terminations for cause don't go unnoticed, and the employee grapevine will assuredly carry the news of a termination around your organization. That's a good thing because it's important for employees to understand that bad acts get punished. However, it's generally improper to publicly explain why an individual has been punished; the primary objective is to protect the dignity and privacy of the person who has been punished.

Why Are These Ethical Problems?

Hiring, performance evaluation, discipline, and terminations can be ethical issues because they all involve honesty, fairness, and the dignity of the individual. Rice and Dreilinger[6] say that the desire for justice is a "fundamental human characteristic. People want to believe that the world operates on the principles of fairness; they react strongly when that belief is violated." In fact, the majority of calls to corporate ethics hotlines (discussed more fully in Chapter Ten) relate to precisely these types of issues.

Costs

Much federal legislation exists to protect the rights of individuals in situations that involve hiring, performance evaluation, discipline, and terminations. There are myriad legal remedies for employees who feel they have suffered discrimination. (See Discrimination—Costs in Chapter Three for more details.) In response to increased litigation, Employment Practice Liability Insurance (EPLI) is a hot product among corporations. This insurance covers organizations that are sued by employees over charges such as harassment, discrimination, or wrongful discharge. The insurance, which was virtually unheard of in 1993, has been purchased by half of Fortune 500 companies. This is surely the result of the huge increase in litigation and in settlements. The Equal Employment Opportunity Commission received 15,889 sexual harassment complaints in 1997, up from 6,883 in 1991. Also, the record amount paid in an EEOC case was $10 million in 1998, up from $1.3 million just two years earlier.[7]

In addition to perhaps paying legal costs and fines, organizations that have been charged with discrimination can also expect to pay a price in terms of employee morale and organizational reputation. Research evidence indicates that employees who perceive that they have been unfairly treated are less satisfied, less likely to go the extra mile, and more likely to steal from the organization.[8]

MANAGING A DIVERSE WORKFORCE

Experts predict that the workforce is becoming more diverse and that the key to many managers' success will be how well they can persuade diverse groups to sing together as a well-tuned chorus. Companies that best address the needs of a diverse population will probably be in a better position to succeed than companies that ignore this new reality. The result: managers need to be able to deal with individuals of both sexes, and all ages, races, religions, and ethnic groups. Managers not only need to have this ability themselves, but also need to be able to encourage this ability in team members. Managers must become "conductors" who orchestrate team performance—sometimes teaching, sometimes coaching, always communicating with employees and empowering them to learn and make good decisions.

The second skill set required of the new manager involves positively influencing the relationships among other team members and creating an ethical work environment that enhances individual productivity. Everyone we work with has a range of issues that could affect the ability to perform well. Many people are responsible for children, parents, or other relatives. Many workers have chronic illnesses or conditions or allergies; and those workers who are lucky not to have a chronic condition can suddenly become ill or injured. Other employees have chemical dependencies, such as an addiction to drugs or alcohol. Managers need to be able to accomplish tasks and the mission of a department or team, in spite of the often painful events and conditions that can distract team members.

Since a bias-free person hasn't been born yet, managers also have to be able to counsel team members in their relationships with one another. Because every team will include a wide range of personalities, a manager frequently needs to be a referee: mediating and resolving disputes, assigning tasks to the workers who can best accomplish them, and ensuring that fairness is built into the working relationships of team members.

The examples that follow, though similar to those in Chapter Three, differ because they are written from the perspective of the manager, not the individual. And, as we said earlier in this chapter, managers have a different level of responsibility.

Diversity

> One of your best customers is a very conservative organization—a real "white-shirt" company. Reporting to you is David, a very talented African American who could benefit greatly from working with this customer account—and the customer account would benefit greatly from David's expertise and creativity. The issue is that David dresses in vibrant colors and wears an African skull cap. Your company long ago recognized David's brilliance, and his dress within the company isn't an issue. But you know your customer would react to David's attire with raised eyebrows.

What is it? A diverse workforce consists of individuals of both sexes and myriad races, ethnic groups, and religions. The role of a manager is to create an environment in which the contribution of each individual can be maximized. Since the population of the United States is remarkably diverse, it makes perfect sense to believe that products and services offered to this population should be developed, produced, and marketed by a diverse workforce.

The danger of ignoring this diversity was illustrated during an interview with a chemical company executive. One of the company's products is wallpaper. Even though the wallpaper was of a very high quality and priced competitively, sales were down. This was even more of a mystery since home repairs and renovations, especially by do-it-yourself decorators, were at record numbers.

Baffled by the problem, several senior marketing managers conducted customer surveys and found that the patterns of the company's wallpaper were the problem. Consumers viewed the patterns and styles as being outdated and old fashioned. The managers then investigated the process by which patterns and styles were selected. What kind of market research was performed before patterns were selected for the next season?

They discovered that, even though female consumers made more than 90 percent of all wallpaper purchases, there were no women on the team of chemical company employees who selected patterns for production. All style decisions were made by male employees. The marketing managers and other executives insisted that women and other diverse voices be included on the selection committee. The results were immediate. As soon as the new styles of wallpaper appeared in stores, sales increased substantially.

In the example at the beginning of this section, David's attire could be viewed as problematic by some managers. In this case, and others like it, honesty is the best policy. You may want to tell David frankly that you want him to work on this account because his ability would benefit the customer. You may perhaps say that the customer is conservative and that his attire may distract the customer from his ability. Let David decide how he wants to dress when meeting with the customer.

You may also be frank with your customer: tell him or her that David is extraordinarily talented and is the best person to add value to your relationship. Mention that David often wears ethnic garb as a way to lessen the surprise of the initial meeting. This approach lets David know how the client might interpret his clothing, but it doesn't force him into some narrow corporate box. It also prepares the client to be able to deal with diversity. The point is to balance your interpretation of what a customer might appreciate with David's individuality and diverse voice.

Dress codes tend to raise some people's hackles. The intention of most dress codes is not to restrict individuality, but to ensure a professional appearance in the workplace. Ethnic garb shouldn't really be an issue, as long as it's modest. The aim of most dress codes is to eliminate clothing that could be viewed as immodest or too casual to a customer.

Harassment

Your profession has been traditionally a male-dominated one, and Marcia is the only woman in your department. Whenever Sam—your senior engineer—holds staff meetings, he and the other males in the department compliment Marcia profusely. They say things like, "It's hard for us to concentrate with a gorgeous woman like you in the room," or "you've got to stop batting your eyelashes at us or the temperature in this room will trigger the air conditioning." They compliment her apparel, her figure, her legs, and the way she speaks. Although flattering, their remarks make her feel uncomfortable. She has mentioned her discomfort to you on several occasions, and you've told Sam and the others to cut it out. They just laughed and told you that Marcia was too sensitive. You think that while Marcia was being sensitive, she did have justification for being upset about her co-workers' remarks. (For a review of the legal definitions of sexual harassment, please consult Chapter Three.)

Do compliments constitute harassment? They do when they embarrass someone and serve to undermine an individual's professional standing in front of co-workers. If Marcia is disturbed by the remarks of her co-workers, it's your responsibility as her manager to do something about it. In cases like these, it's sometimes helpful to reverse the situation. Imagine that your department was predominantly female and that the women continually said to the lone male, "You're just a hunk." "We all get aroused when you bat your eyelashes at us." "That's a great suit you're wearing; those slacks really show off your gorgeous thighs." How ridiculous does that banter sound?

In this case, Marcia's discomfort is the issue, and it's irrelevant whether or not you or others think she's being a "little too sensitive." She has already taken the appropriate steps, first by telling her co-workers to stop and then approaching you when they didn't. You should meet immediately with the members of your department, individually or as a group. You could reverse the situation as in the previous paragraph and show the men how ridiculous their comments would sound if the sex of the players was reversed. Explain to them that inappropriate compliments are not acceptable and that anyone who behaves inappropriately in the future will be disciplined. Make it clear that every member of the team has the right to feel comfortable on the team and to be treated with respect. In addition, if you don't act swiftly and firmly, and then back up future offenses with disciplinary action, you may be inviting a lawsuit.

Here's another kind of harassment:

> One of your direct reports, Robert, belongs to a fundamentalist church. Although you have no problems with anyone's religious beliefs, Robert is so vocal about his religion that it's becoming a problem with other employees in your department. He not only preaches to his fellow employees, but he also has criticized the attire of some of his female co-workers and continually quotes the bible in staff meetings. You've received complaints about his behavior from several employees. A few weeks ago, you suggested to Robert that he tone down his preaching, and he reacted as if you were a heathen about to persecute him for his beliefs. His behavior has since escalated.

The job of a manager is to try to maintain a balance between the rights of the individual and the rights of the group—in this case, the attempt by one individual to impose his or her opinions or behavior on other team members. The objectives are fairness and respect for each individual.

In the case of Robert, it appears that he has crossed the line from expressing diverse views to harassment. Although it's important to recognize the value of diverse backgrounds, it's just as important to have an environment where one individual can't constantly attempt to impose his beliefs on other team members. Robert has ignored your requests and those of his co-workers, and has continued his preaching. This kind of behavior will no doubt disrupt the performance of the team and the relationships among team members. In this case, it's probably reasonable to begin documenting Robert's performance since you've already verbally warned him. His hostility and his refusal to respect the opinions of his co-workers and his manager can be viewed as insubordination. In organizations that have a due process approach to discipline, the next step might be a written warning to curb his attempts to influence the religion of his co-workers, or termination will result. Then, if Robert's harassment of his co-workers doesn't stop, he could be fired.

Family and Personal Issues

> One of your direct reports is Ellen, who just returned from maternity leave. She now has two children—her infant is four months old, and her older child is three years old. Ellen is not only a talented worker, but she's also a wonderful person. Before the birth of her second child, she had no problem handling the workload and the demands on her time; she had a live-in nanny who could care for her

child regardless of when she returned home. Recently, however, her live-in left, and Ellen is now sending her children to a day care facility with strict opening and closing times. Although Ellen is very productive when she's in the office, her schedule no longer has any flexibility—she must leave the office no later than 5:00 P.M. This has caused a hardship for all of her peers who must complete team assignments whether or not she's present. Although you don't want to cause problems for her, the situation doesn't seem fair to her co-workers.

Family and personal issues are those situations and conditions that, though not directly related to work, can affect someone's ability to perform. People simply can't leave their personal and family problems at home. The difficulty in situations like these is achieving a balance between maintaining a worker's job commitment, performance, and attendance with his or her right to privacy and with fairness to co-workers. The yardstick is: if someone is performing well, and his or her attendance is satisfactory, there's probably no cause for action on the part of the manager, beyond offering assistance if the worker wants it.

In Ellen's case, she has a temporary inability to match her co-workers' schedules. Sooner or later, every worker must deal with situations that place limitations on the ability to maintain certain working hours. Similar situations could result from a variety of other causes including illness, family responsibilities, home construction, and commuting schedules. The issue here is fairness in attendance, not performance or productivity. The ideal solution may be to build more flexibility into the working hours, not just for Ellen, but for the entire team. The ideal solution would involve confronting the problem head-on by asking the people in your area to collaborate and find a solution. For example, you could make an attempt to hold all team meetings in the middle of the day, when everyone can attend. Individual activities could be relegated to the afternoon, so that it would not be essential that Ellen—or anyone else—stay late to work as a group. If your organization has flexible work hours, you could talk to your manager about the possibility of your area incorporating flexible work schedules, where people could arrive and leave at varying times, but where the office and department would always be covered. The objective is to make life easier for individual employees and fair for the entire group, and as a result enhance the team's overall productivity.

Personal illnesses and chemical dependencies of employees present a different set of issues. These situations can affect not only work schedules, but also an individual's ability to perform. Most corporations have explicit policies for managing employee illness. Generally, employees are guaranteed a specific number of sick days and then go on some sort of disability program. If an employee, however, hasn't received a formal diagnosis and is simply taking sick days, acting erratically, or showing a change in his or her performance, you might suspect a physical or mental illness. Encourage the employee to see a doctor, and consult with the company medical department (if you have one) if you continue to be concerned about an employee's health. It's important to remember that illnesses of any kind—depression, cancer, AIDS—are private and should be kept confidential. These conditions do not cause any danger to co-workers, and many people who suffer from them can resume normal or modified work schedules. Managers can help these employees by protecting the employee's privacy and by being fair and compassionate.

Drug or alcohol abuse is a different matter. Most corporations have policies that prohibit any kind of drug or alcohol use on company premises, and many companies have severe penalties for employees who are caught working under the influence of alcohol or drugs. Both alcoholism and drug addiction are costly in terms of the abuser's health, and they can both cause extreme danger in the workplace. A corporate bond trader who's high on cocaine can wreak havoc on himself, his employer, and his customers. A pilot who's drunk poses obvious risks to an airline and its passengers. Would you like to ride with a railroad engineer who just smoked a few joints, or have the sale of your home negotiated by a real estate broker who's inebriated, or have your child's broken leg set by a doctor who's on amphetamines?

If you suspect that one of your employees is abusing drugs on or off the job, keep track of any changes in behavior and performance, in writing. (Even if an employee uses drugs or alcohol only off company premises, the residual effects of the substance may affect job performance.) This is an important step because some medications smell like alcohol on the breath, so it's important to be sure that you're dealing with abuse and not a medical condition. Once you're fairly certain that you're dealing with abuse, contact your human resources department. Substance abuse is considered an illness (and generally not an offense that will get the employee fired—at least in many large corporations), and the employee usually will be counseled by human resources. If abuse is present, most large employers offer substance abuse programs for employees and will probably insist that your employee participate in such a program. In most large companies, employees are given one or two chances to get clean. If the problem recurs, substance abusers can be terminated. The important issue here is to get fast help for the employee—for the sake of the employee, the company, and your customers.

Why Are These Ethical Problems?

These are all ethical issues because they concern fairness and respect for the individual. A large percentage of the ethical issues that arise in business are related to human resources, and they can usually be addressed by local managers, who act quickly, fairly, and with compassion.

Costs

The personal, professional, and corporate costs of discrimination and sexual harassment are described earlier in this chapter and in Chapter Three. The costs for mishandling most issues connected to diversity are not clear-cut, and they're often difficult to quantify.

To glimpse how costly the publicity associated with such cases can be, we have to look no further than the now infamous Texaco case. Texaco executives were heard on tape complaining about Hanukkah and Kwanzaa interfering with the celebration of Christmas, and recounting the destruction of documents connected to a pending discrimination case.[9] In the wake of a firestorm of bad publicity, Texaco was forced to settle the case for $176 million. As one writer said at the time, "What the Texaco case proved is that if you can create enough bad publicity, depicting a company as hopelessly racist, you can win without ever going to trial. Though the media are predictably bored by the dry facts of job discrimination, they will almost always bite on colorful news about slurs and jokes."

Obviously, the costs to Texaco—both financially and in damaged reputation—were significant. Yet those costs are just the tip of a giant iceberg. If we could combine all of the fairness issues—performance evaluation systems, harassment, subtle and not-so-subtle discrimination, and how managers handle family, substance, and illness issues—and figure out how much it costs businesses when employees are treated unfairly, the result would probably be astronomical, and not just in terms of financial costs and damaged reputations. How many people leave a job because of unresolved problems with a co-worker? How many people choose not to go the extra mile because the organization doesn't treat its employees fairly? How many of the best performers choose to work for a company that allows them flexible hours to care for a child or an aging parent? How many people are depressed and frustrated because they're picking up the slack for a co-worker who's a chronic alcoholic? The toll in human suffering, morale, loyalty, productivity, and lost opportunity is inestimable.

MANAGING UP AND ACROSS

Gone are the days when a person could advance in an organization by impressing only the next level of management. The new team structures mandate that workers treat everyone well. An example of how some corporations are institutionalizing this approach is an increasingly popular method of performance appraisal that some companies call 360 degree feedback. This means that a manager appraises not only a worker, but also co-workers and his or her manager. Feedback of this sort, which comes from all directions, is probably a much more effective barometer of performance than old methods that measure only how well people manage up. Of course, it means that workers need to carefully consider all of their work relationships: up, down, and across. It's also an indicator of what astute workers have always known: since you never know who you might end up reporting to, or who is going to be crucial to your success in the future, it's critical to effectively manage all of your work relationships.

In team situations, managers can still have a profound impact on your future. They sign off on or approve performance appraisals, pay raises, transfers, and generally are a primary influence on your career mobility and trajectory. It can be difficult to overcome a poor relationship with a manager unless you have solid relationships with individuals on or above your manager's level. That's why it's important for you to cultivate your manager's respect.

Although it may appear that your peers don't have as direct an impact on your career as your manager does, they nevertheless can have a profound effect on your future success. Since you generally "get as good as you give," if you don't cooperate with your peers, they'll probably refuse to cooperate with you, and that lack of cooperation could cripple you. In addition, peers can be promoted to management positions, which can prove to be truly unfortunate if you haven't developed good relationships with them.

Honesty Is Rule One

Michael is a lawyer who reports to Paula, the corporate counsel for a chemical company. During one particularly busy period, Paula asks Michael to prepare a summary of all pending lawsuits and other legal activity for the company's senior management. Since Michael has several court appearances and depositions cluttering his schedule, he assigns the report to one of his paralegals, who completes the report in several days. Since he's so busy, Michael simply submits the report to Paula without reviewing it. When Paula asks him what he thinks of the report, he assures her that it's fine. The next day, Paula asks Michael into her office and says that she has found a major omission in the report. Michael has no choice but to admit that he didn't have time to review it.

There's probably nothing that trips up more people than the temptation to lie or stretch the truth. There's also probably nothing that will trip up your career faster than a lie or an exaggeration. In business, your reputation is everything, and lying or exaggerating can quickly undermine it.

Michael has basically lied to his manager. Even if he can weasel his way out of the hot seat by saying he didn't have time to thoroughly review the report, he has created an indelible impression on Paula. She may question not only his future reports, but also his activities in general. Michael could have told Paula up front that he didn't have time to prepare a report. He could have suggested that one of the paralegals prepare it. He could have asked for more time so that he could carefully review it. Paula may not have been thrilled with his analysis of the situation, but she probably would have understood and helped him look for another solution. However, by implying that he had completed and reviewed the report, when in fact he hadn't looked at it, Michael has severely damaged his reputation with his manager. A worker's responsibility includes identifying a problem and then proposing a solution. If you provide a solution when you report a concern, you stand a good chance of having your idea implemented. If you just report an issue with no solution, you'll probably have one imposed on you.

Managers and peers rely on the information they receive from the people who report to them and who work with them. Obviously, that information must be truthful and accurate, or someone else's work will be skewed. Once someone has reason to doubt your veracity, it may be impossible for you to recover. As one executive said, "Lying will end someone's relationship with me, period." The caveat is: Be completely honest about all aspects of your work, including your ability, the information you provide, and your ability to meet deadlines. Keep your promises.

Standards Go Both Ways

It began when Bruce asked Andy to lie to his wife about his whereabouts. "If Marcia calls, tell her I'm in Phoenix on a business trip," he told Andy. Of course, he had also confided to Andy that in case of an office emergency, he could be reached at a local golf tournament or at a nearby hotel where he was staying with another woman. Since Bruce was senior to Andy and was a powerful contributor in the department, Andy went along with his request. When Marcia called, Andy told the lie about Bruce being in Phoenix. Bruce asked several more "favors" of Andy, and Andy complied. Then Bruce asked for a big favor: he instructed Andy to inflate monthly sales figures for a report going to senior management. When Andy objected, Bruce said, "Oh, come on Andy, we all know how high your standards are."

Just as it's important for managers to set standards within their departments, it's equally important that workers set ethical standards with their managers and peers. The best way to ensure that you're not going to be asked to compromise your values is to clearly communicate what people can expect from you.

In Andy's case, he made his first mistake by going along with Bruce's lie to his wife. Although it's tempting to help out a colleague—especially one who's powerful and senior to you—you're sliding down a slippery slope when it involves a lie. And the chances are excellent that Bruce would not have asked Andy to lie about the monthly sales figures if he hadn't already known that he could manipulate Andy. If Andy had refused to lie for Bruce on that first occasion, Bruce would probably have vastly different expectations of him. When Bruce asked Andy to lie to his wife, Andy could have replied, "Hey, Bruce, don't drag me into that one! I'll tell her you're not in the office, but I'm not going to outright lie to her." Andy could have said it in a nonthreatening way and Bruce probably would have understood. Bruce might even have been embarrassed. But once Andy got caught up in Bruce's conspiracy, Bruce felt he would probably go along with other untruths. The caveat: Say it politely but say it firmly and unequivocally. If a co-worker or manager asks you to betray your standards—even in the tiniest of ways—refuse to compromise your standards or you'll end up being confronted with increasingly thorny dilemmas.

When It's Impossible

John and Maria were peers in a large corporation's marketing department until John accepted a transfer to another area within the company. They had an unusually close working relationship and parted as good friends and colleagues. After John was in his new position, they continued to meet for lunch, and they called one another frequently. Since they had worked so creatively together, it took a while for Maria to adjust to John's absence. In a few months, however, Maria had created a new team in the department and was producing highly acclaimed projects with her new partner. When Maria's manager, Carol, retired, she recommended Maria as her successor. However, the senior manager in charge of the area ignored Carol's recommendation and brought John back as department manager. Now that Maria reports to John, their relationship has changed dramatically. John tries to aggressively manage her in an effort to exert his authority, and the more aggressively he behaves, the more Maria resists, since she feels cheated out of a promotion and resents the dramatic change in his attitude.

It's not unusual in business to end up reporting to someone you dislike, don't respect, or find it extremely difficult to work with. Perhaps the touchiest situation is one like the case above, where an individual suddenly finds herself or himself reporting to a former peer, who may even be a friend. This situation is so tricky to manage that it should be avoided unless the position represents a unique career opportunity.

In Maria's case, her real problem is not only with John, but also with the next level of management, which ignored her ability and contributions, and installed someone else (anyone else) to manage the department. It's a clear signal to Maria that she should either transfer to another area of the company or look for another job. If she can't or won't look for another position, she's going to have to manage her relationship with John.

Her first step is to stop reacting to John and ask him for a truce. They both need to negotiate rules for their new working relationship. In the real case on which this example is based, John and Maria didn't negotiate a truce. They talked about one another to co-workers and in innumerable ways betrayed the relationship they had previously had with one another. The resulting cat fight took a tremendous toll on both of their careers. Their behavior was frowned on by their management chain (even though they had created the problem), and they both looked out of control. Both finally left the company, but the period of fighting was an emotionally draining time for each of them. And they both lost a close friend.

The lesson to be learned from John and Maria is that it's foolhardy to take things personally. Treat everyone as if you might someday report to them because someday you might. Those people who can find a way to work with everyone are the people who are most valued by organizations. Negative emotions like jealously, dishonesty, and betrayal will serve no purpose except to make the participants look ridiculous to observers. Work is work—you don't have to make love to someone you work with, or live with them, or get so emotionally charged over a situation that you lose control. As soon as you see a relationship start to get out of control, call a truce, discuss the situation, and establish rules for future dealings. If that doesn't work, find a way to get out of the situation.

Why Are These Ethical Problems?

Honesty is obviously an ethical issue because it involves the truth. Setting standards and knowing how to deal with "impossible" relationships are not ethical problems. They are preventive measures to help you avoid getting caught up in situations that could damage your career.

Costs

Honesty, setting standards, and knowing how to handle relationships are critical skills for the establishment of your reputation. As one executive says: "A good reputation is a prerequisite for success. The way to cultivate a good reputation is to be cooperative, do a good job, treat people with respect, keep your promises, meet deadlines, and be accurate and fair in your appraisal of events and activities." Effectiveness at work is all about influence, and reputation is one important key to influence.

CONCLUSION

Employees are strongly influenced by the conduct of management. That's why it's so critical that individual managers understand how employees view them and the impact managers can have on how decisions will be made in their area. It's also critical that managers understand that if they set high standards, foster good communications, and act as role models, they will have the power to create an environment that encourages employees to behave ethically. It's equally important that workers appreciate the importance of managing their relationships with the manager and their peers, and how to alert the company's senior executives to wrongdoing in the safest way possible.

MORE SHORT CASES FOR DISCUSSION

Employment Basics

You've recently been promoted to a supervisory position and are now responsible for coordinating the work of four other employees. Two of these workers are more than 20 years older than you are, and both have been with the company much longer than you. Although you've tried to be supportive of them and have gone out of your way to praise their work, whenever there is some kind of disagreement, they go to your boss with the problem. You've asked them repeatedly to come to you with whatever issues they have; they just ignore you and complain to other workers about reporting to someone your age. Design a strategy for dealing with these workers and your manager.

Managing a Diverse Workforce

After two years of sales calls and persuasion, a large, multinational petroleum company—Big Oil Ltd.—decides to sign with your employer, Secure Bank. Since Big Oil is headquartered in Saudi Arabia and most of the meetings with the client have been in the Middle East, Secure Bank's senior executive in charge of oil and oil products companies—Julie—has not attended. Although the Secure Bank employees who have met with the company have told the Big Oil executives that the lead on their account will be a woman, the news must not have registered, perhaps because of language difficulties. Today, the Big Oil reps are in Chicago to sign on the dotted line and meet with Secure Bank's senior managers, and of course, they've met with Julie. A member of the original Secure Bank sales team calls you to say that Big Oil's senior team member has told him that Julie will not work on their account, period. Because of cultural issues, Big

Oil execs are uncomfortable dealing with women from any country. As Julie's manager, what do you do?

Managing Up and Across

As an operations professional, you need to be able to interface effectively with many internal customers—from corporate managers to field representatives. One of your peers is Jessica, who is a talented operations professional but who is downright rude to her internal customers. Her attitude is so bad that people around your company ask specifically to deal with you instead of Jess. You've heard many tales about her sarcasm and her unwillingness to deliver anything other than the absolute minimum to other employees. You've thought about talking to Bruce, the manager to whom both you and Jess report—but you and everyone else knows that they're dating. In the meantime, your workload is increasing because of Jessica's reputation. How do you handle Jess and Bruce?

DISCUSSION QUESTIONS

1. Why should performance be measured as an ongoing process, and not just as a once-a-year event?

2. Should high performers be allowed to work by rules that are different from those that apply to other workers? Why or why not?

3. Imagine that you're the manager of a facility where 200 layoffs are scheduled. Design an action plan for how the layoffs would occur. How would you handle those being laid off and the survivors?

4. Are there ways in which managers can avoid harassment issues among employees who report to them? What would your strategy be?

5. Imagine that someone who reports to you is on a prescription medication that makes this employee's breath smell like alcohol. How would you handle this situation?

6. Imagine that one of your employees complained that a co-worker was harassing him or her. Also imagine that you suspect the motives of the person who is complaining to you. How would you handle this situation? Is there a way you could discern motivation, or does it matter? When would you involve your company's human resources department?

7. As a manager, how would you respond when a worker's performance has declined and you suspect a problem at home is the cause?

8. List ways you can communicate your ethical standards to your employees and to your peers.

NOTES

1. Halper, J. 1988. *Quiet desperation, the truth about successful men.* New York: Warner Books.

2. Ball,G., Treo, L., & Sims, H. P., Jr. 1994. Just and unjust punishment incidents: Influence on subordinate performance and citizenship. *Academy of Management Journal* 37: 299–332.

3. Rice, D., & Dreilinger, C. 1991. After downsizing. *Training and Development Journal,* May: 41–44.

4. Brockner, J. 1992. Managing the effects of layoffs on survivors. *California Management Review,* Winter: 9–28.

5. Labich, Kenneth. 1996. How to fire people and still sleep at night. *Fortune,* June 10, 1996: 65–71.

6. Rice & Dreilinger, After downsizing.

7. Solomon, J. 1998. Fire, flood, and now . . . sexual-harassment insurance. *Newsweek,* March 16, internet edition.

8. Greenberg, J. 1990. Employee theft as a reaction to underpayment inequity: The hidden cost of pay cuts. *Journal of Applied Psychology* 75: 561–164.

9. Leo, John. 1997. Jelly bean: The sequel. *U.S. News & World Report,* February 10, 1997: 20.

CHAPTER 7

Managing for Ethical Conduct

INTRODUCTION

Managers need simple and practical tools for managing ethical conduct. Therefore, this chapter introduces some basic management concepts that provide a foundation for understanding how to manage for ethical conduct in organizations. These principles can be applied at the department level or at the level of the entire organization. Consistent with the focus of the book, each section concludes with practical implications for managers. Underlying our recommendations to managers are several key assumptions:

1. That managers want to be ethical

2. That managers can and should work to develop their own ethical decision-making skills (see Chapters Four and Five)

3. That, based on their experience, managers will have insight into the unique ethical requirements of the job

4. That managers will want their subordinates to be ethical as well

IN BUSINESS, ETHICS IS ABOUT "BEHAVIOR"

In business, when people talk about ethics, they're talking about "behavior." In this context, ethics isn't mysterious or unusual, nor does it depend on the individual's innate goodness, religious conviction, or understanding (or lack thereof) of philosophy. People find themselves in work situations every day where they're faced with questions of right and wrong where values are in conflict. Should I hire, fire, promote, or demote this individual? Should I offer or accept a gift in this or that situation? How should I respond when my supervisor asks me to act against my own beliefs?[1]

The study of ethical behavior in business has to do with understanding the factors that influence how people behave in these situations. Although we've seen that internal factors such as individual moral development are important, ethical conduct depends, to a large extent, on such external factors as the rules of the context they're in, the reward system, what their peers are doing, what authority figures expect of them, the roles they're asked to play, and more. We're going to focus on these external factors because they're the ones that managers can influence the most. Once managers understand how management principles apply to ethical conduct, they can manage ethical behavior more proactively and effectively. On the other hand, if managers fool themselves into thinking that ethical conduct is determined exclusively by some mysterious character trait, they'll throw up their hands and walk away from situations that they could proactively manage. Or they'll think that by simply getting rid of a "bad apple," unethical conduct won't recur. This kind of thinking is a copout. Unethical behavior is rarely as simple as a "bad apple." It's often something about the work environment that allows the bad apple to behave badly. And the work environment is managers' responsibility. Top managers are responsible for the broad organizational culture (as we'll see in Chapter Nine). But, in most cases, lower-level managers can do a lot to influence the subordinates in their own departments.

Practical Advice for Managers

What are the practical implications for managers? First, think of ethics in concrete behavioral terms. Specifically, what kind of behavior are you looking for in your subordinates, and how can you create a context that will support ethical conduct? Specifying concrete goals for ethical behavior means going beyond abstract statements, such as "integrity is important around here" to more concrete statements, such as "I expect sales representatives to be absolutely honest with our customers about such things as the characteristics of our products and our ability to deliver by a certain date." Finally, it's the manager's responsibility to create a work environment that supports ethical behavior and discourages unethical behavior just as much as it's the manager's responsibility to manage for productivity. Don't just set ethical behavior goals. Follow up to make sure that they're achievable and that they're being met, and model ethical conduct yourself. Your people will pay more attention to what you do than to what you say. Take advantage of opportunities to demonstrate the ethical conduct you expect.

OUR MULTIPLE ETHICAL SELVES

To understand ethics at work, we must understand that people are socialized to accept different behavior depending on the context. Cultural anthropologists have known for years that we have multiple selves and that we behave differently depending on the situation we confront.[2] Children in our society are taught very early that it's alright to be loud and boisterous on the playground, but they must be reverent at the church, synagogue, temple, or mosque. Table manners are important when visiting, but eating with one's fingers may be acceptable at home. As adults, we play highly differentiated roles, and we assume that each social context presents different behavioral expectations. Football players are expected to tackle each other deliberately and aggressively on the playing field, a behavior that they would be arrested for on the street. Business people are expected to be aggressive against competitors but gentle with their spouses and children. Game jargon is often applied to business dealings—like the term *playing field*—which makes the business dealings less subject to moral scrutiny. One "bluffs" and conceals information in business negotiations the same way one "bluffs" in a poker game. "Bluffing" sounds a lot better than lying, and the game analogy helps to distinguish business behavior from morality in other situations. So, although we might prefer to take a single ethical self from situation to situation, reality suggests that most people are willing to accept different rules for different contexts. All of this means that we can have multiple ethical selves.

The Dennis Levine Example Dennis Levine's personal account of his 1980s insider trading activities suggests multiple ethical selves. He described himself as a good son, husband, and father, and a man who had been encouraged by his parents to "play straight." "I come from a strong, old-fashioned family . . . [my father] taught me to work hard, believe in myself, and persevere . . . as a kid I always worked."[3] Levine's wife, Laurie, had no idea that he had been secretly and illegally trading in stocks for years. In fact, the family lived in a cramped, one-bedroom apartment for nearly three years after their son was born despite Levine's huge insider trading profits. So, the fact that someone is "from a good family" or is "a family man or woman" is no guarantee of ethical behavior in the office. At the office, the manager is dealing with the "office self" who may be very different from the "family self" or the "religious self" where the expectations and norms are different.

Levine was a good son, husband, and father. But he separated his family self from his insider trading self. Why was his insider trading self allowed to exist? We can only speculate that this office self fit into an environment where peers were crossing the ethical line and not getting caught. Most important, his continuing huge profits led him into a downward spiral of unethical behavior that he found difficult to stop despite his recognition that it was illegal.

Practical Advice for Managers

So what should managers do? The ideal is to make the organizational environment one that supports ethical conduct and "integrity." Integrity is defined as that quality or state of being complete, whole, or undivided. So the ultimate goal is to bring these multiple ethical selves together—to support the idea that a business person can be equally ethical at the office and at home. But managers should pursue that goal with the practical understanding that many people find it quite possible to divide themselves into multiple ethical selves.

Begin by analyzing yourself. Get to know your own office ethical self. Is it consistent with your personal ethical self? If not, what will be required to bring the two together? Again, you're an important role model for your subordinates. If you're clearly a "whole" person of integrity, they're more likely to aspire to "wholeness" themselves.

Then, be realistic. When thinking about your subordinates, make no assumptions about ethics at work based on a person's background, religious affiliation, family life, or good deeds in the community. Instead, find out what norms and expectations guide their office selves and make sure that they support ethical behavior. You can learn a great deal simply by keeping your eyes and ears wide open. But the best way to find out how your people think about these issues is to ask them, either in person or in survey form. You may be surprised what they'll tell you. And you're sending an important symbolic message about what concerns you just by asking. Do they feel, as many surveys have suggested, that they must compromise their personal ethics to get ahead in your organization? If so, what do they think can be done about it?

Find out what influences their thoughts and behavior in ethical dilemma situations. Find out what inhibits them from being the best they can be—from doing the right thing. You can base your questions on real or hypothetical situations. Most supervisors have never bothered to ask the question. Is it any wonder then that most subordinates end up believing that their managers don't really care about ethics? Once you've had this type of discussion, it's essential that the organization follow up in ways that support ethical conduct. A number of practical ideas for how to do that follow.

REWARD SYSTEMS

People Do What's Rewarded and Avoid Doing What's Punished

Reward systems are probably the single most important formal influence on people's behavior at work. Ask any manager about reward systems, and he or she can probably recite a few basics recalled from a college psychology or management class. For example, most of us remember something about reinforcement theory—people are more likely to behave in ways that are rewarded, and they're less likely to do what's punished. That seems simple enough. But we often fail to recognize the power of these simple concepts. People in work organizations are constantly on the lookout for information about rewards and punishments—especially if this information isn't explicit. In fact, the more ambiguous the situation, the more people search for clues. They know that to be successful at work they'll have to determine what's rewarded and do those things while avoiding behaviors that are punished.

How Reward Systems Can Encourage Unethical Behavior

The Electronics Appliance Sales Example   How does this simple idea apply to the management of ethical and unethical behavior? Imagine an employee in an electronic appliance store who works on a modest salary plus commission basis. In other words, the salespeople are paid a percentage on the items they sell. The company frequently advertises specials on certain television models in the local newspaper and, of course, people come into the store asking about those models. But because of the lower profit margin on these sale items, the company also lowers the commission that sales personnel receive on these models. The higher rewards (higher commissions) come with sales of models that aren't on special. The company prefers to sell the higher-priced models but advertises the lower-priced ones to get customers into the store. The company has set sales goals for each salesperson, with higher goals for the higher-priced models. The company offers little sales training. New salespeople spend a day or so working with the store manager, and then they're pretty much on their own. The manager doesn't seem to care how sales are made—just that they are made. The manager's commissions are based on store sales.

If the salespeople value money (and their jobs), and the assumption is that they do, they'll be motivated to sell the higher-priced models. They can do this in a variety of ways. For example, they might simply point out that some of the models not on special have features that the sale models don't have. Some customers will probably listen to the advice and buy the more expensive models. As buyers listen and go along, the connection between selling higher-priced items and positive outcomes (commissions, praise) becomes stronger, and the motivation to sell more of these items grows.

But there are still probably lots of folks who insist on buying the sale models. To sell more of the higher-priced models, the salesperson might be tempted to discuss the importance of features (only available on the higher-priced models) that the customer doesn't really need. The salesperson may try this and find that a good number of people go along. There are more rewards—more money, praise from the manager—and no obvious negative outcomes. This behavior can even be justified or at least rationalized. These customers are getting features they wouldn't otherwise get, right?

Things are going so well that the salesperson might now be tempted to go a bit farther—perhaps playing with the controls to make it look as if the picture on the sale TV is a bit fuzzier than the picture on the more expensive models. That makes it even easier to sell the more expensive models.

Explained this way, the connection between rewards and unethical behavior seems pretty clear. Although no one was explicitly telling salespeople to be unethical, the opportunity was there, management set higher sales goals for higher-priced models, and rewarded the sale of these models with higher commissions. The store manager didn't seem to care how the sales got made and didn't object to the salesperson playing with the controls to deceive customers.

The goal was to sell higher-priced models. But the exclusive focus on goals frequently obscures the means to the goal—how you get there. If managers are concerned about ethical conduct, it's essential that they also focus on how the goal is being achieved. They must let their subordinates know that they're interested in means as well as ends. If individuals are rewarded for meeting goals no matter what methods are used, they're much more likely to try methods that cross over the ethical/unethical line.

Many people have told us of their experience with managers who make a statement something like the following, "I don't care how you do it, just do it."

Or, "I don't want to know how you meet the goal, just meet it." These statements are clearly giving permission to use any means necessary (ethical or unethical) to meet the goal. Managers who have uttered these words shouldn't be surprised to find that unethical behavior is often the result. Goal-setting is one of the most effective motivational methods available to managers. Set challenging and achievable goals and people will do their best to meet them. That's why responsible managers need to be clear about the importance of using only ethical means to achieve the goal.

Practical Advice for Managers About Rewards

Here's the key for managers. People do what's rewarded. And these rewards don't have to be explicit. The company in our example would probably never have dreamed of saying that it was rewarding salespersons for being unethical. In fact, they weren't doing this explicitly. But if the designers of the motivational plan had thought carefully about the plan's potential effects, they might very well have identified its fatal flaw—it focused on ends only and left it to the salespeople to figure out the means (how to accomplish the goals). Managers are more likely to identify these flaws in advance if they put themselves in their employees' shoes. Think about what an individual would be likely to do given the reward system that's in place or the one that's being recommended. What kinds of attitudes and behaviors are being rewarded explicitly or implicitly? How can you find out? Ask your staff. If you have good open communication with them, they'll tell you.

Finally, think about the goals you have set. Have you set goals for ethical conduct (e.g., honesty) as well as for bottom-line performance (e.g., number of TVs sold)? We believe in the ethical pygmalion effect. In tests of the more general pygmalion effect, researchers have found that people in school and work settings generally live up to the expectations that are set for them, whether high or low. Students and workers perform better in response to a teacher's or supervisor's high expectation. With the ethical pygmalion effect, expectations for ethical behavior are set high, and people are expected to fulfill them. This ethical pygmalion effect appeals to people's desire to do what's right. It is also likely to get people to think about how they achieve their goals, not just whether they've achieved them.

Recognize the Power of Indirect Rewards and Punishments

It's equally important to recognize that workers don't have to be individually rewarded for the message to have an impact. An extension of reinforcement theory is social learning theory.[4] According to social learning theory, people also learn from observing the rewards and punishments of others. Recall that we said that workers are constantly on the lookout for information about rewards and punishments. But they don't have to experience the reward or punishment themselves in order for these to have their reinforcing effects. If they see that others get away with lying, cheating, or stealing, they're more likely to try these behaviors themselves, especially if the behaviors are personally rewarding.

The Tailhook Example   As an example of how people learn about rewards and punishments from observing others, think about the 1992 Tailhook scandal in the U.S. Navy. According to many insiders, the type of sexual harassment (of some 90 women) that occurred in the Las Vegas Hilton had been implicitly rewarded (or at least not punished) in the Navy for some time. These harassment rituals were regular events that the male participants experienced as fun (rewarding). The Navy brass was known to turn a blind eye to reports, responding with a "boys will be boys" attitude. Investigations were torturously slow and resulted in little, if any, punishment. The reward system became well known in the Navy, and therefore the men continued to engage in "rewarding" behaviors that weren't punished.

Many (especially women) looked to the Navy's reaction to the Tailhook scandal as an opportunity to change the messages being sent about acceptable and unacceptable conduct in the Navy. Some early signs were encouraging, but the longer term results were disappointing. The Secretary of the Navy resigned his post at the outset of the scandal. Investigations of potential criminal misconduct were also launched. However, the Navy's discussions with 1,500 men resulted in only two suspects. When the Pentagon took over, 140 fliers were accused of indecent exposure, assault, or lying under oath. However, only 80 of these individuals were ever fined or even moderately disciplined. Perhaps most significant, in early 1994, the young woman who filed the first complaint, Lt. Paula Coughlin, resigned from the Navy, explaining that Tailhook "and the covert attacks on me that followed have stripped me of my ability to serve."[5] The Navy's top admiral, Frank B. Kelso, retired two months early "with a flowery note from the Defense Secretary praising him 'as a man of the highest honor and integrity.' " Lt. Coughlin left amid "rumormongering by officers trying to impugn her credibility" and with a "stack of hate mail."[6] In total, 90 women were assaulted, and none of those responsible was court-martialed or seriously disciplined.

The message to Navy men (and women) remains mixed. Yes, the event caused a lot of turmoil, perhaps enough to suggest to Navy men that assaulting their female colleagues isn't as "rewarding" as it used to be. Sexual-harassment sensitivity training is now required. The annual Tailhook convention is now a tame affair. And five admirals have now been discharged for inappropriate sexual behavior committed since Tailhook. But in 1996 *Newsweek* reported that, in the four years since Tailhook, the Navy had received more than 1,000 harassment complaints and more than 3,500 charges of indecent assault. Women still complain that they face reprisals for filing complaints. And, drunken navy carrier pilots still carry on in strip joints in Thailand.[7] As a result, it isn't clear that the Navy has cleaned up its act. Unfortunately, many women in the Navy still believe that if you report sexual assault, you may be the one to resign, not your attacker.

Managers, take note of the messages you're implicitly sending to all of your workers by what you reward and punish (or fail to punish). Employees are constantly on the lookout for these cues. They want to know what's OK and not OK in your work environment. If they observe that people advance by stepping on others, by lying to customers, and by falsifying reports, they'll be more inclined to do so themselves. So, if you become aware of unethical behavior in your group, chances are that it is being rewarded somehow. Ask yourself how the reward system might be intentionally or unintentionally rewarding the undesired behavior, and take responsibility for changing it. On the other hand, if unethical individuals are dismissed, and persons of integrity advance, the ethical lesson is also clear. Integrity is valued around here and unethical behavior won't be tolerated.

Can You Really Reward Ethical Behavior?

Reward systems assume the use of rewards and punishments. However, for years, management writers have preached that managers should use rewards whenever possible—that punishment is inherently a bad management practice. This idea, good as it sounds, may be impractical when the goal is to encourage ethical behavior and discourage unethical behavior. Relying on rewards means rewarding ethical behavior. So, let's think about how a manager might reward ethical behavior. Perhaps he or she could give awards or bonuses to those whose expense reports were honest and accurate or to those managers who didn't harass their secretaries. Ridiculous? Of course. Workers don't expect to be rewarded for behaviors that are expected of everyone—for simply doing the right thing. So in the short term it's quite difficult to reward ethical behavior.

In the long term, yes. On the other hand, if we switch to longer term thinking, there may be rewards for doing the right thing. For example, in most organizations people are aware of how one gets ahead. Do people get promoted despite ethical lapses? If so, the message is clear. If you want to get ahead around here, you have to do whatever it takes. People who make it are likely the ones who have decided to go along to get along or, worse yet, the ones who stepped on others to get ahead. Or, are those who have advanced to the highest levels known for their integrity? If so, a general message about the importance of integrity is being sent. So, rewards are a limited tool for influencing specific behaviors today or tomorrow, but they can certainly set the tone for what's expected and rewarded in the long term.

What About Punishment?

As for punishment, we all know that managers sometimes have to discipline their subordinates, just as responsible parents are expected to discipline their children. It's part of the manager's job to guide an employee who is headed down the wrong path. We also know that punishment works. If people expect their misconduct to be detected and punished, they're less likely to engage in it. So, if it works, why not use it? Well, it turns out that punishment works best when it's carried out in a particular way—when workers perceive it as fair.

If we examine the idea that punishment should be avoided, we find that it's based on old psychological research that was conducted on rats and small children. It has little to do with adults in work settings who can distinguish punishment that's fair (i.e., punishment that is deserved and fairly administered) from punishment that's unfair. Have you ever heard an adult say, "I had it coming, I deserved it"? As Dennis Levine said of his arrest and imprisonment for insider trading, "I've gained an abiding respect for the fairness of our system of justice. . . . When I broke the law, I was punished. The system works." He also said, "my former life was destroyed because I figured the odds were 1,000 to 1 against my getting caught."[8] If he had thought he would be caught and punished, the odds would have been reversed, and he may never have cut an insider trading deal. Once caught and punished, he acknowledged that the punishment was just.

Punishment should be administered fairly. Research evidence[9] suggests that punishment results in more positive outcomes (e.g., the behavior improves and the employee becomes a better corporate citizen) if the recipient perceives it to be fair. As we said in Chapter Six, these positive outcomes are linked primarily to the appropriate severity of the punishment and employee input. The punishment should "fit the crime," and it should be consistent with what others have received for similar infractions. It's also important that you give the employee an opportunity for input—to explain his or her side of the story. Also, the disciplined worker is more likely to respond positively to the punishment if you approach it in a constructive fashion and carefully explain the reasons for the punishment. Finally, if you punish, do it in private. Punishment can be a humiliating experience, and public punishment adds insult to injury.

Recognize punishment's indirect effects. However, the punished employee should not be the manager's only concern. Social learning theory suggests that other workers will be powerfully affected as well. Remember, we learn a great deal from observing the rewards and punishments of others. But if the punishment occurs in private, how will others know about it? Anyone who has worked in a real organization knows about the "grapevine," the communication network that flashes organizational news throughout a department or organization. Good managers are aware of the power of the grapevine and rely on it to transmit important information. And research has discovered that when people are aware that unethical behavior has taken place, they want the violators to be punished.[10] The idea here is that people want to believe that the workplace is "just"—that good guys are rewarded and bad guys are punished. They also want to feel that they aren't suckers who, in a sense, are being punished for following the rules when others get away with breaking them. This is an important reason why managers must discipline unethical behavior when it occurs. There must be no exceptions. High-level rule violators must be held to the same standards. By clearly disciplining all rule violators, managers not only send an unequivocal message to the violator and all observers that this behavior won't be tolerated, but they support the notion that this is a just place to work where the rules are enforced fairly and consistently.

The Thomas J. Watson, Jr.—IBM Example In _Father Son & Co.; My Life at IBM and Beyond,_ Thomas Watson, Jr. discussed the importance of swift, severe punishment for breaches of integrity and the indirect effects of punishing or not punishing. Watson said, "If a manager does something unethical, he should be fired just as surely as a factory worker. This is the wholesome use of the boss's power." But, as he explains in the following excerpt from his book, his managers didn't always follow his advice.

> On one occasion some managers in one of our plants started a chain letter involving U.S. savings bonds. The idea was that one manager would write to five other managers, and each of those would write to five more, who would each send some bonds back to the first guy and write to five more, and so on. Pretty soon they ran out of managers and got down to employees. It ended up that the employees felt pressure to join the chain letter and pay off the managers. I got a complaint about this and brought it to the attention of the head of the division. I expected him to say, at a minimum, "We've got to fire a couple of guys, I'll handle it." Instead, he simply said, "Well, it was a mistake." I couldn't convince him to fire anybody. Now, you could admire him for defending the team, but I think there is a time when integrity should take the rudder from team loyalty. All the same, I didn't pursue the matter any further, and my failure to act came back to haunt me.
>
> A couple of years later in that same division, a manager fired a low-level employee who had been stealing engineering diagrams and selling them to a competitor. Firing him would have been fine, except that the manager handled it in a brutal way. The employee in question had one thing in his life that he was proud of—his commission in the U.S. Army Reserve, where he held the rank of major. Instead of simply going to the man's house and telling him, "You swiped the drawings and we're going to fire you," the manager picked a week when the fellow was in military camp to lower the boom. Somehow the military authorities got involved as well, and the man was stripped of his commission. The humiliation caused him to become insanely angry, and for the next few years he devoted himself to making me uncomfortable. He sent pictures of Tom Watson Jr. behind bars to his senators and his congressman and to every justice of the Supreme Court. And he kept harking back to that chain letter, because he knew we had tolerated the men responsible for it. Eventually he simmered down, but the incident really taught me a lesson. After that I simply fired managers when they broke rules of integrity. I did it in perhaps a dozen cases, including a couple involving senior executives. I had to overrule a lot of people each time, who would argue that we should merely demote the man, or transfer him, or that the business would fall apart without him. But the company was invariably better off for the decision and the example.[11]

Practical Advice for Managers About Punishment

Tom Watson learned the hard way what can happen when breaches of integrity aren't disciplined swiftly and severely. Workers have long memories about incidents such as the chain letter and how management handled them. They tuck that sort of information away for later use. When the employee who stole the engineering drawings was fired in a particularly humiliating way, he was outraged. His severe and public punishment seemed particularly unfair when compared with the way others had been treated. And he reacted in ways that managers are told to expect from punished employees. He was angry at the punisher and the organization.

The important point about punishment is that adults differentiate between fair and unfair punishment. If you use punishment consistently to enforce the rules, employees will expect to be punished when they break them. However, they expect punishment that fits the crime, and that's consistent with how others have been treated. In most cases, if you impose discipline fairly, the problem behavior improves and the subordinate goes on to be a productive organizational citizen.

Finally, remember that you should be concerned about observers who pay a great deal of attention to how rule violations are handled. When the chain letter offenders weren't severely punished, an implicit message was sent to all who were aware of the scheme, and expectations were set up for how management would respond to future breaches of integrity. A "just" organization is one that punishes rule violations fairly and consistently. Workers expect managers to do this, and they're frequently morally outraged when management doesn't do its job.

"EVERYONE'S DOING IT"

People Follow Group Norms

"Everyone's doing it" is the refrain so frequently used to encourage (and rationalize or justify) unethical behavior. We've all heard it. From fraternity brothers who are expected to advise their peers about the content of exams, to college football players who accept booster money, to waiters and waitresses who don't claim all of their tip income for tax purposes, to auditors who sign off on financial statements that haven't been thoroughly checked, to insider traders who share secrets about upcoming financial deals, individuals are much more likely to engage in unethical behavior if they're convinced that others are doing it. It lets them off the hook by providing an acceptable justification and rationale for the behavior.

Rationalizing Unethical Behavior

At least two dynamics may be operating here. For some behaviors, the refrain "everyone is doing it" is used primarily as a rationalization. The employee who inflates his or her expense reports feels that it's justified first because everyone else is doing it (and getting away with it, too). This group may develop other reasons to bolster the rationalization process. For example, inflating expenses may be explained in the group as a way of compensating for the extra hours spent away from home, to pay for the drink at the bar or a movie, and other expenses that aren't deductible under the organization's travel cost reimbursement policy. These rationalizations are often explicitly or implicitly supported by the boss who suggests the behavior or who engages in it himself or herself. Either way, the manager sends a powerful message that it's okay to bend the rules, a message that can easily be generalized to other rules in the organization.

A better way to manage the process is to state the rules clearly and then enforce them. In other words, if it seems reasonable to reimburse a traveling employee for a drink at the bar, a movie, or a telephone call home, then change the rules so that these expenses can be legally reimbursed under the organization's travel policy. Then abuses of the system can be disciplined.

Pressure to Go Along

For other behaviors, the "everyone is doing it" refrain represents not just a rationalization but actual pressure to go along with the crowd. The argument is used to encourage those who are reluctant. "Aw, c'mon everybody does it!" Not going along puts the individual in the uncomfortable spot of being perceived as some sort of "goody goody" who is highly ethical but also highly unlikable, and certainly not someone who can be trusted. The result can be ostracism from the group, and most of us would rather go along than be ostracized.[12] Many individuals will go along with unethical behaviors because of the strong need they have to be accepted. If left to their own devices, they might very well follow the rules. But, in the group situation, they feel that they have no choice but to comply or at least remain silent about what others are doing.

Practical Advice for Managers

So what does this mean for the manager? Above all, you must be acutely aware of the power of group norms that may be consistent or inconsistent with the formal, written rules. They represent what's really happening in the group, and you must be in touch with this reality. Any new employee brought into a group will be quickly schooled in "the way we do things in this group" and will be expected to go along. Loyalty to the group may be the most powerful norm and one that's extremely difficult to counteract. If the group norms support ethical behavior, you have no problem, but if they don't, you face a particularly tough situation. If the group is strong and cohesive, one approach you can use is to identify the informal group leader and attempt to influence that individual, hoping she or he will influence the others. It's also important to consider the reward system. Norms often arise to support behaviors that are implicitly rewarded. If people are doing something, it's usually because they find it rewarding and the system somehow encourages it. Changes in the reward system can lead to changes in group norms.

The Slade Company Case Example   A classic Harvard Business School case explains how a highly productive manufacturing work group with a strong informal leader has created a problematic group norm for punching in and out. After the foreman leaves, all but one of the group members go home. The one person remaining behind punches out all of the other group members. The result is that group members are paid for more hours than they actually work.

On occasion, when a group member is delayed in the morning, the group punches him in. But this is carefully controlled, and the group has developed norms so that it's not abused. Although the punchout practice seems to be clearly wrong, the case is complicated by the fact that management admits that although pay is low, productivity in the group is high. Furthermore, the group is highly cohesive and very willing to work hard when necessary to fulfill last-minute orders or to solve unusual production problems. The workers also value the ability to have some control over the work day. Finally, management has known about the practice for some time and has ignored it.

The solution to the case isn't clear cut. The case writers have suggested that management might be better off leaving well enough alone. "If it ain't broke, don't fix it." However, we believe that this is impossible if the ethical dimensions of the case are brought into focus. Leaving it alone implies tacit acceptance and approval of rule breaking and sends that message not only to this work group but to all of the others as well. Other groups that, for some reason, can't manage to do the same (perhaps because of less cohesion or because their supervisor stays later) will no doubt resent the injustice. Management must also accept some responsibility for tacitly approving this over a long period of time.

Remembering that people do what's rewarded, we believe that the norm is most likely to change via adjustments in the reward system. For example, moving to a five-day salary (somewhat higher than their current average take home pay) rather than hourly pay would reward people for getting the job done rather than staying a certain number of hours on weekdays. Group members could still be paid extra for weekend overtime work when it's available. If the late-arrival norm isn't being abused, it could be institutionalized. If someone must be late, a new rule could state that he or she must inform someone in the work group by a certain time. Like absences, a certain number of late arrivals would be allowed within a specified time period. The informal group leader should be involved in devising the solution with an appeal to his or her concern for fairness to other workers in the organization.

PEOPLE FULFILL ASSIGNED ROLES

Roles are strong forces for guiding behavior, and workers are assigned roles that can powerfully influence their behavior in ethical dilemma situations. Roles can reduce a person's sense of his or her individuality by focusing attention on the role and the expectations that accompany it. It doesn't really matter who fills the role. It's the role requirements that are important. This focus on the role reduces the individual's awareness of the self as an independent individual who is personally responsible for an outcome. This psychological process is called deindividuation.[13]

So, the individual acts "in role" and does whatever is expected. This is fine when behaving "in role" means doing the right thing. But what happens when "in role" behavior involves behaving illegally or unethically? For example, some might argue that the police officers in the Rodney King beatings in Los Angeles were behaving "in role." Aggression has become a necessary part of the police officer's role in this country. Another important part of the police officer role is loyalty to other police officers and protection of one's peers. Police officers often travel in pairs and must rely on each other in difficult, life-threatening situations. Therefore, loyalty, protection, and trust within the ranks serve an important, positive purpose. But loyalty can also end up supporting unethical behavior when, for example, a fellow police officer is unnecessarily aggressive and isn't reported.

The Cagney and Lacey Example   In an old "Cagney and Lacey" television segment, Cagney and Lacey (two female police detectives) were part of a stakeout to catch one of their fellow police officers stealing heroin. They realized that they faced a complex moral dilemma when he told them that he was stealing the heroin for his mother who was dying of cancer and in severe pain. He had clearly broken the law, and the rules clearly said that they must turn him in. But loyalty and protection were important parts of their police role. Their colleague had good intentions—to help his dying mother. After much discussion and individual soul searching, they decided to protect their colleague and keep silent about what they knew. Although we may disagree about whether they made the right decision, the point here is that the peer protection and loyalty aspects of the police officer role were an important part of that decision.

The Zimbardo Prison Experiment

A powerful and widely cited social-psychological study illustrates the power of roles to influence behavior. The researchers[14] created a prison environment in the basement of the psychology building at Stanford University. Twenty-four psychologically healthy subjects (people like us) were recruited and randomly assigned to play the roles of prisoners or guards. General rules were provided regarding how to fulfill the role, but subjects were left free to interact within those general guidelines. With the cooperation of the local police, the guards were actually sent out to arrest the prisoners, book them, and transport them to their simulated cells. The prisoners were given uniforms and were referred to by identification numbers. The guards were given comfortable quarters and a recreation area. The guards wore uniforms and silvered sunglasses, and worked standard eight-hour shifts where they were given a great deal of control over the prisoners, short of physical abuse. With rare exceptions, the guards enjoyed the social power and status of the guard role. Some "guards" were exhilarated by the experience, reinforcing their guard role with aggression, threats, and insults. The "prisoners" quickly began to show dramatic signs of emotional change, including acute anxiety, helplessness, and passivity verging on complete servility. Some became severely distressed and physically ill.

Although the experiment was originally scheduled to last two weeks, it was halted after only six days. "At the end of only six days . . . it was no longer apparent to most of the subjects (or to us) where reality ended and their roles began. The majority had indeed become prisoners or guards, no longer able to clearly differentiate between role playing and the real self. There were dramatic changes in virtually every aspect of their behavior, thinking and feeling."[15]

After the experiment was concluded, guards expressed a combination of excitement and dismay at the darker side of themselves that had emerged. The simulated situation had become real very quickly, and both sides readily assumed the roles expected of them as members of their respective groups (prisoner or guard). This occurred despite the other roles these individuals may have played in their "normal" lives just days before. Finally, when individuals attempted to deviate from the role behavior, the deviation was quickly suppressed by pressure to conform expressed by other group members. The experimental results were used to support the "situational" explanation for prison behavior. In other words, perfectly normal people behaved cruelly and aggressively when placed in a role where these behaviors were either expected or allowed.

Roles at Work

But prisons aren't your average work setting. How do the results of this experiment apply to work organizations? People enter work organizations in a state of "role-readiness."[16] In this state, they're likely to engage in behaviors that are consistent with their organizationally prescribed role, even if those behaviors violate other values they hold (another example of multiple ethical selves). A particularly interesting example is provided by corporate professionals such as lawyers and physicians. Professionals are thought to adhere most closely to their professional roles. In fact, this is part of the definition of a professional. Although there's little research evidence, much anecdotal evidence suggests that many corporate physicians or lawyers identify more closely with their organizational role. For example, Johns-Manville medical personnel conformed to corporate policy and remained silent, despite the known medical dangers of asbestos exposure.[17] In their dual roles of physician and organizational member, the latter took precedence.

Conflicting Roles Can Lead to Unethical Behavior

In their jobs, people play different roles that may make competing demands on them, causing internal conflict and stress that may be resolved via unethical behavior such as lying. For example, professional nurses are taught that patient education and patient advocacy are important aspects of the nursing role. Yet these nursing role expectations may conflict with physicians' orders, or they may be difficult to implement because of time pressures and paperwork that take nurses away from patients. In a research study,[18] nurses responded to scenarios, some of which placed them in role conflict situations. Those nurses who were in role conflict situations said that they would be more likely to lie by misreporting their behavior on the patient's chart.

Managers must be aware that conflicting role demands can pressure their subordinates to be dishonest. The best way to avoid this type of dishonesty is to minimize conflicting role demands. Ask your staff to analyze their jobs and to identify sources of conflict that could cause them to feel that they have to lie to you or someone else in order to successfully accomplish some aspect of their job. Then, see if the job can be redesigned to minimize these conflicts.

Roles Can Support Ethical Behavior

Roles can also work to support ethical behavior. For example, whistleblowing (reporting the misconduct of others) is sometimes prescribed for individuals in certain jobs. This makes a difficult behavior easier to carry out. A survey of internal auditors found that whistleblowing was more likely when the auditors saw auditing as a prescribed job requirement.[19] Therefore, managers should consider the extent to which organizational roles encourage either ethical or unethical behavior. Obviously, those that support and encourage unethical behavior should be changed. Those that encourage ethical behavior (e.g., whistleblowing) should be bolstered. For example, research has found that, although reporting a peer's misconduct is a distasteful and difficult act, people are more likely to report a peer if reporting is explicitly made a part of their role via an honor code or code of conduct.[20] In other words, if their role requires them to report misconduct when they see it, they're more likely to do so. The requirement makes it easier because the behavior becomes a duty, a role responsibility rather than a voluntary ethical act.

Practical Advice for Managers

The key for managers is that roles influence behavior. Think about the roles people play in your department or organization. What are the implications of their role expectations for ethical and unethical behavior? Do some individuals experience conflicts between their roles? For example, are professionals torn between their organizational and professional roles? Or do employees experience conflicts within a role, like nurses who are supposed to play the often conflicting roles of patient advocate and subordinate to the physician? Again, the individuals who hold the jobs are probably the best source of information about their role expectations and potential conflicts. Once you've analyzed roles and role conflicts, determine whether jobs need to be altered to reduce conflict. If change isn't possible, at least you can anticipate the problems that are likely to arise for people in these jobs.

PEOPLE DO WHAT THEY'RE TOLD

In a "60 Minutes" segment aired on October 4, 1992, Americans working for a Japanese company in the United States reported that their supervisor told them to unpack machine tools manufactured in and shipped from Japan, remove the "Manufactured in Japan" label, change a few things, replace the label with a "Manufactured in the U.S." label, and recrate the machine tools for shipping. These products were then shipped as if they had been manufactured in the

United States to, of all places, the American military (where U.S. manufacture of machine tools was a requirement). An American accountant at the firm finally blew the whistle, but when the workers who had been doing the unpacking and recrating were asked why they did it, they replied that they were doing what their supervisor had told them to do. One of the men who had attempted to protest was told that he could find another job if he didn't like it. So he continued doing what he was told to do.

This is just one of many examples we could cite of workers at all levels doing what they're told by managers. Participants in the Watergate break-in in 1972 referred to their unquestioning obedience to superior orders in testimony before the Senate investigating committee, as did Nazi SS officers in war crimes trials and participants in the Iran-Contra affair.[21] Organizations (corporate, political, or military) are authority structures whose members accept the idea that, to be members in good standing, they must give up a certain amount of independence and autonomy. They expect that managers will tell them what to do. That's the managerial role. They also assume that they should do what's expected of them. That's the subordinate role. These assumptions and expectations allow organizations to avoid chaos and function in an orderly fashion. Also, individuals often feel that they owe the organization and their manager their loyalty, further reinforcing the pressure to comply.

The Milgram Experiments

Classic social-psychological studies conducted by Stanley Milgram[22] provide uncomfortable insights into how normal adults behave in authority situations. Most adults will carry out the authority figure's orders even if these orders are contrary to their personal beliefs about what's right.

In a number of laboratory experiments, Milgram paid subjects recruited from the New Haven, Connecticut, area to participate in a one-hour study on the effects of punishment on learning. The subject was asked to play the role of teacher in a learning experiment, while a second individual (a part of the research team who unbeknownst to the teacher/subject was in on the experiment) was asked to play the role of learner. The learner was strapped into a chair with an electrode attached to his or her wrist. The teacher/subject was seated at a shock generator and posed questions to the learner. Each time the learner provided an incorrect response to a question, the teacher/subject turned a dial to administer an increasingly severe shock. As the shocks intensified, the learner verbally expressed increasing discomfort, finally screaming and then going silent. During the experiments, many teacher/subjects would question the experimenter and express the desire to stop. The experimenter, dressed in a white lab coat, would say, "Although the shocks may be painful, there is no permanent tissue damage, so please go on." If the teacher/subject continued to resist, the experimenter would respond with three successive prods: "the experiment requires that you continue"; "it is absolutely essential that you continue"; "you have no choice, you must go on." If the teacher continued to resist, the experiment was finally terminated.

To the surprise of Milgram and other observers, about 60 percent of the teacher/subjects in these experiments continued to the end, obeying the authority figure's instructions despite the conflict they felt and expressed. It's not that they felt OK about what they were doing. In fact, their emotional appeals to the experimenter suggested that they very much wanted to stop. But most of them didn't. They may have felt that refusing to continue would challenge the experimenter's authority, the legitimacy of the experiment, and that they would risk embarrassing themselves.[23] They acted as if they were constrained to do as they were told by the authority figure, rather than as independent adults who could end the experiment at any time. We should also note that teacher/subjects who were at the principled level of cognitive moral development (see Chapter Five) were more likely to challenge the experimenter's authority and that they were more likely to stop giving the electric shocks.

Obedience to Authority at Work

The obedient behavior seen in the Milgram experiments is similar to behavior observed over and over again in work organizations. The notion of legitimate authority is an accepted tenet of organizational life. In 1968, American military men massacred hundreds of innocent civilians at MyLai, Vietnam. They didn't ask questions. They did what they were told to do. Twenty years later, Colonel Oliver North, who was tried for arranging the illegal sale of arms to the Nicaraguan contra forces, claimed that he was only following the order of his superiors. Individuals who testified to the U.S. Congress about price-fixing practices in the electrical industry were asked why they didn't report these practices to higher authorities. They responded that they felt they couldn't because they reported to a prescribed superior only.[24] And, Roger Boisjoly, who questioned the safety of the O-rings and who attempted to convince managers to cancel the launch of the *Challenger,* never went outside the chain of command to protest.[25]

Practical Advice for Managers

The bottom line is that managers must realize the power they hold as legitimate authority figures in work organizations. Old concepts die hard. And even today in team-oriented organizations, most people will do as they're told. Therefore, authority figures must exhibit ethical behavior, and they must send powerful signals that high ethical standards are expected of everyone. This message should begin at the top of the organization and work its way down through every level. Moreover, when unethical behavior is uncovered, the investigation must consider the explicit or implicit messages being sent by authority figures. Don't assume that the individual acted alone and without influence. Our tendency is to try to isolate the problem, find the one "culprit" (bad apple), and get on with our lives. But the culprit may have been explicitly or implicitly encouraged by a superior and this possibility should be taken into account.

RESPONSIBILITY IS DIFFUSED IN ORGANIZATIONS

In order for a relationship to exist between what people think is right and what they do, they must feel responsible for the consequences of their actions.[26] Therefore, the feeling of personal responsibility is a prerequisite for moral action. If you feel that a decision YOU made to market a particular product might hurt small children or the environment, you are much more likely to seriously consider the moral implications of the decision. But in organizations the individual often becomes disconnected from the consequences of his or her actions and doesn't feel personally responsible for them. Responsibility becomes diffused. No individual feels the need to take responsibility, so in the end no one does, and unethical behavior is more likely.

There are at least four reasons why individuals may not feel personally responsible for their organizational actions. Responsibility is diffused because it is taken away, shared with others in decision making groups, obscured by the organizational hierarchy or by psychological distance to potential victims.

"Don't Worry—We're Taking Care of Everything"

First, at work, individuals are often encouraged to turn responsibility over to those at higher levels. This is related to our earlier discussion of obedience to authority. But in this case, the individual is simply told not to worry—that the problem or decision is someone else's responsibility. For example, an individual who expresses concern about a safety or environmental problem may be told, "we appreciate your concern, but you don't need to worry about it. We're taking care of everything." This type of response absolves the subordinate of feelings of responsibility for the consequences of the organization's action. Someone, particularly someone at a higher level, has taken the responsibility.

However, even if the superiors are highly responsible and highly ethical, the act of absolving subordinates of responsibility may have significant implications for their subsequent ethical behavior. Because of the feeling that they must do as they're told by authority figures, most people feel that they have no choice but to follow superiors' orders. In this case, the orders are to hand over responsibility for decision making and the individual feels that she or he has no choice but to give it up. If this sort of response becomes routine, individuals will come to believe that it isn't their responsibility to be on the lookout for ethical violations and that they may stop bringing potential problems to the attention of superiors.

Diffusing Responsibility in Groups

Second, important organizational decisions are often made in groups. Therefore, responsibility for the decision becomes diffused among all group members. No single individual feels responsible. Diffusion of responsibility in groups is used to explain the results of classic research on the likelihood that bystanders will help a seizure victim.[27] This research suggests that when others are present, responsibility is diffused among all of the bystanders and individuals are less likely to help.

Diffusion of responsibility also operates in group decision making through processes such as "groupthink."[28] Groupthink occurs in cohesive groups where group members have a commitment to the group and a strong desire to remain a group member. A major characteristic of groupthink is the conformity of individual group members to the decision they think the majority of group members prefer. Individual group members find it very difficult to express disagreement and tend to censor themselves even if they disagree with the group decision.

One important symptom of groupthink is the group's "illusion of morality," the sense that the group simply wouldn't do anything wrong. In a classic film on groupthink, a group of managers makes a decision to market a new drug despite disturbing evidence that it may produce dangerous side effects. The illusion of morality is expressed by a group member who states that the company has a well-earned good reputation and would never do anything to hurt the customer.

Clearly, decisions with ethical overtones that are made in a group setting require special attention. The manager must make sure that the ethical implications are identified and carefully analyzed. The group leader should be careful not to state his or her preference up front because group members will tend to censor their own beliefs to conform with those of the leader. Other techniques can be used to make sure that alternative points of view are aired. For example, an individual can be appointed to the role of devil's advocate, or multiple individuals can be appointed to voice multiple alternative perspectives. It's easier for these individuals to take an alternative stance when it's their role to do so. Another alternative is to open the group to outside stakeholders who would come in to present their concerns and perspectives.

Diffusing Responsibility by Dividing Responsibility

Third, responsibility in organizations is often so divided that individuals see themselves as only a small cog in a large machine. Division of responsibility is essential for the kind of specialization required in modern jobs. But this means that organizational members essentially do their jobs with blinders on; they see only what's directly ahead of them, and no one sees (or takes responsibility for) the whole picture.

Scott Peck is a psychiatrist and author of the bestseller, *The Road Less Traveled*. He was part of a group dispatched to study the 1968 MyLai massacre in South Vietnam. At MyLai, American troops slaughtered a village of unarmed women, children, and elderly men. The killing took all morning, and only one person, an observant helicopter pilot, tried to stop it. Peck's interviews with military people revealed a bureaucratic organizational structure that allowed individuals to see only their own narrow part of the problem, thereby allowing them to avoid feelings of responsibility. When he wandered the halls of the Pentagon, questioning those involved in directing the manufacture of napalm and its transportation to Vietnam as bombs, the replies he received were something like the following: "We appreciate your problem and your concerns, but we are not the department you want. We are in ordnance. We supply the weapons, but we don't determine how they're used." Down the hall, another group suggested that the broad issues were also beyond their purview. "We simply determine how the war will be conducted—not whether it will be conducted."[29] Peck termed this process "the fragmentation of conscience." "Any group will remain inevitably potentially conscienceless and evil until such time as each and every individual holds himself or herself directly responsible for the behavior of the whole group—the organism—of which he or she is a part. We have not yet begun to arrive at that point."[30]

Research has documented the diffusion of responsibility process. In a variation on the Milgram obedience to authority experiments discussed earlier, the diffusion of responsibility was simulated by dividing the teacher's role between two people, a "transmitter" and an "executant." The transmitter would inform the executant when a shock had to be administered and at what level. The experiment found that transmitters were significantly more likely to obey than executants.[31] One can imagine that it was easier for the transmitter to rationalize his or her actions. "I didn't actually do the harm—someone else did." This rationalization should become easier and easier, the greater the distance between the individual decision maker and the actual outcome.

Diffusing Responsibility by Creating Psychological Distance

Finally, responsibility can be diffused because of the psychological distance between the decision maker and potential victims.[32] When potential victims are psychologically distant or out of sight, it's more difficult to see oneself as responsible for any negative outcomes. This was exemplified in further variations on the obedience to authority studies in which Milgram[33] varied the closeness of the learner victim to the teacher. For example, when the learner was placed in the same room with the teacher, the level of obedience dropped more than 20 percent (to 40 percent). In another variation, when the teacher was asked to physically force the learner's hand onto the shock plate, the obedience level dropped another 10 percent. In these situations, as psychological distance decreased, the teacher felt personal responsibility more strongly and was less likely to comply with the authority figure's demands to harm the learner.

This research suggests that personal responsibility for the outcomes of our organizational decisions will be less clear in situations where the potential harm is far removed. For example, when the plant is not in our community, but in Mexico or somewhere in Asia, potential negative consequences are more distant, we may feel less personal responsibility, and we may be more willing to make decisions that would harm people.

Practical Advice for Managers

People are much more likely to act ethically if they perceive themselves as responsible for the outcomes of their decisions and actions. As a manager, you can increase this perception of responsibility by making responsibility a highly relevant issue. When a subordinate brings up an ethical concern, don't take it completely off his or her hands. Or, if it becomes necessary to do so, be sure to keep the individual informed of the progress and outcome of the decision. Second, make it clear that every group member will be held personally responsible for the outcome of group decisions. Ask groups to present minority reports or recommendations so that a communication mechanism exists for those who don't agree with the group. Appoint a devil's advocate or multiple advocates to question the assumptions of the group and the group's decision.

The current movement to decrease levels in the organizational hierarchy may have a positive side benefit. With fewer levels, it should become more difficult for organizational members to rationalize their actions in such a way. Also, accountability can be enhanced by spelling out the expectations associated with specific positions in the organization and by holding individuals to those expectations. Finally, personal visits to geographically distant work sites and personal contact with customers should decrease psychological distance and increase the manager's felt responsibility for the outcomes of any decisions or actions that impact people in these locations.

CONCLUSION

You now have some important management concepts that can be applied to the management of ethical and unethical conduct. The remaining challenge is to analyze yourself (or your manager) in relation to these ideas. A common phrase used by today's managers is "walking the talk." If your intention is to be an ethical manager, here are some questions to ask yourself to see if you're "walking your ethical talk."

AM I "WALKING MY TALK?"

1. Do I talk about the ethical implications of decisions with the people who report to me and with candidates I'm interested in hiring? With my peers? With my manager?

2. Have I made it clear to the people who report to me that I don't want to be protected from bad news? Do they understand that they can tell me anything without fear of retribution? Do my reports come to me with ethical concerns?

3. Do I provide guidance on ethical decision making, and have I participated in the ethics training of those who report to me?

4. When evaluating the performance of my staff, do I consider ethical goals as well as performance and quality goals? Do I focus on the means as well as the ends in decision making and performance appraisals?

5. Do I reward ethical conduct and discipline unethical conduct?

6. Do I require my people to take responsibility for their decisions?

7. What are the informal norms in my department? If my employees were asked to list the "rules" of working for me, what would they say? Are any of these "problematic" if ethical conduct is the goal?

8. If I were to die tomorrow, would the people who report to me say that I had integrity? How would my peers describe me? And what would my manager say?

The answers to these questions should form a sound beginning for understanding and managing ethical behavior in your work group. We'll discuss the important broader issue of organizational culture in Chapter Nine.

DISCUSSION QUESTIONS

1. Have you ever been in a situation, especially a work situation, where the norms supported unethical/ethical behavior—where you felt pressured to go along? Explain.

2. Have you ever been in a situation where the rewards explicitly or implicitly supported unethical conduct (ethical conduct)? Explain.

3. Can you think of situations in which unethical behavior was dealt with appropriately (punished justly) or inappropriately? What were the reactions of others in the organization?

4. What do you think would be appropriate punishment for those found guilty of assault or indecent exposure in the Tailhook situation? Why?

5. Have you ever felt obligated to do something you felt was wrong because a person in a position of authority told you to do it?

6. Think about how you might design work to maximize workers' taking responsibility for the consequences of their actions.

7. Evaluate yourself or a manager you know using the "do you walk your talk" questions above.

CASE 7.1

Sears, Roebuck, and Co.:
The Auto Center Scandal

Sears, Roebuck, and Co. began in the late 1800s as a mail-order company that sold farm supplies and other consumer items. Its first retail store opened in the mid-1920s. Responding to changes in American society, such as the move from farms to factories and the presence of the automobile in many homes, hundreds of retail stores opened over the years. The company expanded rapidly, and eventually it diversified to include other businesses: insurance (Allstate Insurance), real estate (Coldwell Banker), securities (Dean Witter Reynolds), and credit cards (Discover). Each of these other businesses became its own division, in addition to the merchandising group which included retail stores, appliances, and auto service centers. By the early 1990s, the company was reporting earnings and revenues in the billions of dollars.[34]

Despite its long history of high earnings and its penetration into the U.S. market, Sears' retail business began to experience serious financial difficulties in the 1980s. Discount retailers such as Wal-Mart and K-Mart were pulling ahead in market share, leaving Sears lagging. Sears responded by adding non-Sears name brands and an "everyday low price" policy. But, despite these efforts, in 1990 Sears reported a 40 percent decline in earnings, with the merchandising group dropping a whopping 60 percent! Cost-cutting measures were planned, including the elimination of jobs and a focus on profits at every level.[35]

In 1991, Sears unveiled a productivity incentive plan to increase profits in its auto centers nationwide. Auto mechanics had traditionally been paid an hourly wage and were expected to meet production quotas. In 1991, the compensation plan was changed to include a commission component. Mechanics were paid a base salary plus a fixed dollar amount for meeting hourly production quotas. Auto service advisors (the counter people who take orders, consult with mechanics, and advise customers) had traditionally been paid a salary. In order to increase sales, however, commissions and product-specific sales quotas were introduced for them as well. For example, a service advisor might be given the goal of selling a certain number of front-end alignments or brake repairs during each shift.[36]

In June 1992, the California Department of Consumer Affairs accused Sears, Roebuck and Co. of violating the state's Auto Repair Act and sought to revoke the licenses of all Sears auto centers in California. The allegation resulted from an increasing number of consumer complaints and an undercover investigation of brake repairs. Other states quickly followed suit. Essentially, the charges alleged that Sears Auto Centers had been systematically misleading customers and charging them for unnecessary repairs. The California investigation attributed the problems to Sears Auto Centers' compensation system.[37]

In response to the charges, Sears CEO and Chairman Edward A. Brennan called a news conference where he denied that any fraud had occurred and he defended Sears' focus on preventive maintenance for older cars. He admitted to isolated errors, accepted personal responsibility for creating an environment where "mistakes" had occurred, and outlined the actions the company planned to take to resolve the issue. These included:

> Elimination of the incentive compensation program for service advisors
>
> Substitution of commissions based on customer satisfaction
>
> Elimination of sales quotas for specific parts and repairs
>
> Substitution of sales volume quotas

According to Brennan, "we have to have some way to measure performance."[38]

Sears also introduced "shopping audits" of its auto centers in which employees would pose as customers, and Brennan published a letter to the company's customers in *The Wall Street Journal* and *USA Today* on June 25, 1992.

Note that the compensation system for mechanics, based on number of tasks performed and parts replaced, was maintained. During the summer of 1992, Chuck Fabbri, a Sears mechanic from California, sent a letter about Sears' wage policy for mechanics to U.S. Senator Richard Bryan. He said:

> It is my understanding that Sears is attempting to convince your committee that all inspections in their auto centers are now performed by employees who are paid hourly and not on commission. This is not the case. The truth is that the majority of employees performing inspections are still on commission . . . .
>
> The Service Advisors . . . sell the repair work to the customer. . . . The repairs that they sell are not only based on their inspections, but to a larger degree based on the recommendations of mechanics who are on commission. . . .
>
> On January 1, 1991 the mechanics, installers and tire changers had their hourly wages cut to what Sears termed a fixed dollar amount, or FDA per hour which varied depending on the classification. At present the mechanic's FDA amount is $3.25 which, based on current Sears minimum production quotas, is 17% of my earnings. What this means is that for every hour of work, as defined by Sears, that I complete, I receive $3.25 plus my hourly base pay. If I do two hours worth of work in one hour I receive an additional $3.25 therefore increasing my earnings.
>
> Sears calls this type of compensation incentive pay or piecework; however, a rose by any other name is still a rose. This is commission plain and simple. The faster I get the work done the more money I make, and as intended, Sears' profits increase. It is therefore obvious to increase his earnings, a mechanic might cut corners on, or eliminate altogether, procedures required to complete the repair correction. In addition to this, since the mechanic often inspects or performs the diagnosis, he has the ideal opportunity to oversell or recommend more repair work than is needed. This would be especially tempting if it has been a slow day or week. In part greed may create this less than ethical situation, but high pressure to meet quotas by Sears' management also presents a significant contribution. I have recently been threatened with termination if my production didn't at least equal Sears' minimum quotas. I might add that prior to this new wage policy, management had only positive response to my production, and my record proves this. . . .
>
> There is no doubt in my mind that before their auto center employees were put on commission Sears enjoyed the trust of its customers. Today presents a

different story. The solution is obvious not only for Sears, but for the industry.[39]

Sears agreed to a multimillion-dollar settlement with the state of California and the 41 other states that had filed similar charges. The company was placed on three-year probation in California. It also settled a number of consumer class-action suits. In July 1992, the U.S. Congress held hearings on fraud in the auto repair industry.

The long-term impact of the scandal is unclear. Sears has now sold off its securities firm, the Discover card, most of its real estate and mortgage business, and 20 percent of Allstate Insurance. At the end of 1992, auto center sales lagged behind prior levels.[40] Also, in 1992, *Business Week* reported that employees in other areas of Sears' business such as insurance and appliance sales, were feeling the same kinds of pressures from sales quotas.[41]

Case-Based Questions

1. Identify the ethical issues involved in the case from a consequentialist and deontological perspective (refer to Chapter Four).

2. Identify the management issues involved in the case. For example, think about the case in terms of multiple ethical selves, norms, reward systems, diffu-sion of responsibility, obedience to authority. What factors contributed the most to the alleged unethical conduct on the part of service advisors, mechanics?

3. How would you evaluate Sears' response to the allegations and the changes they made? Has Sears resolved its problem? Why or why not?

4. What do you think is the potential long-term impact of the scandal on Sears' longstanding reputation for quality and service?

5. Respond to Brennan's comment that, "we have to have some way to measure performance." What can management do to prevent "overselling?" Propose a management plan (including a compensation system) that allows management to measure performance and encourages auto center employees to behave ethically.

6. Should anyone be disciplined? If so, who, and when?

7. Think more generally about Sears management's response to the firm's financial problems. How else could they have increased auto center sales without providing incentives to employees to sell specific products?

Another Short Case for Discussion

You've recently been promoted into the position of marketing manager in the communications division of your company. Your new job involves managing a staff and creating the publications and marketing materials for insurance sales professionals in three regions.

Although you have met the directors of the three regional sales forces before, you ask each one for a meeting to discuss in depth how your team can best meet their needs. Two of the sales directors were very cordial, and each explained what the technical demands of their areas are and how your department can best meet their needs.

However, during your meeting with Bill—the sales director of the third region and one of your firm's biggest money makers—he "lays down the law." He says that his area is the largest of the three regions, and it produces significantly more revenue for your company than the other two regions combined. "You and your people need to know that when I say, 'Jump,' he says, "They need to ask, 'How high?'"

In return, he says, he'll recommend you and your people for every award the company has to offer. In addition, he says he'll personally give you a monetary bonus, based on your team's performance, at the end of the year. Although you have never heard of a manager giving someone a bonus out of his own pocket, you suspect that your company would frown on such a practice.

Case-Based Questions

1. What are the ethical issues in this case?

2. What are some reasons the decision maker in this case might be inclined to go along? not go along?

3. If you were the decision maker, how would you handle the situation?

4. Would you report the conversation to your manager? Why or why not?

NOTES

1. Toffler, B. 1986. *Tough choices*. New York: John Wiley & Sons.

2. Barrett, R. A. 1984. *Culture and conduct: An excursion in anthropology*. Belmont, CA: Wadsworth.

3. Levine, D. B. 1990. The inside story of an inside trader. *Fortune*, May 21: 80–89.

4. Bandura, A. 1986. *Social foundations of thought and action: A social-cognitive theory*. Englewood Cliffs, NJ: Prentice-Hall.

5. Goodman, E. 1994. Nobody deemed accountable for Tailhook. *Centre Daily Times*, February 15: 6A.

6. Waller, D. C. 1994. Tailhook's lightning rod. *Newsweek*, February 28: 31.

7. Vistica, G. L. 1996. Anchors aweigh. *Newsweek*, February 5: 69–71.

8. Levine, D. B. 1990. The inside story of an inside trader. *Fortune*, May 21: 80–89.

9. Ball, G., Treviño, L. K., & Sims, H. P., Jr. 1994. Just and unjust punishment incidents. *Academy of Management Journal*, 37: 299–322.

10. Treviño, L. K., & Ball, G. A. 1992. The social implications of punishing unethical behavior: Observers' cognitive and affective reactions. *Journal of Management* 18: 751–768.

11. Watson, Thomas J., Jr. 1990. *Father son & co.: My life at IBM and beyond*. New York: Bantam.

12. Treviño, L. K., & Victor, B. 1992. Peer reporting of unethical behavior: A social context perspective. *Academy of Management Journal* 353: 38–64.

13. Zimbardo, P. G. 1970. The human choice: Individuation, reason, and order versus deindividuation, impulse, and chaos. In *Nebraska Symposium on Motivation, 1969*. W. J. Arnold & D. Levine, eds. Lincoln: University of Nebraska Press, 237–307.

14. Haney, C. C., Banks, & Zimbardo, P. 1973. Interpersonal dynamics in a simulated prison. *International Journal of Criminology and Penology* 1: 69–97.

15. Zimbardo, P. 1982. Pathology of imprisonment. In *Readings in social psychology: Contemporary perspectives*, 2nd ed. D. Krebs, ed. New York: Harper & Row.

16. Katz, D., & Kahn, R. 1978. *The social psychology of organizations*, 2nd ed. New York: John Wiley & Sons.

17. Brady, F. N., & Logdson, J. M. 1988. Zimbardo's "Stanford prison experiment" and the relevance of social psychology for teaching business ethics. *Journal of Business Ethics*, 7: 703–710.

    Brodeur, P. 1985. *Outrageous misconduct: The asbestos industry on trial*. New York: Pantheon.

18. Grover, S. 1992. Why professionals lie: The impact of professional role conflict on reporting accuracy. *Organizational Behavior and Human Decision Processes*

19. Miceli, M. P., & Near, J. P. 1984. The relationships among beliefs, organizational position, and whistle-blowing status: A discriminant analysis. *Academy of Management Journal* 27: 687–705.

20. Treviño, L. K., & Victor, B. 1992. Peer reporting of unethical behavior: A social context perspective. *Academy of Management Journal* 353: 38–64.

21. Kelman, H. C., & Hamilton, V. L. 1989. *Crimes of obedience*. New Haven, CT: Yale University Press.

22. Milgram, S. 1974. *Obedience to authority; An experimental view*. New York: Harper & Row.

23. Kelman & Hamilton, *Crimes of obedience*.

24. Waters, J. A. 1978. Catch 20.5: corporate morality as an organizational phenomenon. *Organizational Dynamics*, Spring: 3–19.

25. Kelman & Hamilton, *Crimes of obedience*.

26. Schwartz, S. H. 1968a. Words, deeds, and the perception of consequences and responsibility in action situations. *Journal of Personality and Social Psychology* 10: 232–242.

    Schwartz, S. H. 1968b. Awareness of consequences and the influence of moral norms on interpersonal behavior. *Sociometry* 31: 355–369.

27. Darley, J. M., & Latane, B. 1968. Bystanders' intervention in emergencies: Diffusion of responsibility. *Journal of Personality and Social Psychology* 8: 373–383.

28. Janis, I. 1982. *Group Think*, 2nd ed. Boston: Houghton Mifflin.

29. Peck, M., & Scott, M. D. 1983. *People of the lie: The hope for healing human evil*. New York: Simon & Schuster.

30. Ibid.

31. Kilham, W., & Mann, L. 1974. Level of destructive obedience as a function of transmitter and executant roles in the Milgram obedience paradigm. *Journal of Personality and Social Psychology* 29: 696–702.

32. Kelman & Hamilton, *Crimes of obedience.*

33. Milgram, S. 1974. *Obedience to authority: An experimental view.* New York: Harper & Row.

34. Santoro, M. A. 1993. *Sears auto centers.* Boston: Harvard Business School.

35. Ibid.; Kelly, K. 1992. How did Sears blow this gasket? *Business Week,* June 29: 38.

36. Santoro, *Sears auto centers.*

37. Kelly, How did Sears blow this gasket?

38. Gellene, D. 1992. New state probe of Sears could lead to suit. *Los Angeles Times,* June 12, part D: 1.

39. Hearing Before Subcommittee on Consumer of the Senate Committee on Commerce, Science, and Transportation, 102nd Congress, 2nd Sess., July 21, 1992 (Sen. Hearing 102–972), p. 83.

40. Santoro, *Sears auto centers.*

41. Flynn, J. 1992. Did Sears take other customers for a ride? *Business Week,* August 3: 24–25.

SECTION IV

ETHICS AND THE ORGANIZATION

CHAPTER 8

Ethical Problems of Organizations

INTRODUCTION

There's been increased concern in recent years over the state of business ethics. The media has responded to the public's concern about business ethics by providing more coverage of ethical lapses by organizations. With so much bad news, it's easy to wonder if any organization is doing the right thing.

Wonder no more. There are thousands of organizations that work every day to uphold ethical standards and train employees in what those standards mean. If you try to imagine the hundreds of thousands of transactions that occur every day, and then think about how many you hear about as being illegal or unethical, the proportion of wrongdoers is probably quite small. However, there are those few that do cross the line.

In this chapter, we're going to look at a series of business ethics cases within the framework of stakeholders—those individuals or groups who have a stake in what the organization does or how it performs. Many of the cases you'll read about here are well known as major business disasters. You might wonder why we're focusing on disasters instead of typical ethical issues within corporations. Here's why: if you read these cases carefully, you'll discover that many of them started as small issues until mismanagement, denial, or other more malevolent motives caused these seemingly minor situations to mushroom into huge legal, ethical, and public relations nightmares.

Some of the issues we look at in this chapter are similar to the issues we explored in Chapters Three and Six. The difference is that the stakes are much higher, and events can escalate into a debacle much faster. In addition to the business ethics nightmares, we'll also look at some of the positive programs businesses are promoting, and we'll look at some hypothetical cases that we hope will get you thinking.

MANAGING STAKEHOLDERS

Business wasn't always as complex as it is today. At the end of the nineteenth century, many of the country's largest corporations were privately held and consequently their owners had very few constituencies to answer to. The magnates and robber barons of a century ago ruled their companies with an iron hand. There were no unions or laws to protect workers, and the sporadic media attention of the era left the public largely unaware of most corporate abuses. Of course, all of that has changed.

As we've already explained in earlier chapters, modern corporations have multiple stakeholders with myriad and often conflicting interests and expectations. Few corporations today are run unilaterally by one individual, as they well might have been 100 years ago. Even in the handful of companies where an individual founder or owner has a looming presence—like Bill Gates at Microsoft—there are boards of directors, regulatory agencies, and consumer groups that dramatically influence how an organization is managed. Corporations are frequently traded on the various stock exchanges and have numerous task masters—institutional and individual—in the investor community. In addition, because individuals have invested in money market funds and the stock market in numbers unprecedented even a decade ago, the press is vigilant in its coverage of corporate misdeeds or any other factor that could influence corporate earnings.

What exactly is a stakeholder? To fully understand what a stakeholder is, we first must have some idea of what a stake is. A stake is an interest or a share in some effort or undertaking.[1] For example, any couple who has ever planned a wedding understands that there are multiple stakeholders in the grand event, including: the bride and groom, their parents and siblings, friends, business associates, extended families, and all of the vendors who are being paid to make the event happen. The couple will discover that many people feel as if they should be part of the planning process for the event. Various stakeholders will have opinions on the formality of the wedding, the food, dresses, tuxedos, music, flowers, and especially who is to be invited and how much is to be spent. There are many stakeholders in the couple's wedding plans. Similarly, in business, neighbors living near a manufacturing plant will feel as if they should have some say in new plant construction, customers will feel as if they should be consulted when a product is being redesigned, and employees will no doubt think that they should have some input when it comes to revising corporate policy.

A stake can also be a claim, or a right to something. A claim is a demand for something due or something perceived to be due. In the wedding example, the parents of the bride will have more than an interest in the marriage plans, they will surely feel as if they have the right to invite some of their relatives, friends, and business associates if they are paying for the event. In business, employees will probably feel they have a right to privacy, customers will feel that they have a right to receive quality goods and services for their money, and shareholders will feel they have a right to a healthy return on their investment because they have assumed a financial risk.

So, a stakeholder is any individual or group that has one or more stakes in an organization. In other words, a stakeholder is an individual or group that can affect or be affected by business decisions or undertakings.[2]

What do businesses owe their stakeholders? Once we have determined who the stakeholders in a situation are, how do we determine our organization's obligations to them? And if those obligations conflict, how does an organization resolve those conflicts?

Perhaps the easiest way to think about this is to divide stakeholders into primary and secondary groups.[3] Primary stakeholders are those groups or individuals with whom the organization has a formal, contractual relationship: in most cases this means customers, employees, shareholders or owners, suppliers, and perhaps even the government. Secondary stakeholders are other individuals or groups to whom the organization has obligations, but who are not formal, contractual partners. Obviously, organizations should strive to satisfy their obligations to their primary stakeholders while also trying to keep their secondary stakeholders happy. It's a difficult balancing act but a helpful exercise if companies are to be fair to the people and groups they can affect.

The cases that follow are divided into categories representing four of the major stakeholder groups in many business decisions: consumers or customers, employees, shareholders, and the community. In all the cases, more than one stakeholder group is affected; we have categorized the cases under headings that represent the stakeholder group that we feel is most affected. However, as you read through the cases, we urge you to identify all of the stakeholders in each case, and try to discern what each organization's obligations were to all of its various stakeholders.

ETHICS AND CONSUMERS

It might surprise many people to learn that there were few laws protecting consumers before the 1960s. At the turn of the last century, consumers didn't even have the right to sue a manufacturer for defective equipment. The first real consumer law took effect early in the twentieth century when, in *McPherson v. General Motors,* a consumer was given the right to sue the auto manufacturer for a defective vehicle. Until then, the only recourse for the owner of an auto was to go after the dealer who sold him or her the vehicle. Another landmark law was the Pure Food and Drug Act, which was passed in 1906 to prohibit adulteration in food and drugs.[4]

Although more consumer laws were passed in the first half of this century, consumers had to wait until the early 1960s for any real protectionist legislation that positioned consumers as a major stakeholder group. The framework of consumer protection as we know it today was constructed during the Kennedy administration. In his speech to Congress on consumers in 1962, President John F. Kennedy outlined four consumer "rights."[5] The four rights he outlined included the right to safety, the right to be heard, the right to choose, and the right to be informed. This message and the legislation that resulted laid the groundwork for today's consumer movement.

Exactly what do companies and organizations owe their customers? According to some observers, products and services should be produced and delivered according to the "due care" theory.[6] This theory stipulates that due care involves:

1. Design—products and services should meet all government regulations and specifications and be safe under all foreseeable conditions, including misuse by the consumer.

2. Materials—materials should meet government regulations and be durable enough to withstand reasonable use.

3. Production—products should be made without defects.

4. Quality control—products should be inspected regularly for quality.

5. Packaging, labeling, and warnings—products should be safely packaged, should include clear, easily understood directions for use, and should include a clear description of any hazards.

6. Notification—manufacturers should have a system in place to recall products that prove to be dangerous at some time after manufacture and distribution.

Although we've certainly alluded to some organizational responsibilities in earlier chapters, we're going to concentrate on three duties in this chapter: to respect the customer and not engage in activities that conflict with the interests of an established customer base, to produce a safe product that is free from any known defects, and to honestly advertise a product or service.

Conflicts of Interest

Although we usually think of conflicts of interest as situations involving individuals, they can also involve organizations. For example, what happens to Small Bank, a client of a larger financial institution—Big Bank—when Big Bank purchases a small company that supplies other financial institutions with computerized information? Small Bank isn't just a customer of Big Bank; it's also a competitor. Big Bank could, in theory, delay information over the wires until it has had an opportunity to act. Even if Big Bank never takes advantage of the situation, it could appear as if it could delay or manipulate information because it owns the company that supplies information to itself and to other corporations. In an industry like finance, where information is the fuel that drives the engine, it's difficult to imagine how one institution could justify owning an information company to its customers (who also are competitors). In the financial institution where this happened, the information company became a black hole, where the financial institution poured out money and resources until it finally sold the information company. Customers (competitors) could not accept the relationship between the financial institution and its subsidiary.

DISCUSSION CASE

Big Insurance Company is a large supplier of health care services that is under fire from the government to lower costs and increase efficiency. Big Insurance has an excellent reputation and is widely acknowledged as one of the best-managed companies in the country. In spite of its reputation, however, Wall Street has reacted negatively to government efforts to reform the industry as a whole, and Big Insurance's stock price has lost 30 percent of its value in the last year. To counter the effect of possible government intervention, Big Insurance has just purchased Little Company, a discount health care supplier and traditionally one of Big Insurance's feistiest competitors. Wall Street has greeted the acquisition with enthusiasm, and Big Insurance's stock price has rebounded by more than 10 percent since news of the acquisition was made public.

While this acquisition could provide Big Insurance with a foothold in tomorrow's health care industry, a real problem lies in the mission of Little Company. Little has made its reputation by providing objective health care advice to its customers. Now that it's owned by Big Insurance, customers have expressed doubts about how objective Little can be in recommending health care services if it's owned by a health care provider.

As the senior executive charged with bringing Little Company into the corporate fold, how do you proceed? What are your obligations to Big Insurance, Little, and the customers of both? What do you owe to shareholders and the financial community? Are there other stakeholders, and what do you owe to them? What provisions would you include in an ethics code for Little Company?

In Chapter Three, we defined a conflict of interest as occurring when someone could think that your judgment might be clouded because of a relationship you have. The definition is the same for organizations: if an organization's customers or other stakeholder group think that an organization's judgment is biased because of a relationship it has with another company or firm, a conflict exists. Corporate or organizational conflicts are just as risky as those that exist between individuals and should be avoided at all costs.

Product Safety

Obviously, a major ethical obligation of any organization is to produce a quality product or service. Just as obviously, nothing will put a company out of business faster than offering a product that is dangerous, poorly produced, or of inferior quality. The competition in the marketplace generally helps to ensure that goods and services will be of a quality that is acceptable to consumers. However, sometimes a company will become the victim of external sabotage (like Johnson & Johnson), and sometimes a company will make a foolhardy decision (like A.H. Robins), and the result is a product that is not safe. Let's look at a few of these classic cases:

Company: Johnson & Johnson

Industry: Pharmaceuticals

Situation: In September 1982, seven people in the Chicago area were killed when they ingested Tylenol, a painkiller produced by McNeil Labs, a division of Johnson & Johnson. The Tylenol in question was found to have been laced with cyanide, and it was not known for several weeks whether the contamination was the result of internal or external sabotage. A thorough investigation later proved that the poisonings were the result of external sabotage.

How the Company Handled It: First, the company pulled all Tylenol from shelves in the Chicago area. That was quickly followed by a nationwide recall of all Tylenol—31 million bottles with a retail value of over $100 million. Johnson & Johnson sent Mailgram messages explaining the situation and the recall to over 500,000 doctors, hospitals, and distributors of Tylenol. It also established a crisis phone line where consumers could call an 800 number to ask questions about the product. In addition, its CEO, James Burke, and other executives were accessible to the press and were interviewed by a variety of media.

Since Tylenol had captured over a third of the painkiller market before the poisoning, Johnson & Johnson decided to try to rebuild the brand and its franchise. That wasn't going to be easy since consumer fear ran high immediately after the poisoning. In one survey conducted a month after the incident, 87 percent of the respondents understood that Johnson & Johnson was not to blame for the Tylenol deaths, yet 61 percent declared they would be unlikely to buy Tylenol in the future. So even though most consumers knew the poisonings were not the fault of Johnson & Johnson, a majority wouldn't buy the product again. Johnson & Johnson tackled this problem head-on by offering coupons to entice consumers back to Tylenol and, ultimately, by redesigning Tylenol's packaging to be tamper resistant.

The Result: Johnson & Johnson's reaction to the Tylenol poisoning has been hailed as the benchmark for how organizations should react to a crisis. As we've mentioned in other chapters, Johnson & Johnson's reaction to the Tylenol crisis proved that its famous credo wasn't hollow. Its commitment to its consumers was not only the first tenet of the credo, but it was also that concern for the customer—its primary stakeholder—that drove its response to the crisis. By being accessible to the press, its executives displayed concern for the consumer by refusing to dodge responsibility or blame any other party for their difficulties.

The results of the crisis have been far reaching. The tamper-resistant packaging pioneered by Johnson & Johnson has become commonplace in a wide variety of products—from food to pharmaceuticals. Johnson & Johnson's reputation as a quality producer of pharmaceuticals and as a company that cares about its customers is still strong, more than a decade after the crisis. Its former chairman, James Burke, is renowned for his concern about ethical issues and is a sought-after speaker on a wide variety of topics related to ethics. Also, by the mid-1980s, Tylenol had regained almost all of its market share.

Comments: The background of former Johnson & Johnson CEO James Burke was critical to the company's behavior during the Tylenol crisis. Burke was a marketing man, who knew and understood the value of timely, accurate communications. Not many executives are comfortable with open communications, and their natural reticence can be enormously harmful to their organizations when a crisis strikes.[7]

Company: A. H. Robins

Industry: Pharmaceuticals

Situation: In 1970, A. H. Robins, a small, family-owned pharmaceutical company best known as the manufacturers of Chap Stick and Robitussin cough syrup, purchased ownership of the Dalkon Shield, a new intrauterine device (IUD) at the time. Interest in birth control measures had dramatically increased in the 1960s, and big profits were being made from contraceptives. This was a new market for Robins; in fact, it had no obstetrician or gynecologist on its staff. The problems with the Dalkon Shield were present from the very beginning, although A. H. Robins was initially ignorant of the time bomb it had just bought. Because it was a medical device, the Dalkon Shield wasn't required to undergo the rigorous testing the government required of new drugs. And the Dalkon Shield had had precious little testing before Robins purchased the rights to it. Robins aggressively marketed it anyway. By 1975, there were more than four million Dalkon Shields in use by women all over the world, and more than half of those were in use in the United States.

The major problem with the Dalkon Shield was the "tail" that allowed for its removal by a physician. Other IUDs had monofilament tails—the tails were one, solid piece of plastic. By contrast, the Dalkon Shield had a multifilament tail—it was made up of hundreds of pieces of plastic that proved to be an efficient breeding ground for bacteria. This tail could introduce bacteria into a woman's body, and the result could be severe sepsis that could cause massive infection, sterility, miscarriage, or death.

How the Company Handled It:

A. H. Robins stonewalled at every opportunity. Its executives falsified medical data, lost or destroyed key company files and records related to the IUD, and completely denied knowledge of the danger under oath. It finally alerted 120,000 doctors to the danger in 1975. However, it didn't recall the IUD until 1984, when it conducted a massive press campaign to encourage women to have the device removed at Robins' expense.

The Result: The results of their inaction were tragic. Fifteen women died as a result of severe pelvic inflammatory disease, and over 60,000 women suffered miscarriages. Hundreds more women gave birth to children with severe handicaps such as blindness, cerebral palsy, and mental retardation. In 1984, Robins established a fund of $615 million to deal with claims from the Dalkon Shield. Shortly thereafter, it became apparent that with hundreds of thousands of claims against the company, the fund would prove inadequate, and the company declared Chapter 11 bankruptcy in late 1985. In 1988, the company was acquired by American Home Products.[8]

Comments: Part of the tragedy in this case is that A. H. Robins began thinking about stakeholders in 1975, when it alerted physicians across the country that there was a problem with the Dalkon Shield. However, the company didn't take action to prevent harm to its primary stakeholders—the women into whom the IUDs were inserted—for another nine years! Think of how different the outcome of this case would have been if A. H. Robins had protected its consumers in the same way Johnson & Johnson had.

DISCUSSION CASE

As a brand manager at a large food manufacturer, you're positioning a new product for entry into the highly competitive snack food market. This product is low fat, low calorie, and should prove to be unusually successful, especially against the rapidly growing pretzel market. You know that one of your leading competitors is preparing to launch a similar product at about the same time. Since market research suggests that the two products will be perceived as identical, the first product to be released should gain significant market share.

A research report from a small, independent lab—Green Lab—indicates that your product causes dizziness in a small group of individuals. Green has an impressive reputation and its research has always been reliable in the past. However, the research reports from two other independent labs don't support Green's conclusion.

Your director of research assures you that any claims of adverse effects are unfounded and that the indication of dizziness is either extremely rare or the result of faulty research by Green Lab. Since your division has been losing revenue because of its emphasis on potato chips and other high-fat snack food, it desperately needs a low-fat money maker. Since you were brought into the division to turn it around, your career at the company could depend on the success of this product.

What are your alternatives? What is your obligation to consumers? Who are your other stakeholders, and what do you owe them? What is your obligation to your employer and to other employees at your company? What should your course of action be?

As we saw in Chapter Four, one of the most common faults in ethical decision making is to ignore the long-term consequences of a decision. Although most organizations try hard to produce a product or service of high quality (to stay in business, if for no other reason), many don't take the time to identify all stakeholders and think long term about the consequences of their decisions. In issues that involve product safety and possible harm to consumers, thinking long term is critical. Is this product going to harm someone? How serious is the potential harm? Even if it might harm only one person, is there a way that can be avoided? Is there a way we can warn against possible harm? What can we do to ensure this product's safety? If the product is sabotaged by angry insiders or outsiders, or if we discover problems with this product or service at a later date, how can we protect the public, consumers, and ourselves? Do we have a crisis management plan? How closely did the companies involved in the classic cases adhere to the due care theory described earlier? How can you apply the due care theory to the hypothetical case?

Advertising

The subject of ethics in advertising is a murky one, simply because there are varying opinions of exactly what truth is, and furthermore, what responsible is. Does a certain moisturizer really make skin look younger, or is it the 20-year-old model who has a young, dewy complexion? How would that moisturizer work for a 50-year-old? Do automakers and beer makers really need young women in skimpy bathing suits to sell their products? Do companies have a responsibility to respect all consumers? Are certain segments of the population fair game when it comes to the art of selling? Should we attempt to protect children from sugary cereal ads or teenagers from ads for expensive athletic shoes? How truthful, or responsible, does advertising have to be to qualify as ethical? Let's take a look at a classic case:

Company: G. Heileman Brewing Co.

Industry: Beer makers (brewers)

Situation: Although beer sales in general were off by several percentage points in 1991, one segment of the market—the malt liquor segment—was experiencing tremendous growth. Depending on the brand, malt liquors can have almost twice the alcoholic content of regular beer. Heileman's brew, PowerMaster, had an alcohol content of 5.9 percent compared to 3.5 percent for ordinary beer.

The company got into trouble when it focused on inner-city youth as a target market. The company developed commercials featuring rap musicians who glorified in song (rap) the virtues of being a PowerMaster and drinking a beer that was the "power." African-American activists like the Reverend Calvin Butts in New York City, and others, denounced the company's efforts to sell what could be a dangerous product to a group that already had serious problems with drugs and alcohol and gang-related violence.

How the Company Handled It: Pressure from African-American leaders (particularly the clergy) mounted, and their outrage was documented in a wide range of media. However, all calls to discontinue the production of PowerMaster were unheeded until the federal government got involved. The Bureau of Alcohol, Tobacco, and Firearms finally ordered Heileman to stop marketing PowerMaster. Heileman was allowed to sell its remaining inventory—about a month's supply, and the brand died shortly after that.

The Result: This advertising campaign began a wave of controversy, not only about PowerMaster, but about malt liquors in general and the appropriateness of some advertising messages. It's one thing to target a market, but it's another to prey on a vulnerable market. It would be like the liquor industry targeting recovering alcoholics in Alcoholics Anonymous. It also prompted a hard look at how companies target certain groups of consumers. Heileman no longer makes PowerMaster. It does continue to produce Colt 45, another high-alcohol malt liquor.[9] A case like this illustrates the need for companies to consider, not only all of their stakeholders, but also how their products could affect the relationship between primary and other stakeholders.

In advertising, there's a thin line between enthusiasm for a product and high-pressure sales tactics, between optimism and truth, and between focusing on a target market and perhaps tempting that market into unfortunate activities. A classic example of a company tempting consumers into unhealthy activities must be, of course, the tobacco industry. Although the hazards of smoking have been well-documented for over two decades, tobacco companies spent most of that time denying the health risks of smoking and used "benign" advertising devices such as Joe Camel to market their very dangerous products. Another example could be gambling casinos, where consumers are urged to have a good time playing roulette, blackjack, or the slot machines. Are there ethical obligations for casinos, which know that they may be tempting compulsive gamblers into a binge? Who are the stakeholders for the tobacco industry and the casino industry? Another case involves various brands of bottled water, which most consumers believe come from fresh water springs in Maine, Minnesota, or some other location with a reputation for a clean environment. Some bottlers are packaging filtered water from the municipal water supplies of several American cities despite the picture of the mountain on the label. Is it up to consumers to read labels closely, or are companies obligated to represent their products honestly on all labels and in advertisements?

Can you think of any products where outrageous claims have been made? Is it fair to appeal to the emotions of a particular market segment? Why not? Can you think of particular advertising devices or symbols that are used to appeal to a specific group of consumers? How far is "too far" in advertising?

DISCUSSION CASE

As a bottler of natural spring water, your advertising department has recently launched a campaign that emphasizes the purity of your product. The industry is highly competitive, and your organization has been badly hurt by a lengthy strike of unionized employees. The strike seriously disrupted production and distribution, and it caused your company to lose significant revenues and market share. Now that the strike is over, your company will have to struggle to recoup lost customers, and will have to pay for the increased wages and benefits called for in the new union contract. The company's financial situation is precarious to say the least.

You and the entire senior management team have high hopes for the new ad campaign, and initial consumer response has been positive. You are shocked then, when your head of operations reports to you that an angry worker has sabotaged one of your bottling plants. The worker introduced a chemical into one of the machines, which in turn contaminated 120,000 bottles of the spring water. Fortunately, the chemical is present in extremely minute amounts—no consumer could possibly suffer harm unless they drank in excess of 10 gallons of the water per day over a long period of time. Since the machine has already been sterilized, any risk of long-term exposure has been virtually eliminated. But, of course, the claims made by your new ad campaign could not be more false.

List all of the stakeholders involved in this situation. Do any stakeholder groups have more to gain or lose than others? Develop a strategy for dealing with the contamination. How much does a company's financial situation determine how ethical dilemmas are handled?

ETHICS AND EMPLOYEES

Certainly, one of the key stakeholder groups in any corporate situation should be the employees of the organization(s) involved in the case. Organizations have myriad ethical obligations to their employees. Some of these could include the right to privacy, the right not to be fired without just cause, the right to a safe workplace, the right to due process and fair treatment, the right to freedom of speech (whistleblowing), and the right to work in an environment that is free of bias.[10] We've addressed a number of these rights in other chapters. In this chapter, we're going to focus on two specific rights: a safe workplace and the right to keep a job unless just cause can be found for a firing.

Employee Safety

The most basic of employee rights is the right to work without being maimed or even killed on the job. In 1970, the Occupational Safety and Health Administration (OSHA) was created in an attempt to protect workers from hazards in the workplace. OSHA's mission is not only to protect workers against possible harm, but also to ensure that employees are informed of the hazards of their particular industry and job.

Let's look at a classic employee safety case:

Company: Johns Manville

Industry: Asbestos

Situation: For decades, asbestos was the favorite insulator in myriad construction products. Some estimate that over 3000 products contained some kind of asbestos component. Millions of homes, schools, and other buildings contained asbestos insulation; thousands of ship workers in World War II installed asbestos in battle ships and other water craft; and thousands of auto mechanics had fixed innumerable automobile brakes lined with asbestos. The danger of inhaling even minute amounts of asbestos was not publicly known until the 1970s, mainly because the incubation period for many of the asbestos-related lung diseases and cancers is anywhere from 10 to 40 years. However, by the mid-1970s tens of thousands of people who worked with asbestos were beginning to suffer from the fatal diseases we now know are characteristic of asbestos exposure.

How the Company Handled It: According to company documents, Johns Manville became aware of the adverse health effects of asbestos exposure as early as the mid-1930s. (In fact, Prudential Insurance stopped insuring asbestos workers' lives in 1928.) Although some executives were disturbed by the connection between their product and workers' illnesses, the sentiments of the stonewallers prevailed. Warning labels were not placed on asbestos packaging until 1964. In addition, company doctors lied to asbestos workers at Manville facilities and told them they had no health problems. Johns Manville executives hid scientific data; lied to the public, the government, and their employees; and kept quiet about the danger to which tens of thousands of workers were being exposed. The only stakeholder groups considered by Johns Manville during this period seem to be the senior executives and the shareholders. The company appeared to totally ignore the obligations it had to other stakeholder groups.

The Result: By 1982, more than 17,000 lawsuits had been filed against Johns Manville. That was the tip of the iceberg. Many more thousands are expected to be filed as more workers develop fatal diseases that were the result of World War II exposure. Many of these deaths are lingering ones, in which the quality of life is greatly diminished over many years. As a result of the massive litigation, Johns Manville established a fund containing hundreds of millions of dollars to settle claims. The company filed for Chapter 11 bankruptcy protection in 1982, has been reorganized, and has been renamed the Manville Corporation. The new corporation has a strong commitment to funding the costs of the claims filed against its former self, and Manville executives have voiced what appears to be a real commitment to ethics within the corporation in an effort to prevent what happened from happening again.[11]

Comments: One of the real mysteries surrounding this case is: how could so many senior executives over so many years manage to live with themselves while keeping the awful secret of asbestos-related illness? It's one thing to hide something for a few years. But to keep this devastating secret for more than 40 years, throughout many changes in management, is a staggering notion to contemplate. Bill Sells, a manager with Johns-Manville and the Manville Corporation for more than 30 years, wrote a *Harvard Business Review* article in which he analyzed what happened.[12] He contends that management was in denial. "Manville managers at every level were unwilling or unable to believe in the long-term consequences of these known hazards. . . . Had the company responded to the dangers of asbestosis and lung cancer with extensive medical research, assiduous communication, insistent warnings, and a rigorous dust-reduction program, it could have saved lives and would probably have saved the stockholders, the industry, and, for that matter, the product. . . . But Manville and the rest of the asbestos industry did almost nothing of significance—some medical studies but no follow through, safety bulletins and dust-abatement policies but no enforcement, acknowledgment of hazards but no direct warnings to downstream customers—and their collective inaction was ruinous."[13]

According to Sells, the denial was fed by the conviction that asbestos was an essential product—that the world couldn't get along without it. Managers also believed that they were doing enough because Manville's air quality standards were higher than the allowable limit set by the American Conference of Governmental Industrial Hygienists. But how did the company know whether the standard was really safe? They did little to find out. And what about the need for standards to protect those working with asbestos products such as brake shoe installers? Nothing was being done to protect them. Another factor feeding the denial was the fact that asbestos workers who were also smokers were much more likely to get sick. So, managers could blame the tobacco industry and avoid self-blame. In addition, short-term finan-cial consequences took precedence in managerial decision making. And, fi-nally, managers sent a "don't tell me what I don't want to hear" message. So, top managers may have actually been unaware of some of the prob-lems. As Sells points out, however, ju-ries convict companies based on what they "should have known,"[14] not nec-essarily what they did know.

Can you think of examples in other industries where employee safety and health are major issues? Are there health and safety issues in service (nonmanufacturing) industries? Are employers responsible for conditions such as carpal tunnel syndrome, which is a condition where the wrist is injured as a result of repeated movements like entering data into a computer? What recourse do em-ployers have in situations where the performance of a job, in itself, can cause injury? If a company discovers that its employees are at risk for in-jury, is it under any obligation to in-form the public?

Employee Downsizings

Employee downsizings or layoffs can result from many business conditions in-cluding economic depressions, the desire to consolidate operations and decrease labor costs, increased competition and unmet corporate objectives, to list just a few causes.[15] However justifiable the reason may be, the result always involves human misery. Organizations may not have an ethical obligation to keep labor forces at a specific number. They do, however, have an obligation to hire and fire responsibly. One major Fortune 500 company, with recent memories of a painful layoff, sent a directive to all of its managers when conditions began to improve in 1992. The directive stated that no unnecessary hirings were to take place. In other words, "This upturn may be temporary. Don't hire people today who we may have to lay off next year." One of the most contentious downsiz-ing cases in recent years involved a major employer in the Northeast:

Company: Scott Paper Company

Industry: Consumer paper products

Situation: In late 1993, Scott Paper had tired product lines, some extraneous business ventures, and a lagging revenue stream and stock price. Scott's board of directors wanted to breathe some life into the slumbering giant. In April 1994, Albert J. Dunlap, a self-proclaimed "Rambo in pinstripes," was named CEO of Scott Paper, and he immediately created his very own crisis to get the company moving. It was as if he lobbed a fire bomb through the doors of corporate headquarters.

How the Company Handled It: Dunlap began by quickly selling off $2 billion worth of nonessential businesses.[16] He also quickly terminated one-third of the total workforce of Scott—over 11,000 workers lost their jobs. But perhaps the most painful blow to the Philadelphia area was Dunlap's decision to move Scott's corporate headquarters out of the city where it had been founded 116 years earlier to Boca Raton, Florida—where Dunlap had a home. According to some sources, the move was prompted by Philadelphia's climate, which Dunlap didn't like.

The Result: Scott's stock price increased 146 percent in 14 months, and its profits doubled after one year of Dunlap's management. The company was sold in mid-1995 to Kimberly-Clark Corporation for $6.8 billion in stock.[17] Some stakeholders were delirious. Scott shareholders made out like bandits. Wall Street financial types did a jig. But no one was more gleeful than Dunlap, who pocketed $100 million in salary, stock profits, and other perks. Not bad for 15 months of his time.

Comments: There are many people who think of Dunlap as a hero, including Dunlap. Many others, however, think of him as the worst kind of villain, as "Chain-saw Al," as some of his detractors called him. Though painful, many people can understand why measures of that sort might be necessary to turn around a company that could no longer compete. What infuriated everyone in the Philadelphia area, however, was moving Scott's corporate headquarters because Dunlap didn't like the weather in Philadelphia. It is a very capricious reason to move an organization that was an institution in the area for over a century. Scott was not just some company. Rather, it had been an exemplary corporate citizen, providing talent and financing for local cultural and civic organizations. In addition, Dunlap's manner was arrogant, and he showed little or no sympathy either toward the long-term employees who had been axed or to the area he gutted.

Post-script: Al Dunlap went on to become CEO of Sunbeam (maker of electric blankets and outdoor grills) in 1996 after selling Scott Paper Company earlier that year. In typical Al Dunlap fashion, he quickly announced the closing or sale of two-thirds of the company's factories and the firing of half of its 12,000 employees. The stock rose and Wall Street applauded. In March of 1997, Sunbeam bought three companies: Coleman (camping equipment), First Alert (smoke alarms) and Signature Brands (Mr. Coffee). A year later it became clear to Sunbeam's board that the acquisitions had not been well managed and that the company was in financial trouble. They also discovered that the company was using "highly aggressive sales tactics and accounting practices that inflated revenues and profits."[18] In June 1998, Chainsaw Al got the ax himself.

Contrast what happened to Scott Paper with the philosophy of Lincoln Electric Company, in Cleveland, Ohio.

Company: Lincoln Electric Company[19]

Industry: Electrical Components

Situation: Lincoln Electric has had an unusual relationship with its employees since it was founded by John C. Lincoln in 1895. The company has literally been on the cutting edge of worker-friendly efforts. It was among the first companies to offer company-paid vacation in 1923; it was among the first to offer employee stock ownership plans in 1925; the first employee suggestion program was implemented in 1929; and Lincoln employees received their first Incentive Bonus in 1934. Perhaps the most controversial of its programs, however, is its Guaranteed Employment Plan. It works like this: after three years of continuous employment with Lincoln Electric, workers are guaranteed their jobs. In the early 1980s, however, the company experienced tremendous hardship. As a result of inflation, higher energy costs, and a recession in the United States, Lincoln's sales plummeted 40 percent Company managers didn't know if they would be able to keep their promise of guaranteed employment.

How the Company Handled It: The company was severely tested. However, not one Lincoln employee was laid off for lack of work. In fact, Lincoln has not laid off employees in the United States since 1948. The company's loyalty to its employees was returned in 1993, when Lincoln urged its employees to attain record levels of sales and production. Employees voluntarily postponed 614 weeks of vacation in order to meet customer demands.

Results: In 1994, Lincoln added 600 new employees and by 1995 had reached $1 billion in sales. Incentive Management is a cornerstone of Lincoln's culture. As one of the first pay-for-performance systems in the country, it is frequently a subject of research by academics and other companies. Lincoln also has an elected advisory board for direct and open communications between employees and senior managers. It was established in 1914. So loyalty at Lincoln is nothing new.

As we mentioned in Chapter Six, employees have the right to be treated fairly, without bias, and on the basis of their ability to perform a specific job. If a layoff or downsizing is necessary—if it involves one person or many—the layoff should be done with respect, dignity, and compassion. In the two cases we just outlined, what do you imagine are the key differences in philosophy? How could companies become more like Lincoln Electric? What are the pitfalls of Lincoln's approach? What are the pitfalls of Dunlap's? If you had to lay off employees, what factors would you consider in structuring a plan that would be as fair as possible to all involved?

Suppose the country experiences a recession. Should companies begin to lay off employees in order to maintain expected growth rates? to satisfy Wall Street's profit and growth expectations? What other stakeholder groups are affected? Are companies in business only to make a profit for shareholders? Are employee stakeholder groups more expendable than customer stakeholders? How can a company reconcile long-term obligations to all stakeholders with short-term financial crises?

ETHICS AND SHAREHOLDERS

Organizations also have a clear ethical obligation to shareholders and other "owners." This ethical obligation includes serving the interests of owners and trying to perform well, not only in the short term, but also over the long term. It also means not engaging in activities that could put the organization out of business and making short-term decisions that might jeopardize the company's health in the future. As Kotter and Heskett[20] say in their book, *Corporate Culture and Performance,* ". . . only when managers care about the legitimate interests of stockholders do they strive to perform well economically over time, and in a competitive industry that is only possible when they take care of their customers, and in a competitive labor market, that is only possible when they take care of those who serve customers—employees." Thus, taking care of shareholders also means ultimately taking care of other key stakeholder groups. Let's examine how a recent case involving the investment banking giant, Salomon Brothers, impacted shareholders:

Company: Salomon Brothers

Industry: Investment Banking

Situation: In December 1990, the head of Salomon's government bond trading desk, Paul Mozer, decided to test the regulatory resolve of the U.S. Treasury. Annoyed by the federal limits on the percentage of Treasury bonds any one firm could bid for in Treasury auctions—the ceiling was 35 percent—Mozer devised a plan to evade the regulation. He submitted a bid for Salomon Brothers, and he submitted an unauthorized bid in the name of one of his customers. The two bids combined represented 46 percent of the auction—a clear violation of the rules. Mozer got his bonds and repeated this maneuver in February, April, and May 1991.

How the Company Handled It: In April, Mozer described the tactic to these Salomon executives: Chairman John Gutfreund, President Thomas W. Strauss, Vice Chairman John W. Meriwether, and General Counsel Donald M. Feuerstein. These executives told Mozer to stop his scheme but did not report Mozer's activities to the Securities and Exchange Commission (SEC) at that time. (In May, Mozer rigged the bidding again.) In June, the SEC subpoenaed Salomon for its auction records. In August, Salomon finally alerted the SEC to Mozer's activities. Immediately following the disclosure to the SEC, Mozer was suspended from his job, and shortly afterward, the four Salomon executives mentioned above, as well as Salomon's outside law firm, were asked to resign from the firm by the Board of Directors. The Board named one of its own members, Warren Buffett, as interim chairman.

The Result: The publicity generated by the Salomon scandal was devastating to the firm. Its market value dropped by over one-third—$1.5 billion—in the week following the disclosure. Their debt was downgraded by various rating agencies, and major banks reevaluated Salomon's loan terms. Because of the firm's decreased liquidity, its ability to trade was dramatically reduced. In addition to the immediate financial debacle, teams of Salomon Brothers personnel left the firm. For a year after the crisis, the financial press was awash in reports of high-level Salomon employees joining other firms. The defections will no doubt damage the firm for many years. In addition, at a time when the profits of other investment banks were soaring by as much as 50 percent over previous years, Salomon's underwriting revenues were down 26 percent—a huge and humbling disparity. Their profits were off substantially, customers left, and they were barred from some kinds of transactions or were rendered ineffective because of their weakened financial position. It took years for the firm to recover.[21]

Comments: In the investment banking industry, reputation is everything. It's the yardstick by which customers evaluate quality and a firm's ability to do business. There is nothing more devastating for a financial services firm than the loss of reputation. Salomon is lucky it survived. It very well could have gone the way of E. F. Hutton and Drexel Burnham Lambert. E. F. Hutton was acquired by another financial firm after it could not survive pleading guilty to 2000 felony counts of fraud in a check-kiting case. Drexel closed its doors after charges of wrongdoing in the high-yield market effectively crippled its ability to do business. In all cases, the firms put their own interests ahead of the interests of their primary stakeholders: their customers.

DISCUSSION CASE

You work for an investment bank that provides advice to corporate clients. The deal team you work on also includes Pat, a marketing manager, and Joe, who serves as the credit manager for the team, as well as several other professionals. Just before your team is scheduled to present details of a new deal to senior management, Pat suggests to Joe that the deal would have a better chance of being approved if he withheld certain financials. "If you can't leave out this information," Pat says, "at least put a positive spin on it so they don't trash the whole deal."

The other team members agree that the deal has tremendous potential, not only for the two clients, but also for your company. The financial information Pat objects to—though disturbing at first glance—would most likely not seriously jeopardize the interest of any party involved. Joe objects and says that full disclosure is the right way to proceed, but that if all team members agree to the "positive spin," he'll go along with the decision. Team members vote and all agree to go along with Pat's suggestion—you have the last vote. What do you do?

In this hypothetical case, what is your obligation to the shareholders of your organization and to the shareholders of the two organizations that are considering a deal? Are shareholders a consideration in this case? Are customers? Are employees? Could the survival of any of the three companies be at stake in this case? In a situation like this one, how could you best protect the interests of key stakeholder groups?

ETHICS AND THE COMMUNITY

As many people have discovered, companies don't exist in a vacuum. Companies are citizens in their communities, just as individuals are, and because of their size they can have an outsized impact on the communities of which they are a part. Therefore, a major stakeholder in business must be the communities of which corporations and other organizations are a part. Perhaps the most obvious way in which a company can impact its community centers around its approach to the environment.

The public's concern with the effect of business on the environment began in earnest in 1962 with the publication of Rachel Carson's, *Silent Spring*.[22] In her book, Carson outlined the hazards of pesticides, and DDT in particular, to the environment. The public was alarmed by Carson's predictions, and that public outcry resulted in the Environmental Protection Act in 1969 and the creation of the Environmental Protection Agency in 1970. The goal of both the act and the agency is to protect the environment—air, water, earth—from the activities of businesses and individuals. Of course, the ethical obligations implicit for all of us is to think long term about the health of the planet and its environs for ourselves, our children, and other generations to follow. Let's look at some classic environmental cases:

Company: Union Carbide

Industry: Chemicals

Situation: Late in 1984, Union Carbide's plant in Bhopal, India, experienced a catastrophe unparalleled in corporate history. Forty tons of methyl isocyanate (MIC), a lethal chemical used in pesticide production, leaked from a storage tank, formed a toxic cloud, and began heading for the unsuspecting people who lived near the plant. Experts estimate that 2500 people died and more than 300,000 suffered injuries as a result of being exposed to the chemical cloud. In addition to the human casualties, there was significant damage done to the surrounding countryside and to the animals living nearby. A complicating factor in the disaster is that, although Union Carbide was the majority stockholder in the Bhopal plant, the Indian government owned 49.1 percent of the operation, and all of the workers and managers in Bhopal were Indian nationals. The links between the Indian plant and Union Carbide's U.S. headquarters were tenuous. To complicate the situation, only two international telephone lines existed between Bhopal and the rest of the world at the time of the disaster.

How the Company Handled the Crisis: Because of a dearth of accurate information about the disaster, Union Carbide had difficulty ascertaining the exact details of the accident. Even with sketchy information, however, the company's reaction was swift and compassionate, and it recognized its obligations to multiple stakeholder groups. It immediately shut down its other MIC-producing plant in West Virginia. It quickly sent medical supplies and a doctor who was an expert in dealing with the effects of the chemical to India. In addition, and even more impressive, Union Carbide's CEO, Warren Anderson, flew to India the day after the disaster to inspect the damage and lend support to the local Union Carbide management team. Anderson was arrested by Indian officials when he arrived, although he was later released. The company also sent a team of experts to Bhopal to investigate the accident.

Meanwhile, Union Carbide's communications team in Danbury, Connecticut, was gearing up an enormous effort to communicate the company's position to all its stakeholders. In the year following the accident, "press requests increased from an average of 250 per year to more than 5,000; employee bulletins increased from annual levels of 40–50 to more than 200; and employee videotapes increased from 3–5 a year to 45."[23]

The Result: Wall Street investors reacted immediately to the Bhopal disaster, and Union Carbide lost almost $900 million in market value. In addition, the company image took a beating, with 47 percent of the public be-

ing able to identify Union Carbide as the company involved in the Bhopal tragedy. The disaster turned into a five-year nightmare for Union Carbide: besides the negative publicity and a plummeting stock price, the company endured a two-year investigation, an attempted hostile takeover by GAF Corporation, a gas leak at its West Virginia facility, as well as reorganizations, recapitalizations, and major divestitures. In February 1989, Union Carbide paid total damages of $470 million and $58 million in litigation costs. After the debacle, Union Carbide is still whole and profitable, albeit, much wiser.[24]

Comments: A long-term result of the accident is hopefully an increased awareness on the part of multinationals to keep closer tabs on their foreign operations, especially those located in less-developed countries. Although Union Carbide handled the accident with incredible speed and compassion, its original mistake was to allow a foreign facility to operate with lax controls and poor links to the mother corporation.

Company: Exxon

Industry: Petroleum
Situation: In 1989, the Exxon *Valdez,* an oil tanker bound for Long Beach, California, from the Port of Valdez in Alaska, ran aground in Prince William Sound. The *Valdez* contained 52 million gallons of crude oil, 10 million gallons of which began quickly to leak into the pristine Alaskan wa-

ters. The captain of the tanker, Joseph Hazelwood, was later tested for alcohol consumption and showed an increased blood alcohol level. Although it was never proven that Hazelwood was drunk at the time of the accident, he did violate company regulations by not being on the bridge of the tanker when navigating in those waters

In addition, Aleyeska, the consortium of seven oil companies that originally established Alaska as an oil capital with the construction of the Trans Alaska pipeline, was charged with safeguarding Alaska from just such an accident and with providing immediate help should such a catastrophe occur.

How the Company Handled the Crisis: Although Exxon immediately began cleanup efforts, critical equipment was either damaged and in the process of being repaired, or not on the scene. Although CEO Lawrence Rawls did place full-page apology ads in various newspapers one week after the accident, he did not visit Alaska and was roundly criticized for that seeming insensitivity. In addition, Exxon appeared to blame everyone but itself for its problem. And Aleyeska was not much help. Like Exxon, it was unprepared for a crisis of the magnitude of the Exxon *Valdez* spill. As a result, Exxon appeared as if it dropped the ball with this oil spill. It looked as if the firm denied responsibility.

The Result: Although over 800 miles of Alaskan beaches were initially covered with oil, by 1990, 85 percent of them had been cleaned. Wildlife in the area was not so lucky—more than 30,000 birds died, as well as at least 2000 sea otters. In addition, the fish population was contaminated and may take years to recover. Exxon spent more than $2 billion on the cleanup and paid additional hundreds of millions to the city of Valdez and Alaskan fishermen. Captain Joseph Hazelwood was fired for not following the regulation about being on the bridge of the tanker.[25]

What really took a beating, however, was Exxon's image. Environmentalists publicly hammered the company, and approximately 40,000 consumers destroyed their Exxon credit cards in protest.

Comments: The difference between the personality of Exxon CEO Lawrence Rawls and Johnson & Johnson CEO James Burke could be why Exxon received such poor marks on its handling of the *Valdez* crisis. Rawls was an engineer and uncomfortable with the media. His reaction appeared slow and seemingly dispassionate, and the lemon he was handed remained a lemon. Burke knew how to make lemonade.

DISCUSSION CASE

You have just been named CEO of a small chemical refinery in the Northeast. Shortly after you assume your new position, you discover that your three predecessors have kept a horrifying secret. Your headquarters location sits atop thirty 5000-gallon tanks that have held a variety of chemicals—from simple oil to highly toxic chemicals. Although the tanks were drained over 20 years ago, there's ample evidence that the tanks themselves have begun to rust and leech sludge from the various chemicals into the ground. Because your company is located in an area that supplies water to a large city over 100 miles away, the leeching sludge could already be causing major problems. The costs involved in a cleanup are estimated to be astronomical. Because the tanks are under the four-story headquarters building, the structure will have to be demolished before cleanup can begin. Then, all 30 tanks will have to be dug up and disposed of, and all of the soil around the area cleaned.

You're frankly appalled that the last three CEOs didn't try to correct this situation when they were in charge. If the problem had been corrected 15 years ago before the building had been erected, the costs would be substantially less than they will be now. However, as frustrated as you are, you're also committed to rectifying the situation. After lengthy discussions with your technical and financial people, you decide that a cleanup can begin in two years. Obviously, the longer you wait to begin a cleanup, the riskier it becomes to the water supply. Before you begin the cleanup, it's imperative that you raise capital, and a stock offering seems to be the best way to do it. However, if you disclose news of the dump problem now, the offering will likely be jeopardized. But the prospect of holding a news conference and explaining your role in keeping the dump a secret keeps you up at night.

Who are the stakeholders in this situation? What strategy would you develop for dealing with the dump and its disclosure? Are you morally obligated to disclose the dump right away? How will Wall Street react to this news? Does your desire to correct the situation justify keeping it a secret for another two years?

Think about the due care theory presented earlier in this chapter. Can we draw parallels between due care for the consumer and due care for the environment? What if the oil tank dump mentioned in the hypothetical case was located in a foreign subsidiary of a U.S. company and the country in which it was located had no laws against such a dump? Would the CEO be under any obligation to clean it up? Should American companies uphold U.S. laws concerning the environment in non-U.S. locations? How much protection is enough?

Why Are These Ethical Issues?

These are all ethical issues because they involve obligations to primary or key stakeholder groups. Consumers, shareholders, employees, and the community are probably the major constituencies of any organization that is not operating in a vacuum. What groups are more important to a company than the people who pay to have goods made, the people who make them, the people who buy them, and the place where the goods are made? These ethical obligations all involve fairness, safety, and honesty to the four main stakeholders of most organizations.

Costs

As we've seen in the classic cases we've described in this chapter, the costs of bungling an ethical obligation to any of the four primary stakeholder groups can not only be crippling, they also can be fatal. Just as individuals who cross the line can short circuit their careers or end up fired or prosecuted, organizations pay the same kind of price: their ability to function can be severely limited, and they can even be forced out of business. At the very least, if a company's misdeeds are discovered, they will most certainly be excoriated in the press and by the public. Their reputation can suffer long-term damage that may be impossible to repair.

It's impossible to list here all of the regulatory bodies that watch over the rights of these four stakeholder groups. Certainly, as you enter a particular industry or company, you will need to know what laws apply to that sector and what regulatory bodies govern compliance. In general, federal, state, and local governments have agencies charged with protecting the rights of stakeholder groups. Regulatory bodies like the Securities and Exchange Commission, the Comptroller of the Currency, and the Federal Reserve Board guard rights of shareholders. The Food and Drug Administration, the Federal Trade Commission, and the Federal Communications Commission are federal watchdog agencies for consumer rights. Employee rights are protected by a wide range of agencies including the Equal Employment and Opportunity Commission, the Labor Board, the Occupational Safety and Health Administration, and others. Finally, the Environmental Protection Agency is the primary protector of the environment.

CONCLUSION

The cases we've described in this chapter represent a few of the more memorable business ethics cases. No industry, and really no company, has been immune from ethical problems and unethical employees. Even Johnson & Johnson has taken its licks in recent years because of alleged inflated prices for some medications prescribed for chronic medical conditions. The point of examining these cases is that truly smart managers should learn from the mistakes of others.

DISCUSSION QUESTIONS

1. What factors contributed to Johns Manville's long silence on the dangers of asbestos?
2. What role do you think the personality of a CEO plays in the handling of an ethical problem?
3. Imagine that you're the CEO of a large firm like any of the ones described in this chapter. What concrete steps would you take to restore your company's reputation?
4. How much testing is enough testing when launching a new product?
5. How can the interests of multiple stakeholders be balanced?

NOTES

1. Carroll, Archie B. 1989. *Business and society: Ethics and stakeholder management.* Cincinnati: Southwestern Publishing, pp. 55–57.

2. Freeman, R.E. 1984. *Strategic Management: A Stakeholder Approach.* Boston: Pitman.

3. Ibid.

4. Ferrell, O. C., & Fraedrich, J. 1994. *Business ethics: Ethical decision making and cases.* New York: Houghton Mifflin Co., 76.

5. Hay, R. D., Gary, E. R., & Smith, P. H. 1989. *Business & society: Perspectives on ethics & social responsibility.* Cincinnati: Southwestern Publishing Co., 288.

6. Boatright, J. R. 1993. *Ethics and the conduct of business.* Englewood Cliffs, NJ: Prentice-Hall, 332–335.

7. Donaldson, T., & Werhane, P. H. 1988. *Ethical issues in business: A philosophical approach.* Englewood Cliffs, NJ: Prentice-Hall, 89–100, 414–424.
   Hartley, R. F. 1993. *Business ethics: Violations of the public trust.* New York: John Wiley & Sons, 295–305.

8. Donaldson & Werhane, *Ethical issues in business.*

9. Hartley, *Business ethics.*

10. Carroll, *Business and society.*

11. Donaldson & Werhane, *Ethical issues in business.*

12. Sells, B. 1994. What asbestos taught me about risk. *Harvard Business Review,* March/April: 76–90.

13. Ibid., p. 76.

14. Ibid., p. 84.

15. Carroll, *Business and society.*

16. Knox, A. 1995. What will Albert Dunlap do next at Scott? *The Philadelphia Inquirer,* May 16, p. E4.

17. Gorenstein, N., & Mayer, C. 1995. Scott, Kimberly-Clark to merge. *The Philadelphia Inquirer,* July 18, p. C1.

18. Byrne, J. A. 1998. How Al Dunlap self-destructed. *Business Week,* July 6: 58–65, p. 61.

19. Lincoln Electric Company Web Site @www.lincolnelectric.com; A Century of Excellence, A Future of Innovation; and Career Opportunities.

20. Kotter, J. P. and Heskett, J. L. 1992. *Corporate culture and performance.* New York: The Free Press, 46.

21. Smith, C. W. 1993. *Ethics and markets. Restructuring Japan's financial markets.* Homewood, IL: Business One Irwin, 335–345.

22. Wood, D. J. 1994. *Business and society.* New York: HarperCollins, 664.

23. Smith, A. L. 1991. *Innovative employee communications.* Englewood Cliffs, NJ: Prentice-Hall, 41–44.

24. Hartley, *Business ethics.*

25. Ibid.

CHAPTER 9

Ethics as Organizational Culture

INTRODUCTION

"Culture" has become a common way of thinking about and describing an organization's internal world—a way of differentiating one organization's "personality" from another. In this chapter, we apply this culture concept to organizational ethics. We will propose that organizations can proactively develop an ethical organizational culture and that organizations with "ethics problems" should take a culture change approach to solving them.

A "COOKIE CUTTER" APPROACH WON'T WORK

The theme of this chapter is that a "cookie cutter" or "one size fits all" approach to developing an ethical organization simply will not work. Ethics is an integral part of the organization's overall culture. Therefore, designing an ethical organization means systematically analyzing all aspects of the organization's culture and aligning them so that they support ethical behavior and discourage unethical behavior. This kind of analysis and alignment requires a substantial and sustained effort over a long period of time and the full involvement of senior executives.

Organizations Don't Have Cookie Cutter Ethical Problems

Standard cookie cutter ethics programs are likely to be ineffective because organizations don't have cookie cutter ethical problems. Although common ethical problems exist across virtually all organizations, organizations may vary in terms of the ethical problems that are most common or important for them. For example, a growing regional bank, a manufacturer involved in downsizing, and an inner-city university probably have different ethics program needs. Forgery or embezzlement may be key ethical issues at the bank. Layoffs may be the hot

This chapter has been adapted with permission from Treviño, L.K. 1990. Developing and changing organizational ethics: A cultural approach. *Research in Organizational Change and Development,* 4:195–230.

ethical issue for the manufacturer, and research misconduct issues may be the major ethical concern at the university. Thus, each organization must identify and address the unique ethical problems that it faces.

Cookie Cutter Programs Are Superficial

Second, no matter how well-intentioned they are, cookie-cutter efforts are likely to be short lived or ineffective because they tend to be superficial, leaving deeper organizational systems unanalyzed and untouched. For example, a one-day training program that emphasizes "doing the right thing" won't have any impact if the organization's incentive system rewards unethical behavior. The reward system is still there, awaiting employees when they return to the job.

"Ethics for a Day" Breeds Cynicism

As interest in business ethics has grown, more and more consultants are offering packaged lectures and seminars. "The rule in ethics was spray and pray. Consultants sprayed some ethics over [big companies] and prayed that something happened."[1]

These spray and pray programs can breed cynicism because they raise employees' awareness of ethics problems, while simultaneously suggesting, in many cases, how little the organization is doing about them. "We had our ethics-for-a-day training program. Now we're back to doing things the way we've always done them."

Many companies employ consultants to help them design their ethics initiatives. In order for these initiatives to go beyond superficial cookie-cutter prescriptions and "spray and pray" programs, they need to be based on an in-depth analysis of the company and its current ethical culture. Many consultants provide this kind of service. But unfortunately, what firms sometimes receive is an off-the-shelf report with standard prescriptions that could apply to any firm. So, companies that are looking for advice from consultants need to scrutinize the consulting firm and its practices, making it clear that they expect a unique plan that is designed to fit their firm's needs and culture and that they're willing to pay for it.

Proactively Develop an Ethical Organizational Culture

Align Multiple Systems to Support Ethical Behavior   Rather than the cookie-cutter approach, organizations that are serious about ethics must proactively develop an ethical culture. Cultures are complex combinations of formal and informal organizational systems. To create an ethical culture, these systems must be aligned to support ethical behavior. For example, if the formal ethics code tells people that honesty is highly valued in the organization, and high-level managers routinely tell customers the truth about the company's ability to meet their needs, employees receive a consistent message about the organization's commitment to honesty. The systems are aligned. On the other hand, if the same organization regularly deceives customers in order to land a sale, the organization is out of alignment. Its code says one thing while its actions say quite another. Deceit is what the organization is really about, despite the ethics code.

Dow Corning—An Organization Out of Alignment? An organization out of alignment may be lulled into thinking that its ethical house is soundly constructed (because it has an ethics code or program, for example), only to find that the roof has been leaking and it's about to cave in. This may be what happened to Dow Corning.

Dow Corning had been recognized as a corporate ethics pioneer. It was among the first to establish an elaborate ethics program in 1976. Then-chairman John S. Ludington set up a Business Conduct Committee, comprised of six company executives each of whom devoted up to six weeks a year to the committee's work and reported directly to the Board of Directors. Two of these members were given responsibility for auditing every business operation every three years. In addition, three-hour reviews were held with up to 35 employees who were encouraged to raise ethical issues. The results of these audits were reported to the Audit and Social Responsibility Committee of the Board of Directors. John Swanson, manager of Corporate Internal and Management Communication, headed this effort and was quoted as saying that the audit approach, "makes it virtually impossible for employees to consciously make an unethical decision."[2]

This impressive program failed to help the organization avoid its problem with breast implant safety, however, despite documented warnings from a company engineer in 1976 that suggested that the implants could rupture and cause severe medical problems. It isn't entirely clear why this well-intentioned ethics program failed. It's likely that, although it was designed to cultivate an overall environment of ethical conduct, aspects of the ethical culture were out of alignment—giving employees different messages.[3] "Layering in a bureaucracy is no substitute for a true corporate culture. Workers have a genius for discovering the real reason for a system and learn quickly how to satisfy its minimum requirements."[4] The system relied on managers to identify the key ethical issues covered by the auditors. Were these managers likely to alert the auditors to their most severe ethical problems? What would the consequences be? The system also relied on periodic planned audits. Did commitment to ethics peak during the planned audit sessions, only to disappear into the woodwork after the auditors left?[5]

Audit of the Ethical Culture The only way to determine if the culture is aligned to support ethical behavior is to conduct a comprehensive audit of all relevant aspects of the ethical culture. This chapter provides guidelines for how to conduct such an audit. If the ethics audit determines that aspects of the current culture do not support ethical behavior, and the goal is to produce an ethical organization, then the culture must change.

ORGANIZATIONAL ETHICS AS A CULTURAL PHENOMENON

What Is Culture?

Anthropologists define culture as a body of learned beliefs, traditions, and guides for behavior shared among members of a society or a group.[6] This idea of culture has been found to be particularly useful for understanding work organizations and the behavior of people in them.[7] The organizational culture expresses shared assumptions, values and beliefs and is the social glue that holds the organization together.[8] Organizational culture is manifested in many ways, including norms, physical settings, modes of dress, special language, myths, rituals, heroes, and stories.[9]

Organizational cultures can vary widely, even within the same industry. For example, IBM has been known for its formal culture, exemplified for a long time by a dress code that mandated dark suits, white shirts, and polished shoes. Apple Computer, on the other hand, was known for its informality. Particularly in its early days, tee shirts, jeans, and tennis shoes were the expected Apple "costume." According to *Fortune* magazine, "IBM is the sensible, wingtip, Armonk, New York, computer company, not part of that sneaker-wearing, tofu-eating Silicon Valley crowd."[10]

Strong versus Weak Cultures

Organizational cultures can be strong or weak.[11] In a strong culture, standards and guidelines are known and shared by all, providing common direction for day-to-day behavior. Citicorp's culture was so strong in the 1980s that when Katherine Nelson traveled to Citicorp offices in the Far East to deliver ethics training, she felt right at home (despite huge differences in national culture). "You could tell that you were in a Citicorp facility," she said, "whether you were in London, Tokyo, or New York." Kate facilitated an ethics training session for Japanese managers. She presented them with a common ethical dilemma—what do you do if you have raised an important ethical issue with your manager and nothing is done? In fact, the manager discourages you from pursuing the issue. The potential answers included do nothing, go around the manager to the next level, raise the issue in writing to the manager, or take the issue to a staff department such as Human Resources.

The Japanese managers unanimously gave the "correct" answer according to Citicorp's culture and policies. They said that they would go around their manager and take the issue to the next level. Kate was shocked at their response, thinking that it conflicted with the wider Japanese culture's attention to authority, seniority, and honor. So, she asked these managers, "Doesn't this conflict with Japanese culture?" To which, they responded, "You forget—we are much more Citicorp than we are Japanese." Citicorp's culture proved to be so strong that standards and guidelines spanned continents and superseded national culture. This experience has since been verified by some of our international students who worked for U.S.-based multinationals before returning to school for the MBA degree. For example, one student worked for Baxter Healthcare in a country known for corruption and bribery. Baxter's strong ethical culture clearly didn't allow such conduct, and employees were proud to be a part of such an organization.

In a weak organizational culture, subgroup norms are more influential than cultural norms. As a result, subcultures within divisions or departments are more likely to guide behavior. Many large public universities can be thought of as having weak cultures. Departmental subcultures are often stronger than the overall university culture, with the romance languages department operating very differently from the accounting department, for example. Among students at a large state university, the fraternity/sorority subculture coexists with the political activist subculture, the devout Christian subculture, the jock subculture, and many other subcultures, and behavior is quite different within each. It's important to note that weak doesn't necessarily mean "bad." In some situations, strong subcultures are desirable. They allow for diversity of thought and action. However, in a weak culture, behavioral consistency is difficult, if not impossible to achieve.

Norms—"The Way We Do Things Around Here"

Norms are rules or standards of behavior that are accepted as appropriate by members of a group. They exert a powerful influence on individual behavior in organizations, and they can serve to support ethical or unethical conduct. For example, imagine an individual entering a sales job who is told immediately that customers should always be dealt with honestly because long-term customer relations are important. Here, the norm supports ethical conduct—honesty. On the other hand, consider the individual who begins a new job and is told by his or her boss that making the sale is all that counts. This norm supports unethical conduct. Either kind of norm (ethical or unethical) can become "the way we do things around here." In a strong culture, norms are consistent across the organization. But in a weak culture, subculture norms become more important.

Socialization versus Internalization

Employees are brought into and are taught the organization's culture through a process called enculturation or socialization.[12] Through socialization, employees learn the prevailing norms—they learn "the ropes." Socialization can occur through formal training or mentoring, or through more informal transmission of norms by peers and superiors. When effectively socialized, employees behave in ways that are consistent with cultural norms. They know how to dress, what to say, and what to do.

With socialization, people behave in ways that are consistent with the culture because they feel that they are expected to do so. Their behavior may have nothing to do with their personal beliefs, but they behave as they are expected to behave in order to fit into the context and to be approved by people they care about.[13] An IBM employee whose personal preference is to work in jeans and a sweat shirt will nevertheless dress appropriately according to the more formal IBM culture because of socialization. Similarly, individuals who don't personally believe in giving kickbacks—but are taught that it's the organizational norm—feel that if they don't go along they'll risk disapproval or they won't fit in. Those who conform to expectations are retained and promoted. Those who don't fit into the culture are likely to leave voluntarily. Obviously, socialization can support either ethical or unethical behavior.

Individuals may behave according to the culture for another reason—because they have internalized the norms. With internalization, individuals behave according to the norms because they have adopted the external cultural standards as their own. Their behavior, though consistent with the culture, also accords with their own beliefs about what's right. For example, an individual who prefers formal dress fits in with IBM's cultural expectations about attire. The standards are internalized and are therefore easily followed.

Organizational culture is created and maintained through a complex interplay of formal and informal organizational systems. Formally, leadership, structure, selection systems, orientation and training programs, rules, policies, reward systems, and decision-making processes all contribute to culture creation and maintenance. Informally, the culture's norms, heroes, rituals, stories, and language keep the culture alive and indicate to both insiders and outsiders whether the formal systems represent fact or facade. The next section will describe and provide examples of each of these important ethics culture components.

FORMAL CULTURAL SYSTEMS

Leadership

Leaders Create Culture   Leadership is a critical component of the organization's culture because leaders can create, maintain, or change culture.[14] The founder of a new organization is thought to play a particularly important culture-creating role.[15] Often, the founder has a vision for what the new organization should be. He or she may personify the culture's values, providing a role model for others to observe and follow, and guiding decision making at all organizational levels. For example, Thomas Jefferson founded the University of Virginia. Although he's long gone, it's said today that when the governing board of the university is faced with a difficult decision, they're still guided by "what Mr. Jefferson would do."

The same has been said of Walt Disney. The question, "What would Walt do," has been asked for many years since Disney's death. Walt Disney's moral influence is represented in the introduction to the company's code of ethics. "Walt Disney believed that the right kind of entertainment would appeal to all people . . . .Walt believed that our audience would accept, above anything else, quality and good taste in entertainment. Time and time again throughout his career, he virtually bet his entire organization on this belief . . . often in the face of skepticism and predicted failure by others. His philosophy rejected gimmicks and the fast buck, embracing instead a different and vastly more difficult philosophy . . . to produce a quality family entertainment product. This philosophy has brought to the name "Disney" a hard-earned public trust unparalleled anywhere else in the entertainment business."[16]

Interestingly, Disney's reputation for producing quality family entertainment drives public expectations of the company, creating tough issues for an increasingly diversified company. For example, religious groups in the United States have protested Disney's provision of partner benefits for its gay employees, its toleration of "gay days" at theme parks, and the company's 1997 decision to support the "coming out" of the lesbian main character on ABC's "Ellen" sitcom. (Disney now owns ABC.)

Leaders Maintain or Change Culture   Current leaders can also influence culture in a number of ways.[17] They can help to maintain the current culture, or they can change it by articulating a vision, by paying attention to, measuring, and controlling certain things, by making critical policy decisions, by recruiting and hiring personnel who fit their vision of the organization, and by holding people accountable for their actions.

Jack Welch, CEO of GE since 1981, is held up as an example of a leader who has changed the staid bureaucratic culture of GE into a lean and highly competitive organization. Welch began the culture change effort by clearly articulating his vision that the new GE would be number one or number two in the world in each of its businesses. Businesses that could not measure up would be sold.

Traditional GE employees had been attracted to the job security of the old GE. But Welch wanted to encourage competitiveness, risk taking, creativity, self-confidence, and dynamism. He recruited managers who were interested in doing a great job and then moving on, if GE no longer needed them. Many of the old-line GE employees found themselves out of sync and out of a job.

Welch also focused on identifying and eliminating unproductive work in the organization. He told managers to eliminate reports, reviews and forecasts, to speed decision cycles, and to move information more quickly through the organization by eliminating unnecessary bureaucratic layers. All of this has contributed to the "leaner and meaner" GE culture he created.

Leadership and Ethical Culture   Leadership may be the single most important component of an organization's ethical culture, as integrity (or the lack of it) flows from the top down. Employees watch what leaders do, and they make sense of the organization's culture based on leaders' communications and, most importantly, their actions. According to a report from the Business Roundtable, a group of senior executives from major American corporations, "to achieve results, the Chief Executive Officer and those around the CEO need to be openly and strongly committed to ethical conduct, and give constant leadership in tending and renewing the values of the organization."[18]

This view was echoed by Vin Sarni, former CEO of PPG Industries, a large multinational firm, in a speech to Penn State business school students. Sarni said that the title CEO stands for chief ethics officer, a statement that recognizes how important it is for the organization's leader to set the firm's ethical standards. As CEO, Sarni eschewed the use of special staff departments to investigate ethical complaints. Rather, he personally headed the firm's ethics committee, comprised of line officers, the organization's leaders. The symbolic message was clear. Ethical problems are important enough to be handled by leaders at the highest organizational levels.

Research has found that ethical leadership is important to employees. In a recent study, employees were more committed to their organizations, and unethical behavior was lower in organizations that had an ethical culture characterized by top executives who represented high ethical standards, regularly showed that they care about ethics, and were models of ethical behavior.[19] According to Carl Skooglund, vice president and ethics director at Texas Instruments,

> Leadership makes all the difference in the world because the leaders' actions come across very clearly to people in the organization. Even more important, the leader's actions tend to be reflected all the way down the line. If the order of the day is to make the forecast at all costs, that message is going to filter down. . . . I've seen leaders who said that personal integrity was the most important thing. And I don't doubt for a minute that they meant what they said. But at the same time, they put incredible pressure for performance on their organization, to the point that you could be publicly slaughtered if you weren't meeting an objective. Pressure to make the goals, that's what counted. But, at the same time, the leaders were saying and believed that personal integrity, doing it right, was the most important thing. Hey gang, you can't have it both ways—performance at all costs AND personal integrity.
>
> So, leaders have to be perfectly clear about their expectations. Leaders . . . also have to continually stress their concern over the means that are used to attain the ends. I heard one person say 'reward noble failure.' If someone has made an effort and for whatever reason it didn't work, or maybe they had to walk away from a profit opportunity because it didn't taste or sound or feel right— recognize that effort. It sends a good signal.

Kent Druyvesteyn, former staff vice president, ethics, General Dynamics Corporation, made a similar point about leaders as ethical role models. "People in leadership need to . . . set the tone by the example of their own conduct. We could have had all the workshops in the world. We could have even had Jesus and Moses and Mohammed and Buddha come and speak at our workshops. But, if after all of that, someone in a leadership position then behaved in a way which was contrary to the standards, that instance of misconduct by a person in a leadership position would teach more than all the experts in the world."

Similar to business leaders, coaches of college sports are expected to set and enforce ethical standards. Joe Paterno, the legendary Penn State football coach, and Dean Smith, former coach of the University of North Carolina basketball team, are coaches who are held up as examples of positive ethical leadership. They set high expectations (for performance and ethics), create rules and policies, and enforce them.[20]

Coaches are also held responsible when ethical violations are discovered among players, assistants, and boosters. A number of coaches have lost their jobs or have resigned because of these violations.[21] When wrongdoing occurs in any type of organization, top managers are frequently held accountable even if they weren't personally involved. For example, the chairman of Dow Corning was quickly replaced as a result of the controversy over breast implant safety in 1992.

Robert D. Haas is the 50-something chairman and chief executive of Levi Strauss, the maker of Levi's jeans, Dockers, and other casual clothing. He is also the great-great grand nephew of the company's founder, Levi Strauss. Since its founding in 1850, the company has been known for its extraordinary commercial success as well as its commitment to high ethical standards and social responsibility. Haas is following in a long company tradition with what he dubs "responsible commercial success"—combining profit making with making the world a better place. When he took over as CEO in 1984 (after stints as a Peace Corps volunteer, a White House fellow, and a McKinsey consultant), the company had become bureaucratic and bloated. Haas took the company private through a $2 billion leveraged buyout of nonfamily stockholders. When announcing the buyout, Haas not only discussed its financial benefits but also claimed that the buyout would allow management to "focus attention on long-term interests [and] would be the most appropriate way to ensure that the company continues to respect and implement its important values and traditions."[22] This chairman "guru" is known within and outside the company for his efforts to promote diversity, openness, empowerment, and ethical management practices. "He won't tolerate harassment of any kind. He won't do business with suppliers who violate Levi's strict standards regarding work environment and ethics. A set of corporate 'aspirations,' written by top management, is to guide all major decisions."[20] Some have asked if the company would behave differently if it were publicly traded. Haas replies, "It would take a lot more fortitude on the part of Levi's executives," but he insists that "it's a matter of leadership."[23]

Another example of ethical leadership is Monsanto's CEO, Robert Shapiro. Monsanto is a huge company that sold $9.3 billion worth of goods and services in 1996. According to *Fortune* magazine, Shapiro "is betting billions" to transform Monsanto into a "biotech powerhouse capable of helping feed the planet's exploding population at the same time it heals a damaged environment." He has committed the company to what scientists call "sustainable development." Shapiro argues that, by providing planet-friendly products, the company can "do good for people, the planet, and his shareholders." The long-term goal is "to transform Monsanto into a 'life sciences' enterprise, devoted to improving human health by seeking synergies in biotech, pharmaceutical research, and food products." At a three-day company offsite in a Chicago hotel, an employee, taken with Shapiro's vision, walked up to him and said, "I want you to know I am with you. As a pledge of loyalty, I'd like to give you this." She removed her nametag from around her neck and placed it around his. Others followed her lead, and by the end of the evening, Shapiro was wearing over 100 nametags. Today, he keeps the nametags in his office, "enshrined atop a glass-enclosed wooden pedestal." He says they symbolize "something I want so deeply and I care so much about."[24]

Unfortunately, leaders have as much influence on the development of an unethical culture. if the organization's leaders seem to care only about short-term financial results, employees quickly get that message and act accordingly. In 1995, *Business Week* conducted interviews with 50 current and former executives of Bausch & Lomb (B&L), the optical products company. According to the report, B&L's CEO, Daniel Gill, held tenaciously to double-digit annual growth goals, and he pressured managers to achieve results, accepting no excuses for failure. Managers learned to cut corners and used tactics that were costly for the company in the long run but produced short-term sales for which they were rewarded handsomely. For example, beginning in 1989, in an attempt to compete with Johnson & Johnson's disposable lenses, the contact-lens division took the Optima lens which it had been selling since the 1970s (for about $70), repackaged and relabeled it, and sold the exact same lens as a frequent-replacement brand (for $7.50). When consumers discovered the deception, they were irate and filed a class action lawsuit. Then, in December 1993, U.S. distributors were coerced into taking large stocks of old Optima contact lenses so that the B&L manager could book an extra $23 million in year end sales. When almost all of the lenses were returned in 1994, the Securities and Exchange Commission decided to investigate the company for accounting irregularities. In 1994, after 12 years of double-digit growth, earnings fell 54 percent. The SEC investigation sparked changes to more conservative management practices, but observers are waiting to see how deep the changes go and how long they will last. The CEO took little personal responsibility for the problems. In a video sent to remote locations to discuss 1994's disastrous financial results, Gill blamed individual division presidents for the company's problems. One executive said, "it was like slapping the hands of children when they were really acting on Daddy's orders."[25]

Most top managers are neither ethical nor unethical leaders. They fall into an ethically "neutral" category. This is probably because they don't realize how important they are to the organization's ethical culture, so they simply don't provide leadership in this crucial area. They don't set ethical goals. They don't talk about the importance of ethical business practices. They also don't tell employees to meet business goals at any price. There is simply no ethics message. But silence is a message. In the context of all the other messages being sent in a highly competitive business environment, employees are likely to interpret silence to mean that the leaders really don't care how business goals are met, and they'll act on that message.

Selection Systems

Organizations can avoid many ethical problems by recruiting the right people to join the organization and by building a reputation that precedes the organization's representatives wherever they go. Although there are no fool-proof integrity tests available, companies can certainly let prospective employees know about the importance of integrity in their organization. Coach Joe Paterno was outspoken on this topic in our interview with him. He claimed that the Penn State football program avoids lots of problems faced by other college sports organizations by being absolutely clear up front about its commitment to education for its athletes and to doing things "by the [NCAA] book," as he shows in the following quote.

> I think our reputation eliminates most problems before we start. Because we do have a reputation. If a kid is looking for some kind of a deal, he generally won't fool around with us. But, I remember one kid whose Dad openly said, "He can't live on that. He's gotta have more money than that." I said, "That's all we can do." He said, "Well somebody will give it to us." I wished the kid luck and walked out of the house.

Because the Penn State football program has a reputation for integrity, Coach Paterno and his staff rarely face such requests. Those who are looking for money under the table know to look elsewhere.

Organizational Structure

In Chapter Seven we learned that individuals should take responsibility for their own behavior and question orders to behave unethically. However, the organizational structure frequently reinforces, and sometimes creates, problems of authority and responsibility.

Most modern organizations are bureaucratic,[26] meaning that they have a hierarchy of authority, a division of labor or specialization, standardization of activities, and a stress on competence and efficiency. Bureaucracy provides many advantages, and large organizations require a certain amount of bureaucracy in order to survive. However, certain characteristics of bureaucracy such as specialization, division of labor, and hierarchy of authority can present problems for the organization's ethical culture.

Authority, Responsibility, and Ethical Culture   With bureaucracy comes the idea of legitimate authority. Look at any organizational chart. It will tell you who supervises whom—who has authority over whom. These authority figures serve important bureaucratic roles. They direct work, delegate responsibility, conduct performance appraisals, and make decisions about promotions and raises.[27]

But the idea of legitimate authority can present problems for the ethical culture. First, recall from Chapter Seven that people tend to obey authority figures no matter what they are ordered to do.[28] This natural tendency toward unquestioning obedience can be a real threat to the organization's attempt to build individual responsibility into its ethical culture.

Second, managers tend to expend a great deal of energy avoiding blame.[29] Their greatest fear is that when it comes time to blame someone, the finger will point their way, and their job will be at risk. By delegating responsibility to those at lower levels in the organization, the authority figure can often avoid blame for mistakes or ethical blunders. When it comes time to blame someone, the finger of blame frequently points down. Underlings, in particular, fear becoming the scapegoat for mistakes made at higher levels. CYA ("cover your ass") memos proliferate as managers look to blame someone in a relatively powerless position who is considered to be expendable.

The structure of an organization can also fragment jobs and roles.[30] It isn't necessarily that individuals don't want to take responsibility. But jobs and roles get so divided up that they simply can't see the big picture.[31] We saw in Chapter Seven how military bureaucrats passed the buck for responsibility during an investigation of the MyLai massacre. They saw themselves only as cogs in a machine. No one felt responsible for the larger outcomes of their actions.

The ethical culture must incorporate a structure that emphasizes and supports individual responsibility and accountability at every level. Each person must be encouraged to take responsibility for his or her actions and must be held accountable for negative consequences when they occur. However, tracking responsibility is difficult and time consuming and is rarely done well. Many organizations don't do this kind of recordkeeping at all, perhaps preferring to keep responsibility ambiguous and scapegoating a viable possibility. Special Prosecutor Lawrence Walsh's attempt to track responsibility in the U.S. government's Iran-Contra affair provides a case in point. It's arguable that Colonel Oliver North served as a relatively low-level scapegoat. He received most of the blame, while others in Ronald Reagan's administration were able to claim (rightly or wrongly) that they were "out of the loop."

New Organizational Structures   Organizations today are developing structures designed to remove bureaucratic layers, push responsibility down, and empower individuals to make decisions at every organizational level. Take the example of Herman Miller Inc. (HMI), the manufacturer of office and health care facility furniture that is committed to the values of "open communication," "the dignity of each individual," and "quality relationships based on mutual trust and integrity." Kevin Knowles, a crew leader for six years, said, "What always surprises me is that everyone in the company . . . is free to talk with anyone in management about whatever they'd like to talk about." Managers at HMI cite workers' ability to go over their managers' heads as a major reason for the company's success. "There's no fear of retribution if you call someone three levels above." HMI touts a process its chairman calls "roving leadership" that allows anyone to be a leader on a particular issue.

Here is an example of how roving leadership was tested successfully. An employee with AIDS decided that he should let others know about his illness. A co-worker took the roving leader responsibility and informed the human resources manager. Quickly, the entire plant was informed, and a physician from headquarters flew in with a training videotape and a question and answer session. According to the "roving leader," what's important is that HMI's value system "allows us to act on our instincts and know the company will support us. Because the value of each individual is important to us, we were able to stop the manufacture of furniture for one day to take care of Peter."[32]

These recent structural changes have powerful implications for taking responsibility and for ethical decision making, and they increase the importance of having a strong ethical culture. When individuals are independently making decisions, with less direct supervision, they need a strong ethical culture to guide them. An important part of this strong ethical culture is a structure that supports taking individual responsibility for ethical action.

Policies and Codes

Many organizations guide employees' behavior through formal organizational value statements, mission statements, credos, policies, and formal codes of ethical conduct. Generally, value and mission statements, and credos are abstract, general statements of guiding beliefs. Formal ethics codes are longer and more detailed, providing guidance about behavior in specific situations. Policy manuals are even lengthier and include more detailed lists of rules covering a multitude of job situations. An extended discussion of policies and codes follows in Chapter Ten.

Formal ethics codes are most common, with most ethics codes being introduced within the past 20 years. In a study of the Fortune 1000, 98 percent of the firms reported addressing ethics and conduct issues in formal documents. Of those 98 percent, 78 percent had separate codes of ethics.[33]

Research has found that employees working in organizations with codes of ethics report that they engage in less unethical behavior.[34] However, codes vary so much in content and implementation that it's difficult to generalize about their impact. We do know, however, that the existence of an ethics code alone will not solve all organizational ethics problems and can actually cause problems if it is implemented without attention to the rest of the ethical culture. A code can prescribe behavior. If that behavior isn't followed, we end up with an organization out of alignment (an organization that says one thing and does another). We also have cynical workers who can cite one more instance of organizational hypocrisy.

Most companies with codes now distribute them quite widely. In a survey of Fortune 1000 firms conducted in 1995, 75 percent of responding companies reported distributing their code or policy to at least 80 percent of their employees.[35] This may be a byproduct of the Sentencing Guidelines (discussed in Chapter Two) which specify communication of compliance standards to all employees as a guiding principle. Some firms even distribute their codes beyond their own employees. For example, in 1993, Wakefern Food Corporation (Shop-Rite supermarkets) distributed its code to its suppliers along with a letter, signed by the president, that said:

Dear Business Associate:

As the holidays draw near, we are mindful of the mutually satisfying and mutually profitable relationship which exists between Wakefern and our suppliers. We look forward to many more years of successful growth together through our joint efforts to provide our customers with quality products, excellent service and low price.

In recent years, we have found many of our staff members embarrassed by well-intentioned gifts from those with whom we do business. Our Board of Directors approved the enclosed Code of Ethics for Wakefern which clearly states our policy prohibiting Wakefern Associates from accepting gifts from our suppliers and customers. We feel that this policy should apply during the holidays as well as throughout the year.

With so much attention being given to practices which bring the business community's ethics into question, we urge your support of our efforts to maintain the respect and confidence of the industry for the objectivity of our dealings with suppliers.

Since failure to comply with our policy will result in disqualification from further business dealings with us, we request that you distribute this letter to those in your company who have business dealings with Wakefern Food Corporation and its subsidiaries.

The most significant means of expressing your appreciation to Wakefern staff continues to be your efforts to help us grow together by anticipating and meeting the changing consumers' needs and wants.

If you have any questions regarding this policy, please contact . . .

With our best wishes for happy holidays and a healthy and prosperous 1994.

Research on honor codes in colleges and universities suggests that students cheat less in institutions with codes.[36] A recent study found, however, that students' perceptions of their peers' cheating had a more profound influence on their own cheating behavior than the existence of a code. In addition, the certainty of being reported and the severity of penalties were found to be important, supporting the idea that the code alone is not the most important influence.[37] It must act in concert with other aspects of the ethical culture. The code must not only be distributed, but it must also be enforced and be consistent with other cultural systems. Otherwise, codes of conduct are more likely to serve as mere "window dressing" while being disregarded as guides for actual behavior.

Managers, especially middle managers, want to have a stated organizational policy or code when it comes to serious ethical matters. Remember, cognitive moral development research tells us that most people are looking outside themselves for guidance, and stated organizational policy can be an important source of that guidance. To determine where policy is needed, the organization can survey managers about areas of ethical concern and their perception of the need for policy in each area. In one study, managers made it clear that policy was needed in such areas as filing expense claims, gifts and bribes, and treatment of competitor information.[38]

Reward Systems

The importance of reward systems was discussed in Chapter Seven. Here, we will focus on the reward system as a key component of the ethical culture and, in particular, the essential role it plays in alignment or misalignment of cultural systems.

Rewarding and Punishing Behavior   To understand the ethical conduct of individuals in the organization, we need to look more specifically at the behaviors that are rewarded and punished, and how this system aligns with (or doesn't align with) the rest of the ethical culture. When managers are asked about ethics in their organization, reward systems are frequently cited as a significant problem. They report that concern about the bottom line often conflicts with and overwhelms concern about ethics. Employees are rewarded for reaching a particular goal or for selling a certain amount of product, with little attention to how the goal is achieved. Because people tend to do those things that are rewarded, management must ensure that performance goals are realistic and can be achieved without resorting to unethical behavior. A classic case occurred at a GM plant several years ago. The plant manager had installed a device that periodically speeded up the assembly line beyond the rate agreed to in the union contract. When confronted, he pointed out that the firm's production specifications assumed that the line would run at maximum allowable speed 100 percent of the time. He installed the device to make up for inevitable down time.[39]

Misalignment of the reward system with other aspects of the ethical culture is quite common. We frequently hear this from managers who work in an organization with a code of ethical conduct that isn't enforced. Think about what happens when these cultural systems conflict. For example, imagine an organization where everyone knows that the top sales representative's sales depend on unethical practices. Not only does the unethical conduct go undisciplined, but the sales representative receives large bonuses, expensive vacations, and is celebrated at annual sales meetings. Members of the sales force recognize that the reward system carries the "real" message, and so the code becomes meaningless, or worse yet, an example of top management's hypocrisy.

Joe Paterno, in our interview with him, was clear about the importance of rules and their enforcement with every player. "The players know what the penalties are. They have a pretty good idea of what's going to happen to them if they break the rules. . . . If I tell the players we have a rule, we have to enforce it and apply it to everyone. You can't say this is the rule and it's for everybody but your top quarterback." Paterno showed how he held players accountable when the Penn State team played its 1998 bowl game without two star players. One had academic problems, and the other had been accused of taking a gift from a sports agent. The team lost, but the program's integrity was intact. Interestingly, Paterno's rule enforcement extends to alumni and boosters who have gotten other football programs in big trouble with the NCAA. Penn State regularly informs alumni of their responsibility to uphold the integrity of the football program. And, according to Paterno, alumni have lost their rights to buy tickets because of past violations.

Carl Skooglund echoed the philosophy that employees at all levels must be held accountable. "It's very important that you send a signal that you are going to discipline people for unethical conduct. And you have to be sure that you are disciplining high enough in the organization. But when you move up in the organization, you use different criteria. Somebody at a lower organizational level may do something that's wrong, but then you need to ask if they knew it was wrong. If they didn't know it was wrong, then you ask, why. Is it because the manager didn't meet his or her responsibility to communicate and train them properly? So the manager may need to be disciplined. If you don't discipline you aren't sending the signal that you're serious."

The Reward System and Whistleblowers   The organization's treatment of whistleblowers is a relevant reward system concern[40] and a frequent source of misalignment. In today's organizations, fewer employees are directly supervised. Therefore, organizations must rely more on their employees to report misconduct. However, as we all know, powerful norms exist against blowing the whistle. The words we use to describe this behavior, "tattling," "squealing," "snitching," "informing," and "ratting," all have negative connotations. In fact, there isn't a nice or even a neutral word to describe it.

Whistleblowers frequently suffer retaliation, particularly when whistleblowers report managerial or organizational misconduct.[41] They're punished rather than rewarded for doing what they think is right. If an organization claims that it's attempting to develop an ethical culture, retaliation against a whistleblower is a powerful example of misalignment. Again, the workers view this "punishment" of the whistleblower as an example of the organization's "real" ethical beliefs.

Roger Boisjoly, a Morton Thiokol engineer blew the whistle on his employer regarding O-ring safety and management problems leading to the space shuttle Challenger disaster. He lost his job as a result of his "ethical" behavior, sending the clear message to other employees that blowing the whistle gets punished. According to Boisjoly, "if you believe in practicing what you preach, it can mean career suicide."[42]

The ethical organization, however, should view the whistleblower as an important cog in its control system and must find ways to make whistleblowing a safe activity. Some organizations even reward whistleblowing. For example, in 1996, *Fortune* magazine published "memos from the chairman" of Bear Stearns, the witty chairman considered responsible for the success of one of the best managed Wall Street firms. Two of the eight memos the magazine published concerned the importance of whistleblowing and the company's policy to provide cash awards to whistleblowers whose accusations are well-founded. This memo was addressed to senior managing directors, managing directors, and associate directors in 1993.

> We need your help. Please help us get a message out to every associate. It is essential that once again we stress that we welcome every suspicion or feeling that our co-workers might have about something they see or hear that is going on at Bear Stearns that might not measure up to our standards of honesty and integrity . . .
>
> We want people at Bear Stears to cry wolf. If the doubt is justified, the reporter will be handsomely rewarded. If the suspicion proves unfounded, the person who brought it to our attention will be thanked for their vigilance and told to keep it up.
>
> Forget the chain of command! That is not the way Bear Stearns was built. If you think somebody is doing something off the wall or his/her decision making stinks, go around the person,** and that includes me. . . .
>
> *Get these messages out loud and clear.*

** We have had some senior people who resented "end runs." They quickly became associated with more conventional firms—you can draw your own conclusions about whether their career change worked out for the best.[43]

This leader sent a clear message that whistleblowing was encouraged and rewarded. In the second memo, he shared information about a specific instance in which two administrative assistants detected that fictitious taxicab vouchers were being submitted by an employee. The employee was terminated, and the administrative assistants were provided an immediate cash award.

But most people don't want a reward for doing the right thing. They just don't want to be punished for it. In an attempt to protect whistleblowers, many organizations have installed hotlines and ombudspersons. Whistleblowers can call these hotlines and speak confidentially and without fear of retaliation. Examples of how these work are included in Chapter Ten.

Thus, reward systems are important in themselves because they provide guidance about expected behavior, but they're particularly important in the sense that people look to them to reflect the "real" message about what is valued in the organization. Is there consistency between what the organization says (e.g., codes) and what it does (rewards and punishments)? Reward systems frequently represent the source of "cultural misalignment" that can lead to cynicism about organizational ethics.

Orientation and Training Programs

Socialization is often begun through formal orientation programs and reinforced through ongoing training. The organization's values and guiding principles can be communicated in orientation programs. More specific guidance in ethical decision making can be provided in subsequent training programs. Recently, an increasing number of firms have added ethics training to their list of management development programs. Most Fortune 1000 firms provide some ethics training at least every few years. However, as of 1995, more than 20 percent of large firms still provided no ethics training whatsoever.[44]

A former chairman and CEO of Allied Corporation said, "Through our ethics seminars, we encourage people to gain a broader perspective of their responsibilities at Allied. Our managers must be capable of recognizing the ethical dimensions of their business decisions."[45] By providing ethics training, the organization not only offers specific skills to managers, but indirectly communicates that ethical behavior is valued and that ethical dimensions should be considered in decision making. More specific examples of ethics training are included in Chapter Ten.

The ethics training must be consistent with the ethical culture because a training program that is out of alignment is thought of, at best, as a pleasant day away from the office. At its worst, the ethics training will be taken as a joke, when managers attempt to reconcile what they're hearing with their experience in the organization.

Decision-Making Processes

Ethical decisions are influenced by the organization's formal decision-making processes. For example, managers may ignore the ethical dimension of decisions unless leaders state that ethical concerns must be a formal part of organizational decisions. This emphasis on ethics can also be reinforced by regularly addressing ethical concerns in meetings and by making them an expected part of managers' reports regarding new products or business ventures. Some organizations are creating special high-level "ethics" committees charged with reviewing major organizational level decisions from an ethical perspective.[46] Others have advocated the implementation of moral quality circles, groups set up to assess the morality of business decisions.[47]

Overreliance on Quantitative Analysis Decision-making processes can also contribute to unethical behavior. For example, in Chapter Five, we discussed the decision-making process that kept the Ford Pinto from being recalled. In that situation, exclusive reliance on a quantitative cost/benefit analysis to the exclusion of moral considerations had disastrous consequences. In another example, Johns Manville, the former corporate giant and producer of asbestos, was brought down by decision-making processes that focused on the bottom line to the exclusion of worker health. More than 40 years ago, top management began to receive information implicating asbestos inhalation as a cause of severe lung disease in workers. Managers and medical staff suppressed the research and concealed the information from employees. During testimony, a lawyer reported on a confrontation with the corporate counsel about the failure to share X-ray results with employees. The lawyer reported asking, "You mean to tell me you would let them work until they dropped dead?" The lawyer replied, "Yes, we save a lot of money that way." It was apparently cheaper to pay workers' compensation claims than to develop safer working conditions. A New Jersey court found that the company had made a "conscious, cold-blooded business decision to take no protective or remedial action."[48] Obviously, organizational decision makers must rely on quantitative analysis in making business decisions. However, their reliance on numbers, to the exclusion of moral considerations, is problematic. Discussions about whether the decision is the "right" thing to do must accompany discussions about the effect of a particular decision on the bottom line.

Burden of Proof In 1986, Beech-Nut Nutrition Corporation, the second-largest U.S. baby food manufacturer, pleaded guilty to 215 felony counts and admitted to selling apple products that were a blend of synthetic ingredients. How did this happen? There were many causes, among them the company's financial difficulties, the belief that other companies were selling fake juice (industry norms), and the belief that the juice was perfectly safe.

A chief cause may also have been the decision-making processes that were used. When Jerome LiCari, director of Research and Development, recommended changing suppliers in 1981 (because he suspected adulteration), Operations Head John Lavery turned the traditional burden of proof around. Generally, baby food manufacturers would switch suppliers if the supplier couldn't demonstrate that the product was genuine. In this case, Lavery said that if LiCari wanted to go with a more expensive supplier, he would have to prove that the concentrate they were buying was adulterated (rather than genuine). Given the technology available at the time, this was difficult, and the supplier was retained.[49]

A similar decision-making criterion was used in the decision to launch the space shuttle Challenger despite engineers' concerns about O-ring failure in cold weather. In previous launches, engineers had been required to show evidence that the launch was safe (which would have been difficult, if not impossible). In the case of the Challenger, the burden of proof was changed. Engineers who balked at the impending launch decision were asked to prove that it was unsafe.

These examples suggest that it's relatively easy to alter decision-making processes to support whatever decision managers have already made. That's why it's extremely important that organizations design decision-making processes in good financial times and before a crisis occurs. Then, when trouble strikes, they can rely on these effective decision-making processes to guide them. The space shuttle Challenger might never have been launched if engineers had been required to prove that the launch would be safe, rather than unsafe. Managers must be particularly alert to changes in traditional decision-making criteria, particularly in times of crisis.

INFORMAL CULTURAL SYSTEMS

In addition to the formal systems described above, organizational culture is kept alive informally and symbolically through informal norms, heroes, rituals, myths, and stories. Information about these is carried through informal communication systems such as the grapevine. In this way, people come to know what behaviors are "really" rewarded, how decisions are "really" made, and what organizational leaders "really" expect. If the formal and informal systems are out of alignment, people are more likely to believe the messages carried by the informal system. Therefore, management of these informal systems is extremely important.

Informal Norms

As discussed above, organizational norms are a powerful factor influencing organizational behavior. At a fast-food restaurant, new employees may be told about a rule against eating food without paying for it. However, once on the job, they may see co-workers eating while the supervisor looks the other way. These co-workers may rationalize their behavior because of their low pay, poor working conditions, or because the supervisor doesn't seem to care. Encouraged to join them, the new employee is likely to do so, having learned the informal or "real" norms. Thus, despite rules, regulations, codes, and credos, informal norms are frequently the most influential behavior guides.

Heroes and Role Models

Heroes personify the organization's values.[50] They're symbolic figures who set standards of performance by modeling certain behaviors. These heroes need not even be present in the organization. Tom Watson, former president and son of the founder of IBM, is still very much alive in the organization. Stories about his values and exploits continue to influence daily organizational behavior. Thus, a hero who champions integrity and stands up for what is right may influence the behavior of many in the organization.

When asked to identify the organization's heroes, Penn State students in a management class on organizational culture inevitably name football coach, Joe Paterno. "Joepa" as he is affectionately known around campus is not only the formal leader of the football team, but a cultural hero as well. His values, including education first for college athletes, and winning by sticking to the rules of the game,[51] are considered by many to extend far beyond the football program to permeate Penn State's culture. On campus, "Joepa" and his wife are also known for their philanthropy. Most recently, they showed their leadership in the fundraising campaign for a much needed university library addition to be known as the Paterno Library addition. Some say that Penn State is the only university whose sports arena is named after a former president, while the library addition is named after its football coach.

Much organizational socialization is informally conducted by role models and mentors who may be superiors or more experienced co-workers. Individuals who are passing through organizational "boundaries," such as new hires, or individuals who are transferring from one part of the organization to another, are most vulnerable to these socialization influences.[52] The mentor or role model may emphasize the importance of integrity and resistance to pressure to behave

unethically, or the role model may indoctrinate the individual into accepted unethical practices, making it difficult for the individual to redefine the job to exclude them.[53] The new accounting graduate who was told by his superior in a
public accounting firm, "you're too honest to be an auditor," received a powerful message about ethics (or the lack thereof) in that organization.

Rituals

Rituals tell people symbolically what the organization wants them to do and
how it expects them to do it.[54] Rituals are a way of affirming and communicating culture in a very tangible way.[55] For example, General Motors of Canada
introduced its new vision and values by asking each manufacturing unit to create a small float representing one of the key values. These floats were part of
a parade that kicked off a full day of culture-building ritual surrounding the
theme, "customers for life" and the motto, "I am GM." During the day, the CEO
unveiled a large painting of the group vision and told a story about their future. To reinforce the "I am GM" motto, employees were asked to see themselves as being responsible, at any moment, for the company, its products, and
services. The day ended with the "GM Acceleration Song" performed by the 100-
person Up With People singing and dancing group. The song had been revised
to incorporate the new values created by the leadership team.[56]

Other companies have awards ceremonies that convey the values of the organization. What values are celebrated at these ceremonies? Is it success with
integrity, or is it just the bottom line? Are the rituals consistent with the formal
rules and reward systems?

Myths and Stories

Another extremely important way organizational culture is communicated and
kept alive is through the informal communication network. People invent stories to give meaning to their world and life.[57] Organizational myths and stories
explain and give meaning to the organizational culture. They're anecdotes about
a sequence of events drawn from the organization's history. The story's characters are employees, perhaps company heroes, and the moral of the story expresses the organization's values.[58]

At IBM, a story that has been told and retold describes how a low-level employee denied Tom Watson, the former IBM president, entry into a restricted
area of the company because Watson was not wearing his IBM identification
badge. Watson praised the employee, suggesting the importance of upholding
company rules and applying them to everyone.

In his book, *Paterno by the Book*,[59] Paterno recounted a powerful story from
the Penn State football program's history about a leader standing up for what
he believes at a critical moment.

> The Miami game was a turning point for me. . . . Late that night, as we waited to
> board our charter plane, Jim O'Hara and I strolled around the terminal replaying

the joys of our victory when I saw something that stopped our conversation cold. I looked again and sure enough two of our best players were standing at a not-too-visible spot of the airport bar, each fingering a glass of beer. . . . "You're in trouble," I told them. "You know that you're never to be seen standing at a bar." Naturally they protested that they were having only one, that they were coming down after the great game, that nobody around here knew them. "Never means never," I said. Nobody on the squad could possibly have the faintest doubt about my rule: We don't want a Penn State football player to drink in a public place. . . . He throws a bad light on the entire team, putting every member under suspicion. Furthermore, . . . football players are public figures, watched and talked about. Also they're role models. I reminded the two guys of the one loophole in my rule: You can sit down with your folks privately and have a glass of wine. You can even have a couple of beers on a Saturday night—in private, with personal friends. That won't make you victims of hearsay. But if I see you standing at a public bar, you're in trouble.

So now these two kids had forced the decision on me. One of them had previously got himself in a minor jam with the police. It made a mention in the paper. "You're gone," I said. That meant for good. Off the team. To the other I said, "This is the first trouble I know about. You get one more chance, but you're suspended for the next two games." On Monday evening the captains . . . came to see me. The whole squad was meeting at that moment, they said, and had sent the captains to tell me that they felt the penalties were too harsh. They wanted me to take the first guy back and lift the suspension on the second—and they wanted to return to the meeting with my changed decision.

There are moments in the life of a manager when his ability to maintain control teeters on a hair. He can only manage with the consent of the managed, unless he's a prison warden. On the other hand, he can only manage by unambiguous assertion of authority. Those are opposites, in a sense. If the manager, who sometimes has to choose in a split second, chooses the wrong one of those two, his effectiveness is finished.

"Go back to your meeting and I'll be there myself in five minutes," I said. The sentence was harsh, I said to myself, but the rule they had broken was perfectly clear, defensible, and necessary. The morale and support of the entire squad hung in the air. If I backed off, the message was clear as a bell: I'm afraid of you guys. Ignore this rule. Ignore any rule that itches as much as this one does. And if there's a rule that itches less, try me on that, too.

Five minutes later, that squad room was a tableau of sullen, hard faces. I looked around, eye to eye, then talked. "A rule that protects us all was broken. The decision I made was the best one for all of us. I have no choice but to stand with it." Faces stayed frozen, waiting. I couldn't read them. "If anybody here can't live with it, go. Right now. If you stay, you do it my way, the right way, living by the rules. If you decide to stay and do it that way, we'll have a great football team. I'm going to walk out of here right now. A minute later I'm coming back in. Whoever's here, that's who we're going to play with."

As I walked bravely out of there, imitating John Wayne the best I could, my knees were shaking. In the promised minute, I returned. Every frozen face that was there during my first visit was still there, although still frozen.[60]

This story represents a critical event in the history of Paterno's tenure as Penn State's football coach. It symbolizes the idea that rules are valued and enforced in a culture of high integrity and accountability. To the extent that the story has become a part of the organization's culture, it serves to reinforce the culture's emphasis on the value of rules.

Language

Cultures develop and use language to communicate values to employees. The old joke that business ethics is an oxymoron suggests that many consider the language of ethics to be out of place in the business context. A number of the corporate ethics officers we interviewed suggested that the word "ethics" is "charged" and "emotional" for employees who often react negatively to any hint that their ethics might not be okay. When possible, they use other words to describe what they're trying to do. For example, employees seem to be more comfortable talking about integrity or shared values than ethics.

Research suggests that managers are reluctant to describe their actions in moral terms even when they are acting for moral reasons, a phenomenon referred to as moral muteness. This reluctance can be attributed to managers' avoidance of the interpersonal confrontation that may take place if they question an organizational practice or decision, to the value placed on "efficient" decision making such that moral talk can be thought of as a distraction, and to the desire to appear powerful and effective. Moral talk can appear idealistic and utopian and inconsistent with the expectation that managers can solve their own problems.[61]

Getting people to talk about ethics has also been likened to sex education. Although parents agree that sex education is a good thing, they find it difficult to broach the subject with their children. Similarly, managers may find it difficult to begin a conversation about ethics with other managers or with their subordinates. If these topics are typically not discussed, the manager who brings it up may feel like a "goody goody" or a spoil sport.[62] But managers who become comfortable talking about ethics will be role modeling important behaviors for their subordinates.

Kent Druyvesteyn told us an anecdote about the early development of ethics training at General Dynamics.

Early on, at General Dynamics, we declared that our ethics training workshops were to be small and interactive, and that they were to be led by managers. And, we heard some complaints from managers who said, "We don't know anything about this." They thought we were going to have them teach Aristotle and Kant, but that's not what we were trying to do. We also had people in training say, "We can't have people in management do this. There won't be any quality control."

At that point I said, "Let's consider what it is we're trying to do here. What we are trying to do is raise awareness, to increase knowledge of company standards and stimulate commitment to those standards. That's the most important thing." Here's an analogy I'd like you to consider. You have some small children and you decide that you want to teach them about sex. There are a number of ways that you could do this. You could hire an expert—someone who knows all about sex, who knows the right words to use, who knows all the latest terminology, who is pedagogically very skilled. You could hire this person to come into your home, sit down in your living room with your children, and teach them about sex. I mean, isn't that good management technique—to delegate it to someone? On the other hand, you could do it yourself. You may have limitations. You don't know everything. You might be embarrassed or tongue tied. In the end though, who do you think would be more effective? To have the expert do it or for you to do it yourself? I have never had a person say that the expert would be more effective.

Top managers can also make ethics an acceptable topic of conversation by sending a message that it's not only OK, but expected, to talk about one's ethical concerns. They can do this by leading discussions about ethics, discussing the ethics code and its application in a videotape that is shown to employees, and otherwise openly discussing ethical problems with managers and employees. Senior managers can also build "moral talk" into the fabric of the organization by requiring routine discussion of moral issues and inclusion of ethical issues in business proposals.[63]

Empire Southwest, a company in Phoenix, Arizona, supports "moral talk" in its code of conduct: "It is not enough that you are honest, but vital that you speak out for honesty and honor. The courage to confront a violator, even though embarrassing, is necessary if we are to remain trusted. One act of dishonesty can hurt the entire group, and it is the responsibility of each to act in safeguarding all."[64]

It's difficult to imagine discussing questions of organizational ethics without an acceptable vocabulary to support the discussion. Both educators and employers have a role to play in providing students and workers with the language that can be used to discuss and analyze organizational problems from an ethical perspective. It could be as simple as using words such as "right," "wrong," "honesty," "integrity," "values," and "character." How often does your organization ask whether the decision is the right one, in a moral as well as a business sense? Is this the "right" thing to do for customers, suppliers, the community? How often is a job applicant evaluated for integrity, values, and character, in addition to performance? How often is potential harm to all stakeholders considered when making a business decision?

The use of ethical language may be related to decision-making behavior. In one study,[65] individuals who discussed their decision-making process using the language of ethics were more likely to be the ones who made an ethical decision. These people talked about ethics, morals, honesty, integrity, values, and good character. Those who had made the unethical decision were more likely to recount the decision in the more traditional business language of costs and benefits. This research suggests a link between language and ethical decision making. The implication for organizations is that their employees may need to be taught the language of ethics and its appropriateness for business decision making.

Special organizational language can also be used to avoid the moral implications of actions. For example, in Nazi Germany, the code names for killing and genocide were "final solution," "evacuation," and "special treatment." This use of euphemisms allowed people to avoid confronting the true meaning of their behavior.[66] Similarly, in recent years companies have created euphemisms to avoid the pain of downsizing decisions. "Rightsizing" and "targeted outplacement" are just a couple of the terms we've encountered. It may be easier to impose a "targeted outplacement" than a layoff, but are the moral considerations as obvious with "targeted outplacement" as they are with layoffs?

DEVELOPING AND CHANGING THE ETHICAL CULTURE

We can conclude from this cultural analysis that ethics at work is greatly influenced by the organization's culture. Both formal and informal organizational systems and processes channel and reinforce certain kinds of behavior. Each of the systems on its own can support either ethical or unethical conduct. In addition, these multiple systems can work together or at cross purposes to support ethical or unethical conduct in the organization. Imagine an organization with an ethics code that forbids giving kickbacks but then promotes the salesperson who is widely known for giving them. This "we say one thing, but do another" approach leads to widespread cynicism. The code loses all credibility as workers pay more attention to what's done than to what's said. On the other hand, the organization that fires the kickback giver reinforces the code, supporting its ethical stance with its workers.

Developing or changing organizational ethics, then, involves simultaneously developing or changing multiple aspects of the organization's ethical culture. If the effort is to be successful, this ethical culture development or change should involve the alignment of all relevant formal and informal organizational systems.

Changing organizational culture is more difficult than developing it. In a new organization, workers are quite open to learning and accepting the culture of their new organizational home. However, anthropologists and organizational scientists agree that changing culture is an extremely difficult process.[67] This view is consistent with an idea basic to all organizational change and development efforts—that changing individual and group behavior is both difficult and time consuming. The human tendency to want to conserve the existing culture is referred to as "cultural persistence" or inertia. Culture has an addictive quality, perhaps because culture members are aware that culture components cannot be altered without affecting other, cherished values and institutions.[68] Also, an unethical culture tends to feed on itself. Why would successful (but unethical) managers want to change? They wouldn't. They would tend to hire people like themselves and perpetuate the culture that exists.

In general, the catalyst and pressure for culture change come from the organization's environment. For example, companies in deregulated industries (banking, telecommunications, airlines) were forced to change their cultures to become more innovative and more marketing oriented.

The pressure to change organizational ethics can come from stockholders, the government, and other outside stakeholders. The public's general mistrust of business executives[69] and the threat of increased government regulation may encourage leaders to look more closely at their ethical cultures. In addition, organizations whose members have been "caught" engaging in unethical behavior, or those faced with costly lawsuits are prime candidates for such ethical culture change attempts. Finally, the government's new sentencing guidelines for corporate crime have turned the attention of many organizations to an evaluation of their ethical cultures.

The influence of bad publicity and costly lawsuits extends beyond the targeted organization. Organizations scan the environment for information that is relevant to their concerns. When one organization in an industry is called on the carpet for a legal or ethical violation, other organizations in the industry may take notice and act. Exxon's mishandling of the *Valdez* oil spill in 1989 sullied the reputation of the entire oil industry. And insider trading scandals put the entire financial industry on alert. Thus, any organization that senses increased vulnerability to external pressure is also more likely to consider the need for attention to the management of its ethical culture.

A CULTURAL APPROACH TO CHANGING ORGANIZATIONAL ETHICS

Any attempt to develop or change organizational ethics can benefit from an organizational change approach that includes a systemwide, long-term view. In addition, it should be based on the assumption that human beings are essentially good and capable of development and change.

A Cultural Systems View

The cultural approach relies on the idea that to be successful any attempt to develop or change the organization's ethics must take the entire cultural system into account.[70] The change effort must target multiple formal and informal organizational subsystems. All of these must work together to create clear, consistent messages about what is and is not appropriate behavior in the organization. If subsystems conflict, confusion and mixed messages will result. Thus, the entire range of formal and informal subsystems must be analyzed and targeted for development and change.

This complex, multisystem approach to managing organizational ethics argues against any short-term, quick-fix solutions that target only one system. The idea that an organization could solve its ethics problem simply by establishing a code of ethics or by hiring a consultant to deliver a one-hour ethics training program becomes ludicrous when the complexity of the ethics culture is understood. The management of ethical conduct must be complex because it's influenced by multiple systems, each of them complex in itself. Thus, the complexity of the solution must match the complexity of the problem. A solution that isn't sufficiently complex will miss important information, make incomplete diagnoses, and produce overly simple and short-sighted solutions. The organization that creates a code of ethics in response to external pressure and files it away without making changes in other systems such as the reward system and decision-making processes is more likely making a negative statement about organizational ethics rather than a positive one. The informal message is that management is hypocritical and that the code of ethics serves no useful purpose beyond the creation of a false facade.

Shirley Peterson, former vice president for ethics and business conduct at Northrop Corporation, emphasized the importance of this systems view in our interview with her.

> Values or guiding principles have to be woven into the fabric of all corporate systems—in hiring practices, in succession planning, in pay for performance and appraisal, and the education of management on how to manage their people. If those values aren't woven into all of the systems, you're going to have values conflicts that will cause more problems than you had before values were articulated.

> If management is going to publish a statement of guiding principles, they really need to be reminded of the danger zone they're getting into. The danger zone is not quite understanding what the commitment is because once they've gone to the effort to put that all in writing, now the employees have something to stick right in their face. What is this? We value people? We treat one another with respect? We recognize contribution to diversity and we have few black or female line managers out there?

The bottom line about systems thinking is understanding that, if an organization decides to get into the "ethics business" with a code or a training program, employees are likely to expect follow through in other parts of the organization. And, the failure to follow through will be interpreted as hypocrisy.

A Long-Term View

The development of organizational culture takes place over a number of years. Effective culture change may take even longer, as much as 6 to 15 years.[71] It requires alterations in both formal and informal organizational systems that take time to implement and take hold. Resistances must be overcome. New rules and values must be reinforced via training programs, rites and rituals, and reward systems. Although not all organizational change efforts take this long, deep interventions in the organizational culture should be considered long-term projects.

Assumptions about People

Mainstream economics rests on the assumption that human beings are driven by self-interest and opportunism and are likely to shirk responsibility.[72] Acceptance of this assumption logically leads to change efforts focused almost exclusively on behavioral control.

We believe, however, that human beings are essentially good and open to growth and change. Most employees prefer being associated with a just organization that supports ethical behavior and disciplines unethical behavior. Given this type of environment, most individuals can be expected to choose ethical behavior. Individuals who engage in unethical behavior should not simply be labeled "bad" people. They are often responding to external pressures or are behaving according to organizationally sanctioned definitions of what's appropriate. Although unethical behaviors must be disciplined, the organization should also treat unethical behavior as a signal to investigate itself and the cultural context in which the behavior occurred. Through culture, the organization can change definitions of what is appropriate and inappropriate, and relieve pressures to behave unethically.

Diagnosis—The Ethical Culture Audit

Formal attempts to develop or change organizational ethics should begin with diagnosis. Diagnosing culture calls for time-consuming techniques such as auditing the content of decision making, coding the content of organizational stories and anecdotes, and holding open-ended interviews with employees at all levels.[73] It also requires systematic analysis of formal organizational systems such as the structure and criteria for rewards and promotion.

The framework presented in this chapter can provide guidance for an audit of the organization's ethical culture.[74] The audit should include probes into the formal and informal organizational systems that are maintaining the ethics culture in its current state. First, formal organizational systems can be analyzed in a number of ways. Through surveys, interviews, observation at meetings, orientation and training sessions, and analysis of organizational documents, perceptions of how formal organizational systems either encourage or discourage ethical behavior can be identified. A sample of the kinds of questions that can be asked are listed in Table 9.1.

Audit of informal systems is equally important. The culture can be analyzed to identify the organization's heroes, as well as the behaviors that are reinforced through stories, rituals, and language. This can be accomplished through open-ended interviews, observation of organizational rituals, and analysis of the organization's stories. Some questions that might be asked in an audit of the informal system are offered in Table 9.2. The questions in Tables 9.1 and 9.2 are designed to suggest the general direction of an ethical culture audit. Specific questions that arise out of the particular system being analyzed must be developed to tap that system's unique problems and needs. Canned approaches to discovering culture that assume they can identify the relevant dimensions in advance are bound to fail.[75] In addition, the multisystem nature of organizational culture suggests that responses must be compared within and across systems to answer the key question of whether formal and informal systems are aligned within themselves and with each other.

As you may have determined by now, a full-fledged ethical culture audit is a complex process that the average manager isn't prepared to conduct. Although

TABLE 9.1   Selected Questions for Auditing the Formal System

1. How are organizational leaders perceived in terms of their integrity?

2. How are ethics-related behaviors modeled by organizational leaders?

3. Are workers at all levels encouraged to take responsibility for the consequences of their behavior? To question authority when they are asked to do something that they consider to be wrong? How?

4. Does a formal code of ethics and/or values exist? Is it distributed? How widely? Is it used? Is it reinforced in other formal systems such as reward and decision making systems?

5. Are whistleblowers encouraged and are formal channels available for them to make their concerns known confidentially?

6. Is misconduct disciplined swiftly and justly in the organization?

7. Are people of integrity promoted? Are means as well as ends important?

8. Is integrity emphasized to recruits and new employees?

9. Are managers oriented to the values of the organization in orientation programs? Are they trained in ethical decision making?

10. Are ethical considerations a routine part of planning and policy meetings, new venture reports? Is the language of ethics taught and used? Does a formal committee exist high in the organization for considering ethical issues?

large organizations may have staff with the required expertise, many organizations will find that they will need to hire consultants to assist with these diagnoses and intervention efforts. When dealing with a sensitive topic such as ethics, outsiders may be preferable for other reasons as well. Employees may be more willing to discuss these sensitive issues with a trusted, external consultant. On the other hand, understanding the cultural issues addressed in this chapter can help any manager become more sensitive to the complex nature of organizational ethics and the importance of cultural alignment.

TABLE 9.2   Selected Questions for Auditing the Informal System

1. Identify the organization's heroes. What values do they represent? Given an ambiguous ethical dilemma, what decision would thay make and why?

2. What are some important organizational rituals? How do they encourage or discourage ehtical behavior? Who gets the awards, people of integrity who are successful or individuals who use unethical methods to attain success?

3. What are ethical messages sent to new entrants into the organization—must they obey authority at all costs, or is questioning authority acceptable or even desirable?

4. Does analysis of organizational stories and myths reveal individuals who stand up for what's right despite pressure, or is conformity the valued characteristic? Do people get fired or promoted in these stories?

5. Does acceptable language exist for discussing ethical concerns? Is this language routinely incorporated and encouraged in business decision making?

6. What informal socialization processes exist and what norms for ethical/unethical behavior do they promote? Are these different for different organizational subgroups?

Ethical Culture Change Intervention

Once the audit is complete, the data should be discussed with employees who can then be enlisted in the development of a culture change intervention plan. The plan will be guided by the diagnosis and the cultural, multisystem framework shown in Figure 9.1. Complementary changes in both the formal and informal organizational systems should be a part of any recommended change effort (see Figure 9.1.)

Though difficult, changing formal systems is a more straightforward process than changing informal systems. Gaps and problems identified in the diagnosis can be addressed in a number of ways. Structure can be altered to encourage individuals to take responsibility for their behavior and to discourage unquestioning deference to authority. Codes of ethics can be designed participatively, distributed, and enforced. Reward systems can be designed to punish unethical behavior. Whistleblowers can be encouraged and provided formal communication channels and confidentiality.[76] Orientation programs can be designed to incorporate the organization's values, and training programs can be set up for the individuals most likely to be faced with ethical dilemmas in their work. Integrity can be emphasized in selection and promotion decisions. Decision-making processes can incorporate attention to ethical issues by devoting time at meetings and space in reports.

It's more difficult to change the informal systems, particularly those that have been found to maintain unethical behavior in the organization. However, these changes must be undertaken if the total change effort is to be effective. These changes require attention to the "art" rather than the science of management and are consistent with ideas about the importance of "symbolic management." With

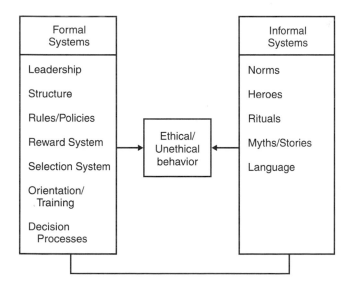

Figure 9.1 Developing and changing organizational ethics—a multisystem cultural framework

symbolic management, organizational leaders and managers are encouraged to create rituals, symbols, and stories that will influence those they manage.[77]

The organization may have to be "remythologized"[78] by reviving myths and stories of its founding and resurrecting related tales that can guide organizational behavior in the desired direction. For example, Alexander Bell's comment, "Come here, Watson, I need your help," set up Bell's concept of service that was so important to AT&T's success for many years. However, myths must also be frequently evaluated for their continuing usefulness. New ones may have to be found or developed in order to fit the current needs and goals of the organization. Remythologizing should be done carefully and infrequently. Employees generally know what's "really going on" in the organization. If the revived myth doesn't fit with organizational reality, it will only increase their cynicism. Also, myths can't be changed frequently. Their strength and value in the culture come from their stability across time.

Ethical Culture Change Evaluation

As with any organizational change and development effort, results should be evaluated over an extended period of time. Evaluation, like diagnosis and intervention, should be guided by the multisystem framework. Surveys and interviews can be repeated regularly to determine if norms have changed and to pinpoint potential problem areas. Documents can be analyzed to determine if ethical issues are being consistently considered. Other outcomes, such as number of lawsuits or reports of unethical behavior can also be tracked. However, interpretation may need to go beyond simply the numbers. Increased reporting to a hotline, for example, may only mean that ethical sensitivity has been raised and can be viewed as a positive outcome rather than a negative one. This is probably the part of culture building that is most neglected. Most organizations are unwilling to make the investment in evaluation, and therefore they really can't calculate the effectiveness of their efforts.

THE ETHICS OF MANAGING ORGANIZATIONAL ETHICS

An effort aimed at changing organizational ethics requires us to face a particularly knotty ethical dilemma. Whose values or ethics are to prevail? We believe that a change effort that involves employees is not manipulative or coercive and is most consistent with a concern for the ethics of the change effort itself. Employees should participate in the problem diagnosis and planning process. They should be aware of what's happening and should take part in identifying problems and recommending solutions.

CONCLUSION

This chapter has proposed a cultural framework for thinking about ethical and unethical behavior in the organizational context. Although individual character traits may predispose a person to ethical or unethical behavior, the cultural context in the organization also has a powerful influence on the behavior of most employees. An organization that wishes to develop or change its ethical culture must attend to the complex interplay of formal and informal systems that can support either ethical or unethical behavior. Quick-fix solutions are not likely to succeed. A broad, multisystem approach to developing and changing organizational ethics was outlined to guide organizations in diagnosing and, if necessary, changing their ethical culture.

Although most managers are not prepared to conduct a broad culture change effort themselves, this chapter has provided managers with the understanding that organizational ethics is a complex cultural phenomenon. With this knowledge, the manager can begin to assess the ethical culture of the organization and will know what questions to ask the consultant who is brought in to help with a culture change effort.

DISCUSSION QUESTIONS

For the following questions, focus on an organization with which you are familiar. Or if you are a student without significant organizational experience, discuss the questions with someone who is currently in a managerial role.

1. Does your organization address ethical issues in a formal, systematic way? If so, is it a cookie cutter, one size fits all approach, or has the organization customized an ethical culture to match its unique needs?

2. To the best of your ability, use the questions in Tables 9.1 and 9.2 to conduct an ethics audit of the formal and informal systems in your organization.

3. Having conducted the ethics audit, identify the formal and informal systems that are in need of attention. Design a change program to address weaknesses and to align formal and informal systems into a strong ethical culture.

$\langle$ **CASE 9.1** $\rangle$

VideoTek Corporation

Jeremy Campbell is the chief executive officer and chairman of a relatively young, publicly held, Boston high-tech company we'll call VideoTek (for video technology). VideoTek was founded in 1980 by Earl Mantz who created a device that could convert black and white computer monitors into color monitors and would sell for $85.

The company started with two people and grew quickly to a core of 35 people who respected Earl as a visionary. Some in the founding group described him as a "deep thinking, spiritual type of person, with high ethical standards." The company culture evolved naturally out of his style. It was a hard work/high trust culture. Good people were hired and trusted to work hard and well for the company, and they did. It was common for people to work 60 to 80 hours a week for VideoTek. They believed in what they were doing and they believed in their product.

The company grew explosively from just two employees in 1980 to 1500 employees and over $200 million in sales in 1994. In 1989, when the company had achieved approximately $40 million in sales, it went public. A professional manager, Jeremy Campbell, was recruited from a large company to bring operational sanity to this small company that was growing out of control. He was named president and CEO. Earl, now a multimillionaire, happily became a member of the Board.

Jeremy brought in his own team—big company types—to manage the company. However, he recognized the value of Videotek's culture, and he vowed to perpetuate it. Management today still prides itself on the company's flat organizational structure (e.g., few layers of management) and efficient, open communication via the company's electronic mail system originally set up by Earl. Just about everything that needs to be communicated within the company is communicated by electronic mail. Employees who are on the road keep in touch via their laptops. In support of communication openness, a unique feature of the system allows messages to be sent anonymously.

But all is not rosy at VideoTek. Not long after Jeremy's arrival, long-time employees began to question top management's commitment to all aspects of the culture. They felt that he especially liked the "hard work" part,

but what happened to "high trust"? Something was amiss. Jeremy seemed to be big on words but short on follow through. He was doing some things that seemed highly questionable and supporting the questionable conduct of his friends. The key question seemed to be, "Could this top management team be trusted?"

Finally, the company has been experiencing a slowdown in growth. It needs new products to sustain its growth, but so far new products introduced under Jeremy's leadership have had disappointing results.

Following are two ethics-related electronic mail messages. The first is a message sent to all employees by Jeremy Campbell in response to an incident of unethical behavior that the grapevine was buzzing about. The second communication is an electronic mail message also sent to all employees a month later by an anonymous employee.

E-MAIL COMMUNICATION FROM THE CHAIRMAN AND CEO
From: Jeremy Cam@VTK 1-MAR-1993
To: All Staff
Subj: Ethical Conduct. Actions, Not Words.
The VideoTek Philosophy is a blueprint for action, a template for daily life at VideoTek. The second we forget that, we are vulnerable to internal challenges which threaten the very foundation of our continued success.

One precept of the VideoTek Philosophy must not be compromised under any circumstances: we live and work ethically. It is imperative to remind ourselves of certain key values which support this commitment:

The goal of any business is to make a sound profit. Our dedication to quality will help us realize that goal. We do not compromise our integrity in the name of profits.

VideoTek is changing the way people do business. Because we truly have an impact on people's lives, we must set a positive example of leadership and credibility in all things we do.

We are honest and fair in all transactions with our customers, suppliers, shareholders and each other.

As specific challenges to these values have arisen, we have addressed them swiftly and decisively. In order to maintain focus on ethical behavior throughout the organization, I have formed a task force consisting of Joe Donaldson, Bill Sykes, Alan Golden, and Joyce Eldridge. This group will examine the following issues in depth and provide me with specific recommendations for corrective action:

- Relationships between VideoTek employees and customers and suppliers
- Outside business activities of VideoTek employees
- Protection of company assets and intellectual property rights

Beyond your own conduct, you have an obligation to report circumstances which you believe to be in conflict with VideoTek's ethical standards. Our ethics committee—composed of Joe Donaldson, Leslie Bolton, Alan Golden, and Joyce Eldridge—has been established to hear these reports and recommend the appropriate response.

VideoTek has been successful because of our ethics, not in spite of them. Only by remaining true to ourselves—resolute in our beliefs and consistent in our actions—will we continue to fulfill our mission. This requires both courage and wisdom, the very same qualities that have made us the company that we are today.

Jeremy.

E-MAIL COMMUNICATION FROM ANONYMOUS EMPLOYEE
From: SECRET@VTK 1-APR-1993
To: All Staff
Subj: Preliminary Report from VideoTek Ethics Committee

The VideoTek Ethics committee, consisting of Joe Donaldson, Leslie Bolton, Alan Golden, and Joyce Eldridge has been meeting to ensure that all VideoTek employees act in the most ethical possible manner. We must all remember the timeless words of our president Jeremy Campbell: "One precept of the VideoTek Philosophy must not be compromised under any circumstances: we live and work ethically."

In light of this, we have prepared the 1992 Spearshaft of Ethics awards for cases of outstanding ethical behavior within VideoTek.

For instance, the Ethics Committee has received nominations from a few employees for one particular director of VideoTek who is also a major stockholder in one of VideoTek's customers, and whose son, a former employee of VideoTek, is also involved with this customer. Moreover, according to these employees, VideoTek has spent large sums of money and plans to spend even more to develop products for this customer, despite the fact that they have not lived up to the terms of their initial agreement with VideoTek. However, to avoid the slightest tiniest hint of a conflict of interest, the director in question stepped out of the meeting when the Board of Directors voted to approve the deal. Well, he didn't actually step out of the room, but he didn't vote on it, and that qualifies him for the Golden Spearshaft of Ethics. Even if VideoTek eventually loses money on the deal, we can still be proud to have lived by the highest of ethical standards.

From another employee who even read the annual report, we learned that the eight-person Board of Directors voted in 1992 to give all seven of the nonemployee directors stock options. We think that it was very important that the directors get these stock options. The directors do not have nearly enough money. In fact, some of them are practically living on the brink of poverty, or at any rate on the brink of being merely well off. For the eight of them to generously give the seven of themselves these options was the least they could do. After all, the options are only worth $850,000 between them. Because of this generous and self-sacrificing move we are awarding the entire Board of Directors the Silver Spearshaft of Ethics.

Don't believe the rumor that top management has been inconsistent in ethical word and deed. The malcontents who are spreading this rumor are woefully misinformed about a recent incident. As everyone knows, Amy Masterson has been one of our finest sales representatives for several years. However, her commitment to the firm recently came into question when she steadfastly refused to release customer confidential information, even when encouraged to do so by some highly placed VideoTek managers, and even when releasing the information would have clearly contributed to VideoTek's bottom line. Nor would Amy accept the $150,000 top management offered her to go quietly. The entire top management team has been awarded a Bronze Spearshaft of Ethics for their unending support of unquestioning loyalty to the firm. (By the way, donations to help Amy defray her legal expenses on her unjust discharge lawsuit may be sent directly to her home.)

Sadly, it has also come to our attention that some employees have said that our Human Resources Policies do not live up to

VideoTek's ethical philosophy. Nothing could be further from the truth. The Human Resources Policies have been reviewed and considered as broadly as possible within the company. For instance, the company policy on nepotism was carefully evaluated by both Jim and Dana Swift. The company policy on termination of employees was scrutinized by a tremendous number of VideoTek employees within the BW and TC Divisions [two new product divisions that have been shut down, millions of dollars in losses, and hundreds of layoffs]. The ethics committee will also be inviting the employees who made the Spearshaft of Ethics nominations to personally review the termination policy, as soon as we can learn their names. Finally, VideoTek's policy on fair compensation was exhaustively studied by Jeremy himself, with the assistance of *Business Week* magazine, and he said he is fully satisfied that VideoTek is paying fair compensation.

In fact, the executive compensation committee has determined that the company's performance in 1992 was so outstanding that Jeremy has fully earned his compensation of $375,426 plus $50,000 bonus plus options, even though the company's performance was so average that it would be totally unreasonable for any employees to receive bonuses for 1992. In light of this, we are jointly awarding the Tin Spearshaft of Ethics to the entire Human Resources Department and the executive compensation committee.

There are so many outstanding feats of ethical behavior within this company that we are sorry we can only honor an outstanding few. We hope that this will inspire everyone within the company to try harder in the coming year to live up to VideoTek's high ethical standards.

Lastly, we offer a few words from Jeremy himself: "I am personally chagrined that anyone could have any perception that any VideoTek employee would do anything unethical. Whoever you are, you had better just change your perception, Buster!"

Joe Donaldson, Leslie Bolton, Alan Golden, and Joyce El dridge—NOT! April Fool's!

Case-Based Questions

1. Evaluate Jeremy Campbell's e-mail communication. Assume that this was the only "formal" communication employees had received from him regarding ethics (aside from a "Ten Commandments" type brochure handed to every new employee at orientation). Do you think electronic mail is an appropriate medium for this message? Why or why not? How would you evaluate the content of the communication itself?

2. Next, think about the anonymous e-mail communication. Assume that this communication represents the thinking of a large number of other employees, not just a lone dissenter. What does it say about the

alignment or misalignment of VideoTek's ethical culture? For example, what does the communication say about the perception of ethical leadership, reward systems, honesty, and decision processes in the firm?

3. Shortly after this anonymous communication was sent, the ability to send anonymous communications was eliminated from the firm's electronic mail system. What kind of symbolic message do you think that action sent?

4. Earl Mantz, the founder, was a cultural hero while he ran the company during its early years. He had created and maintained the hard work/high trust culture and had the respect of the people who worked for him. Now, however, many see him as someone who sold out, and a growing number of people from the original committed group are leaving to join other companies. In fact, less than 5 people remain from the original 35. They get together for a beer occasionally and reminisce about old times. Recently, one of them went on about how money and power can corrupt, "I wonder if the culture was ever real?" What has happened to the hard work/high trust culture? What happened to Earl's ability to provide decision-making guidance? Is there any hope for culture change in this organization? For remythologizing?

ANOTHER CASE—CULTURE CHANGE AT DENNY'S?[79]

In April 1993, Denny's settled a federal suit that charged the firm with discriminating against African American customers in California. In the end, Denny's paid $54 million to 295,000 minority customers and their lawyers.

Apparently, there were serious problems throughout the Denny's organization. In 1990, a consulting firm brought in to address Flagstar's financial problems identified the lack of diversity as a problem for the organization. In response, the CEO at the time said, "I'm sure you're right about our being behind on diversity, but I just never thought about it."[80] The leadership didn't take the racial problems seriously at first. They just didn't recognize the extent of the problem. But a white waitress in a California restaurant declared in court that "the N word" was commonly used and that management didn't want to "encourage black customers to stay in the restaurant." A manager of another California restaurant said that staffers would actually close the restaurant when they were concerned that too many African Americans were there. They had a name for the policy—"blackout." When the manager discontinued the policy, he was threatened with firing. Procurement officers claimed that it was difficult to find minority suppliers. But minority vendors who tried to do business with Denny's claimed that they were ignored by the company's buyers.

Shortly after the lawsuit was settled, a new CEO, Ron Petty (former head of Burger King, USA), was hired to help repair the company's shattered reputation. A new CEO also entered the picture at Flagstar, Denny's parent company and a holding company that owns several restaurant chains. Jim Adamson, the new Flagstar CEO, was also a Burger King veteran. Both CEOs worked together to implant diversity into the entire Flagstar corporate culture. At his first meeting with employees, Adamson said that he was "going to do everything possible to provide better jobs for women and minorities. And I will fire you if you discriminate. Anyone who doesn't like the direction this train is moving had better jump off now."[81] Adamson's background prepared him well for his task. The son of a general, he was born in Japan and grew up on army bases all over the world where he played with children from all kinds of backgrounds. He was often the only white kid around. After a few months with Adamson as CEO, only four of the previous top officers remained. A Hispanic man and an African American woman were among the replacements. The new leaders also implemented a selection program that screens job applicants for racial bias. They created new management training programs that help move minorities onto the fast track for executive leadership positions and prepare them to become successful franchisees. They also created a diversity training program for employees that emphasizes equal treatment for all customers. Employees who resisted the program had to participate in advanced sensitivity training in an all-day intensive program conducted by outside consultants. Some employees who have continued to resist the culture change have been fired. Denny's ads were changed to feature a minimum of 30 percent African American or other minorities. By 1996, the number of minority executives had risen from zero in 1993 to 11 percent. The number of directors, jobs just below vice president, increased from zero in 1993 to 20 percent in 1996. The number of African American franchisees increased from one in 1993 to 27 in 1996. Minority vendors are being contacted by Denny's new director of minority business development, and deals are being made. Higher goals in all of these areas have been set for the future.

Case-Based Questions

1. Identify the ethical culture problem at Denny's in 1993.

2. Based on the facts in the case, evaluate the culture change effort that is underway. What cultural systems have been targeted in the culture change effort? What systems are missing? What else might management do that they haven't already done to make the culture change successful?

3. How long might such a culture change take?

NOTES

1. Byrne, J. 1992. The best laid ethics programs. *Business Week,* March 9: 67–69.
2. Murphy, P. 1989. Creating ethical corporate structures. *Sloan Management Review* 30 (2): 221–227.
3. Ibid.
4. Wesslund, P. 1992. Ethics are no substitute for the real thing. *Business Week,* April 7.
5. Murphy, Creating ethical corporate structures.
6. Barrett, R. A. 1984. *Culture and conduct: An excursion in anthropology.* Belmont, CA: Wadsworth.
7. Deal, T. E., & Kennedy, A. A. 1982. *Corporate cultures.* Reading, MA: Addison-Wesley.

   Louis, M. R. 1981. A cultural perspective on organizations: The need for and consequences of viewing organizations as culture-bearing milieux. *Human Systems Management,* 246–258.

   Martin, J., & Siehl, C. 1983. Organizational culture and counterculture: An uneasy symbiosis. *Organizational Dynamics,* Autumn: 52–64.

   Pettigrew, A. M. 1979. On studying organizational cultures. *Administrative Science Quarterly* 24: 570–580.

   Schein, E. H. 1985b. *Organizational culture and leadership.* San Francisco: Jossey-Bass.

   Smircich, L. 1983. Concepts of culture and organizational analysis. *Administrative Science Quarterly* 28: 339–358.
8. Smircich, L. 1983. Concepts of culture and organizational analysis. *Administrative Science Quarterly* 28: 339–358.
9. Deal & Kennedy, *Corporate cultures.*
10. Morris, B. 1997. He's smart. he's not nice. he's saving Big Blue. *Fortune,* April 14: 68–81.
11. Deal & Kennedy, *Corporate cultures.*
12. Van Maanen, J., & Schein, E. H. 1979. Toward a theory of organizational socialization. In L. Cummings & B. Staw (Eds.), *Research in organizational behavior,* vol. 1. New York: JAI Press.

    Fisher, C. D. 1986. Organizational socialization: an integrative review. In K. Rowland & G. Ferris (Eds.), *Research in Personnel and Human Resources Management,* vol. 4. Greenwich, CT: JAI Press, 101–145.
13. Barrett, *Culture and conduct.*
14. Schein, *Organizational culture and leadership.*
15. Pettigrew, On studying organizational cultures.

    Schein, E. H. 1985a. How culture forms, develops, and changes. In R. H. Kilmann, M. J. Saxtion, & R. Serpa (Eds.), *Gaining control of the corporate culture.* San Francisco: Jossey-Bass, 17–43.

    Selznick, P. 1957. *Leadership in administration.* New York: Harper & Row.
16. Manley, W. W. II. 1991. *Executive's handbook of model business conduct codes.* Englewood Cliffs, NJ: Prentice-Hall.

17. Schein, *Organizational culture and leadership.*

    Selznick, P. 1957. *Leadership in administration.* New York: Harper & Row.

18. Business Roundtable. 1988. *Corporate ethics: A prime business asset.* New York: Business Roundtable.

19. Treviño, L. K., Butterfield, K., & McCabe, D. in press. The ethical context in organizations: Influences on employee attitudes and behaviors. *Business Ethics Quarterly.*

20. Paterno, Joe. 1989. *Paterno by the book.* New York: Random House.

21. Borden, R. C. 1989. Sherrill's termination released. *Bryan College Station Eagle,* March 3: 1.

    Hamilton, A. 1989. Switzer resigns. *Centre Daily Times,* June 20: D1.

    Status of sports investigations on college campuses. 1989. *The Chronicle of Higher Education,* June 7: A34.

22. Lacter, M. 1985. Levi's buyout—It's official. *San Francisco Chronicle,* July 16: 51.

23. Managing by values; Is Levi Strauss' approach visionary—or flaky? 1994. *Business Week,* August 1: 46–51.

24. Ibid.

25. Maremont, M. 1995. Blind ambition; how the pursuit of results got out of hand at Bausch & Lomb. *Business Week,* October 23: 78–92.

26. Weber, M. 1947. *The theory of social and economic organizations.* Translated by A. M. Henderson and T. Parsons. New York: Free Press.

27. Sjoberg, G., Vaughan, T. R., & Williams, N. 1984. Bureaucracy as a moral issue. *Journal of Applied Behavioral Science* 20 (4): 441–453.

28. Milgram, S. 1974. *Obedience to authority: An experimental view.* New York: Harper & Row.

29. Jackall, R. 1988. *Moral mazes: The world of corporate managers.* New York: Oxford University Press.

30. Kanter, R. M. 1983. *The changemasters.* New York: Simon and Schuster.

31. Kelman, H. C., & Hamilton, V. L. 1989. *Crimes of obedience; Toward a social psychology of authority and responsibility.* New Haven, CT: Yale University.

32. Nelson-Horchler, 1991. The magic of Herman Miller. *Industry Week,* February 18: 11–12, 14,17.

33. Weaver, G. R., Treviño, L. K., & Cochran, P. L. in press. Corporate ethics practices in the mid-1990s: An empirical study of the Fortune 1000. *Journal of Business Ethics.*

34. McCabe, D., Treviño, L. K., & Butterfield, K. D. 1996. The influence of collegiate and corporate codes of conduct on ethics-related behavior in the workplace. *Business Ethics Quarterly* 6 (4): 461–476.

35. Weaver, Treviño, & Cochran, Corporate ethics practices in the mid-1980s.

36. Bowers, W. J. 1964. *Student dishonesty and its control in college.* New York: Bureau of Applied Social Research, Columbia University.

    Campbell, W. G. 1935. *A comparative investigation of students under an honor system and a proctor system in the same university.* Los Angeles: University of Southern California Press.

    Canning, R. 1956. Does an honor system reduce classroom cheating? An experimental answer. *Journal of Experimental Education* 24: 291–296.

37. McCabe, D. L., & Treviño, L. K. 1993. Academic dishonesty: Honor codes and other situational influences. *Journal of Higher Education* 64 (5): 522–528.

38. Nel, D., Pitt, L., & Watson, R. 1989. Business ethics: Defining the twilight zone. *Journal of Business Ethics* 8: 781–791.

39. Labich, K. 1992. The new crisis in business ethics. *Fortune,* April 20: 167–176.

40. Graham, J. W. 1986. Principled organizational dissent: A theoretical essay. In L. Cummings & B. M. Staw, *Research in organizational behavior,* vol. 8. Greenwich, CT: JAI Press, 1–52.

    Near, J. P., & Miceli, M. P. 1987. Whistleblowers in organizations: dissidents or reformers? In Cummings & Staw, *Research in organizational behavior.* Research in organizational behavior, 321–368.

41. Glazer, M. P., & Glazer, P. M. 1986. Whistleblowing. *Psychology Today,* August.

42. Murray, T. J. 1987. Ethics programs: Just a pretty face? *Business Month,* 130 (3): 30–32.

43. Greenberg, A. C. 1996. Memos from the chairman. *Fortune,* April 29: 173–175.

44. Weaver, Treviño, & Cochran, Corporate ethics practices in the mid-1990s.

45. Allied Corporation. 1984. Ethics education for managers. *Ethics Resource Center Report* 2: 1.

46. Schwartz, H., & Davis, S. M. 1981. Matching corporate culture and business strategy. *Organizational Dynamics,* Summer: 30–48.

47. Tiger, L. 1988. Stone age provides model for instilling business ethics. *Wall Street Journal,* January 11: 18.

48. Gellerman, S. 1986. Why "good" managers make bad ethical choices. *Harvard Business Review,* Winter: 15–19.

49. Welles, C. 1988. What led Beech-Nut down the road to disgrace? *Business Week,* February 22.

50. Deal & Kennedy, *Corporate cultures.*

51. Paterno, *Paterno by the book.*

52. Van Maanen, J., & Schein, E. H. 1979. Toward a theory of organizational socialization. In Cummings & Staw (Eds.), *Research in organizational behavior,* vol. 1.

53. Waters, J. A. 1978. Catch 20.5: Corporate morality as an organizational phenomenon. *Organizational Dynamics,* Spring: 3–19.

54. Deal & Kennedy, *Corporate cultures.*

55. Beyer, J. M. & Trice, H. M. 1987. How an organization's rites reveal its culture. *Organizational Dynamics* 15 (4): 5–24.

56. Channon, J. 1992. Creating esprit de corps. In *New traditions in Business; Spirit and leadership in the 21st century.* San Francisco: Berrett Koehler Publishers, 53–66.

57. Mitroff, I. & Kilmann, R. H. 1976. On organizational stories: An approach to the design and analysis of organization through myths and stories. In R. Kilmann, L. Pondy, & Slevin (Eds.), *The management of organization design; Strategies and implications.* New York: North-Holland.

58. Martin, J., & Siehl, C. 1983. Organizational culture and counterculture: An uneasy symbiosis. *Organizational Dynamics,* Autumn: 52–64.

59. Paterno, *Paterno by the book.*

60. Ibid.

61. Bird, F. B., & Waters, J. A. 1989. The moral muteness of managers. *California Management Review,* Fall: 73–88.

62. Berney, K. 1987. Finding the ethical edge. *Nation's Business,* August: 18–24.

63. Bird & Waters, The moral muteness of managers.

64. Berney, Finding the ethical edge.

65. Treviño, L. K. 1987. The influences of vicarious learning and individual differences on ethical decision making in the organization: An experiment. Unpublished doctoral dissertation, Texas A & M University, College Station, Texas.

66. Kelman & Hamilton, Crimes of obedience.

67. Barrett, *Culture and conduct.*
    Uttal, B. 1983. The corporate culture vultures. *Fortune,* October 17: 66–71.

68. Barrett, *Culture and conduct.*

69. Ricklees, R. 1983. Ethics in America series. *Wall Street Journal,* October 31–November 3: 33.

70. Tichy, N. 1983. *Managing strategic change.* New York: John Wiley & Sons.

71. Uttal, The corporate culture vultures.

72. Nord, W. R. 1989. OD's unfulfilled visions: Some lessons from economics. In R. W. Woodman & W. A. Pasmore (Eds.), *Research in organizational change and development.* Greenwich, CT: JAI Press, 39–60.

73. Uttal, The corporate culture vultures.

74. Wilkins, A. L. 1983. The culture audit: A tool for understanding organizations. *Organizational Dynamics,* Autumn: 24–38.

75. Luthans, F. 1989. Conversation with Edgar H. Schein. *Organizational Dynamics,* 17 (4): 60–76.

76. Near & Miceli, Whistleblowers in organizations. In Cummings & Staw (Eds.), *Research in organizational behavior.*

77. Peters, T. 1978. Symbols, patterns, and settings: An optimistic case of getting things done. *Organizational Dynamics,* Autumn: 3–23.

78. McWhinney, W. & Batista, J. 1988. How remythologizing can revitalize organizations. *Organizational Dynamics* 17 (2): 46–79.

79. Rice, F. 1996. Denny's changes its spots. *Fortune,* May 13: 133–140.

80. Ibid., p. 135.

81. Ibid., p. 134.

CHAPTER 10

Creating an Ethical Organizational Culture: Model Ethics Programs

INTRODUCTION

Chapter Nine presented ethics as organizational culture. But it may have raised as many questions as it answered, such as "What are real organizations actually doing to create and communicate an ethical organizational culture?" This chapter is more concrete and is designed to answer that question. It focuses on explicit examples from model ethics programs—corporations that manage and communicate ethics in ways that are consistent with their cultures. We focus primarily on the successful ethics management practices of two Texas companies, one large and one small.

Texas Instruments (TI) is a large, multinational electronics firm headquartered in Dallas with over 40,000 employees in more than 25 countries. It published its first written code of ethics in 1961. As the business continued to grow and become more complex, it introduced a more comprehensive and formal ethics program in 1987. In recognition of its exceptional efforts in the ethics management area over the years, TI has received three awards: the David C. Lincoln Award for Ethics and Excellence in Business (1991), the American Business Ethics Award (1994), and the Bentley College Center for Business Ethics Award (1994).

Most discussions of ethics programs focus on large organizations and their formal ethics programs. But most people work for smaller firms, and we wanted to explore how ethics can be managed in this smaller firm environment. Holt Companies, headquartered in San Antonio, Texas, provides an excellent example of how a smaller firm that is highly committed to ethics can address the ethics management issue. At the end of the chapter, we will describe Holt's exceptional "Values-Based Leadership" approach.

Whatever your organizational level, you should find this chapter helpful. If you're at a high organization level, it could give you ideas about how to create an ethical culture in your firm. If you're at a lower or mid-management level, it should help you to understand your own organization's approach to ethics management and how it relates to what other organizations are currently doing. If you're a student, you will know what to look for during the job-seeking process.

STRUCTURING ETHICS MANAGEMENT: THE ETHICS INFRASTRUCTURE

Many organizations are allocating significant resources toward formal ethics and legal compliance programs. One CEO recently estimated that his firm spends a million dollars per year on such programs.[1] This increasing attention to formal ethics management programs has come about because of management's increasing awareness of the U.S. Sentencing guidelines (see Chapter 2); because organizations such as the Conference Board have held business ethics conferences for a number of years at which formal ethics management systems are encouraged; and because some corporate leaders are simply committed to the importance of ethics in their organizations.[2]

Who Manages Formal Ethics Programs?

Some organizations delegate ethics management responsibilities widely, finding that a strong statement of values and a strong ethical culture can bind the ethics management effort together. This approach may be particularly effective in smaller firms. However, most large ones are deciding that ethics initiatives need to be coordinated from a single office to ensure that all of the program's pieces fit together and that all of the U.S. Sentencing Guidelines requirements are being met.

The corporate ethics office concept is relatively new. It can be traced to 1985 and General Dynamics, then the second largest U.S. defense contractor. The secretary of the navy, out of concern about the allowability of certain indirect expenses that had been billed to the government, directed General Dynamics to establish and enforce a rigorous code of ethics for all employees, with sanctions for violators. The company turned to a nonprofit consulting firm in Washington, DC, the Ethics Resource Center, for help in developing the code. As part of this process, an ethics office was set up and an ethics officer was hired.[3]

The 1991 U.S. Federal Sentencing Guidelines gave further impetus to the move toward naming ethics officers and establishing formal ethics offices in many more firms. The guidelines list seven requirements (see Chapter Two) for due diligence and an effective compliance program. One of the requirements calls for the assignment of specific high-level individuals with responsibility to oversee legal compliance standards. This responsibility can be held by one executive, or it can be divided among a number of individuals such as the legal counsel, internal auditors, or human resource professionals.

Until the mid-1980s, the title "ethics officer" didn't exist in American business. However, there are enough of these high-level ethics executives today that they now have their own professional organization, the Ethics Officer Association (EOA). The organization's stated mission is "to promote ethical business practices, serving as a forum for the exchange of information and strategies." The organization began in 1991 when over 40 ethics/compliance officers met at the Center for Business Ethics at Bentley College in Waltham, Massachusetts. The organization was officially launched later that year and began holding annual meetings in 1993. As of the end of 1997, the organization had members representing nearly three hundred companies. The organization also now holds regular workshops and provides training for ethics officers.

Ethics Officers

Approximately one-third of the corporate respondents to a 1995 survey for Fortune 1000 firms reported having an ethics officer function.[4] Many firms designate their general counsel as the ethics officer. Others create a title like vice-president or director of ethics, compliance, or business practices, director of internal audit, or just plain ethics officer. Most firms locate the ethics officer at the corporate level, and these high-level executives generally report to a senior executive, the CEO, the board of directors, a committee of the board, or some combination. These individuals are expected to provide leadership and strategies for ensuring that the firm's standards of business conduct are communicated and upheld.

Insiders versus Outsiders An ethics officer may be an insider or someone brought in from the outside. We talked to past and present ethics officers who represent both categories. The consensus among them seems to favor a respected and trusted insider who knows the company's culture and people. Results of the 1995 survey support the insider preference. Eighty-two percent of the firms responding to the question hired their ethics officer from inside the firm. However, if the organization needs to make a drastic change, the CEO may feel it necessary to bring in an unbiased outsider who can help guide the organization through a culture change process.

Ethics Officer Background The job of ethics officer has been called "the newest profession in American business."[5] These individuals come from many backgrounds. With insiders, the job is often assigned to someone in a staff function (e.g., someone in the Corporate Secretary's Office, Office of the Legal Counsel, Audit, Human Resources, or Public Affairs). According to the 1995 ethics officer survey, law was the most common background. But some believe that lawyers shouldn't be considered for the job because corporate lawyers face a potential conflict of interest. They're hired to defend the corporation and therefore can't objectively handle an ethical issue that calls the corporation's behavior into question. The ethics officers we interviewed agreed that there is no single preferred background. What seems to be most important is that the individual is respected for being fair, trustworthy, credible, and discreet.

Carl Skooglund, TI's vice president and ethics director, has spent most of his career at Texas Instruments. He worked his way up through engineering and manufacturing and held a variety of operational jobs. He was a product department manager, a division manager, and head of quality training and development and procurement, before being asked to set up the ethics office in 1987. When interviewed, Carl said,

> A lot of people have asked me why I was selected for this job and I think it's probably because I had a lot of experience on the factory floor. People also tell me I come across as non-threatening. I've always dealt with people well. I've had good communication relationships both up and down the organization. People at lower levels have generally felt that I'm approachable and I guess they trusted me. If you were to ask me what are the characteristics I would look for if I were selecting an ethics officer, it would be somebody who would be reasonably well known and trusted, somebody who has had experience on day-to-day workplace issues and the kinds of pressures that people are under, and clearly somebody who is perceived to be very discreet.

The Ethics Office, the Organizational Structure, and the CEO

Ethics offices can be centralized or decentralized. The decision to centralize or decentralize may depend on the overall structure of the firm and on whether different business units have different ethics management needs. If the firm's other staff functions are highly decentralized, it may be difficult to centralize the ethics function. Also, a local ethics office might better meet the needs of different units that are in different businesses. But decentralized ethics offices can be difficult to manage effectively because they must communicate with each other constantly to ensure consistency and commitment to the organization's key values.

Texas Instruments has a single ethics office that manages and coordinates all corporate ethics activities. This centralized ethics office is the central point of communications for the global firm. Given the size of the firm, the ethics office at TI is small. Carl Skooglund has a staff of four that handles all ethics issues worldwide. Such a small ethics staff makes it essential that the ethics office work closely with people in line and staff positions throughout the company in order to assess the state of ethics in the organization, develop standards and programs, and implement and evaluate those programs.

TI has been working hard to extend the global reach and effectiveness of the ethics office through a Global Business Practices Council. Council representatives, who represent TI's three major markets (Europe, Japan, and Asia Pacific), are selected on the basis of how they are positioned to do two things: (1) help disseminate ethics office communications so that there is consistent communication worldwide, and (2) help the ethics office understand how to communicate its message in different cultures and markets in the most appropriate manner. For example, these representatives helped the ethics office develop its new booklet entitled "Values and Ethics of TI" so that it would reflect the values and ethics of ALL TIers. The booklet, introduced in December 1997, has been translated into twelve languages and is being distributed globally.

Ethics officers seem to agree that, whatever other reporting relationships exist, the ethics officer should have a direct reporting relationship to the CEO. They were particularly concerned about the ethics function being "stuck" under law, human resources, audit, or finance where it could "have its strings yanked" and where it would be just another part of the "silo mentality" that still exists in many organizations. Ethics would then be perceived as Audit's job or HR's job rather than as part of the total culture. The person who leads the ethics office is in a much better position to "press the envelope" if he or she reports directly to the CEO.

The Corporate Ethics Committee

In some organizations, ethics is managed by a corporate committee staffed by senior-level managers from a variety of functional areas. This committee is set up to "provide ethical oversight and policy guidance for CEO and management decisions."[6] It also represents an affirmation that top management really cares about ethics.

At Texas Instruments, the TI ethics committee is composed of eight high-level managers, including the general counsel, the chief financial officer, the vice chairman, and the human resources director. The committee has two functions. First, it is a steering body for the ethics office, reviewing and approving major initiatives, and meeting three times per year. For example, the ethics committee recently approved a newly revised code of conduct. Second, the committee convenes on an ad hoc basis if issues come up that require high-level deliberation. Such an issue might be the decision to voluntarily disclose to the Justice Department that an employee has violated the law (in accordance with the U.S. Sentencing Commission Guidelines).

COMMUNICATING ETHICS

Within the ethics infrastructure, good communication—downward, upward, and two way—is essential if an organization is to have a strong, aligned ethics culture. The organization must evaluate the current state of ethics communication and initiatives. It must communicate its values, standards, and policies in a variety of formal and informal ways that meet its employees' needs. These communication efforts should be synergistic, clear, consistent, and credible. They also need to be executed in a variety of media, because people learn things in different ways. In general, the old advice to speech writers still holds. "Tell 'em what you're going to tell 'em, then tell 'em, then tell 'em what you told 'em." In addition to downward communication from management, employees must also be provided opportunities to communicate their ethical concerns upward. Finally, an open communication environment must be created that says it's OK to ask questions and it's OK to talk about ethics. In the following section, we begin with some corporate communications basics—principles that should guide all ethics communication initiatives.

A number of the executives we interviewed, particularly the ethics officers, were sensitive to the negativity often attached to the word "ethics." Employees can get defensive when they hear the word. They think to themselves, "Why are you here talking to me about ethics? Mine are fine." Kent Druyvesteyn, former ethics officer at General Dynamics, put it this way. "When you first stand up and say, 'Hi, I'm here to talk about ethics,' don't expect people to cheer. Don't expect people to say, 'Oh I'm really glad, I can't wait to talk about ethics. I just love ethics.' No, the response is going to be largely negative and defensive. They're not happy to see you. People are going to ask, 'Why are you talking to ME about ethics?' Using the word ethics unfortunately implies that somebody has a deficiency. So, I would urge you not to use that word at least until you can make clear what you mean by it."

Basic Communications Principles

Corporate Credibility—Align the Formal and Informal Communication Systems When most people think of a corporate communications system, they think of the obvious—the company newspaper, the annual report, and other written materials. However, like culture, a corporate communications system consists of formal and informal components. Formal communications include all written communication such as newspapers, magazines, memos, recruiting literature, policy manuals, annual reports, and advertising, as well as formalized oral communication such as meetings and speeches. But perhaps the most powerful component in a corporation's communications system is the informal component—the grapevine.

The grapevine—a continual stream of information among employees about "what's really going on"—exists in every organization. It contains news, rumors, impressions, and perceptions. Surprisingly, research has shown that from 70 to 90 percent of the information that passes through the grapevine is accurate.[7] In survey after survey of employees in numerous and varied businesses, the grapevine is where they said they received most of their information about their employer. (In those same surveys, most people said that they would rather receive information from their managers.) The grapevine can be examined to shed light on a corporation's credibility since most employees are plugged into it, it provides information fast and continually, and it contains the "inside" scoop on corporate events.

One way to determine corporate credibility on various issues—especially ethics—is to compare the messages on the formal and informal communications systems. For example, suppose that XYZ Company has a policy prohibiting employees from excessively entertaining customers. The policy is spelled out in a manual, and the president of XYZ has reinforced the policy in speeches to employees. Now imagine that XYZ's head of marketing repeatedly wines and dines clients. The costs of the lavish entertainment are detailed in expense reports that are approved by management and that are processed by clerical and financial control employees. In addition, other employees are invited along when the clients are entertained, and still more employees observe the head of marketing entertaining guests in expensive restaurants. Regardless of how strongly XYZ's formal communications system states the official policy, the informal communication system—the grapevine—will communicate what's really going on: XYZ is saying one thing and doing another. The company says it prohibits lavish entertainment, yet it condones that forbidden behavior in at least one high-level employee. As a result, XYZ's ethics culture is out of alignment, and it has no corporate credibility on the subject of customer entertainment. Furthermore, its credibility on other ethical issues is probably suspect.

Now, imagine another situation. LMN Company has a strongly worded policy regarding sexual harassment. Moreover, LMN's senior executives have frequently stated that sexual harassment will not be tolerated. Suppose a manager, Pat, is accused of sexual harassment. The charge is investigated, found to be accurate, and Pat is fired. The exact details of the incident may not be on the grapevine, but in most cases, just the bare bones of that story will send a strong message. The messages on the grapevine will match what's said by LMN's formal communications system. Employees will get the word very quickly that LMN means business on the issue of sexual harassment, and the corporation will have increased its credibility by "walking the talk."

The importance of informal communications can't be overstated. Since truth and honesty are at the core of any ethics effort, if a company is saying one thing and doing another—if the messages on its formal communications system and its grapevine don't match—it has little or no credibility and probably shouldn't attempt a formal ethics communications effort until it has regained its credibility. How can you compare the formal and informal messages? Ask employees. Employee surveys and focus groups can provide feedback that will serve as the beginning of an effective comparison. How does an organization establish or regain credibility? Designing consistent policies and enforcing those polices are the only route an organization can take to gain credibility on ethics issues. If policies are enforced for only part of the employee population, or if there are different rules and treatment for different employees, there's little an organization can do to gain credibility until consistency is established.

Analyze the Audience   The first thing to do when designing a communications program is to analyze your audience's needs. Consider what employees already know, what they need to know, what biases and abilities they have, what the desired and required behaviors look like, when they should be asking questions, and where they can go to report their concerns and to ask for help.

When designing ethics communication for a typical employee population, organizations need to consider three kinds of people. (We use military jargon to describe the three types because it's easy to visualize and remember.)

Good soldiers. Group I are "good soldiers"—these people understand and follow the rules and policies of the organization, and they have good ethical compasses. They have the judgment or experience required to discern the difference between right and wrong, and they have the moral grounding to do the right thing. Be careful to note that these aren't just soldiers who follow orders, right or wrong. They know that "good" soldiers are expected to question an order they believe to be illegal or morally wrong—and they would.

Loose cannons. Group II is called "loose cannons"—they're people who may have good ethical compasses, but they don't know their corporation's policies, and they may not even be familiar with general ethical standards in business. Loose cannons may be inexperienced; or they may have transferred from another, unrelated industry with very different norms; or they may never have read a policy manual. Whatever the reason, loose cannons may be well meaning, but they're naive. Without guidance, ethics may not even be a consideration.

Grenades. Group III are "grenades," and they're neither ignorant nor benign. These people may or may not know the rules, but they don't care. They have their own agenda, and they lack any company or professional loyalty. We call this group grenades because their activities can blow up suddenly and severely damage the organization.

Although the communication needs of the three groups overlap, the emphasis for each specific group is clear. Good soldiers need support because good people often feel as if they need to compromise in order to "fit in." Good soldiers need to know that their instincts are right and that their behavior is not the exception. It represents the organizational model. Loose cannons need to be educated; they need to know and understand basic norms of ethical conduct and specific company policy and standards. Grenades need to know unequivocally that ethical lapses will not be tolerated. They need to see good behavior rewarded and ethical lapses dealt with swiftly, consistently, and firmly.

There are probably few grenades in any organization. But they surely exist everywhere, and the system must be prepared to deal with them. Good soldiers may account for a substantial portion of employees but perhaps not the majority. Since very few employees ever read a policy manual cover to cover—most people learn policy on a need-to-know basis—it is safest to assume that the majority of employees fit into the loose cannon category. The challenge in designing effective ethics communication programs is meeting the needs of all types of employees.

This focus on the ethics audience assumes that most employees don't come to the organization perfectly principled and perfectly prepared to make the right decision in every situation. Recall from earlier chapters that most employees are highly susceptible to influence from outside themselves, so the organization has to provide guidance, and, despite advances, the perfect integrity test hasn't been invented. Since polygraphs were outlawed for most types of employee screening in the United States, more organizations have turned to paper-and-pencil honesty or integrity tests to screen prospective employees. Most of these tests attempt to predict the prospective employee's propensity to steal from the organization, although others have a more general focus on workplace deviance. Integrity tests have recently been evaluated by the American Psychological Association and the government's Office of Technology Assessment. The two organizations' reports generally agree that research on integrity tests is improving and that evidence supporting the tests' ability to predict dishonest behavior has increased.[8] Nevertheless, many problems remain, and organizations will continue to have imperfect employees who need guidance on ethical issues.

Evaluate the Current State of Ethics Communications Before beginning the actual design of an ethics communication program, it's essential to conduct an evaluation that asks the following questions:

What kinds of ethical dilemmas are employees likely to encounter? In addition to common ethical dilemmas faced by employees everywhere, organizations need to identify the kinds of issues and dilemmas that might be unique to their particular industry. For example, a chemical company needs to pay special attention to environmental and safety dilemmas. A financial firm should pay extremely close attention to fiduciary and confidentiality issues. A manufacturing company may have to look at the ethical issues involved in worker safety, product quality, product liability, and labor relations. In addition to identifying issues specific to their industry, companies also need to examine the various jobs within their organization to uncover what specific professional dilemmas their communication program will have to address. For example, an internal auditor will face one set of dilemmas, whereas a manufacturing supervisor will face an entirely different set. Once typical dilemmas are identified, it's possible for an organization to develop a program that's useful for employees—one that shows them how to deal with the most common dilemmas.

What don't employees know? Is the company hiring numerous midcareer hires, who may come from other industries with different standards of conduct? Does the company regularly hire large numbers of recent college or business school graduates who may have little knowledge of business standards, much less specific corporate policy or industry standards? The communications program needs to target the specific needs of these different groups.

How are policies currently communicated? How is policy communicated now? Does the policy manual weigh in at 40 pounds? When a manager has a policy question, what does he or she do—look it up in the manual, ask human resources, ask a colleague, or guess? Is corporate policy ever discussed in orientation or training programs? No one is ever going to memorize a policy manual. Therefore, an ethics communications program needs to take a "snapshot" of key policies and concentrate on communicating those, as well as the message that employees need to know when to ask questions and that the organization encourages employees to inquire. Companies generally do a very good job of telling new hires how to succeed; what they usually don't do nearly as well is telling new hires how they're going to fail or get fired or worse. It's key that new employees understand their employer's standards. What does the company expect from them?

What communications channels exist? How do employees receive messages from management? How does management receive messages from employees? Is "management by walking around" a common practice, or is senior management isolated from most employees? Is there a suggestion program? If so, do suggestions get responses? Are employees generally comfortable approaching their managers with problems, concerns, and questions? Is there a grievance process or a whistleblowing procedure? Do most employees know where to go for help if their managers are unavailable or if their manager is part of the problem? Are human resources, legal, and audit professionals accessible to most employees? Analyzing the answers to these questions will give an organization a good idea of where effective communications channels exist, where they don't, and where to build new ones.

Multiple Communications Channels for Formal Ethics Communication

The company's ethics message can and should be communicated in a variety of ways. The most obvious ethics communication channels include a mission or values statement, a code of conduct, policy statements, a formal whistleblowing process, and communications from leaders. In addition to these, the ethics message needs to be reinforced in all print communication materials, including recruiting and orientation materials, newsletters, and magazines. Specific ethics-related materials can also be developed. Finally, most companies are now communicating with their employees electronically through their websites, intranets, and electronic mail. For example, Texas Instruments' ethics office has decided to use electronic distribution for most of its ethics communications. With the exception of its ethics code booklet and brochures that focus on specific ethics issues, the office's communications are now being distributed electronically.

The following list suggests just some of the types of communications materials that can contain an ethics message:

Website. The company's website is an important source of information about the company and its values. Stakeholders such as potential employees, customers, and suppliers are likely to use the company's website to gather information about the company. Many firms post their mission or values statements and even their codes of conduct on their websites.

Recruiting brochures. These can include the mission or values statement, a discussion of corporate values, and a description of how people in the organization succeed and fail. Ethical conduct can be highlighted.

Orientation materials. These can include the mission or values statement, descriptions of common ethical dilemmas and advice for handling them, explanations of resources to help employees make ethical decisions, and how to raise an ethical issue or report an ethical concern.

Newsletters/magazines. These can include the mission statement, stories about corporate "heroes"—employees who illustrate the corporate values, features that describe ethical dilemmas with comments from employees and managers about how they would deal with the problems. These can also be targeted to specific groups of employees with specific needs. For example, in 1995 Texas Instruments' ethics office started publishing a newsletter it calls "Ethical & Legal Leadership 200: A Management Publication of the Ethics Office," which it distributes to TI's senior managers, those who supervise two hundred people or more. Recent issues of the newsletter have announced new ethics initiatives, advised top managers of their responsibilities vis-a-vis ethics, and listed the U.S. Sentencing Guidelines due diligence requirements (see Chapter Two). They have also focused these senior managers' attention on timely topics of ethical and legal interest to senior managers such as trade regulations in different parts of the world and TI's commitment to the environment.

Booklets. These can be whatever they need to be given employees' need for information. Texas Instruments places resource racks in strategic locations and fills them with brief brochures on specific topics such as "Product Safety," "Expense Reporting," "Business Intelligence," "Benchmarking," "Working with Competitors," "Working with Suppliers," and "Designing for the Environment." Employees can take the brochures they need, without having to deal with issues that aren't as important to their particular job. The brief brochures can also be easily updated or added to, making the program flexible to the dynamic business environment.

Texas Instruments publishes another brochure it calls "The Ethics Tool Box," which briefly outlines all the pieces of the company's wide-ranging ethics programs and initiatives. It tells the employee where to go for answers to ethics-related questions, how to contact the ethics office, and how to use the office's electronic communication system, and it lists available brochures, posters, and videotapes for training. It is a toolbox full of materials designed to help employees understand the firm's ethical expectations and know how to get information to make the best decisions.

A Novel Approach to Ethics Communication at Texas Instruments

To help employees learn from each other, Texas Instruments introduced an internal corporate communication tool it calls "Instant Experience," aimed at helping employees deal with everyday kinds of ethical crises that they may not have experienced themselves. "Instant Experience" uses the corporate electronic mail system to transmit information about ethical issues weekly to the 30,000 or so employees on *T-News,* the company's worldwide electronic newspaper, and to interact with employees about ethical issues. It frequently posts anonymous ethical questions and the ethics office's answers. This allows employees to raise timely issues quickly and without a lot of bureaucracy, and it provides the ethics office with a constant line to the ethical pulse of the organization.

The idea was the brainchild of Glen Coleman, a retired Air Force helicopter pilot and an aerospace engineer who joined TI's ethics office about eight years ago. Coleman admitted that, in Vietnam, he and his fellow helicopter pilots sometimes made potentially life-threatening mistakes. But, on their return, they would freely enter their "stupid mistakes" into a book they called "Instant Experience" so that their buddies wouldn't make the same mistakes and lives could be saved.

Coleman thought that something like this could work at TI. In a variation of the idea that not everyone should have to get burned to find out that the stove is hot, he reasoned that the ethics office could be a clearinghouse for ethical experiences that members of the organization were willing to share with others. As a result, these "instant experiences" are regularly transmitted to all employees on an electronic mail communication system and are retained on the system so that new employees can get up to speed and ongoing employees can check the system whenever they wish.

Here's an example of an anonymous question posed by a TIer that was posted on the communication system on May 20, 1991.

> Suppose I'm in a restaurant and I happen to overhear a conversation from behind me. It's two TI competitors discussing sensitive, competitive information that would be very valuable to TI. What do I do? Continue to listen? Put my fingers in my ears? Tell them to stop? And what should I do with the information that I've already heard? Forget it and pretend it never happened? Mark it TI STRICTLY PRIVATE and distribute it?
>
> I didn't go out looking for the information and I couldn't change my table location to get away from the conversation. It seems a little ridiculous to just throw away an opportunity to use valuable information that I've acquired but didn't solicit in any way. What's the right course of action?

And, here's how Carl Skooglund, TI's ethics director, responded:

> There is nothing illegal or unethical about accidentally being in the right place at the right time and overhearing a competitor's conversation. They must accept the responsibility for irresponsibly discussing sensitive information in a public place. If you have overheard the conversation, your best course of action is to document to your best ability what you heard and notify TI Legal, telling them how you acquired it. The TIer who raised this question is correct. It would be ridiculous to pretend that you never heard the information. Under these circumstances you can share the information with TI. The competitor must accept responsibility for his carelessness. Our ethical principles do not exclude common sense.

Skooglund's response then took the issue a step further, asking TIers if the response should be different if the TIer had intentionally sat at a table adjacent to known competitors. Many TIers responded, and over 95 percent of the responses agreed that intentional eavesdropping was clearly unethical. Here are some of their responses:

> "We are not in the spy business. It's totally unethical."
>
> "I was disappointed that you would even ask us this."
>
> "Spying is spying."
>
> "What happened to the golden rule?"
>
> "My grandmother told me that if something makes you feel guilty, don't do it."
>
> "If our customers knew about this, would their opinion of us suffer?"
>
> "I would be ashamed."
>
> "It's unmitigatedly unethical."
>
> "Would I be proud to have my TI badge on?"
>
> "Let's leave trickery to magicians."
>
> "Stay far enough away from legal limits so that TI's character is never questioned."

Skooglund agreed with the large majority of responses and assured the respondents that their ethical compasses were pointing in the right direction. This instant experience system is useful because it allows employees to openly share their ethics-related questions and experiences and everyone in the organization can learn from the open exchange. In an organization without such a system, this individual may have struggled silently with the issue or may have asked a few peers or a manager for advice. But, with the system, the entire organization learns from one individual's experience.

"Instant Experience" is one of the most creative ethics communication tools we've discovered in talking with ethics managers. In addition to the weekly transmissions and interactions, a collection of the weekly articles is retained on the Instant Experience system with a chronological and a subject index. As of December 1997 the system had archived nearly four hundred separate articles—everything from ethical issues surrounding fax machine use to guidelines on the use of frequent traveler programs. A recent question submitted by a TIer helped to demonstrate that you can't have a rule or policy for everything, but that TI's values and principles can usually help an employee make the right decision. Here is the question that was asked:

> I have a question with respect to dealing with suppliers. Let's say I am organizing a volleyball competition and several vendors have volunteered to help out by offering catered refreshments and prizes for the winners. Another vendor wants to give away T-shirts with the TI and event logos on them. Is it ethical to allow the vendors to help out? The event is open to groups within a large TI organization, and the contestants must pay their own entry fee.

And, here is Carl Skooglund's response:

> Obviously, there will not be a rule or policy to cover such a specific and unique situation. . . . However, we will need to understand some of the basic principles of conducting business and examples of how our values are employed into our everyday work life. . . . We have taken the position that anything of value received from a supplier has to be treated as a gift. Likewise, we may not accept gifts from suppliers that are of excessive value or in poor taste. These are basic principles that can be used to make our decision. In this case, the "gifts" are refreshments, prizes and T-shirts. The refreshments and shirts are of low value and would normally be acceptable. However, our position is not to allow the supplier to sponsor the team because of another important principle—that all of our suppliers must feel that they have a fair and equitable opportunity to do business with us. To allow one supplier to provide even modest financial support, but in a manner that is quite visible (sponsoring names on T-shirts) might send the wrong signal to other suppliers. Would those other suppliers feel that they have a fair shot at our business?
>
> Is there a policy to cover every situation? Of course not. But an understanding of the TI values and principles will help us work through to a good decision. This becomes a personal responsibility in the truly empowered workplace. There are many places you can get help in working through the process. We recommend starting with the supervisor or manager, but there are other sources, such as TI Legal, Human Resources, and the TI Ethics Office. If you are having trouble in making that decision or you just want another place to check it out, try any or all of these resources.

The Instant Experience archive can be used by new employees or anyone with a question. A recent survey of TI employees found that 30 to 40 percent read it every week and 70 to 80 percent read it at least monthly. Supervisors are also encouraged to print the messages and post them on a bulletin board.

We think this system is particularly effective because it fits TI's culture and is based on sound communication principles. First, TI is a high-tech company where electronic communication is an essential part of the culture. So, e-mail ethics discussions are a natural extension of that culture. Second, electronic mail is appropriate for "ethics" discussions because it allows for interaction with reflection. Ethical issues generally require some introspection, perhaps even a trip to the file cabinet to check the code of conduct. The "instant experience" system allows employees to think about the issue and then participate in relatively informal discussions with other TIers. Finally, research suggests that people are less inhibited when communicating electronically. Therefore, they may be more willing to discuss sensitive ethical issues electronically than they would be face to face, contributing to the "it's OK to talk about ethics" atmosphere.

Mission or Values Statements

In recent years, many corporations have developed mission or values statements. A mission statement, values statement, or credo is a succinct description of "how we do business"—the corporate principles and values that guide how business is to be conducted in an organization. A mission statement is a codification of essential corporate behavior. It's a sort of "Ten Commandments" for an organization. If it's to be effective, it should be short, memorable, and in plain language so that everyone can be clear about its message. It's also essential that the organization's own employees have input because a mission statement must accurately reflect the organizational culture. A mission statement scribed by outsiders just won't ring true and is likely to end up the subject of a Dilbert cartoon.

As a result of input from twenty focus groups worldwide, TI recently "retired" its mission statement, The "TI Commitment," and replaced it with three values and six principles.

VALUES	**PRINCIPLES**
Integrity	Respect and Value People
	Be Honest
Innovation	Learn and Create
	Act Boldly
Commitment	Take Responsibility
	Commit to Win

According to Carl Skooglund, the old statement served well posted on the wall. But it didn't serve the purpose of providing us a set of "take them with you" tools. "The values and principles represent a small set of key words that are relevant to our business priorities, that place these priorities into ethical perspective (explaining HOW we will act in pursuit of them) and make them easy to remember and to apply day-to-day."

Obviously, it's possible to have a meaningless mission and values statement when the words are posted on bulletin boards but aren't really a part of the organizational culture. To be meaningful, corporate values must guide corporate and individual decision making on a regular basis. For example, TI's commitment to integrity should be clear from their consistent and growing ethics management efforts over many years. The role of the "customer first" value that guided Johnson & Johnson's decision making in the Tylenol crisis is perhaps the most famous single example of a corporate value being meaningfully applied. However there are many others. At Alcoa, for example, worker safety has become a top priority value. According to a number of Alcoa's top executives, corporate decisions are not made without considering their implications for worker safety.

Policy Manuals

A policy manual is important because it's the one place where all relevant company rules are housed. Generally, policy manuals describe not only laws and regulations pertaining to the company and its industry, but also all company policy, including human resources policy. Although it's critical for a corporation to define its policies and communicate them—it's one of the stipulations of the

U.S. Sentencing Guidelines—most employees don't read policy manuals cover-to-cover. Employees consider policy manuals to be reference manuals, and, as a result, employees consult policy manuals in the way they use a dictionary—periodically and on a need-to-know basis. Many managers never consult a policy manual, however—it's much easier to ask someone than to look up the rules in a voluminous book—and, depending on whom they ask, they may or may not get the right answer.

The very nature of policy manuals—they're usually large and written in "legalese"—makes them a poor way to communicate the rules. Also, since all policy is detailed, all policy may be viewed as having the same importance. Obviously, some policies are much more important than others and should receive special emphasis.

When designing policy communications, analyze the audience. Who needs to know all the policy? Does some corporate policy only apply to a portion of the employees? What do employees really need to know, and what's nice for them to know? Here are some guidelines to follow:

> **Communicate relevant rules to the people who need them.** Although there's certainly policy that applies to everyone, there's surely some policy that applies only to specific employee groups. For example, if accountants in the organization need specific policy, either separate it from the main manual under a specific heading, or leave it out of the main manual and distribute accounting policy only to accountants. If some policy applies to all employees, it can be incorporated into the code of conduct.

> **Prioritize policy.** The material describing confidentiality is more important than a description of how to code a time sheet for sick time. Policy should be presented in a way that lets employees see, at a glance, what the most important rules are.

> **Make it understandable.** First, eliminate the legalese—the only people who like legalese are lawyers. The rest of us like simple English. Second, tell employees what the policy means. Most policy manuals prohibit conflicts of interest, yet few employees can define what a conflict is. Give examples of conflicts and tell employees what a conflict looks like. If people can't tell you what a conflict is, it will be difficult for them to avoid one.

> **Make policy come alive.** Effective communication occurs not when you send the message, but when people receive it and understand it. Policy needs to be communicated in short brochures (like TI's booklets) that highlight important rules, and communicated in person in staff meetings, orientation programs, and training sessions.

Codes of Conduct

As stated in Chapter Nine, a code of conduct is not a substitute for an ethics program; a code is only the start of an ethics effort. Codes come up frequently because most ethics programs, good or bad, have them. Codes vary substantially in length, content, and readability, but they're generally perceived as the main road map, the ground rules for ethical conduct within the organization.

It's probably fair to say that the longer the code, the less employees are likely to read it. On the other hand, the shorter the code, the broader and more abstract the guidelines. In 1998, Texas Instruments shortened its code from 32 pages to 14 pages. The page reduction represents acknowledgment that the company can't have rules to cover the hundreds of choices employees make every day. Rather, a focus on the values that should guide decision making can help employees make the best decisions in a wide variety of situations.

Many organizations deal with a longer code by dividing the code into parts. The first part provides the broad guiding principles. These are followed by a more detailed section that includes more specific application to cases, answers to commonly asked questions, and reference to more detailed policy manuals. Some organizations create separate booklets, in order to supplement a more general code, for workers in particular functions such as purchasing or human resources management. These can provide details and answers to questions that are likely to arise in that particular type of job, and the individuals in that job are more likely to read those details.

Code content may vary depending on the industry and the degree to which the firm has entered the global marketplace. Specific issues are addressed depending on the industry. Firms in the defense industry carefully outline the guidelines for charging one's time to particular government projects. If the firm is global, the code almost certainly deals with issues such as bribery. We'll talk more about this in the next chapter.

If the code is to be taken seriously, it should be updated regularly and redistributed throughout the organization. For example, Texas Instrument's code of ethics has been revised five times since 1961. The most recent version was published in 1998.

TI's newly revised ethics code is organized around TI's values of integrity, innovation, and commitment. Each of these three broad values is introduced by a quote from a current or former leader of TI. For example, integrity is introduced with this 1997 quote from Tom Engibous, president and CEO of TI. "One of TI's greatest strengths is its values and ethics. We had some early leaders who set those values as the standard for how they lived their lives. And it is important that TI grew that way. It's something that we don't want to lose. At the same time, we must move more rapidly. But we don't want to confuse that with the fact that we're ethical and we're moral. We're very responsible, and we live up to what we say." Each value is then explained in more detail. For example, integrity means respecting and valuing people (treating others as we want to be treated) and being honest (representing ourselves and our intentions truthfully). Each of these actions is then explained in further detail through bullet points that represent what they mean in practice.

For example, being honest has seven bullet points including, "respecting the rights and property of others, including their intellectual property." Attached to the booklet are information about how to get answers to one's questions, wallet-sized cards with information about where to go for answers, TI's Ethics Quick Test, and a cutout cube representing the values, for display on one's desk. The booklet is also available on the Ethics Office's TI Values website.

Many organizations ask employees to sign a statement acknowledging that they have read the company code and abided by it during the previous year. Opinions differ as to whether this is a wise or necessary practice. Some see it as a necessary step that can convince workers that the company is serious about the code and expects it to be followed. Others see such statements only as efforts by the organization to cover itself in case of a lawsuit. If workers see it this way, they may end up with a cynical attitude toward the statement signing and the organization.

Here's what Carl Skooglund had to say about the card-signing issue:

> I have actually polled our managers and about 80 percent of them said "No"; it comes across as a CYA for the company and that's not the kind of tone that we want. Now, I am not saying it's wrong. There are other companies that have taken the card-signing track and used it very effectively. If you are doing a corrective action type of program then it's a very useful tool. Fortunately, we were trying to reinforce a culture that was already there. We hadn't had an event that we were trying to work our way around.

Communicating About Change

What happens when something in the organization changes? How should that affect ethics communications? Texas Instruments divested its defense businesses in 1997. As a member of the defense industry, TI's ethics program had focused to a large extent on industry-related issues such as government contracting. With the divestiture, the company wanted to be sure that TIers understood that the firm's commitment to ethics was unchanged despite the fact that they had divested their highly regulated defense businesses. They revised their ethics code and communication materials to reflect the change and to reaffirm their commitment to their longstanding values.

Ethics Training Programs

Values statements, policy manuals, and conduct codes aren't enough. Organizations that are serious about ethics distribute these materials widely and then provide training in their meaning and application. Effective training programs are ongoing efforts to train everyone from new recruits to high-level managers. Most executives charged with responsibility for ethics don't claim to "teach ethics," however; as George Sammett, Jr. (retired ethics officer, Martin Marietta Corporation) said in a 1993 speech at the Conference Board conference on business ethics: "We don't teach ethics, we teach ethics awareness. I got half way through Aristotle and quit. We teach what the company expects of you and what kind of company we want to be, what kind of climate we want."

Training should be designed to suit the group of individuals being trained. A new employee needs different training from a manager who has been with the firm for ten years. An assembly-line worker might only require an hour of training, with regular refresher sessions, whereas a manager might require days of training that address a variety of issues.

New Recruits

Many firms provide ethics training to new recruits through new employee orientation. For example, all new Texas Instruments employees are introduced to ethics on their very first day. They view a videotape and are oriented to TI's values and code. The Human Resources organization actually does the training, in coordination with the ethics office. This is a way of integrating ethics into the total organization; it isn't just the ethics office's job.

Existing Employees

Training is also provided to existing employees. Some companies provide a basic ethics training module to all employees, whereas other firms target the training to specific groups. Texas Instruments has taken the latter approach. For example, TI has merged with or acquired a number of firms over the past ten years. In the merger and acquisition process, the ethics office asks questions about the ethical climate of the company. Once a decision is made to go ahead with the relationship, ethics training is designed for the new employees. TI's ethics office has also developed a workshop on ethics in the procurement process that is offered to all employees who interface with suppliers in any way.

Top Management Involvement

When organizations conduct ethics training for the first time, many of them use a method that begins the training at the top of the organization. "Cascading" is a term frequently used to describe ethics initiatives that begin at the top of the organization and work their way down, level by level. This technique is often used because of the importance of leadership to the credibility of ethics training.

Although top executive involvement is generally considered to be important, few organizations have gone as far as Syntex, a 50-year-old California pharmaceutical company with 10,000 employees in a dozen countries. The vice chairman and chief executive officer, Hans Wolf, addressed the Conference Board meeting on ethics in 1992. He discussed the fact that he personally conducted ethics training on a regular basis. Imagine the symbolic meaning of the simple fact that the vice chairman would be willing to spend this much time dealing with real ethical issues faced by the firm's managers! Five hundred U.S. and international managers had participated in his ethics training program in groups of from twelve to thirty. Here's how it works. Managers request a workshop with Mr. Wolf. He then solicits a brief description of situations these individuals have actually encountered on the job in which it was hard to decide what to do. The entries can be anonymous. He then creates cases that can be discussed in the workshop setting. He has learned that the concern for good ethical behavior is not just an American concern. Requests come from their managers at multiple locations around the world.

Local Management Involvement

Some organizations recommend having local management conduct the ethics training, using common everyday ethical dilemmas as the basis for discussion. TI subscribes to that model. According to Carl Skooglund, training sessions are more useful and effective if they address real ethical issues that people face every day. When he conducts the training himself, he uses examples of calls that have come in to the ethics office. He was inspired to do this in part by focus groups he held early in his tenure. He wanted to find out what people were thinking, what questions they had, and what they thought about TI and ethics. He was shocked to learn that many employees felt that what they did on a day-to-day basis didn't have any impact on TI's ethics.

TIers make ethical decisions every day. Anybody who reports the time that they work or decides how to divide their time across different government contracts, or decides whether they are going to engage in some kind of an outside business activity that might be in conflict with their TI job—these are all ethical decisions. Using common everyday issues in training gives employees a feeling of comfort that the issue they've faced has faced other TIers and that they're not some screwball who's worrying about something that doesn't matter.

Finally, ethics training must be refreshed regularly. This doesn't necessarily have to be done in formal classroom training sessions. But, regular updates are important for a variety of reasons: (1) people forget; (2) ethical issues change with changes in law, technology, and so on; and (3) refreshers send the signal that the organization is constantly thinking about ethics—it isn't a one-shot deal.

A Model—The Ethics Game

A powerful example of how to communicate a corporate ethics message is through an ethics game. As mentioned in Chapter One, Katherine Nelson, coauthor of this book, created the first corporate ethics game, "The Work Ethic: An Exercise in Integrity" when she was head of human resources communications at Citicorp. "The Work Ethic" has been used widely within Citicorp—over 40,000 employees have participated in sessions in over 60 countries. In addition, it was translated into seven languages besides English.

The game works like this: a group of employees is divided into teams. A facilitator then positions the exercise with the following messages:

> "We're playing a game about ethics because we want to make sure we get your attention."

> "We want to make sure you know integrity is important here."

> "This is an opportunity for you to practice making ethical decisions in a risk-free environment."

"We're doing this to give you an overview of corporate policy and how things are done here."

"We're also going to outline all of the resources available to you if you think you'd like some help or advice if you're faced with an ethical dilemma."

The facilitator presents the teams with a series of ethical dilemmas related to such topics as sexual harassment, reporting ethical concerns, responsibilities of customers, the need for confidentiality, and conflicts of interest. The ethical dilemmas are written so that they do not have a clear right answer.

For each issue, the teams take a few minutes to discuss what they think the appropriate action would be. Then, based on a consensus among team members, they choose one of four possible courses of action. Once the teams choose, the facilitator plays devil's advocate and questions the entire group on why they voted the way they did. The discussion can get very heated with participants and teams loudly defending their positions. The facilitator then reveals the scores for each course of action (scores are predetermined, preferably by the management of the organization where the game is being played). If the participants disagree with the scores, they can appeal them to an appeals board of senior managers. Again, the discussions get quite impassioned and lively. And the competition for the best scores keeps interest high.

The senior management appeals board is one of the most important aspects of the ethics game. The very presence of senior managers for 90 minutes or so sends a strong message that integrity and ethics must be important in this company, or all these executives wouldn't be spending so much time talking with employees about it. In addition, when discussing an appeal, the appeals board often communicates messages about company standards and expectations better than anything else. Along the way, employees can see how senior managers work through an ethical dilemma and what factors they consider important in making decisions.

Groups can disagree with the scoring of a question and appeal to these senior managers who have the power to change scores if they're convinced. This somehow "stamps" participating managers as approachable. Managers who participate in appeals boards frequently report there is a marked increase in the number of employees seeking them out and asking for advice. One manager described how he had been stopped in hallways, rest rooms, cafeterias, and even on the street to be asked advice by employees who had seen him as a judge on an ethics game appeals board. Most companies would do just about anything to have their employees seek advice from managers on ethical issues.

Senior managers can also learn a lot from participating in the game. It provides an opportunity for employees to raise issues directly to management. In one session, several male managers were made aware of how offensive young female trainees found any kind of sexual stereotyping. The young women were so determined to let management know how strongly they felt on this issue that the discussion continued at a reception after the game had officially ended.

Since the game usually raises more questions than it answers, it's crucial to have a debriefing. At the end of the game, the facilitator gives advice on how to solve ethical dilemmas, and outlines the resources that are available to help people if they find themselves in need of advice.

The ethics game meets many communication and training goals, but it's especially effective in raising awareness, creating a dialogue, and describing expected dilemmas and how employees might handle them. However, in order for an ethics program to be effective over the long term, training and communications should continue over time. A game is an excellent beginning and can be used repeatedly with different dilemmas. However, it can't exist in a vacuum or be all things to all people. It needs to be part of an integrated ethics program with other media and complementary messages.

Although some may view an ethics game as heresy, those who have seen these training programs in action are quickly convinced of their effectiveness. Other companies have developed their own versions of the game and are using them successfully. For example, Lockheed Martin has developed a similar ethics game but with a new twist. The company received permission from Scott Adams, author of the Dilbert cartoons (popular with employees), to use the Dilbert character in their game. Chairman of the Board, Norm Augustine, appears with Dilbert in an introductory video, and the game includes a humorous "Dogbert answer" to each ethical question.

Another Model—The Northrop "When Things Went Wrong" Video

Northrop Corporation (now Northrop Grumman) surprised a lot of people when it created a case study called "When Things Went Wrong," which was about a devastating incident that took place in the late 1980s at a small thirty-person Northrop site in Pomona, California. At the time, Northrop had about 46,000 employees. In the company's own words, "the incident shook the company to its roots and damaged its reputation." Because of testing irregularities, the facility was closed, the manager and engineer connected to the incident were fired and imprisoned, the division to which the facility reported was suspended from government contracting for two years, the company paid a $17 million fine, and it incurred legal and business costs in the many millions.

The company decided, however, that this painful incident could be used in a positive way to raise the ethical awareness and sensitivity of all Northrop employees. It also decided that the use of the case study would make it difficult for Northrop employees to claim that "it can't happen here." So the company created a videotape. In frank interviews, the CEO, Department of Defense representatives (the customer), and the managers of the parent division discuss the facts and the causes of the incident. These causes include an interplay of both individual and organizational factors. Then, the video identifies what employees and the organization can do to prevent a recurrence.

Thousands of employees viewed and discussed the video with their manager and co-workers. The response was overwhelmingly positive. "It helped heighten everyone's awareness of just what is needed from us as individuals when serious problems arise," one employee commented.

Communicating Senior Management Commitment to Ethics

In *Corporate Culture and Performance,* Kotter and Heskett[9] pointed to one factor that could turn around a company that was heading in the wrong direction—a strong leader who could communicate the culture. They cited corporations like Xerox and General Electric and described how their top managers led.

> Visions and strategies were communicated with words—spoken simply, directly, and often—and with deeds . . . they encouraged people to engage in a dialogue with them, not allowing the communication to flow in one direction only. In almost all cases, the leaders became living embodiments of the cultures they desired. The values and practices they wanted infused into their firms were on display in their daily behavior; in the questions they asked at meetings, in how they spent their time, in the decisions they made. These actions gave credibility to their words. The behavior made it clear to others that their speeches were serious. And successes, which seemed to result from that behavior, made it clear that the practices were sensible.

Without the buy-in and active support of senior management, ethics initiatives are doomed. But senior managers don't have a great track record in communicating a vision, ethical or otherwise. In a survey of professional and management employees[10] respondents revealed a lack of trust in their senior executives. Most said that their company's leaders failed to communicate a "clear understanding of a corporate vision, mission, and goals." They also said that they trust their top management only about 55 percent of the time.[11]

Nevertheless, most employees want to hear from senior executives. Another study of 14,250 employees in seventeen companies in the United States and Canada found that "62 percent of employees list top executives as their preferred source of information, but only 15 percent say they actually get their company news from this source."[12]

What can senior managers do to establish better communications and more trust with employees? How can they begin to build an organization in which ethics are valued? They can take a look at the advice that Peters and Waterman[13] offered over a decade ago in their classic book, *In Search of Excellence.* "An effective leader must be the master of two ends of the spectrum: ideas at the highest level of abstraction and actions at the most mundane level of detail. The value-shaping leader is concerned, on the one hand, with soaring, lofty visions that will generate excitement and enthusiasm. . . . On the other hand, it seems the only way to instill enthusiasm is through scores of daily events." With this advice in mind, here are some concrete steps senior managers can take:

Set high standards and communicate them loudly and repeatedly in public and in private.

Act swiftly and firmly when someone violates the standards. Be consistent—don't have special rules for special people.

Insist on complete candor from your direct reports. Tell them that you don't want to be protected, especially from bad news.

Never, never shoot the messenger.

Talk to a wide variety of employees on different levels and in different locations. Get out there and find out what's really going on. Don't be satisfied with others' interpretations.

In a crisis, take responsibility, be accessible, and be honest. Take the high road. If you do, the company will probably pull through the crisis with a minimum of damage. This is why Union Carbide received generally high marks for the handling of the Bhopal crisis (CEO Warren Anderson quickly flew to India) and why Exxon received horrible marks for its handling of the *Valdez* oil spill (CEO Lawrence Rawls didn't visit Alaska until three weeks after the incident).

Finally, put your money where your mouth is—fund and support ethics initiatives. Without supporting systems, most corporate value statements are collections of empty platitudes that only increase organizational cynicism.[14] To develop ethics initiatives, get help from your communications and training professionals. Don't leave your ethics strategy just to the lawyers.

Formal and Informal Systems to Resolve Questions and Report Ethical Concerns

An organization with a strong ethical culture will be one where employees feel free to speak openly about ethical issues, question authority figures, and report concerns and where managers are approachable and listen to their people. Carl Skooglund said it this way.

> This is probably the most important thing—to set up an environment of candor in your organization. Open up the communication lines. Make sure people feel that they can discuss their opinions, their ideas and their thoughts. But most of all, set up an environment where people feel that they can sincerely bring up and resolve problems without being embarrassed or without fear of retribution. Now, employees are going to come to you with little problems, and then they may come to you with really big problems. But, the first time you blow your stack, or jump down somebody's throat at a point where they really don't deserve it, you've probably capped the level of problem that you're ever going to hear. All I can say is, sometimes you need to do a lot of lip biting. The first time you shoot the messenger who brings you bad news, you've taken the first step towards squelching the ethics of the environment. Easy words for me to say, but I tell our managers: open up those communication lines and let people discuss their problems.

Although most organizations encourage employees to bring their concerns to their immediate supervisor first, employees sometimes want to ask a question anonymously, or they may have a concern about their supervisor's behavior. Also, the U.S. Sentencing Guidelines require that organizations "take reasonable steps to achieve compliance with written standards through monitoring, auditing, and other systems designed to detect criminal conduct, including a reporting system free of retribution to employees who report criminal conduct." As a result, many firms have established a more formal system for raising concerns. This generally takes the form of a telephone line employees can call to ask for help in resolving an ethical dilemma or to report an ethical problem or behavior they've observed in the organization. A number of names have emerged for these—"Communication Lines," "Guideline," "Open Line," "Helpline." These phone lines generally ring in the ethics office if there is one. Some large organizations provide separate reporting lines for each business unit. In a few firms, the line actually rings on the chairman's desk. Other firms have hired an outside consulting firm to take the calls at an 800 number and then transfer the information to the company.

At Texas Instruments, the telephone line rings in the ethics office, and all three professionals in the office take these calls. According to Carl Skooglund, it's important for ethics office staff to talk with callers because they need to be in touch with what's going on in the organization. If they delegate the task, they lose the tone and perspective of the callers. For example, the nonverbals that would come through on the phone can easily get lost in a paper report. In the past, the system defaulted to a voice mail system if no one was in the office. But callers tended to hang up without leaving a message. Therefore, the ethics office recently contracted with an outside firm to offer "overflow capability." That means that if the phone rings four times without being answered (because the entire ethics office staff is out or because it's after hours), the contractor takes the call. Around-the-clock answering capability is essential for a global business. The ethics office has explained the decision to hire an outside contractor to employees as its solution to the "overflow capability" problem rather than as any change in the basic policy of answering the phone in the ethics office. The TI phone line receives about 50 to 75 calls a month, and, as in most companies, the majority are human resource-related issues. In addition to this secure phone line, employees have the option of sending an anonymous e-mail message to a computer that sits on Carl Skooglund's desk. Interestingly, Skooglund reports that in recent years, more employees have been calling on the office's regular office line, or they've been using the regular e-mail system to ask questions. He believes it's a good sign that employees feel they don't necessarily need to use a secure and confidential system.

One concern often raised about these reporting lines is that individuals will make nonvalid reports—"tattling" on people they don't like. That's one reason why confidentiality is so important within the entire reporting and investigative system. Both the identity of the reporter and the alleged violator must be protected throughout the process. The alleged violator must be protected because allegations can result from simple misunderstandings. The reporter must be protected from any retaliation from the accused.

Organizations that have experience with telephone reporting lines find that a large majority of the calls are for information clarification. The individual says, here's what I want to do. Is it okay? Does it follow procedure? Many calls also relate to relatively minor personnel issues.

Carl Skooglund said,

> "We were concerned about nonvalid reports. But we've found that most people call about valid issues. Their motives may not always be noble, but the content is usually correct. Most of the people who use the communication line are using it because they sincerely have a question or concern about something or a question about something that they think is wrong. They may be misinformed. They may be blowing something out of proportion, but I think they use it for positive reasons. I would be willing to bet that only a very small percentage are untruthful allegations made to try to hurt somebody for a vindictive reason. It just hasn't been a problem."

Another relevant question concerns how to interpret the meaning of the number of calls and letters. Obviously, if an organization institutes and promotes an easy way to ask questions, express concerns, and report violations, the number of calls should increase dramatically. Does this mean that there are more ethical problems? Probably not. The executives who run these programs generally interpret such increases as evidence that their programs are working. However, Skooglund suggests that in an ideal world, the ethics office should aim to put itself out of business. In other words, ethical conduct should become so institutionalized that there would be no reason for people to call. They would handle issues locally, with their managers. Like the Maytag repairman, the ethics officer would have a very boring job. On the other hand, a quiet telephone may also signal a number of other positive or negative conditions:

1. lack of concern or recognition of ethical problems (negative),
2. an intimidating environment where people fear retribution (negative),
3. good problem solving at the local level (positive), or
4. no one knowing the ethics office exists (negative).

Ultimately, it is up to the ethics office to devise ways to determine what the numbers and changes in the numbers mean.

Finally, confidentiality and protection of callers remains an important issue. Some firms have hired outsiders such as Pinkerton Services Group (PSG) to manage their reporting lines.[15] Other companies have hired outside individuals often called "ombudspersons" who may answer the reporting line, provide information, investigate complaints, serve in an alternative dispute resolution role, and report problems to a corporate compliance or audit committee while maintaining the confidentiality of the reporter.[16]

Whether a telephone line, an ombudsman, or some other formal procedure is most appropriate for a particular corporate culture, the important thing is to have some way for employees to raise issues without fear of retribution. If there's no way for employees to raise issues without such fear, the first time an executive hears about a problem may be from a district attorney, a regulator, or a newspaper reporter.

EVALUATING THE ETHICS PROGRAM

Many organizations have committed significant resources to their ethics efforts—hiring high-level executives, developing values statements and codes, designing and implementing training programs, and so on. Few organizations however, have systematically evaluated these efforts. Evaluation is particularly important at this relatively early stage in the development of formal ethics programs so that the organizational community can learn what works both in general and under specific circumstances. By evaluation, we don't mean asking employees at an ethics training program whether they "liked" it. Many employees will respond affirmatively just because they "liked" the idea of a few hours or a day away from the office. Whether or not they "liked" it should be secondary. The most important question is, Is the program accomplishing its goals?

Surveys

Most large organizations already conduct regular employee attitude surveys; some have added ethics to the list of survey topics. Surveys can target knowledge, attitudes, skills, and behaviors. For example, if ethics training has been recently required of all employees, surveys can evaluate the extent to which employees understand the company's expectations and standards. Baseline data can be collected before ethics training is begun and then several months after it's completed to analyze whether positive change has occurred. Surveys can help to evaluate employees' skill at recognizing and resolving ethical issues, and they can measure the extent to which employees observe unethical conduct in the organization. Finally, attitudes toward ethics management programs and processes can be evaluated. For example, Texas Instruments recently asked its employees to respond to the following survey statement, "I understand that TI is very serious about ethics and integrity." Seventy-three percent of respondents answered either "strongly agree" or "agree."

The Ethics Resource Center has recently been combining data from a number of organizations across industries so that individual organizations can be compared to this overall data. They reported some disturbing findings at the 1993 Conference Board meeting on business ethics. For example, 33 percent of respondents said that they occasionally observed violations of the company's ethical standards, and 9 percent said they often did. Only about half of the respondents who observed a violation actually reported it. Thirty-six percent of respondents said that nothing was done in response to their report, whereas 27 percent said they never heard about the outcome and 19 percent claimed to be victims of retribution for reporting the violation.

Survey results must be evaluated carefully. For example, many of the firms that call upon the Ethics Resource Center for help do so because they are in some kind of trouble. Thus, these cross-company results may be skewed in a negative direction. Also, because ethics is such a sensitive topic, it may be difficult to get employees to share their honest thoughts and feelings. They may be telling you what they think you want to hear, although the above findings suggest that this isn't the case. Furthermore, the numbers generated by a survey are ultimately ambiguous. Employees who are angry about a recent downsizing may evaluate the "ethics" of the organization more harshly than they otherwise would. A final suggestion from Carl Skooglund regarding surveys is that questions shouldn't be asked if you don't really want to know and you're not willing to accept the answer. He also suggests leaving the legal department out of the survey process. "They'll make it as content free as they possibly can, because, according to the lawyers the safest way to communicate is—don't."

Johnson & Johnson's former chairman, James Burke, had been on the board of IBM Corporation in the 1980s and became impressed with IBM's employee survey program. He decided that one way to keep the Johnson & Johnson Credo alive would be to survey employees about how the company was doing relative to the credo. The survey went through a number of iterations after being tested on employees at a variety of locations. The first survey was conducted in the United States in 1986–1987. The first international survey was conducted the following year. The first part of the survey includes 118 items and takes about twenty-five minutes to complete. It asks employees to rate things like the company's "customer orientation" on five-point scales. The second section is open-ended for written comments. One of the findings has been the impact of top leadership and corporate culture on survey results. For example, former Chairman Burke had emphasized the customer above all. President David Clare emphasized safety first. In an analysis of the survey results, ratings on these two survey dimensions were highest. Most of all, the survey is viewed as a way to keep the Credo alive, a way of "closing the loop on this thing called the Credo."[17]

VALUES OR COMPLIANCE APPROACHES

Formal corporate ethics initiatives can be categorized as emphasizing either a values or compliance approach to managing ethics. The values approach is proactive and aspirational. It emphasizes expected behavior and an effort to achieve high standards represented by the spirit of the law and organizational values. It relies on such techniques as leader communication and role modeling to affirm the organization's commitment to its stated ethical values and goals. Employees learn that these are not empty words, but words that organizational leaders believe and live by. Ethics becomes a point of pride in the organization. "We're so good we don't have to cheat!" The response to a values-oriented program is generally good until violations occur. Then, employees expect that commitment to be backed up with sanctions against the violator(s).

With a compliance emphasis, the focus is more on required behavior—obeying the letter of the law rather than aspiring to lofty ethical principles. Disciplinary procedures for violators are also important to compliance efforts. Many organizations that are motivated strictly by the U.S. Sentencing Guidelines mandate a compliance approach. Employees are told that compliance with the law is essential and that employees who break the law will be punished. The danger with a compliance-only focus is the possibility that employees will believe anything goes as long as there isn't a rule against it or that the company is interested only in protecting itself, not in helping them.

An effective ethics program needs to have both values and compliance components. By themselves, abstract values statements can appear hypocritical to employees. "Management makes these lofty statements, but they don't tell us what we should do." Values must be translated into rules for behavior, and, to give the rules meaning, violators must be disciplined. Employees welcome information that reduces ambiguity about what they can and can't do. And if enforcement is applied consistently across all organizational levels, they are likely to perceive the system as fair and just.

On the other hand, employees often view a strictly compliance-oriented program with cynicism. Without a strong value base, compliance programs seem to focus on catching employees doing something wrong rather than on aspiring to do things right. Employees translate this emphasis into mistrust and a "CYA" approach. Either "the organization doesn't trust its employees," or "the organization is just out to protect its own behind." The best programs aim to focus on aspiring to a set of values first and foremost, supported by just and fair enforcement of the rules.

Texas Instruments recently introduced its "Know What's Right, Do What's Right" theme for TI's ethics program. This theme positions legal compliance as a natural extension of their ongoing values-based ethics initiatives. To help explain the ongoing commitment to ethics, the ethics office published a brief booklet called "Building on the Cornerstone of Ethics," which outlines TI's perspective on ethics as it has developed from 1930 to the present. It begins with the following statement: "We've built a world-class company—with a history spanning more than six decades—by conducting our business in a way that makes others want to associate with us." It goes on to say that the firm's commitment to ethics is built on the founders' principles of honesty, integrity, and fairness. This statement is followed by highlights from the company's history and ethics-related developments. It is clear that legal compliance is simply part of a long-term commitment to "knowing what's right and doing what's right."

ETHICS MANAGEMENT AT THE HOLT COMPANIES

The fastest growing segment of the economy is comprised of smaller firms that are less likely to have the formal ethics structures just described. We are delighted to be able to share the example of the Holt Companies—a smaller company that is a model of values-based approaches to management.

The Holt Companies, headquartered in San Antonio, Texas, include the Holt Company of Texas (a Caterpillar dealership that sells and services new and used Caterpillar machines and engines), the Holt Company of Ohio (also a Caterpillar dealership), and Holt Consulting Services, Inc. (a consulting organization that helps client organizations develop their own values-based leadership management approaches—see below). It includes over twelve hundred employees in fourteen Texas and Ohio locations.

Holt Companies began as a family business a century ago. Benjamin Holt built a horse-drawn "Link Belt Combined Harvester" in the mid-1880s in California. He produced some of the earliest steam traction engines and invented the first successful track-type tractor, the "Caterpillar." Holt eventually moved tractor manufacturing to a more central Illinois location where Caterpillar Inc. remains today. The company went on to develop additional military and farm applications, merge with other companies, and expand to include a Caterpillar dealership in Mexico.

Peter Holt, Benjamin Holt's great grandson, joined the company in 1983. He found a company "marked by poor communication between employees and management, mistrust and attrition, lack of focus, genuinely low morale and low productivity. In short, there was considerable pain."[18] Holt had a vision of something different. He wanted to reinforce the family tradition of quality products and service to customers. He wanted to leave behind the "how much" and "how many" management style he found when he joined the company. He wanted an organization that would operate on the basis of shared strategic values, where employees would truly believe in what they and the company were doing.

Holt enlisted the help of consultants, and, by 1988, the company had developed a process it now proudly calls "Values-Based Leadership (VBL)"—a "synthesized, pervasive, and unwavering commitment to the continuous application of the core values of the organization by all members of the organization."[19]

Since beginning the VBL approach, the Holt Companies have been extremely successful. The employee base has grown, while turnover has declined and satisfaction has increased. Sales and profits have increased substantially. These very tangible results have been accompanied by a spirit of shared responsibility and collaboration. Management attributes all of these successes to the VBL program.

Values

Because the VBL program at Holt revolves around the company's values, we present these first. Development of these values involved the entire company in a rigorous process of deciding which values are central to what Holt stands for. The idea was to develop a set of strategic values that would guide everything the company did, from what services to offer customers to how to treat each other. The stated values, in priority order, are as follows:

ETHICAL "By doing the right thing"
- Being honest
- Showing integrity
- Being consistent
- Providing fair treatment

SUCCESS "By consistently achieving targeted goals"

- Achieving established goals and objectives
- Demonstrating competence
- Recognizing the achievements of all

EXCELLENCE "By continually getting better"

- Exceeding established goals and objectives
- Developing superior skills and abilities

COMMITMENT "By being here to stay"

- Demonstrating a caring attitude
- Being loyal
- Sharing a mutual desire to succeed
- Acknowledging our previous accomplishments

DYNAMIC "By pursuing strategic opportunities"

- Being creative
- Initiating change

Notice that "ethical" is the first of the five stated values and that it comes before success. It means doing the right thing, being honest, showing integrity, being consistent, and being fair. This value, along with the others, defines the culture of the organization and guides individual and organization actions. Putting "ethical" first was a very conscious decision. The spirit of the values is captured in the Holt Companies' Vision Statement.

> We manage by our business values to provide a productive, fulfilling work environment for employees, legendary service for customers, enhanced value for shareholders, and mutually beneficial outcomes for all stakeholders.

Structure

Compared with many larger firms such as TI, Holt has little formal structure for handling ethics. For example, it has no formal ethics office and no separate ethics officer. Rather, ethics is managed by making sure that it is integrated into every aspect of the broader culture of the firm. The company's designated ethics officer is the corporate vice president for human resources. Everyone in the firm is thought to be responsible for ethics, including (and especially) the CEO, Peter Holt. The Executive Committee of the corporation acts as the "Ethics Committee." This committee meets four times per year and consists of the CEO, the general managers of the operating companies, the vice president for human resources, and the vice president for finance. Every meeting is opened with "Values in Action" stories that highlight recent values-relevant events that have occurred, how they were handled, and how the company can learn from them. This regular high-level attention to the company's values and to learning serves to reinforce the idea that values-based leadership is a process that is continuously attended to and reinforced. The operating companies have similar committees of seven to eight senior managers who meet at least monthly. These committees go through a similar "values in action" process at their meetings.

Here's an example of a values in action story. Holt customers love to get merchandise that has the Caterpillar logo on it. Workers in the Parts Department were using their own judgment about when to give hats to customers for free. This issue was raised as one that could cause divisiveness among customers. Some got the hats for free; others paid for them. After much discussion, a decision was made not to give hats away at all, but to make them available to everyone at the same price. The decision was based on the "be ethical" value that means all customers should be treated fairly and consistently.

Leadership

Peter Holt refers to the process of developing the VBL approach as a "journey that changed my life." In talks to ethics officers and executives, he discusses the personal and spiritual turmoil and compartmentalization that characterized his own life. He describes himself as something of a "lost soul" at the time the company began to develop VBL. The VBL development process focused his attention on the values that were guiding his entire life, not just his life as CEO. He emphasizes the importance of the chief executive in developing a values focus in any firm. Values development must start at the top, and the leader must "walk the talk." "Today, I still use my personal power and position to get this program across. People must see that the CEO is TOTALLY committed before THEY buy in. That's part of being ETHICAL. How can I expect you to embrace this system if I don't?"[20] Managers will follow your lead, and then employees will come long. "Employees are watching you all the time to see if you practice what you preach."

Holt now sees himself as the "steward and guardian" of the company's values. He keeps after the values development process "like a bulldog," checking constantly to see that his and the company's actions are in alignment with the values. One of the big challenges, according to Holt, is that VBL requires the leader "to continually look at yourself as you really are." For example, as part of the firm's 360 degree feedback process, he has sometimes received feedback that was less than flattering. "If you get out of line, you hear about it!" For example, he found out that his need to dominate sometimes worked against him. So, he needed to get his own behavior in alignment with the values. Holt is convinced that the VBL approach encourages creativity, confidence, and innovation, and that it frees people to do their best and find the best solutions to problems, solutions that are consistent with the company's bedrock values.

Communication

Much is written about VBL in Holt's internal documents and on the website. But the most effective communication of the values-based leadership approach comes from the CEO himself. Twice a year, Peter Holt visits each of fourteen company locations to conduct two-hour employee meetings. At these meetings, he discloses financial information because he wants employees to understand how the company is doing. He also talks about the company's values, emphasizing each employee's responsibility for implementing them every day. He then makes himself available to answer any question employees want to ask, with the exception of private personnel issues. People write out their questions and deposit them in a question box. Peter reads the questions and responds. For questions that he can't answer on the spot he makes sure that the employee gets an answer later. He also makes himself available to talk with employees individually. All of this leads to an environment of unusual candor and respect between the organization's leader and its employees. Therefore, Holt Companies has not felt the need to establish a formal mechanism for reporting misconduct. Employees are expected to report problems to their managers, but they are also free to go outside the chain of command if necessary. Because Peter, the CEO, is so open, he gets letters from employees on occasion. Some are anonymous; some are not. Whatever the issue, Peter works through the top person in that organization and makes sure that something is done.

Training

New employees are asked to understand, accept, and practice the company's values. Everyone who begins work for the company (from janitors to senior managers) attends a two-day orientation and training session on VBL where they learn about the company's values and discuss values-related cases. These orientation programs are run by the operating companies and are generally delivered by training managers. Peter Holt, the CEO, participates frequently, contributing to the credibility of the values training. He tells participants how important the values are and why he thinks they represent a competitive advantage. Line managers often get involved in delivering the training as well, using leader discussion guides designed to help them lead the case discussions. Their involvement is important because they can speak to how the company's values have actually affected specific business decisions, how the focus on values has changed the character of the company, and how it has influenced them personally.

The cases used in the training were developed based on focus groups, so they represent real events and situations that Holt employees are likely to encounter. Training participants work in groups and use the company values to think through the cases and their solutions. For resolving ethical issues, employees are taught the "Ethics Check" questions from Blanchard and Peale's (1988) *The Power of Ethical Management*. These are:

1. Is it legal?

    Will I be violating either civil law or company policy?

2. Is it balanced?

    Is it fair to all concerned in the short term as well as the long term? Does it promote win–win relationships?

3. How will it make me feel about myself?

Will it make me proud?

Would I feel good if my decision was published in the newspaper?

Would I feel good if my family knew about it?[21]

In addition to the values orientation, the company values have been incorporated into other training programs such as customer service training and conflict resolution training. Cases are included that focus on the values. Participants are encouraged to identify the values that are affected and to consider key stakeholders' needs and priorities. Finally, the Holt Companies also deliver a two-day case-based ethics awareness course for all managers and supervisors. To emphasize the importance of this awareness training, and to provide his personal perspective, Peter Holt participates in all of these programs.

Evaluation and Reward Systems

Management believes that successful implementation of the VBL program depends on ongoing assessment and adjustment. Holt's management is dedicated to "continuous reassessment, alignment, corrections, and follow-through."[22] A key to the success of the VBL system is the performance management process (PMP) that is used to guide and assess all managerial and supervisory employees. Here is a statement from management that emphasizes the importance of the PMP. "The performance management system is a funnel that takes macro goals down to individual jobs and behaviors. Without such a system, critical business issues will fail to be addressed, and values will not turn into behaviors. In short what gets measured and rewarded gets done." In the performance management process, jobs are described in terms of key responsibilities, key competency areas, and key measurement areas. On an annual basis, all managers and supervisors set goals for themselves and meet with their managers to negotiate and refine those goals. The process asks these individuals to identify the Holt value(s) that is associated with each goal.

In addition, a portion of each individual's evaluation (approximately 15 percent or more) is based on personal development goals. So, the focus is not exclusively on the organization's financial ends. Each goal has a "not later than" date so that goal attainment occurs throughout the year. Managers meet monthly with their direct reports to discuss goal progress and to determine how they can help their direct reports with goal achievement. On occasion, goals are also renegotiated at these meetings. Annual bonuses are based on goal attainment.

This values-based performance management process has worked well for Holt. The values are its bedrock, and trust makes it work. But Holt managers caution other companies not to jump into such a program too quickly. General Manager Larry Axline says, "It can take three to five years to develop enough trust in a VBL program that it can become the basis for the performance appraisal system. People must believe that the values have been truly integrated into management decisions and actions before they will buy into a values-based performance management system."

Part of the PMP at Holt is a 360 degree evaluation system in which individual supervisors and managers receive feedback from their direct reports, their peers, their managers, and sometimes from internal and external clients. All feedback is anonymous with the exception of the manager's feedback. Raters complete surveys on computer disks that list about fifty behavioral traits under three categories: self-management, influencing, and problem solving and planning. A fourth category is optional and includes key competencies specific to a job such as technical skills. Each trait is evaluated in two ways: in terms of its importance and its frequency (e.g., "how often do I observe this person engaged in this behavior?"). Holt's values are integrated into this evaluation process. For example, questions ask how the individual demonstrates each of the values. Finally, open-ended comments are included. The 360 degree review has a self-development focus. The ratings and comments are summarized and fed back to the individual, usually by a member of the human resources staff. This information becomes the basis for the following year's goals, which may focus on performance improvement in various areas.

The company has a number of other methods for evaluating how it is doing with regard to its values. These include surveys of customers and employees, and focus groups, all of which aim to assess the alignment between the company's vision, mission, and values and the company's ongoing business practices. An employee survey, called TrendTracker™ is perhaps the most important regular assessment method. This 101-item employee survey is administered annually. Items relate to productivity and effectiveness issues as well as each of the stated company values. Employees are asked to respond to questions on a five-point scale from strongly disagree to strongly agree. Here are a few examples of survey items, listed with their associated values.

ETHICAL
—Being honest

" 'Honesty' is practiced by employees in my work unit."

—Showing integrity

"'Integrity' is practiced by employees in my work unit."

—Being consistent

"People in our work area consistently try to do the right thing."

—Providing fair treatment

"I feel I am treated fairly at Holt Company of Texas (or Ohio)."

SUCCESS "By consistently achieving targeted goals"
—Achieving established goals and objectives

"Our work unit consistently achieves its goals and objectives."

—Demonstrating competence

"Our organization uses advanced technology . . . when necessary to improve productivity."

—Recognizing the achievements of all

"I am recognized and appreciated for my achievements at Holt Company of Texas."

EXCELLENCE "By continually getting better"

—Exceeding established goals and objectives

"Many times our work unit will exceed the goals it has set."

—Developing superior skills and abilities

"I am encouraged to develop superior skills and abilities."

COMMITMENT

—Demonstrating a caring attitude

"The people I work with care about my concerns and my well being."

—Being loyal

"Our company demonstrates loyalty to its customers and the community."

—Sharing a mutual desire to succeed

"Employees in my work unit share a mutual desire to succeed with others."

—Acknowledging our previous accomplishments

"My supervisor expresses genuine and meaningful appreciation for the work I do."

At the end of the survey, employees are asked to expand on one statement with which they agreed or strongly agreed and another with which they disagreed or strongly disagreed. They are then asked an open-ended question about how the company can more effectively match its behaviors with the stated core business values. These comments are analyzed for emergent themes and issues. Following each survey administration, focus groups meet to learn about and discuss the survey results and its implications for needed change in the organization. These focus groups are essential for making sense of the survey results and deciding what, if anything, needs to be done.

A wide variety of changes and improvements have been made as a result of TrendTracker™, especially in the areas of recognition and communication. According to Larry Axline, "These two factors tend to be the lowest on Holt's annual survey, even though significant improvements have been made over the years. Although both of these factors receive positive ratings of almost 80 percent, there's always room for improvement. Communication and recognition are maintenance functions, and we can never achieve perfection. We measure progress not perfection." An example of a change in the area of recognition is the addition of "Legendary Service Awards," which are presented monthly to employees who go out of their way to deliver exceptional customer service.

Here is an example of how the VBL program translates into the bottom line. A large customer, Redland Stone, in San Antonio, operates fifty pieces of CAT equipment worth over $30 million. After a certain amount of time, the equipment must be totally rebuilt for anywhere from $150,000 to 300,000 per unit. Holt estimates a price for each rebuild. If the job turns out to be bigger than originally thought, Redland will pay the additional cost. If it takes less time to do the rebuild, Holt will charge less than the estimate. This agreement works only because Redland trusts Holt to be honest and do the right thing. It benefits Holt's bottom line because the company can bill Redland for their costs. As a result of the strong relationship between the two companies, Redland now has Holt perform all of these rebuilds. There are no more competitive bids to file, and sales people don't have to visit them. So far, 23 machines have been rebuilt for Redland, generating over $4.6 million in revenues.

The Holt Companies managers have been so delighted by their success with VBL that they started a consulting organization called Holt Consulting Services, Inc. that helps other organizations implement values-based leadership in their own organizations. It offers organizational development services as well as products such as training materials and other management aids to support the implementation of values-based leadership programs. Consultants meet and interview key personnel to assess the organization's readiness and to develop a unique approach tailored to the specific client. Employees help to draft a set of guiding principles or code of conduct, and design relevant cases for use in training sessions. Post-training evaluation is conducted via surveys or focus groups. The key to successful values-based leadership is commitment and follow through over time.

Interestingly, Peter Holt has now taken the VBL process to other organizations in which he has a financial interest. For example, Mr. Holt is the principal owner, chairman, and acting CEO of the San Antonio Spurs NBA basketball team. In 1997, VBL was introduced into that organization. At the time this book went to press, it was too early to evaluate the long-term effects at the Spurs organization. However, early reports suggest very favorable reactions to VBL in this atypical setting. Professional sports franchises are not always receptive to a values-based approach where the primary method of keeping score is winning.

CONCLUSION

This chapter has offered specifics about how ethics can be effectively managed in business. Large businesses that are committed to ethics are likely to have formal ethics management systems such as an ethics office, ethics officer, explicit ethics training, and a telephone counseling/reporting line. The best of these formal ethics management programs, like TI's, have a values-based approach that incorporates legal compliance within the framework of a broader set of company values. Smaller firms with a strong commitment to ethics, such as Holt, are less likely to have separate formal ethics management structures and systems. At Holt, values have been successfully "baked into" the organizational culture to the degree that ethics and values are simply a part of everything they do. Whether large or small, the keys to effective ethics management are commitment to ethics from the very top of the organization, involvement of leaders and employees at every level, and recognition that ethics management is an ongoing journey.

DISCUSSION QUESTIONS

1. Imagine that it's your responsibility to select an ethics officer for your organization. What qualities, background, and experience would you look for? Would you ever be interested in such a position? Why or why not?
2. What are the advantages of having an ethics office or officer report to a company's chief executive officer, the legal department, human resources, or audit? What are the disadvantages?
3. Think about an organization where you've worked. What kinds of ethical dilemmas are unique to that organization? To that industry? What might be the best way to prepare employees to deal with those dilemmas?
4. Which of the following exist in the organization? Are they consistent and credible? Mission or values statement, policy manual, code of conduct, ethics training (who conducts it), hotline?
5. Is senior management committed to ethics? How do you know?
6. Are leaders at all levels held accountable for their ethical conduct? If so, how? If not, why not? What would you recommend?
7. What recommendations would you make for handling frivolous calls to the hotline?
8. Does the organization evaluate its ethics initiatives? How? If not, why not?
9. Would you characterize the ethics efforts in this organization as taking a values, compliance, or combination approach? Is it effective? Recommend improvements.
10. How would you raise an ethical concern in this organization? List all of the resources available to you. Which ones would you be likely to use? Why or why not?
11. Imagine that you're the CEO of a small manufacturing company. An employee has dumped toxic waste in a nearby stream. Who would you call into your office, and what would you want to know? Develop a short-term and long-term action plan for dealing with the crisis. Who would you communicate with and why?
12. Evaluate the ethics program at your organization from the perspective of "fit." Has the ethics program been designed to "fit" the organization's overall culture? If so, how? If not, what could be done?

CASE 10.1

What's Wrong with this Picture?

You're a management consultant who has been asked by Green Company to help design an ethics communication and training program for all Green Company employees. Your meetings to date have been with the head of human resources, and your contract with the company has been negotiated with him. Once the papers have been signed, you begin your research and are quickly stymied by Green's corporate counsel. He says that you will not be allowed to ask employees about ethical dilemmas that have occurred at Green. He specifically asks that you get your information from other sources such as press accounts of problems in the industry, or from other organizations with which you've worked. In addition, the head of human resources has told you that you'll be unable to meet the three most senior executives because they're busy negotiating a large acquisition. You will have access to other high-level managers who can tell you what they think the seniors want. You're instructed to write a code of conduct for the company and a mission statement, and prepare presentations for the senior managers to give to employees sometime next month on corporate expectations and values.

Case-Based Questions

1. Based on what you know about developing ethical cultures and programs, identify the problems presented by this case.

2. Why do you think the corporate counsel has responded in this way? What will be your response to him, if any?

3. As a consultant, what are your ethical obligations, if any?

4. How will you proceed?

NOTES

1. Barbakow, J. C. 1995. The ethics patrol. *Chief Executives,* July/August: 58–61.
2. Weaver, G., Treviño, L. K., & Cochran, P. 1998. Corporate ethics programs as control systems: Managerial and institutional influences. Unpublished working paper.
3. Personal communication, Kent Druyvesteyn, 1994.
4. Weaver, G., Treviño, L. K., & Cochran, P. *Journal of Business Ethics.* in press.
5. Austin, N. K. 1994. The new corporate watchdogs. *Working Woman,* January: 19–20.
6. Towne, P. L. 1991. Training employees and communicating ethical standards. In *Corporate ethics: Developing new standards of accountability.* Conference Board Report No. 980. New York: The Conference Board, 25–26.
7. Simmons, D. G. 1985. The nature of the organizational grapevine. *Supervisory Management,* November: 39–42.

8. DeAngelis, T. 1991. Honesty tests weigh in with improved ratings. *APA Monitor,* 7.

   Ones, D. S., Ziswesvaran, C., & Schmidt, F. 1993. Comprehensive meta-analysis of integrity test validities: Findings and implications for personal selection and theories of job performance. *Journal of Applied Psychology,* 78: 679–703.

   Sackett, P. R., Burris, L. R., & Callahan, C. 1989. Integrity testing for personal selection: An update. *Personal Psychology,* 42: 491–529.

9. Kotter, J. P., & Heskett, J. L. 1992. *Corporate Culture and Performance.* New York: Free Press.

10. Smith, A. L. 1991. *Innovative employee communication: A new approach to improving trust, teamwork and performance.* Englewood Cliffs, NJ: Prentice-Hall.

11. Ibid.

12. Ibid.

13. Peters, T. J., & Waterman, R. H. Jr. 1982. *In search of excellence: Lessons from America's best-run companies.* New York: Harper & Row.

14. Hammer, M., & Champy, J. 1993. *Reengineering the corporation: A Manifesto for corporate revolution.* New York: HarperCollins.

15. Powell, J. M. 1994. Pinkerton responds to the Federal Sentencing Guidelines. *Corporate Conduct Quarterly,* 3(1): 10.

16. Miller, S. S. 1991. The ombudsperson. In Corporate ethics: Developing new standards of accountability. Conference Board Report No. 980. New York: The Conference Board, 29–30.

17. Johnson & Johnson's credo survey: Genesis and evolution. 1993. *Ethikos* 7, No. 2, September/October: 2.

18. Axline, L., & Holt, P. Values-Based Leadership: How to Do It. manuscript in progress.

19. Ibid.

20. Ibid, p. 41.

21. Blanchard, K. & Peale, N. V. 1988 *The power of ethical management.* New York: Fawcett Crest, p. 20.

22. Axline & Holt, Values-Based Leadership, pp. 61–62.

ETHICS AND THE WORLD

CHAPTER 11

Managing for Ethical Conduct in a Global Business Environment

INTRODUCTION

With the increasing globalization of business, more managers are finding themselves in an international environment full of ethical challenges. If managing for ethical conduct is a challenge in one's own culture, Imagine how the difficulties multiply when the culture and language are foreign, and the manager is under increased stress.

Particularly in developing nations, business people face cultures, customs, and norms that may conflict with their own ethical standards. Although large multinational corporations with years of experience in the international arena sometimes provide their managers with training and policies to guide their actions, many representatives of American business are left to fend for themselves with little or no guidance.

In this chapter, we will address the difficulties of foreign assignments in general terms. Then, we will focus on the specific challenges of dealing with ethical issues that arise in the context of international business. These issues concern individuals' specific decisions about the conduct of business in different cultures as well as broader organizational issues concerning whether and how to conduct business in foreign nations, and how to guide employees working in a global business environment.

FOCUS ON THE INDIVIDUAL EXPATRIATE MANAGER

We begin by focusing on the individual expatriate manager, the difficulties inherent in foreign business assignments, and the importance of cultural understanding, sensitivity, and openness.

The Difficulties of Foreign Business Assignments

The globalization of business has contributed to a huge increase in interactions between people from different cultural backgrounds. These interactions may occur during brief business trips or more lengthy overseas assignments. Unfortunately, many overseas assignments end early and unsuccessfully because of the expatriate manager's (and his or her family's) inability to adjust to the foreign work environment. The estimated cost of these failures to U.S. business has been estimated to be over $2 billion a year.[1]

The Need for Training and Guidance

Despite these failures and their costs, studies have found that many American businesses don't provide cross-cultural training to their managers who are assigned to work overseas. Top managers seem to believe that an effective manager in New York can be an effective manager in Beijing, Beirut, Buenos Aires, or Budapest with no cross-cultural training. This isn't surprising given that only a small number of top managers of American multinational corporations have substantial international experience.[2]

Studies have found that cross-cultural training can be highly effective. For example, training contributes to:

1. Greater feelings of well-being and self-confidence for the American manager
2. Improvement in relationships with host nationals
3. The development of correct perceptions of host culture members
4. Better adjustment to the new culture
5. Higher performance[3]

Foreign Language Proficiency

One kind of training that can improve one's international business experience is foreign language training. Language is an essential part of cultural learning that can contribute to productive international business relationships. The expatriate manager's effort to learn the language is generally taken as a symbol of his or her interest and commitment to understanding. Those who are fluent in a foreign language know that much cultural learning occurs implicitly as one develops fluency. For example, some languages have words for things that other languages take a tortured phrase or sentence to convey, or can't convey at all. Yet Americans speak fewer foreign languages than their trading partners[4] and some have argued that Americans pay a high price for this "monolingual arrogance."[5]

One senior executive of a Fortune 500 company frequently talks with business school student groups about how to be successful in their future business careers. He recommends, above all, that students find some way to experience an international environment and that they learn to speak a foreign language fluently. After they have learned one language, he suggests that they start on a second.

Language fluency isn't a matter of just knowing the words, but knowing how they are used within the particular cultural context. For example, an old story goes that a Scottish visitor to Japan had worked hard to develop a good relationship with his Japanese host. After several weeks, the Japanese host asked (in Japanese), "Can I sleep with you?" Luckily, the Scot was sophisticated in cross-cultural communication and didn't react negatively or dismiss the question while his mind raced to attempt to understand its meaning. Despite his confusion, he agreed to the apparently odd request. The Japanese host had a second mattress brought to the visitor's room, and the two slept through the night, comfortably and without incident. He later discovered that his Japanese host had paid him the highest compliment. The Japanese believe that an individual can easily be killed in his sleep. Therefore, the request indicated a relationship of total trust.[6] A note of caution—you might not want to try this one today. Our students tell us that "Can I sleep with you?" now carries the same meaning in Japan as it does in the United States!

Learning About the Culture

Culture has been defined as "collective mental programming."[7] This definition of culture suggests that patterns of believing differ across cultures and that individuals use these patterns to interpret the world and to guide action. If an individual operating in a foreign culture doesn't understand its particular patterns of believing and behaving, the individual will interpret experience purely in terms of his or her own culture, inevitably misinterpreting and misunderstanding.

In order to understand how this collective mental programming can lead to misunderstanding, we will focus on two cultural dimensions, developed by Geert Hofstede[8] that are relevant for understanding international business ethics.[9] Readers who are heading overseas are encouraged to learn about the additional cultural dimensions that are more relevant for other aspects of the overseas business experience.

Individualism/Collectivism Individualism represents the extent to which people in a society think of themselves as autonomous individuals who are responsible primarily to themselves and their immediate families. This contrasts with collectivism, which emphasizes collective purposes over personal goals and group harmony over individual achievement. Americans, Canadians, Australians, and most Northern Europeans are individualists. They define themselves in terms of personal characteristics and achievements, and they generally value personal welfare over group harmony. For example, Americans are quick to praise individual accomplishment and individuals' ability to make good decisions independently. They aim to hire people with the highest educational and professional achievements.

Most Asian and Latin American countries represent collectivist societies. They value conformity to the group and define themselves in terms of their group memberships and their contributions to the success of those groups. A common Japanese saying reflects this collectivist orientation—"the nail that sticks out will be pounded down." Hiring in collectivist cultures is based on qualifications, but a person's ability to work well with co-workers and to make collaborative decisions is as important as individual technical proficiency. Knowing an applicant or his or her family is considered an important "qualification," and the hiring of family members is common and expected. An American without cultural knowledge would probably consider this approach to hiring to be wrong—biased and discriminatory. Indeed, many American firms have rules against nepotism. But a collectivist would consider the Americans' individualistic approach to hiring to be wrong—disloyal to friends and family as well as ineffective. To a collectivist, knowing someone is the best way to ensure that the person will work well with others in the group. Furthermore, in a collectivist culture such as Japan, giving gifts is considered to be an important part of relationship building. Giving a gift can also be an important step toward acceptance and becoming a member of the group.[10] In individualistic cultures, gift giving is more likely to be considered to be a bribe—an attempt to influence an individual's business decisions.

Power Distance Power distance represents the extent to which people in the society accept a hierarchical or unequal distribution of power in their organizations and in society. High power distance in a culture reflects acceptance of inequality and respect for social status or class boundaries. In these cultures, employees are more likely to accept the idea that the boss has power simply because he is the boss, and bypassing the boss is considered insubordination. Titles, status, and formality are important in these societies, and those with high status are given much leeway in their behavior. For example, when President Nixon was forced to resign, members of high power distance cultures found it hard to understand. They focused on the fact that he was president, after all, a high status position.[11] Americans, on the other hand, were more likely to focus on Nixon's illegal behavior, regardless of his position or title. Some of the highest power distance countries include India, the Philippines, Mexico, and Venezuela.

Low power distance cultures are more likely to deemphasize status and class distinctions. The United States, Israel, and most Northern European countries (with the exception of France and Belgium) are lower on power distance. In these cultures, a boss's power is accepted because he or she has knowledge, not just because he or she is the boss. Therefore, workers in a low power distance culture may be more willing to question the boss's authority or even to blow the whistle on an unethical manager.

Recognizing the Power of Selective Perception

Human beings are constantly bombarded with information. Therefore, they must perceive selectively, or they would be totally overwhelmed. This selective perception process is largely determined by culture. For example, in collectivist Latin cultures, people pay more attention to social relationships than to behavior. Thus if a close relative commits a crime, it may not even be perceived as a crime because the relationship is more important than the action. Therefore, it is essential to recognize that the visitor to another culture will notice things that are important at home but may not be important in the target culture. The visitor is also likely to overlook important behaviors, roles, and values because of selective perception. These aren't important at home, so they aren't even noticed. Furthermore, members of the target culture are equally selective, perhaps not noticing things that seem crucial to the visitor.[12]

With effective cross-cultural training, managers can be trained to be on the lookout for things that would otherwise be ignored, and they will be more able to interpret their international business experiences in light of the belief patterns of the particular culture. These interpretations are extremely important because actions are likely to vary depending on the interpretation.[13]

Assumption of Behavioral Consistency

Understanding culture doesn't guarantee success, however. Much of the theory and research on international business conduct is grounded in an inaccurate key assumption—that if we understand cultural behavior (how people think and behave in their native environment), we'll understand how a particular group will behave in relation to cultural outsiders. In other words, if I understand the Japanese culture better, I can predict how my Japanese counterparts will behave toward me, what their expectations will be, and so on. And, if I understand all of that, I'll know how to behave with them.

People are amazingly adaptable, however, and, just when you think you have them figured out, they change their behavior. They may be trying to figure out how to behave with you as much as you're trying to figure out how to behave with them. A colleague recently related a story about a meeting between business and philosophy professors on his campus. Recognizing the cultural differences between the two departments, the philosophy professors decided to leave their khakis at home and dress up for the occasion—sporting crisp shirts and ties. The business professors all showed up in jeans! The moral of this story is that people adapt their behaviors to what they believe others expect of them, making it very difficult to predict behavior.

Here's another example from the international business environment. By all accounts, American women should experience great difficulty succeeding in some foreign business environments, particularly in cultures (e.g., Asia, the Middle East) where women have not attained the rights that American women have come to expect. We expect foreign nationals to think about and treat American women as they treat women in their own cultures. Yet a major study of North American women working as expatriate managers in a number of countries around the world found that these women are successful beyond anyone's expectations.[14] "Women succeed because they are seen as foreigners who happen to be women, not as women who happen to be foreigners."[15] The foreign nationals adapt their behavior in relation to these women rather than expecting an American woman to behave like a Japanese or Saudi Arabian woman. Foreign leaders' acceptance of Madeline Albright as the United States' secretary of state supports the study's findings.

A study of cross-cultural business negotiations also challenges the behavioral consistency assumption. Adler and Graham[16] found that, when dealing with an individual from a different culture, negotiators adapted their negotiation behavior to that of the negotiation partner. However, an important study result was the finding that the American negotiators were the least flexible, making fewer adjustments in response to their negotiation partner's behavior than Canadian or Japanese negotiators.

What can we learn from these studies? Although learning about the culture is an essential first step, don't assume that simply learning about another culture is enough. The foreign nationals you deal with in business interactions may behave differently with you than they would with individuals from their own culture. Thus, understanding cultural norms and behaviors is only a starting point. The foreign individuals you deal with may adapt their behavior based on what they expect you to do. Therefore, you must be flexible and open to learning from the situation at hand, despite research findings suggesting that flexibility is not the American manager's strong suit. Perhaps one of the most important things to learn, in preparation for a cross-cultural experience, is that you can't be fully prepared—that there will be surprises and daily opportunities for further learning and understanding.[17] The successful international business person will be open, flexible, and tolerant of ambiguity.

Assumption of Cultural Homogeneity

We should also not assume homogeneity within a culture—that individuals within a culture are all the same. Imagine if someone assumed that all Americans were like the characters in American films. Obviously, this kind of simplistic thinking and stereotyping leads to grossly inaccurate expectations. Individual personalities and experiences vary widely within any culture, leading to behavioral differences. For example, a Japanese business person with an American MBA may behave quite differently from a Japanese business person who has never left the country.[18] Be open to learning as much as possible about the individuals you are dealing with. The most effective international managers are those who modify stereotypes or discard them completely in the light of contradictory evidence. Ineffective international managers are likely to cling to stereotypes and treat individuals who act differently as exceptions. For example, Germans are often stereotyped as hard-working. The ineffective international manager who meets a lazy German employee will view this individual as an exception, while maintaining the stereotype of Germans as hard-working. A more effective international manager would say that some Germans are hard-working, whereas others seem to be lazy. It depends on the individual.[19]

Assumption of Similarity

Another problematic assumption is the assumption of cultural similarity. Many companies begin the internationalization process in countries that they believe to be more similar to their own because they believe that success will come easier in a more familiar culture. But research[20] suggests that this perceived similarity can cause performance failures because managers are less likely to prepare for the cultural differences that do exist. The researchers call this the "psychic distance paradox." Rather than being easier to do business in a country that is "psychically close," it may actually be quite difficult. A study of Canadian retailers entering the American retail market found that familiarity often led to carelessness. Decision makers at Canadian retail companies had preconceived notions that the U.S. market was quite similar to the Canadian market and that what had worked for them in Canada would work in the United States. Therefore, they didn't work as hard at understanding the American retail culture, and they tended to misinterpret information. So, if you're being sent to a country that you perceive to be similar to your own, don't assume similarity. Find out as much as you can about doing business in that country, just as you would about countries that you perceive to be different.

Ethics-Related Training and Guidance

International business assignments require training in areas more specifically related to ethics such as how to recognize the ethical issues that are likely to arise in a particular environment, how to negotiate in a particular culture, and how to handle requests for payoffs and bribes.

Recognizing and Dealing with Ethical Issues   Beyond general training in the culture, training with respect to business ethics beliefs and practices is essential. First, the expatriate manager must be prepared to recognize the ethical issues likely to arise in a particular business setting. Just as ethical issues at home vary somewhat from industry to industry (e.g., manufacturing versus hospitality) and profession to profession (e.g., marketing versus accounting), the ethical issues that are likely to arise vary from culture to culture. The treatment of employees (e.g., child labor, worker safety) may be more of a problem in one culture, whereas the disposal of toxic wastes may be more likely to arise in another, and bribes may be more problematic in yet another culture.

Second, the expatriate manager needs help making ethical decisions in the more ambiguous international business context. At home, where we are familiar with community standards, it's easier to rely on simple guidelines such as "The New York Times Test." But simple guidelines often fall short when home culture norms conflict with those of the host country.[21] Individual expatriate managers shouldn't be left to fend for themselves in these unfamiliar circumstances. The organization owes it to them to help navigate these unknown ethical waters. Some suggestions for how to do this will be offered later in the chapter.

Negotiating across Cultures   The frequency of business negotiations is increasing with growth in foreign trade, joint ventures, and other interorganizational agreements. When working within one's own language and culture, being an effective negotiator requires the utmost in sensitivity, understanding, and communications skills. These requirements multiply when negotiating in an international business environment.

A number of studies detail differences in negotiation styles and tactics across cultures.[22] Most relevant, given our focus on ethics, is an understanding of the use of "dirty tricks" and "psychological warfare"—negotiation "tactics designed to pressure opponents into undesirable concessions and agreements."[23]

The use of dirty tricks is possible in any negotiation, but it becomes more complex in an international negotiation because of possible misinterpretation. For example, Brazilians expect deception among negotiators who are not well acquainted. Therefore, they're more likely to use deception during early negotiation stages than are Americans. Consequently, it may be wise for an American negotiator to expect phony facts to be a part of the initial negotiation stage with a Brazilian counterpart.

It's also important to recognize that what seems like deliberate deception may not be. Eastern Europeans have limited authority to finalize agreements and are expected to check with their superiors about any changes. However, Americans often have wide authority to make important decisions at the negotiation table. Without this cultural knowledge, an American might interpret the Eastern European's claims about limited authority to be an attempt at deception when it isn't.

Psychological warfare—"tactics designed to make the other person feel uncomfortable"[24] and want to conclude the negotiation quickly—also has different meaning in different cultures. For example, too much touching or too much eye contact may make Americans extremely uncomfortable. Again, it's important to be able to distinguish real attempts at psychological warfare from the expression of typical cultural behavior. For example, Latins tend to touch more than Americans or Canadians, who touch more than Scandinavians. Arabs maintain greater eye contact than Americans, who use eye contact more than the Japanese. An understanding of the culture one is dealing with can help to prepare the negotiator to correctly interpret these types of behaviors. The more knowledge each side has of the other's culture, the more options are available in terms of negotiation styles and strategies. But if negotiators are totally unfamiliar with each other's cultures, it is likely best to hire agents to represent each side.[25]

Dealing with Payoffs and Bribes   Probably the most frequent source of anxiety for American business persons operating abroad is the expectation of payoffs and bribes. A bribe is a payment to someone to secure a sale or to obtain approval or assistance from an individual or organization (often a government bureaucrat). Although an accepted part of commercial transactions in many Asian, African, Latin American, and Middle Eastern cultures, it is often against the law in these very same countries.

On arrival in a foreign airport, many a business person has faced a government official's extended hand and the suggestion that payment was needed to facilitate the delivery of product samples to the hotel—no payment, no product. Without previous preparation, the expatriate is at a loss to know what to do. What is the meaning of this request in the context of the culture? Is making the payoff against U.S. or local law? What exactly is local custom? How much is expected? What's likely to happen if I don't pay? Will payment really expedite matters? What are the options? How will my company respond if my work is delayed?

American business people generally prefer to conduct business in a way that's consistent with the U.S. and local law. They would prefer not to make illegal payments to anyone. Despite local laws, however, bribes and payoffs are the custom in many cultures, dating back centuries.[26] Therefore, American business people frequently feel that they are at a competitive disadvantage if they are prohibited from making payments, especially if competitors make them freely.

Survey results[27] suggest that U.S. business professionals hold wide-ranging opinions on the acceptability of payments to foreign officials, despite the illegality of bribery. Survey respondents were given the following vignette:

> A company paid a $350,000 "consulting" fee to an official of a foreign country. In return, the official promised assistance in obtaining a contract that would produce a $10 million profit for the contracting company.

Responses varied from almost half saying that the behavior was "never acceptable" to 32.5 percent who said that it was "sometimes acceptable" to 18.5 percent who said that it was "always acceptable." Those who believed that it was never acceptable relied on their personal beliefs that bribery is illegal and that payoffs are always wrong. Others suggested that if you pay once, you'll be stuck doing it forever. Even if others operate that way, you shouldn't give in to the temptation. However, those who believed that it was sometimes acceptable suggested that it was customary in other cultures, practiced by the competition, and was at times the only way to do business. Some went so far as to say that Americans shouldn't impose their cultural values on others, particularly in countries where bribery is not illegal.

In the 1970s, the Securities and Exchange Commission found that the practice of bribing foreign officials was widespread among U.S. multinational corporations and that the amounts paid were becoming "excessive." For example, in the mid-1960s, a major Korean political party asked Gulf Oil for a $10 million donation. The CEO personally negotiated it down to $4 million, which was still a huge sum. In a notorious incident, Lockheed made an estimated $25 million in payments in connection with sales of its Tristar L-1011 aircraft in Japan. In all, 450 companies, including more than 100 Fortune 500 firms, admitted to making questionable foreign payments in amounts totaling more than $300 million.[28]

The U.S. Congress passed the Foreign Corrupt Practices Act (FCPA) in 1977,[29] making it the only nation with a law prohibiting bribery abroad. The act prohibits representatives of U.S. corporations from offering or providing significant payments to foreign political parties, candidates, or government officials for the purpose of inducing the recipients to misuse their powerful positions to assist the company to obtain, maintain, or retain business—"to make a decision or take an action that he/she otherwise might not take."[30]

The law does allow for small payments to lower-level figures, so-called grease payments or facilitating payments that might be needed to persuade officials to perform their normal clerical or ministerial duties faster or better. Americans might think of these facilitating payments as "tips," a little extra for the individual involved, to assure courteous or efficient service. In order to be classified as a facilitating payment, it must not significantly change the final decision or result. It's against the law and considered to be subversion of the free market system if the money is paid to sway high-level people to make decisions they would not otherwise make. Companies are required to keep records of all such transactions, and these transactions are not tax deductible as they are in many other countries such as Japan. Extortion payments are not prohibited under the law. For example, if a company official is kidnapped overseas and held for ransom, a company can legally pay the ransom.[31]

Although the number of prosecutions under the act has not been large, most corporations work hard to avoid even the appearance of impropriety because Justice Department investigations can be costly and time consuming. A guilty verdict is usually devastating. For example, in 1995, Lockheed Corporation pleaded guilty to conspiring to pay a one million dollar bribe to a member of the Egyptian parliament. Fines and penalties to the company totaled $24.8 million. In addition, a former Lockheed executive was sentenced to 18 months in prison.[32]

The FCPA has been criticized by some who argue that U.S. firms cannot compete effectively when they are constrained by this law while companies from other countries are not.[33] There is now some evidence to support this claim. A recent study by a Harvard economist, James R. Hines, found that U.S. direct investment and exports declined in so-called corrupt countries after the act was passed, whereas investments and exports in these same countries increased for non-U.S. competitor companies.[34]

But some American companies contend that the FCPA helps them because if they come under pressure for kickbacks or bribes, they can cite the law. And more companies have been working to convince locals of the benefits of playing by the rules. One clear benefit of playing by the rules is that business definitely flows to places that have controlled corruption. For example, Hong Kong became a leading international financial center largely because of its reputation for integrity. Corruption has been kept in check by a powerful local law enforcement agency called the Independent Commission Against Corruption (ICAC) which was given broad powers to control corruption and white-collar crime. The ICAC established the Hong Kong Ethics Development Center in 1995. The center provides a number of services to businesses, including consultation on developing codes of conduct, training for staff, and seminars on ethics. However, analysts question what the future of the ICAC and business ethics will be in the new Hong Kong which, as of July 1997, came under the control of mainland China, a country known for corruption.[35]

Attention has been focused on corruption in international business by Transparency International, a nongovernmental international organization founded in 1993 and headquartered in Berlin. It aims to "support global integrity systems both nationally and on the international level." The organization publishes an annual "Corruption Perception Index" (CPI) that is based on international surveys of business people, political analysts, and the general public. In the 1997 index of 52 countries for which data were available (see Table 11.1). Scandinavian countries were at the top of the list, perceived as being the least corrupt. The United States was listed as the sixteenth least corrupt nation. The na-

TABLE 11.1   Transparency International Corruption Perception Index, 1997

Country	1997 Score	Country	1997 Score
LEAST PERCEIVED CORRUPTION = 10			
Denmark	9.94	Czech Republic	5.20
Finland	9.48	Hungary	5.18
Sweden	9.35	Poland	5.08
New Zealand	9.23	Italy	5.03
Canada	9.10	Taiwan	5.02
Netherlands	9.03	Malaysia	5.01
Norway	8.92	South Africa	4.95
Australia	8.86	South Korea	4.29
Singapore	8.66	Uruguay	4.14
Luxembourg	8.61	Brazil	3.56
Switzerland	8.61	Romania	3.44
Ireland	8.28	Turkey	3.21
Germany	8.23	Thailand	3.06
United Kingdom	8.22	Philippines	3.05
Israel	7.97	China	2.88
USA	7.61	Argentina	2.81
Austria	7.61	Vietnam	2.79
Hong Kong	7.28	Venezuela	2.77
Portugal	6.97	India	2.75
France	6.66	Indonesia	2.72
Japan	6.57	Mexico	2.66
Costa Rica	6.45	Pakistan	2.53
Chile	6.05	Russia	2.27
Spain	5.90	Colombia	2.23
Greece	5.35	Bolivia	2.05
Belgium	5.25	Nigeria	1.76
		MOST PERCEIVED CORRUPTION = 1	

tions perceived to be most corrupt were Russia, two South American countries, and Nigeria. China was listed as number 41.

Publication of the CPI has had a profound political impact in a number of countries, such as Pakistan, Malaysia, and Argentina, as government leaders reacted strongly to the results. These leaders are aware of the relationship between perceived corruption and direct foreign investment. Some of them are beginning to take action, working with national chapters of TI to reduce corruption levels in the future.[36] Others have noted that "it takes two parties for bribes to occur," suggesting that those who export to the most corrupt countries should be considered corrupt as well. In a recent survey conducted by a German researcher, U.S. and Swedish exporters were listed among the least corrupt of eighteen exporting countries. Belgium, France, and Italy ranked as the most corrupt exporters.[37]

How Different Are Ethical Standards in Different Cultures?

Certain ethical standards are universally accepted in all human societies. For example, the prescriptions, "thou shalt not kill" and "thou shalt not steal" are universal. Furthermore, the golden rule, "do unto others as you would have them do unto you" appears in the teachings of every major religion from Judaism to Buddhism.

> Buddhism: "Hurt not others in ways that you yourself would find hurtful."
>
> Christianity: "Whatsoever you wish that men would do to you, do so to them, for this is the law and the prophets."
>
> Confucianism: Tsze-Kung asked, saying, "Is there one word which may serve as a rule of practice for all one's life?" The Master said: "Is not reciprocity such a word? What you do not want done to yourself, do not do to others."
>
> Hinduism: "This is the sum of duty: Do naught to others which would cause pain if done to you."
>
> Judaism: "What is hateful to you, do not to your fellow man. This is the entire Law: all the rest is commentary."
>
> Islam: "No one of you is a believer until he desires for his brother that which he desires for himself."[38]

These commonalities suggest some basis for common ethical understanding across cultures. But beyond them, the world gets more complicated. For example, other values are comparable but are interpreted differently in different cultures. For example, honesty is valued in most cultures, but the meaning of honesty may differ from culture to culture. The notion of "caveat emptor" (buyer beware) is considered dishonest, and therefore wrong in the United States, but it may simply be considered good business in other cultures. Furthermore, an individual from a collectivist culture may deceive a business partner in order to maintain harmony, saying "maybe" when the answer is "no."

Still other values are clearly in conflict. For example, as we suggested earlier, many U.S. firms have rules against nepotism and gift giving. Nepotism is viewed as creating a conflict of interest, and gift giving is viewed as a form of influence on objective decision making. But both nepotism and gift giving are deeply embedded in collectivist cultures and are supported by the value these cultures place on relationships and family.

Finally, some values are completely incompatible and will require clear rules against them. For example, child labor may be the best example of an incompatible value. However, figuring out how to address such incompatibilities is a challenge that is addressed in the next section.

Some argue that U.S. executives see the United States, Canada, and Northern Europe as being relatively comparable with regard to ethical business practice because Canada and Northern Europe are culturally most similar to the United States, sharing comparable values. They view Southern Europe as presenting greater ethical challenges because of fewer comparable values, and they regard developing countries, particularly those with autocratic governments, as presenting the greatest challenges because these cultures and their values are most different.[39]

David Vogel[40] has argued that a substantial "ethics gap" remains between the United States and the rest of the developed world. He attributes the greater importance Americans place on business ethics to a number of sources including (1) the legal and regulatory environment in the United States where there are more laws and regulations governing business behavior and they are more strictly enforced. (2) Higher public expectations in comparison with Europe and Japan. The American public is more interested in social investing, they pay more attention to published rankings of corporations on their social responsibility, and there are more boycotts of companies because of their social policies. (3) Business values in the American culture owe a great deal to the Protestant work ethic and its expectation that business managers will behave morally. Despite Americans' cynicism toward business ethics, there is significantly more cynicism in Europe and Japan. In Europe, "the moral status of capitalism has traditionally been problematic,"[41] making the pursuit of profit morally questionable. (4) Because of the emphasis on the individual in American culture, the individual business person is expected to make ethical decisions based on his or her own moral compass. As a result, more American corporations provide avenues for individuals to express moral concerns, and the American legal system offers more protection to whistleblowers.[42]

On the other hand, recent developments suggest increasing interest in business ethics in other countries and increasing similarities across countries in terms of the enactment of environmental and sexual harassment legislation and the prosecution of insider trading. For example, in Great Britain, reports on British business practice are beginning to identify business ethics as important, and a number of organizations and interest groups are raising the business ethics issue.[43] The bottom line seems to be that those involved in international business need to stay informed about the changing legal and ethical landscapes in the countries in which they work.

Development of Corporate Guidelines and Policies for Global Business Ethics

Given the wide diversity of opinion among managers, the ambiguity of legal requirements, and the continued existence of cultural differences and corruption, firms doing business abroad have a responsibility to develop guidelines and policies to guide their employees' ethical conduct.

We learned in Chapter Seven about our "multiple ethical selves," the fact that people are frequently willing to accept different rules for different contexts. When applied to the international business ethics environment, the concept becomes cultural relativism. "When in Rome, do as the Romans do" is the guiding slogan of cultural relativists who claim that "no culture has a better ethics than any other."[44] Tom Donaldson,[45] a leading business ethicist, argues convincingly that ethical relativism must be rejected because, at the extreme, relativists would have to honor any practice that is accepted within another culture, even murder.

But Donaldson[46] also rejects the opposite of relativism, ethical imperialism. Ethical imperialism assumes absolute truths that would require exactly the same standards and behavior in every culture. An absolutist would have to choose a single standard as the best for all situations. However, how would one choose between the American belief that individual liberty is a more important value than loyalty to a community and the Japanese belief that loyalty comes before liberty? Donaldson also points out that ethical imperialism can lead to disastrous mistakes. He offers the example of a large U.S. firm operating in China. When an employee was caught stealing, the manager followed company policy and turned the employee over to provincial authorities. The employee was immediately executed.

So, how can companies help their employees to balance these extremes of ethical relativism and absolutism? First, Donaldson[47] proposes that firms develop an "ethical threshold" for corporate behavior abroad based on core values such as the golden rule, respect for human dignity, respect for basic human rights, and good citizenship. These generalities then must be translated into more specific guidelines. For example, companies can respect human dignity by treating employees, customers, and suppliers as persons with intrinsic value and by creating safe products and a safe workplace. They can respect human rights by protecting employees' and customers' rights. And they can be good citizens by protecting the environment.

Some activities would not be allowed because they cross the ethical threshold. Levi Strauss's global sourcing guidelines are a good example. They were adopted in 1992 to ensure that products were being produced in a manner consistent with the corporation's values. The first guideline bans the use of child labor. Others limit working hours, and mandate safe working conditions and environmental responsibility. Haas reported that the company had terminated relationships with 5 percent and requested change in 25 percent of its sourcing operations because of guideline violations. Implementing a company's standards such as a ban on child labor can be complicated, however. For example, Levi Strauss found that two contractors in Bangladesh used workers who appeared to be under the age of 14, the age set as reasonable by international standards. In analyzing the situation, they realized that there was no proof of age for these children and that the children contributed substantially to their families' income. Firing them might push them into more inhumane work such as begging or prostitution and create hardship for their families. To comply with Levi's standards, the contractor hired a physician who used growth charts to identify the underage children, and they were removed from the factory. The contractor continued to pay these children wages as if they were still working, and Levi Strauss paid for uniforms, tuition, and books so that they could attend school. At the age of 14, they would be rehired. The contractor also agreed not to hire additional underage workers. The contractor was willing to comply with Levi Strauss's standards because they wanted to continue doing business with the firm.

Haas acknowledges that adhering to these standards increases costs. Contractors have to add emergency exits and staircases, improve ventilation or bathroom facilities, and install water treatment systems. These costs are passed along to the firm. But he believes that decisions that focus only on costs do not serve the company's long-term interests.[48]

In other kinds of situations, values may be in conflict, but cultural traditions do not violate any of the core human values. In those situations, Donaldson[49] proposes that managers respect cultural traditions and take the context into account when deciding what is right and wrong. For example, gift giving is an important part of the Japanese culture. An absolutist might judge gift giving to be wrong. However, a corporate ethics code that respects local traditions would likely allow some forms of gift giving and receiving and would provide managers with specific guidance to help them differentiate among acceptable and unacceptable gift-giving situations. Gift giving does not violate a core value as long as there are limits on its scope and intention. Similarly, many U.S. firms have rules against nepotism because they believe that the act of hiring and supervising one's family members presents an inappropriate conflict of interest. However, in cultures that have a deeper tradition of extended family and clan loyalty, nepotism is not only approved, but it is expected. Companies are expected to hire employees' children, for example. Donaldson (1996) argues that, although nepotism conflicts with Western concepts of equal employment opportunity, it is not necessarily wrong when viewed from the perspective of a culture that values family relationships and has high unemployment.

Donaldson offers Motorola's code of conduct as a model global code. First, the code states the company's core values: "How we will always act: [with constant] respect for people [and] uncompromising integrity." The code then goes on to be much more specific. In a section on bribery, for example, it states that the "funds and assets of Motorola shall not be used directly or indirectly for illegal payments of any kind." An illegal payment is defined in the code as "the payment of a bribe to a public official or the kickback of funds to an employee of a customer." The code also outlines specific procedures for handling other specific situations that could involve bribes. Finally, the code allows for individual judgment in culturally sensitive situations. For example, employees may sometimes accept small gifts "in rare circumstances where the refusal to accept a gift" would harm Motorola's "legitimate business interests" and "so long as the gift inures to the benefit of Motorola" and not "to the benefit of the Motorola employee."

In addition to providing guidance to employees through a code, one U.S. executive who talked with us about these issues emphasized the importance of explaining to overseas business partners why you're required to behave in a particular way. Make it clear that this behavior is required by your home culture and your company's code of conduct and request their respect and their cooperation.

Finally, organizations must take care to match their performance appraisal and reward systems to ethical goals. If ethical conduct is the goal, the organization must make it clear that the expatriate manager will not be punished, either explicitly or implicitly, for upholding the organization's ethical standards even if it costs the organization business. Because it's difficult, if not impossible, to monitor expatriate managers' or representatives' behavior from afar, organizations tend to focus on outcomes (the bottom line) to evaluate the expatriate's performance. For example, they set sales or production goals and evaluate performance in light of goal achievement. However, if the organization focuses only on outcomes, with no attention to how those outcomes are achieved, the expatriate manager is likely to do the same, and ethical goals are more likely to be compromised. On the other hand, if the organization recognizes the potential ethical dilemmas to be faced by the expatriate manager in trying to do business in a particular culture, they will be more likely to openly acknowledge that lost business is a possibility and to reward the manager for conducting business within ethical guidelines.

By talking about aligning global codes and reward systems, we are essentially recommending that companies develop a global ethical culture that will guide employee behavior. But can a multinational corporation's ethical culture be effective if it is inconsistent with the national culture of the country in which it is doing business? The answer may depend on the nationality of the employees in question. Expatriate managers who are on temporary assignment in a foreign country would be inclined to follow the firm's conduct code, as long as they are not punished for doing so. However, research suggests that this may be less true for foreign nationals who work for a multinational company in their own country. National culture has a powerful impact on employees' attitudes and behaviors, and its influence may be more powerful than organizational culture. For example, managers working for one multinational firm in ten different countries expressed strong cultural differences.[50] "When working for a multinational corporation, it appears that Germans become more German, Americans become more American, Swedes become more Swedish, and so on."[51] Working for a foreign-owned company may magnify cultural differences and may cause individuals to identify with their own cultures even more. These research findings suggest that multinationals wishing to develop global standards of ethical conduct should take cultural differences into account if they want these standards to be effective with all of their employees.

THE ORGANIZATION IN A GLOBAL BUSINESS ENVIRONMENT

Although more small businesses are venturing into the global marketplace, large multinational corporations still represent much of international business, and the ethical expectations of them are often greater because of their size and visibility. These corporations face business ethics environments that vary widely from country to country. International law is often not particularly helpful, and it is often unclear whether a particular country's legal system has regulatory authority over global transactions.[52] Therefore, a firm's own ethical standards become an important guide for its workers. Multinational corporations also face questions of legitimacy that may cause them to consider whether they should even involve themselves in a foreign culture. If they do decide to do business in a particular foreign environment, what are their responsibilities?

Deciding to Do Business in a Foreign Country

American businesses are aggressively pursuing foreign markets. They face increased competition in the global marketplace, requiring them to become cost effective in a variety of ways, including manufacturing goods abroad or buying from foreign suppliers who can often produce goods more cheaply.

The Challenge to Legitimacy Numerous ethical challenges accompany these forays into the international business environment. For example, in some environments, the very legitimacy of the company may be challenged. Particularly in developing countries, the company's motives may be questioned as:

Managerial lifestyles are perceived as overly materialistic.

Labor-saving technology conflicts with the perceived need for jobs.

Paying market wages is viewed as exploitation.

Expanding locally is perceived as furthering control and dependence.[53]

Furthermore, differences in the sociopolitical environment raise a host of other ethical questions. Should American companies invest in, or do business in, countries that practice racial discrimination, pollute the environment, or violate the human rights of their citizens? Does doing business in these countries or with these organizations tarnish a company's ethical reputation simply by association? Is it all right to do business in the country as long as the company avoids engaging in the unethical practices itself? Furthermore, is it all right to do business in a country if the company creates and sticks to its own standards with regard to issues such as racial discrimination, pollution, or safety? For example, should a company that manufactures children's sleepwear be required to meet U.S. safety (fire hazard) standards when selling this product in countries that do not have such strict standards?

Some U.S. firms have taken their ethical standards abroad. For Alcoa Aluminum, worker safety is a top priority. As Alcoa puts it, the company simply doesn't want to hurt anyone. This commitment to worker safety applies equally to foreign operations where Alcoa safety standards and practices often surpass host country expectations. When a fatality occurs at an Alcoa operation anywhere in the world, the CEO shows up to find out why.

Other firms are moved to reconsider their overseas ethical standards when media attention turns their way. For example, media attention to sweatshop conditions in overseas factories has recently raised legitimacy questions with regard to a number of large corporations, including Wal-Mart and Nike. As globalization continues to expand and the world continues to shrink, companies that ignore working conditions in suppliers' factories risk their valuable reputations. Video cameras take consumers inside factories that, for many years, were out of sight and out of mind. When consumers learn about the working conditions, they demand change. Since the public furor over the fact that Kathie Lee Gifford's line of Wal-Mart clothing was made in sweatshop conditions in Honduras, both Wal-Mart and Kmart have announced new codes for overseas contract labor.

Doing Business in South Africa   The question of whether to do business in South Africa, a country that has now dismantled its longstanding policies of racial segregation and apartheid, was a prominent ethical issue for multinational businesses for many years. Some U.S. firms chose to stay out of South Africa completely during the apartheid years, many feeling pressured to do so by institutional investors such as pension funds that prohibited investment in companies doing business in South Africa. Others elected to do business there while adhering to "The Sullivan Principles," a list of standards for U.S. multinationals doing business in South Africa, drafted by Leon Sullivan, an African-American minister. These principles called for integration of the races in work facilities, equal and fair employment practices, equal pay for equal work, training programs to prepare nonwhites for higher level jobs, the movement of nonwhites into those jobs, and contribution to the quality of employees' life outside of work.[54]

Levi Strauss, as part of global training on ethics, teaches managers how to use a decision tool called the "Principled Reasoning Approach" which can be used to work through tough ethical dilemmas. The approach was recently used by a cross-functional and multinational task force that met over several months to decide whether to enter the South African marketplace. Members conducted research on the history of apartheid, identified stakeholders, visited South Africa, and interviewed members of the government and community organizations. The task force recommended that it would be appropriate to enter the South African marketplace under certain conditions, including free elections. Since free elections were held, the company has opened marketing and production facilities in South Africa.[55]

Marketing Infant Formula in the Developing World   Once engaged in business in a foreign country, companies must also consider whether practices that are perfectly acceptable at home are appropriate in the foreign environment. This is perhaps best exemplified in the now-classic case of marketing infant formula in developing countries, particularly in the 1970s and early 1980s. The Swiss conglomerate, Nestle, was singled out among companies that were engaging in practices that encouraged new mothers in these countries to give up breastfeeding and switch to formula.[56]

In addition to more routine advertising that inaccurately suggested that bottle-fed babies would be healthier, companies used so-called milk nurses to promote their products in maternity wards. These women, though dressed as nurses, were actually sales representatives who received a commission for selling formula.

Unfortunately, the switch to formula posed a serious health risk to the infants for three reasons. First, the formula must be mixed with water, which is contaminated in many of these areas. Therefore, infants fed the formula were at high risk for infections and diarrhea. Second, mothers in these areas often cannot afford to continue buying formula. Therefore, they dilute it or substitute cheaper products that contribute to health problems, including malnourished babies. Finally, and perhaps most important, women who give up breast feeding cannot simply change their minds and return to it. After a short time, their own milk production diminishes, and they are no longer able to feed their babies themselves. They are forced to rely on formula. In response to organized protests and boycotts from numerous activist groups, the company finally agreed to alter its marketing practices.

Although some might argue that the marketing practices just described would be questionable even at home, they would not seriously compromise babies' health here as they do in the developing country. Thus, the very same practice could be considered ethical in one setting but highly unethical in another.

Deciding What to Do about Human Rights   Other issues also arise once a firm has decided to do business in a developing country. Many of these issues have to do with basic human rights and how to deal with incompatible values. We have already learned about how Levi Strauss dealt with the issue of child labor. Since 1992, the Reebok Corporation, manufacturer of athletic shoes, has made human rights an integral part of its corporate strategy. Its formal worldwide code extends its coverage to workers employed by third parties, mostly in Asian factories. The code covers such areas as nondiscrimination, working hours, overtime requirements, fair wages, child labor, and forced or compulsory labor. Regular on-site visits are conducted by independent auditors and include inspections of facilities and interviews with employees. Reebok will terminate its relationship with factories that are found to be in violation of the code. A company that decides to hold itself accountable for protecting human rights in its overseas operations (including those of its suppliers) is taking on an expensive task that can be difficult to implement.

Development of a Transcultural Corporate Ethic

Many business people hope for the day when there will be fewer incompatible values and more agreement about appropriate business conduct. Some progress has been made in that direction through the efforts of government organizations, multinational companies, and private organizations interested in international business ethics.

First, a number of efforts have been underway to battle bribery and corruption. For example, the Organization for Economic Cooperation and Development (OECD) has twenty-nine members, including the nations of North America, Western Europe, and the industrialized democracies of the Pacific. At the end of 1997, the OECD approved the first treaty to outlaw bribery in international business. The treaty would make bribery a criminal offense, and a monitoring system would be set up to enforce it. Some argue that the treaty is weak because it does not require minimum penalties, does not ban gifts to political parties, and does not outlaw tax deductibility for bribes. However, it is a step in the right direction. The treaty will go into force if it is ratified by five of the ten largest OECD members by the end of 1998.[57] The Organization of American States (OAS) has thirty-five members, which include all of the independent republics of the Americas except Cuba. The majority of members signed the Inter-American Convention Against Corruption, which took force in 1997. This binding treaty does not outlaw bribery, but it does require members to develop policies and practices that aim to reduce corruption.[58]

Movement toward "a transcultural corporate ethic"[59] has occurred as a result of a number of other intergovernmental agreements reached during the last half of this century. These combine to set out normative guidelines for the business conduct of multinational corporations. The guidelines that emerge from these agreements cover the areas of employment practices and policies, consumer protection, environmental protection, political payments and involvement, and basic human rights and fundamental freedoms, and are based on four principles:

1. The inviolability of national sovereignty—Multinationals are expected to respect the "host country's economic and social development and its cultural and historical traditions."[60]

2. Social equity—Pay scales are expected to ensure equity between genders, as well as racial and ethnic groups.

3. Market integrity in business transactions—Restrictions on political payments and bribes assume that these "inject non-market considerations into business transactions."[61]

4. Human rights and fundamental freedoms—This principle is based on belief in the inherent worth and dignity of every individual and the equality of rights of all human beings. However, this principle often competes with other principles, especially the first, national sovereignty. For example, South Africa's apartheid system was based on the denial of human rights to its black citizens, and women are denied rights in many cultures and government systems.

An important question remains: Do these agreements influence multinationals to behave differently? Multinational corporations are not explicit parties to these intergovernmental agreements, and they are not directly bound by them. However, they are indirectly affected to the extent that countries enact laws requiring companies to comply. The agreements may also be contributing to a more informal type of compliance as they contribute to the development of accepted cross-cultural moral standards. The more multinationals become aware of these standards, the more likely they will be to comply.

Business leaders have also been working to develop worldwide corporate responsibility standards. A group representing American, European, and Japanese multinationals, calling itself the Caux Round Table, began meeting in Caux, Switzerland in 1986. Their mission was to focus attention on global corporate responsibility. The group has developed a set of standards for global business behavior that are based on two principles: human dignity and the Japanese concept, *kyosei*—"the ideal of living and working together for the common good to enable mutual prosperity." Although, again, the standards are not binding, it is hoped that businesses around the world will rely on them to develop their own standards.[62] See the appendix at the end of this chapter for the full text of these principles.

Other initiatives are more regional in nature and involve partnerships between governments, companies, and private organizations. For example, the Merck Company Foundation has provided a $980,000 grant to establish the Gulf Center for Excellence in Ethics (GCEE) in the United Arab Emirates (UAE). "The GCEE will promote government and private sector initiatives to focus on ethical standards in the Gulf region and foster better business practices."[63] The effort is the result of a collaboration between the Ethics Resource Center, a nonprofit consulting group in Washington, DC, the GCEE, and other UAE institutions. John Taylor, executive vice president of the foundation, said, "It is our belief and sincerest hope that the UAE ethics center will result in better business and ethical practices—effecting systemic change and improving the quality of life throughout the entire Gulf region."[64]

Because none of these agreements is yet binding, Richard DeGeorge[65] has proposed the following seven moral guidelines designed specifically to help multinational corporations (MNCs) make more ethical business decisions.

1. MNCs should do no intentional direct harm.
2. MNCs should produce more good than bad for the host country.

3. MNCs should contribute to the host country's development.

4. MNCs should respect employees' human rights.

5. MNCs should pay their fair share of taxes.

6. MNCs should respect the local culture to the extent that it does not violate moral norms.

7. MNCs should work with the local government to develop and enforce just institutions such as taxes, and health and safety standards.[66]

CONCLUSION

From the individual's perspective, a foreign assignment is full of ethical challenges. Training and guidance, along with openness and flexibility, can go a long way toward preparing the expatriate manager to survive with integrity and sanity intact—perhaps even to enjoy the richness of the international business experience. Organizations can help their employees by developing a set of broad core values as well as specific guidelines for ethical business practice. The expanding interest in business ethics abroad and the development of international guidelines to guide business behavior across cultural boundaries will help to level the playing field and contribute to making the international business experience a richer and more satisfying one for all concerned.

DISCUSSION QUESTIONS

1. If you were going on your first overseas business assignment, what would you do to ensure that you were prepared to deal with ethical dilemmas you would face? What questions would you ask your superiors in preparation for the trip?

2. Your firm is expanding globally and is sending executives overseas for the first time. What will you do to be sure these individuals are prepared to deal with the ethical dilemmas they will face?

3. Imagine that someone from another culture asked you to provide information about business ethics when dealing with American managers. What would you say?

4. Talk with someone from another culture. Ask for information that would be helpful to you if you had to do business in their culture. What did you learn that you didn't know before? How might you behave differently because of what you know?

5. Discuss the following statement from the chapter—"Women succeed [overseas] because they are seen as foreigners who happen to be women, not as women who happen to be foreigners." Can you think of other groups to whom this statement might apply?

6. Imagine yourself in a situation where you had to bribe someone or lose the deal? How would you think about it? What do you think you would do? Why?

7. Assume the role of corporate decision maker in a decision about whether to do business in a foreign country in the developing world. What criteria will you establish for making the decision from an ethics and social responsibility perspective? Why are these the most important criteria?

8. What are the costs and benefits of developing a transcultural corporate ethic? Whose responsibility should it be to develop such an ethic— governments, corporations, intergovernmental organizations, all of these?

CASE 11.1

The Gift

You're an account executive with a multinational financial firm, and one of your biggest accounts is that of a shipping magnate in Greece. Several months after you've arranged very complex financing to build a new fleet of oil tankers for this customer, he asks if you and your wife would attend the christening of the first tanker. You, of course, agree to attend—it would be an insult to him if you didn't. When you arrive, he asks your wife to break the traditional champagne bottle over the bow of the tanker. Two weeks after the christening, your wife receives a package from your customer. In it is a gold bracelet with her initials and the date of the christening in diamonds. To return the gift would insult your customer, but accepting it would clearly violate your company's policy? What should you do?

Case-Based Questions

1. What kind of an ethical issue is this?

2. Why would it be against corporate policy to accept such a gift? Do you agree with the policy? Why or why not?

3. Put yourself in the "shoes" of each of the parties? How might they think about the issue?

4. Imagine that you are the corporate vice-president in charge of business ethics and conduct for your firm. Would you be willing to change this policy? Why or why not?

Caux Round Table Principles for Business

SECTION 1. PREAMBLE

The mobility of employment, capital, products, and technology is making business increasingly global in its transactions and its effects.

Laws and market forces are necessary but insufficient guides for conduct.

Responsibility for the policies and actions of business and respect for the dignity and interests of its stakeholders are fundamental.

Shared values, including a commitment to shared prosperity, are as important for a global community as for communities of smaller scale.

For these reasons, and because business can be a powerful agent of positive social change, we offer the following principles as a foundation for dialogue and action by business leaders in search of business responsibility. In so doing, we affirm the necessity for moral values in business decision making. Without them, the stable business relationships and a sustainable world community are impossible.

SECTION 2. GENERAL PRINCIPLES

PRINCIPLE 1. The Responsibilities of Businesses: Beyond Shareholders Toward Stakeholders

The value of a business to society is the wealth and employment it creates and the marketable products and services it provides to consumers at a reasonable price commensurate with quality. To create such value, a business must maintain its own economic health and viability, but survival is not a sufficient goal.

Businesses have a role to play in improving the lives of all their customers, employees, and shareholders by sharing with them the wealth they have created. Suppliers and competitors as well should expect businesses to honor their obligations in a spirit of honesty and fairness. As responsible citizens of the local, national, regional, and global communities in which they operate, businesses share a part in shaping the future of those communities.

PRINCIPLE 2. The Economic and Social Impact of Business: Toward Innovation, Justice, and World Community

Businesses established in foreign countries to develop, produce, or sell should also contribute to the social advancement of those countries by creating productive employment and helping to raise the purchasing power of their citizens. Businesses also should contribute to human rights, education, welfare, and vitalization of the countries in which they operate.

Businesses should contribute to economic and social development not only in the countries in which they operate, but also in the world community at large, through effective and prudent use of resources, free and fair competition, and emphasis upon innovation in technology, production methods, marketing, and communications.

PRINCIPLE 3. Business Behavior: Beyond the Letter of Law Toward a Spirit of Trust

While accepting the legitimacy of trade secrets, businesses should recognize that sincerity, candor, truthfulness, the keeping of promises, and transparency contribute not only to their own credibility and stability but also to the smoothness and efficiency of business transactions, particularly on the international level.

PRINCIPLE 4. Respect for Rules

To avoid trade frictions and to promote freer trade, equal conditions for competition, and fair and equitable treatment for all participants, businesses should respect international and domestic rules. In addition, they should recognize that some behavior, although legal, may still have adverse consequences.

PRINCIPLE 5. Support for Multinational Trade

Businesses should support the multilateral trade systems of the GATT/World Trade Organization and similar international agreements. They should cooperate in efforts to promote the progressive and judicious liberalization of trade, and to relax those domestic measures that unreasonably hinder global commerce, while giving due respect to national policy objectives.

PRINCIPLE 6. Respect for the Environment

A business should protect and, where possible, improve the environment, promote sustainable development, and prevent the wasteful use of natural resources.

PRINCIPLE 7. Avoidance of Illicit Operations

A business should not participate in or condone bribery, money laundering, or other corrupt practices: indeed, it should seek cooperation with others, to eliminate them. It should not trade in arms or other materials used for terrorist activities, drug traffic, or other organized crime.

SECTION 3. STAKEHOLDER PRINCIPLES

Customers

We believe in treating all customers with dignity, irrespective of whether they purchase our products and services directly from us or otherwise acquire them in the market. We therefore have a responsibility to:

- provide our customers with the highest quality products and services consistent with their requirements;
- treat our customers fairly in all aspects of our business transactions, including a high level of service and remedies for their dissatisfaction;
- make every effort to ensure that the health and safety of our customers, as well as the quality of their environment, will be sustained or enhanced by our products and services;
- assure respect for human dignity in products offered, marketing, and advertising; and
- respect the integrity of the culture of our customers.

Employees

We believe in the dignity of every employee and in taking employee interests seriously. We therefore have the responsibility to:

- provide jobs and compensation that improve workers' living conditions;
- provide working conditions that respect each employee's health and dignity;
- be honest in communications with employees and open in sharing information, limited only by legal and competitive restraints;
- listen to, and where possible, act on employee suggestions, ideas, requests, and complaints;
- engage in good faith negotiations when conflict arises;
- avoid discriminatory practices and guarantee equal treatment and opportunity in areas such as gender, age, race, and religion;
- promote in the business itself the employment of differently abled people in places of work where they can be genuinely useful;
- protect employees from avoidable injury and illness in the workplace;
- encourage and assist employees in developing relevant and transferable skills and knowledge;

- be sensitive to serious unemployment problems frequently associated with business decisions and work with governments, employee groups, other agencies and each other in addressing these dislocations.

Owners/Investors

We believe in honoring the trust our investors place in us. We therefore have a responsibility to:

- apply professional and diligent management in order to secure a fair and competitive return on our owners' investment;
- disclose relevant information to owners/investors subject only to legal requirements and competitive constraints;
- conserve, protect, and increase the owners/investors' assets; and
- respect owners/investors' requests, suggestions, complaints, and formal resolutions.

Suppliers

Our relationship with suppliers and subcontractors must be based on mutual respect. We therefore have a responsibility to:

- seek fairness and truthfulness in all of our activities, including pricing, licensing, and rights to sell;
- ensure that our business activities are free from coercion and unnecessary litigation;
- foster long-term stability in the supplier relationship in return for value, quality, competitiveness, and reliability;
- share information with suppliers and integrate them into our planning processes;
- pay suppliers on time and in accordance with agreed terms of trade;
- seek, encourage, and prefer suppliers and subcontractors whose employment practices respect human dignity.

Competitors

We believe that fair economic competition is one of the basic requirements for increasing the wealth of nations and, ultimately, for making possible the just distribution of goods and services. We therefore have a responsibility to:

- foster open markets for trade and investment;
- promote competitive behavior that is socially and environmentally beneficial and demonstrates mutual respect among competitors;

- refrain from either seeking or participating in questionable payments or favors to secure competitive advantages;
- respect both tangible and intellectual property rights; and
- refuse to acquire commercial information by dishonest or unethical means, such as industrial espionage.

Communities

We believe that as global corporate citizens, we can contribute to such forces of reform and human rights as are at work in the communities in which we operate. We therefore have a responsibility in those communities to:

- respect human rights and democratic institutions, and promote them wherever practicable;
- recognize government's legitimate obligation to the society at large and support public policies and practices that promote human development through harmonious relations between business and other segments of society;
- collaborate with those forces in the community dedicated to raising standards of health, education, workplace safety; and economic well-being;
- promote and stimulate sustainable development and play a leading role in preserving and enhancing the physical environment and conserving the earth's resources;
- support peace, security, diversity, and social integration;
- be a good corporate citizen through charitable donations, educational and cultural contributions and employee participation in community and civic affairs.

NOTES

1. Black, J. S., & Mendenhall, M. 1990. Cross-cultural training effectiveness: A review and a theoretical framework for future research. *Academy of Management Review* 15 (1): 113–136.

2. Adler, N. 1992. *International dimensions of organizational behavior.* Boston: PWS Kent Publishing Co.

3. Black & Mendenhall, Cross-cultural training effectiveness.

4. Adler, *International dimensions of organizational behavior.*

5. Simon, P. 1980. *The tongue-tied American: Confronting the foreign language crisis.* New York: Continuum Publishing.

6. Triandis, H. C., Brislin, R., & Hui, C. H. 1988. Cross-cultural training across the individualism-collectivism divide. *International Journal of Intercultural Relations* 12: 269–289.

7. Hofstede, G. 1980. *Culture's consequences: International differences in work-related values.* Beverly Hills: Sage Publications.

8. Ibid.

9. Adler, N. 1997. *International dimensions of organizational behavior.* Cincinnati: Southwestern College Publishing.

   Carroll, S. J., & Gannon, M. J. 1997. *Ethical dimensions of international management.* Thousand Oaks, CA: Sage.

10. Triandis, Brislin, & Hui, Cross-cultural training across the individualism-collectivism divide.

11. Triandis, H. C. 1984. A theoretical framework for the more efficient construction of culture assimilators. *International Journal of Intercultural Relations* 8: 301–330.

12. Albert, R. D. 1986. Conceptual framework for the development and evaluation of cross-cultural orientation programs. *International Journal of Intercultural Relations* 10: 197–213.

13. Ibid.

14. Jelinek, M., & Adler, N. J. 1988. Women: world class managers for global competition. *Academy of Management Executive* 2 (1): 11–19.

15. Adler, *International dimensions of organizational behavior.*

16. Adler, N. J., & Graham, J. L. 1989. Cross-cultural interaction: The international comparison fallacy? *Journal of International Business Studies* Fall: 515–537.

17. Albert, Conceptual framework for the development and evaluation of cross-cultural orientation programs.

18. Ibid.

19. Adler, *International dimensions of organizational behavior.*

20. O'Grady, S. O., & Lane, H. W. 1996. The psychic distance paradox. *Journal of International Business Studies* 27: 309–333.

21. Donaldson, T. 1992. When in Rome, do . . . what? International business and cultural relativism. In P. M. Minus (Ed.), *The ethics of business in a global economy.* Boston: Kluwer, pp. 67–78.

22. Adler, *International dimensions of organizational behavior.*

23. Ibid, p. 219.

24. Ibid.

25. Ibid.

26. Fadiman, J. A. 1986. A traveler's guide to gifts and bribes. *Harvard Business Review,* July–August: 122–134.

27. Longenecker, J. G., McKinney, J. A., & Moore, C. W. 1988. The ethical issue of international bribery: A study of attitudes among U.S. business professionals. *Journal of Business Ethics* 7: 341–346.

28. Tong, H. M., & Welling, P. 1981. What American business managers should know and do about international bribery. *Baylor Business Review,* November–December: 8.

29. U.S. Government Accounting Office. 1981. Report to Congress, impact of Foreign Corrupt Practices Act on U.S. Business, March 4.

30. Carroll, A. 1989. *Business and society: Ethics and stakeholder management.* Cincinnati: Southwestern Publishing.

31. Behrman, J. 1988. *Essays on ethics in business and the professions.* Englewood Cliffs, NJ: Prentice-Hall.

Grosse, R., & Kujawa, D. 1992. *International Business.* Boston: Irwin.

Singer, A. W. 1991. Ethics: Are standards lower overseas? *Across the Board,* September: 31–34.

32. Nelson, J. 1997. 29 countries commit to pact against bribery. *Los Angeles Times,* November 21: 1.

33. Carroll, *Business and society.*

34. Koretz, G. 1996. Bribes can cost the U.S. an edge. *Business Week,* April 15, p. 30.

35. Schoenberger, K. 1997. Hong Kong's secret weapon. *Fortune,* November 25, pp. 141–142.

36. *Transparency International.* 1997. *Transparency International* published 1997 Corruption Perception Index. Press Release. Berlin, July 31.

37. Steinmetz, G. 1997. U.S. firms appear among least likely to bribe overseas. *Wall Street Journal,* August 25: 1.

38. Barach, J. A. 1985. The ethics of hardball. *California Management Review* 27: 2.

39. Singer, Ethics: Are standards lower overseas?

40. Vogel, D. 1992. The globalization of business ethics: Why America remains distinctive. *California Management Review,* Fall: 30–48.

41. Ibid.

42. Ibid.

43. Mahoney, J. 1990. An international look at business ethics: Britain. *Journal of Business Ethics* 9: 545–550.

44. Donaldson, When in Rome, do . . . what?

45. Donaldson, T. 1996. Values in tension: ethics away from home. *Harvard Business Review,* September–October: 48–62.

46. Ibid.

47. Ibid.

48. Haas, R. 1994. Ethics in the trenches. *Across the Board,* May: 12–13.

49. Donaldson, Values in tension.

50. Laurent, A. 1983. The cultural diversity of Western conceptions of management. *International Studies of Management and Organization* 13 (2): 75–96.

51. Adler, *International dimensions of organizational behavior,* p. 63.

52. Dunfee, T., & Holland, R. C. 1993. Viable ethical standards for global corporations: A glimpse of what might emerge. Unpublished paper. Philadelphia: Wharton School.

53. Carroll, *Business and society.*

54. Ibid.

55. Solomon, C. M. 1996. Put your ethics to a global test. *Personnel Journal,* January: 66–74.

56. Post, J. E. 1985. Assessing the Nestle boycott: Corporate accountability and human rights. *California Management Review,* Winter: 115–116.

57. Coleman, F. 1997. World leaders try to ban business bribery. *USA Today,* November 24: 23B.

58. Getz, K. A. 1997. International instruments on bribery and corruption. Unpublished paper presented at the Conference on Global Codes of Conduct: An Idea Whose Time Has Come. South Bend, IND: University of Notre Dame.

59. Frederick, W. C. 1991. The moral authority of transnational corporate codes. *Journal of Business Ethics* 10: 165–177.

60. Ibid.

61. Ibid, p.168.

62. Solomon, Put your ethics to a global test.

63. Ethics Resource Center. 1997. Merck Company Foundation & ERC launch ethics center in the United Arab Emirates. *Ethics Today* 1(Spring), p.1.

64. Ibid, p. 7.

65. DeGeorge, R. 1992. Ethics and Worse. *Financial Times,* July 3: 12.

66. Hoffman, W. M., Lange, A. E., & Fedo, D. (Eds.). 1986. *Ethics and the multinational enterprise.* Lanham, MD: University Press of America.

Integrative Case: Manville Corporation

INTRODUCTION

John McKinney, CEO of the Manville Corporation, one of the most profitable companies in the history of American business, had just heard a recommendation from his staff that the company file for reorganization under Chapter XI of the Federal Bankruptcy Code. "When I was told of that," Mr. McKinney said, "I went through the roof. I did not think that was right." The company was solvent, in fact profitable, but was required by accounting convention to book a $2 billion contingent liability against its $2.2 billion of assets. The welfare of 28,000 employees was at stake. Though Manville faced 17,000 asbestos-related health claims, of the 4,000 that had gone to trial the company had won half. According to Earl Parker, chief legal counsel for the Manville Corporation, this allowed Manville to settle the remaining cases at reasonable figures. In Mr. McKinney's mind, there was no reason Manville could not continue as it had. It was August 20, 1982.

Asbestos

Asbestos is a grayish-white fibrous mineral that is strong, flexible, and heat resistant. It has been used in over 3,000 applications but is best known as a fire retardant. Asbestos products include asbestos cement roofing tiles, corrugated siding, wallboard, sewing materials, pipe insulations, acoustical insulations, fabric applications, and asbestos-lined hand-held hair dryers. The mineral has been so widely used in numerous applications in public buildings and private dwellings that virtually everyone has had some exposure to asbestos.

But the worst exposures have occurred in the workplace, where asbestos has caused disabling and often fatal disease. Workers who produced asbestos products or installed asbestos insulation—without adequate filtration or ventila-

Case copyright ©1992 by Richard T. Dailey and Scott G. Hibbard. The generous cooperation of the Manville Corporation is gratefully acknowledged. This case was written as a basis for class discussion rather than to illustrate effective or ineffective management policies.

tion systems—were exposed to particularly high concentrations of the asbestos fiber.

Ingested or inhaled asbestos causes mechanical injury to moving tissue, particularly to the lungs, where the constant motion of the lungs during air and oxygen exchange facilitates penetration of these fibers, cutting and damaging the lung tissue in the process. The microscopic fibers are not dissolved or expelled from the body and are nearly impossible to totally filter from the air. Exposure to these fibers can result in asbestosis, lung cancer, or gastrointestinal cancer.

Asbestosis is a nonmalignant progressive and irreversible scarring, thickening, and calcification of the lungs and their linings that makes breathing increasingly difficult—causing shortness of breath and fatigue from climbing even a single flight of stairs. The incidence of asbestosis appears to be directly related to the duration and intensity of exposure to the asbestos fiber. In his 1962–1963 epidemiological studies of workers in the asbestos industry, Dr. Irving J. Selikoff, director of Environmental Sciences at New York's Mount Sinai School of Medicine, found that almost 87 percent of the workers who consistently had been exposed to asbestos in the workplace developed asbestosis, and between 7 percent and 10 percent of asbestos workers died from asbestosis.

The studies conducted by Dr. Selikoff and his associates indicated that asbestos workers had seven times greater risk of developing lung cancer and three times greater risk of developing gastrointestinal cancer than did workers in other industries. His studies also concluded that the degree of fibrosis developed (scarring of the lung tissue) was directly correlated to the length of exposure to asbestos. Dr. Selikoff's studies were funded by the Manville Corporation.

Legal History

Manville faced its first lawsuit in 1968, fourteen years before the bankruptcy recommendation. By 1973 there had been thirteen cases. The caseload did not become alarming until the later half of the 1970s, when several hundred claims were being filed each month. Dick Van Walsh, who managed asbestos cases for Manville, saw the number of cases as being on "some sort of bell-shaped curve," but he did not know where the company was on that curve.

> At that point in time, given the numbers and the lack of real science, I couldn't tell whether we were on an accelerating part of the curve or on the decelerating part of the curve—I just had no way to know. . . . As every year went by, more and more claims came in at a faster rate . . . and we weren't seeing a peak or change in the shape of the curve and so by the late [1970s] . . . the real pressure hit about what is the problem and we'd better really get our hands around this one.

There was also a conception within Manville's management that the epidemiological reports supported a theory that the worst of the asbestos cases had been seen. "We felt that we had already probably paid off or litigated with most of the people who were seriously ill," Mr. McKinney said. "There were only going to be a handful after that."

The magnitude of the issue was difficult to grasp because it was "a sort of creeping problem," Dick Van Walsh said, "not like an airplane crash. This one just kept building every year. And so the psychology of it took time for it to really hit home in a major way."

The "creeping" nature of the asbestos litigation issue began with product-liability law as defined by *Clarence Borel vs. Fiberboard Paper Products Corporation et al.* in 1973. The court ruled that Clarence Borel, an asbestos-insulation worker since 1936, could sue eleven asbestos manufacturers for failure to disclose the foreseeable risk involved in the use of their products. This opened the door for the increasing number of claims that soon followed. By August of 1982, 20,000 lawsuits had been filed against Manville. The company had paid $50 million in claims and settlements.

Insurance Companies

Manville's position was complicated by the nature of its insurance coverage. Whereas most asbestos manufacturers had one or two insurance carriers, Manville had a total of twenty-seven past and present carriers dating back to the 1920s. This led to the "trigger of coverage" argument among insurance companies and between Manville and its insurance companies. As expressed by Earl Parker, Manville's chief legal counsel:

> There was a dispute as to which policy of insurance could be called on to respond to the occurrence. Was it the policy of insurance in effect at the time the person manifested an asbestos-related disease? Or was it the policy in effect at the time that he was first exposed to the asbestos, or was it some combination of those? And that is referred to as exposure or manifestation theories, and some of the insurance companies were arguing for exposure, some for manifestation—of course, depending on where their particular coverage set.

To resolve the impasse between Manville and its carriers, legal proceedings were scheduled to be held in San Francisco. Because of the number of parties involved, Mr. McKinney noted that "they were even refurbishing an old theater to hold the trial in, because there wasn't a trial courtroom big enough to hold that many lawyers."

Meanwhile, the insurance companies had stopped paying claims. Because of this, and because of the increasing volume of claims, Manville adopted a tougher litigation strategy. It was accused of stonewalling, of refusing to settle cases in favor of litigation. According to Mr. Van Walsh:

> that's not really true. . . . We realized that we had to make sure we didn't pay for anything that wasn't a real case. And the only way to do that was to make sure that you work a case very hard so that you get the right facts, right data, and can make the right judgments. . . . We got tougher in demanding good facts . . . we

didn't ever adopt a "hands-off," stonewall policy of "we're not going to pay claims, we're going to try to clog the court system."

The most Manville could litigate in any given year was about 100 cases, of which it was winning roughly half. Total costs of litigation equated to one-third defense costs, one-third plaintiff legal fees, and one-third plaintiff compensation. In the second quarter of 1982, the average cost of case disposition was $40,000. "There are people who say that the litigation expense would have been much less . . . if the companies had not defended the cases," Mr. Parker said. ". . . but you can't lay down your arms and settle cases when the plaintiff's demands are a million or ten million dollars per case." Mr. Parker felt that those cases which it won in court "were responsible for our being able to settle the remaining cases at reasonable figures."

According to Mr. Parker, the insurance companies argued that asbestosis was not accidental, that it was the result of intended actions by Manville. Manville argued that "the state of the medical art was not such that the company knew or could have known that the product was hazardous at the time that it was put into the marketplace." Manville also countercharged that those workers who would not wear respirators after being instructed to do so were guilty of contributory negligence. In those cases where the plaintiff smoked, the defense was able to call into question exposure to asbestos as the cause of the disease.

The U.S. Government

Much of the contention between Manville and its insurance carriers was based on the latency of asbestosis. Twenty to thirty years was needed for the disease to surface after exposure, the most common source of which was the shipyards of World War II. Because of its fire-resistant properties, asbestos was used extensively in the construction and refurbishing of warships. According to Bob Batson (who had primary responsibility for Manville's litigation against the United States), with the heavy use of asbestos-containing materials in ship construction, in a naval battle, "you essentially could be on fire, fight fire, and keep fighting."

The crisis atmosphere of the war demanded that ships be turned out as quickly as possible, with some shipyards turning out a ship a day. To do this, shortcuts were taken, in spite of the fact that information was available to the government which indicated that serious health risks to shipbuilders might be involved. Mr. Batson made reference to court testimony by Dr. Leonard Goldwater, head of medical programs for occupational medicine at the Navy shipyard in Brooklyn during World War II:

> . . . 75,000 workers in the shipyard and Goldwater testified . . . they knew they were at risk . . . they knew there was a number of industrial hygiene measures that could be taken to protect shipyard workers. The fact was, up until October of 1943 we were losing the war because we couldn't build ships fast enough. They were sinking faster then we could build them. So when you talk about the rela-

tive risk here and the importance for building ships and getting them out, they were willing to take the kind of risks that were involved.

. . . you talk to some workers who worked in these facilities during the war and they describe some pretty serious conditions. They talk about working double shifts, working conditions where the ventilation was in disrepair.

Roughly half of the claims filed against Manville were from shipyard exposure during World War II. During the war, the U.S. government imposed mandatory wartime contracts on asbestos manufacturers to supply asbestos-containing materials to shipyards. Much of the specified fiber was from South Africa, which the government would purchase, transport, and sell to manufacturers at a profit. The asbestos-materials manufacturers would then make the required materials as specified by the government, which the government would purchase for use in its shipyards. As a result, Mr. Parker said, " . . . there was a very deep involvement of the government as a commercial party in this asbestos manufacturing experience and as an employer of the people." Because of this, and because the government had control of the materials and the workplace, in Manville's view the government should share the burden of asbestos-related health claims resulting from shipyard exposure. Earl Parker summed up Manville's perspective:

> The predominant argument by the government is that the government is sovereign and cannot be sued in a situation. People often quote that the "king can do no wrong," but the second part of the formula which often goes unquoted is "because the king sees that all wrongs are made right." And we were asking in this case that the sovereign government come in and make right a wrong that had been committed against these people. And, as I said before, the companies were not asking to be absolved but only for some participation, financial participation by the government in the compensation and for the creation of a more efficient means of compensating people rather than continuing the, what we thought was a very wasteful, tort litigation scenario.

Proposed Legislation

The Asbestos Health Hazards Compensation Act was introduced in the U.S. House of Representatives by Representative Millicent Fenwick in 1977 and in the U.S. Senate by Senator Gary Hart in 1980 and 1981. This legislation would have barred victims from filing lawsuits under the tort system and would have administered claims through Workers' Compensation. In so doing, it would have established a Workers' Compensation fund to help compensate asbestos victims. Both bills were sharply attacked by congressmen and asbestosis litigation attorneys as corporate bailouts for the asbestos industry. Both bills were killed in committee.

Manville's Burden

In Mr. Batson's view, the issue was one of "relative knowledge"—that the government knew relatively more about asbestos health hazards than did anyone else. However, "Manville and others in the industry had already been tried and convicted essentially before information about the government came out."

Referring to those cases that Manville did lose, Mr. Parker surmised that "you could say that the courts found that the company did know, or should have known, or had reason to know that the product was unsafe at the time." Mr. Batson, manager of Manville's asbestos litigation, concurred by saying that because the government was fully aware of the health risk, in a relative sense it was safe to assume that Manville was also.

Through the litigation process, documents surfaced which supported a conspiracy between Manville and Raybestos-Manhattan, another asbestos-materials manufacturer. Correspondence between the president of Raybestos and the general counsel of Manville indicated that not only did both companies know of the hazardous nature of asbestos, but also they conspired to cover up that knowledge. This became the basis for punitive damage awards against Manville, depending, according to Mr. Parker, on which parts of the evidence a jury chose to believe.

Product liability law had developed from "buyer beware" to negligence to strict liability. The Borel case was the catalyst in bringing strict product liability to bear in the asbestos issue. The overexposure that occurred in shipyards through World War II and up to the Korean War, as well as the long latency period of the disease, were the other elements which, in Mr. Parker's view, caused the financial crisis for Manville. This situation was exacerbated by inconsistent enforcement of health and exposure regulations within Manville itself. According to Mr. Parker,

> There were instances in the Manville record where managers of local facilities did not observe the policies the corporation had set forth, and I think you can link back to the corporation a failure to insist and enforce those policies in every location. There were instances where people were diagnosed as having asbestos-related disease and were not advised of that diagnosis and were not protected or removed from a dusty occupation. So there were many, many individual and corporate failings which contributed. . . . But I think I feel comfortable in saying that the, at least the financial, liability of Manville and the other asbestos companies was a result of over-exposure and the long latency period and the development of product liability law in the United States.

Manville's Culture

When John McKinney was faced with the decision of whether to file for bankruptcy, the Manville Corporation was ranked 181st on the Fortune 500 list of industrial firms. It was highly centralized and operated from a new corporate campus that it had built outside of Denver. To some it appeared to have a huge image of itself, much like a strutting peacock. For much of its history, Manville was big, and it was insulated. Mr. McKinney said:

> . . . in 1960 probably 80 percent of the profits from the company came from asbestos. And by '77 or so it was down, but what had happened was you had a

whole generation of people who grew up in the company not paying any attention to expenses. Nobody cared. I remember a guy who was head of the asbestos fiber division and coordinating the proposed projects; you know, spend so many million dollars on a plant and his attitude was, "go ahead, we spill more than that every day at the mine." . . . [for] a long time they never borrowed any money, they had never issued any equity, the big deal at the end of every year was to see how many reserves you could set up to depress earnings. . . . I think the lowest cash-on-hand that the company would have during the yearly cycle was about $50 million, this was when the sales were something like $500 million.

There was a sense of family at Manville. It was difficult to get fired. During the depression, the company (then Johns Manville) had no layoffs. In periods of deflation the company deflated salaries rather than cut back on the number of employees. The company instituted a 40-hour week prior to the Wagner Act. A strong sense of personal loyalty to the company was common among employees, with many buying company stock for their pension plans.

Tom Stephens, who became Manville's CEO subsequent to Mr. McKinney's retirement, saw the early Manville culture as having been largely derived from the wealth associated with controlling 70 percent of the world supply of a basic commodity.

So you had a culture built up that [with] almost anything that you did, you could still be successful. And so one of the keys to success is "don't screw up." It's not "go out and do something positive." It becomes a negative. Don't make a mistake. So you build up a culture where you're pretty insulated from the realities of the world.

As a result, Mr. Stephens felt that "too much of the asbestos problem was treated as an accounting entry." He also felt that the blame rested with society as much as with Manville:

Manville as a company really wasn't that different from society in general. They were not a bunch of green monsters that were sitting around a board table at Manville. They were probably some of the more capable people in American industry in those days. But they were a product of the society that they lived in.

Part of the Manville culture involved a code of ethics. To Mr. McKinney's recollection, documents requiring annual signatures were those concerning honesty in general business dealings, that is, testimony that basically had to do with "not cheating," and "the thou shalt nots with respect to the things that could get you into any trust violation." Manville would not allow its employees to bribe foreign or domestic officials even when it was customary to do so. "We never were able to sell asbestos cement pipe in the city of New York because we wouldn't pay anybody off. We never sold any in Chicago because we wouldn't pay anybody off."

In Mr. Stephens' perspective, although Manville was in many respects exemplary in its ethical conduct, its system was not without fault:

> We were way out ahead of most in terms of statements on ethics and employee safety and all that sort of thing. But it still had happened, and why? And the bottom line is the breakdown in getting from those statements of corporate ethics to the actual practices on the plant floor. Having a code of ethics written down is a nice start and you ought to have that. But what you really have to change is the mentality and the culture and the instincts of an organization and that's much more a function of actions in leadership than it is having something on the bookshelf.

Plaintiff Compensation

To more effectively deal with the asbestos health claims, Manville attempted to work with other members of the industry in order to develop a common defense that could settle rather than litigate claims. In so doing, expenditures that were considered by Manville to be wasteful, such as legal fees (defense as well as plaintiff fees) and expert witness fees, could be minimized. This would theoretically allow the claimants to receive, on the average, more compensation per claim at less total expense. In the mind of Chief Legal Counsel Earl Parker, by so doing, less money would be diverted from those most in need. Strict litigation allowed contingency fees as high as 40 percent.

By the early 1980s, it became clear to Manville's management that the claims process could not be managed on a tort system. Manville had been in litigation with its insurance carriers since 1980, and by mid-1982 cases were being filed at a rate of 500 per month. There were a great many more lawsuits than the system was designed to handle.

When Manville settled cases, however, it believed that in many instances it paid people who suffered no significant impairment and therefore deserved no payment. As Mr. Stephens saw it,

> . . . there are people out there that would take all of you they could get. There are people out there that have filed claims that have no physical impairment whatsoever. There are people out there that are in absolute miserable pain and dying. There are people that are not even sick yet.

Some cases were settled for as little as $100, and some were litigated for as much as $1 million. Neither approach appeared to Manville to be particularly fair to all involved or expeditious. Mr. McKinney said:

> . . . even settling a case for $7,000, you can't even open a file in the lawyer's office for $7,000. . . . in the second quarter of 1982 we litigated all cases and settled none. As a result of this our average cost of case disposition went from something like $15,000 a case up to $40,000 a case.

Mr. McKinney wondered if a modified compensation system in which Manville could make awards similar to the most generous federal Workers' Compensation scheme, could be devised. Perhaps in this way a larger percentage of the settlements would go directly to the claimants.

Legal Fees

Manville was well aware that roughly one-third of the awarded payments went to plaintiff legal costs. Mr. McKinney felt that, of the total amount that Manville could expect to pay out over a period of time, "the lawyers are going to pick up 30 to 40 percent of it and that's scandalous. You can justify a contingent fee for one or two cases but you can't for a thousand because you had already been paid for the same work. You do the work on the law one time."

Manville was also concerned that the number of cases being filed was not following the expected bell-shaped pattern. That is, the number of asbestosis victims was expected to increase consistent with the maturation of the latency period of the disease. As the latency period reached expiration, the number of asbestosis cases should decline. "But," Mr. Parker said,

> the relationship between asbestosis and the number of cases filed in court, or claims filed, is not following that pattern. And I think, in part, that's because the lawyers responsible for handling these cases have brought cases for compensation on evidence of minimal exposure to asbestos and not symptom cases where there has been significant impairment or any impairment.

In addition, Manville saw itself being sued by workers who had received federal Workers' Compensation. By law, any compensation collected from other sources subsequent to receipt of Workers' Compensation benefits had to be paid to the government, less legal fees. "So they didn't gain a thing by going for it but their lawyer picked up 40 percent," Mr. McKinney said.

On the other hand, Marianna Smith, a former law school faculty member and former executive of the Trial Lawyers Association, pointed out that Manville did not make it easy for the plaintiffs' bar to prepare their cases:

> One of the things that happens in our legal system is that if you try one case against a manufacturer and produce documents and they're authenticated by the defendant, then typically you could walk into the next court room and that same manufacturer will say, "yes, I'll stipulate that I authenticated these in the last trial." Manville took the position that every case was the first case. So a plaintiff's lawyer spent . . . God knows how much time trying the same case over and over and over again.

She added, "These kind of things get people's dander up."

FASB Rule 5

The Financial Accounting Standards Board (FASB) is a board of accountants that sets standards and rules for the accounting profession. Rule 5, "Accounting for Contingent Liabilities," stipulates that when a company has incurred contingent liabilities of an indeterminate amount and those liabilities can be expressed in a range of low to high, then that company must book a reserve in the amount of the low end of that range. If that figure exceeds the assets of the company, then that company should file for bankruptcy.

In 1981, Manville commissioned a study by an independent firm to determine the expected number of claims to be filed against Manville. Conducted by Epidemiology Resources, Inc., the study predicted a minimum of 52,000 cases, a number that many in Manville were not comfortable with. According to Dick Van Walsh, general counsel at Manville following Mr. Parker's retirement,

> You know when I say good science I mean as good on a scientific or epidemiological approach as we can get as to how many claims are going to exist out in the future. It had never been done, nobody had ever done that kind of study. And not only how many disease claims might there be, but then how many of those people might actually bring a lawsuit.

At $40,000 per case Manville was required to book a reserve to cover a contingent liability of $2 billion. Manville's assets amounted to $2.2 billion. The argument was advanced by senior Manville management that the reserve would essentially wipe out Manville's net worth, thereby crippling its operations, and that bankruptcy was appropriate under these circumstances.

CEO McKinney did not want to hear this. He and other staff felt that the projected number of cases was too high. To test the validity of the commissioned report, Mr. McKinney ordered that a separate group of epidemiologists and biostatisticians be retained to test the methodology of the first study. To Mr. McKinney's disappointment, the second study verified the first. The voices calling for bankruptcy strengthened. Mr. McKinney, having been a patent attorney for twenty years, knew the study could not be challenged, "despite the fact that we thought they were wrong by at least double." The difficulty lay not only in defining an unknown population, but also in predicting their behavior.

Mr. McKinney heard from his staff that if the company were to file for reorganization under Chapter XI of the bankruptcy code, the claimants would then be on the same level as all other creditors. Punitive damage awards would be eliminated, which would allow for more equitable settlements of more claims. Exorbitant legal fees would be reduced. Claimants would not need to go through lengthy litigation and could in fact expect their claims to be settled within 90 days after initiating the claim process. In addition, no better methodology or process had surfaced to handle the volume of claims generated by the asbestos health issue.

The question Mr. McKinney, CEO of one of the largest industrial firms in the world, had to answer was: how could existing and future claims be serviced without destroying a major company? He was greatly concerned that the welfare of Manville's employees and shareholders was at stake, that Manville Corporation remained profitable and no one had ever taken a profitable company into bankruptcy, and that bankruptcy would be based on a potential contingent liability that no one knew for sure was real or accurate and one that Mr. McKinney felt was inflated.

If Manville filed for bankruptcy, Mr. McKinney was concerned that the company would be perceived as evading its corporate responsibility and that it would be the largest bankruptcy ever filed. He also had to wrestle with the reality that declaring bankruptcy went against every grain in his body.

DISCUSSION QUESTIONS

1. Identify the relevant facts.
2. Identify the pertinent ethical issues/points of ethical conflict.
3. Identify the relevant affected parties. Who are the stakeholders?
4. Identify relevant obligations to each stakeholder group.
5. Identify and evaluate the possible consequences of alternative courses of action.
6. Who are the responsible parties? Manville? the government? individuals?
7. Identify the relevant community standards that should have guided a person of integrity at the time.
8. How did Manville's culture affect its behavior?
9. Recommend programs and policies that would better ensure worker safety.
10. Identify arguments for and against bankruptcy that might have been made at the time.

INDEX